THE COMMUNICATION OF EMOTION

THE GUILFORD SOCIAL PSYCHOLOGY SERIES
ROBERT A. BARON AND JUDITH RODIN, EDITORS

THE COMMUNICATION OF EMOTION
Ross Buck

THE COMMUNICATION OF EMOTION

ROSS BUCK

University of Connecticut

THE GUILFORD PRESS
New York London

© 1984 The Guilford Press
A Division of Guilford Publications, Inc.
200 Park Avenue South, New York, N.Y. 10003

Printed in the United States of America

LIBRARY OF CONGRESS CATALOGING IN PUBLICATION DATA
Buck, Ross.
The communication of emotion.

(The Guilford social psychology series)
Bibliography: p.
Includes indexes.
1. Emotions.   2. Nonverbal communication (Psychology)
I. Title.   II. Series.   [DNLM: 1. Emotions.   2. Non-
verbal communication.   BF 531 B922e]
BF531.B78   1984   153.6   83-1613
ISBN 0-89862-110-0

To Marianne

PREFACE

This book takes the view that studies of emotion and emotion communication, carried out for the most part over the past 15 years, allow a considerably more comprehensive understanding of human nature than was previously possible. They allow a new appreciation of the relationship between human and animal communication: that both are based upon emotion and that emotion communication serves as the foundation of the social order in both animals and humans. At the same time, these studies enable us to appreciate the differences between human and animal communication: that in humans language constitutes a system of behavior control that is absent in animals. Research on emotion communication is uniquely relevant to the analysis of the relationship between the individual and the social order. On the one hand, emotional expression is clearly grounded in the individual and related to how the individual adapts to the environment. At the same time, emotional expression determines emotion communication, and makes possible the sorts of behavior coordination that are basic to the social order.

This book presents a view of human nature that can be summarized in the following propositions, to be discussed extensively below. First, human behavior is seen to be a function of several systems of organization. The first involves innate motivational/emotional systems which occur at various levels in the nervous system—reflexes, instincts, drives, primary affects, and so on—which at base are special-purpose processing systems concerned with bodily adaptation and the maintenance of homeostasis. These systems involve a holistic and "syncretic" cognition—knowledge by acquaintance—which is generally associated with the right cerebral hemisphere. The second system of organization includes influences that are a product of learning from experience which are incorporated into the cognitive system. This is a general-purpose processing system concerned with making sense out of the external and internal environment, and it involves a sequential, analytic cognition–knowledge by description— which is generally associated with the left cerebral hemisphere. These two systems of organization are the bases of two sorts of communication: *spontaneous communication* involving emotional expression and *symbolic communication* involving specific propositions.

These systems of organization, and these types of communication, can be seen and studied in both animals and humans. In humans, however, analytic cognition is dominated by language, which constitutes a further kind of organization which supports uniquely human patterns of logic and reasoning—and a sense of self—that make human behavior and communication qualitatively different from animal behavior and communication. There are kinds of behavioral organization that occur in humans that do not occur in animals. However, the converse is not the case. Patterns of behavioral organization that can be seen clearly in animals also occur in humans, but they are often hidden by our powers of language. One of the great contributions of the study of nonverbal communication it that it has shown how human communication, and by extension the human social order, is based upon and influenced by the same motivational/ emotional systems and fundamental learning experiences as is animal communication.

This book begins in Chapter 1 with a definition of communication and in Chapters 2 and 3 with discussion of the basic nature of motivation and emotion. A *readout* model is presented in which emotion is seen as the readout of motivational systems in adaptive/ homeostatic responses, expressive behaviors, and subjective experience. Models of each of these readout processes, termed Emotion I, II, and III, are presented. The book then considers emotion communication, including the processes by which the individual comes to know and understand his or her own feelings, and how such knowledge is influenced by, and influences, emotion communication. Chapter 4 examines how this process occurs in animals, and considers the similarities and differences between animal and human emotional development. The importance for the child of emotion communication in determining emotional *response accessibility* and the *education of attention* are considered. Also, the implications of the uniquely human ability for language are discussed, along with the phenomenon of human cognitive development and the related process of *emotional education.*

Chapter 5 summarizes studies of nonverbal sending accuracy, including evaluations of different techniques of study and methods of analysis. Chapter 6 discusses processes in which the spontaneous emotion display is altered, defining *inhibition* and *repression* as the direct attenuation of the emotional readout to others and oneself, respectively. There is evidence that these may be based upon common subcortical/paleocortical neural systems. In contrast, *deception* and *coping* are defined as the products of learned rules respectively involving the expression and experience of emotion, in which emotional processes may be attenuated or accentuated. Chapter 7 summarizes studies of nonverbal receiving ability, with evaluations of different methods of measurement and analysis, while Chapter 8 considers the implications of emotion communication to a most active area of current research: the analysis of interaction. The methodological analyses in Chapters 5, 7, and 8 all argue, among other things, for the promise of the *segmentation technique* in the analysis of emotion communication, and throughout the book the importance of cerebral lateralization to the understanding of emotion and emotion communication is repeatedly emphasized.

This book is based upon the conviction that we have the knowledge *now* for a comprehensive theory of human nature, but that it will not be realized until investigators using different approaches take the time and trouble to learn about and appreciate other points of view and other approaches to the understanding of behavior. As it is, there is a general reluctance to go beyond one's chosen approach. In science as in politics, such territoriality can be constructive, but it is usually destructive. Investigators avoid topics of study that are potentially relevant to another discipline, perhaps in part for fear of attack from an unfamiliar quarter. As a result, to use Geschwind's (1975a) apt analogy, a topic which should be an area of common ground becomes a no-man's land.

This is particularly true of the topics of motivation and emotion. Few topics are so inherently multidisciplinary. Every psychologist, from the most "simple-minded" positivist to the most "muddle-headed" existentialist, has something to say about motivation and emotion. Typically, of course, they are very different things, and typically each denies the importance or relevance of what the other has to say. There is an ancient parable about ten blind men arrayed around an elephant, each trying to describe the nature of the beast from his own restricted experience, and arguing violently. Like them, investigators studying motivation and emotion from different points of view have often failed to listen to one another with sympathy and understanding, and have instead argued for the superiority of their own positions. However, if one accepts each point of view as a valid but restricted picture of the phenomenon in question, it becomes possible to build up a comprehensive view which has important and far-reaching implications indeed. A comprehensive view of motivation and emotion is potentially an important area of common ground, not only for psychology but also anthropology, communication, ethology, medicine, neurology, psychiatry, political science, and philosophy.

There can be no doubt about the importance of arriving at an increased understanding of human motivation and emotion, particularly as they apply to communication and form the basis of the social order. We live on an increasingly crowded world, whose resources are being depleted and whose environment is being poisoned, where the threat of nuclear holocaust appears very real. We seem to be careening toward destruction. However, there is still time to discover the sorts of political and economic systems that can allow all humans to live in freedom, prosperity, and peace in a culturally diverse world. To do that, we must understand more about human motivation, emotion, and communication, and apply that understanding to the process of discovery.

I am pleased to acknowledge the contribution of many colleagues to this book. Its origins can be traced to my experience at the Department of Clinical Science at the University of Pittsburgh School of Medicine, working in a unique multidisciplinary setting with Robert E. Miller and William F. Caul under the direction of the late Arthur F. Mirsky. My recent sabbatical with Robert Rosenthal at Harvard and at the Aphasia Research Unit of the Boston Veterans Administration Hospital under the direction of Harold Goodglass was also very important in the writing of this book. The support of the University of Connecticut Research Foundation in a number of studies reported here is gratefully acknowledged.

I would particularly like to thank Reuben Baron, Joan Borod, Albert Dreyer, Barbara Montgomery, Kathleen Reardon, and Don Tucker for reading and commenting on portions of the manuscript, and Robert Baron and Judith Rodin for their excellent editorial assistance. In addition, my collaborations in recent years with Peter Blanck, Robert Duffy, David Kenny, Elissa Koff, Jay Lerman, Antonia Maxon, and Ronald Sabatelli have been valuable. Students in my Nonverbal Communication and Interpersonal Communication seminars have also offered many useful suggestions; Jennie Boomer and Lucy Tilton have provided valuable secretarial support; and Ray Blanchette has contributed many excellent drawings for figures. Needless to say, these colleagues and students have contributed to the strengths of this book, but they are in no way responsible for its weaknesses. Finally, I wish to thank my family and especially my wife, Marianne, to whom this book is dedicated.

Ross Buck

Storrs, Connecticut

CONTENTS

PART IV. EMOTION COMMUNICATION AND SOCIAL INTERACTION

THE COMMUNICATION OF EMOTION

PART ONE

INTRODUCTION

1

COMMUNICATION, NONVERBAL BEHAVIOR, AND EMOTION

The past few years have witnessed a major resurgence in interest in two related areas of behavior: the study of emotion and the study of nonverbal communication. These aspects of behavior were relatively ignored during the years of the domination of psychology first by learning theories and later by cognitive approaches. The concept of emotion has proved particularly troublesome to behaviorally oriented researchers because the classic behavioral manifestations of emotion—overt behavior, self-reported experience, and peripheral physiological responding—often relate to one another in complex and confusing ways. However, it has become increasingly clear that the study of nonverbal behavior can provide a major means for making emotion accessible for study by behavioral techniques. At the same time, new techniques for studying the central nervous system mechanisms underlying emotion have become available, so that great advances in our understanding of these systems is taking place.

This research has exciting implications for the analysis of individual emotional expression. For example, there is increasing evidence that how we express our feelings has important implications for our physical health and well-being. However, this research also has important implications for the analysis of social processes. It is now clear that human communication involves more than an exchange of ideas and propositions. A great part of human communication is emotional communication, involving minute signals of affect, attention, approach and avoidance, and dominance and submission, that convey information of central importance to human social organization.

All of this means that the emotional tendencies of the individual cannot be fully understood outside the social context. One of the major qualities of the research on nonverbal communication is that, unlike many areas of psychology (including much of social psychology), it does not focus upon the individual as the unit of analysis. Instead, it focuses upon the communication process in which at least two individuals must be involved: a sender and receiver. The data gained from the study of this process may be translated to investigate the characteristics of the individuals involved, as we shall see when considering how individuals differ in their nonverbal skills. At the same time, the study of the communication process may be directed toward the analysis of the interaction between individuals. Such study allows a unique perspective on how the process of interaction is structured independently of the characteristics of the individuals involved.

This book focuses upon the nonverbal communication of emotion—the process by which one signals one's emotional state to others, and comes to know the emotional state of others—and how it is related to symbolic or propositional communication. This introductory chapter defines communication and examines the relationship between verbal and nonverbal communication. I shall suggest that a distinction between spontaneous and symbolic communication is fundamental to this analysis—more fundamental even than the distinction between "verbal" and "nonverbal" communication. The chapter then considers the basic features of any communication process, introducing and defining terms that shall be used throughout the book. Finally, this chapter spells out the scope and limits of this book.

THE DEFINITION OF COMMUNICATION

SPONTANEOUS VERSUS SYMBOLIC COMMUNICATION

This book defines communication as occurring whenever the behavior of one individual (the sender) influences the behavior of another (the receiver). Such influence may be rigorously defined in information theory terms: Behavior can be defined as communicative to the extent that it reduces uncertainty in the behavior of another. Observations made across time determine whether the presence or absence of the behavior of one interactant (the sender, A) alters the probabilities of the behavior of another interactant (the receiver, B). In other words, A's behavior X1 is defined as communicative given the following:

> The conditional probability that act X2 will be performed by individual B given that A performed X1 is not equal to the probability that B will perform X2 in the absence of X1. (Wilson, 1975, p. 194)

This definition of communication is general and can be applied to any species.

Some would argue that such a definition is too broad, and that communication occurs only when messages or propositions are transferred from sender to receiver via symbols. For example, Weiner, Devoe, Rubinow, and Geller (1972) define communication as necessarily involving a socially shared signal system, or code, which is symbolic in nature. However, such definitions of communication do not allow the possibility of communication via spontaneous expressive behaviors which are nonpropositional and nonsymbolic, and which signal their meaning in a biologically based relationship with that which is signified. In effect, such communication involves a biologically shared as opposed to a socially shared signal system.

Many of the most interesting findings in the field of nonverbal communication involve influences via such spontaneous behaviors, but we shall see that nonverbal behavior can also be symbolic and that verbal behavior can under some circumstances be virtually spontaneous and functionally nonsymbolic. In this sense the distinction between *spontaneous* and *symbolic* communication is more fundamental than the distinction between nonverbal and verbal behavior.

The notion of biologically shared signal system is implied in Darwin's (1872) analysis in *The Expression of the Emotions in Man and Animals*. Darwin's theory and its implications shall be discussed in more detail in Chapter 2. In brief, Darwin argued that facial expressions and other such displays have adaptive value in social animals because they reveal something about the inner state of the responder and are thus useful in social coordination. This implies (1) that the inner state of the responder must be encoded into an expressive display, (2) that the receiver must be able to receive the expressive display via sensory cues, and (3) that the receiver must be able to decode the display, that is, respond appropriately to it. Thus Darwin's thesis requires that both sending mechanisms and receiving mechanisms have evolved in order for the adaptive value of a system of emotion expression to be realized.

In essence, the reasoning behind the evolution of sending mechanisms is that, given that the communication of a certain motivational/emotional state is adaptive to a species, individuals who show evidence of such a state in their overt behaviors which are visible or otherwise "accessible" to others will tend to be favored, so that over the generations these behaviors will become *ritualized*; that is, they will become *displays* of motivational/emotional states which are characteristic of the species (cf. Buck, 1981a). The same reasoning applies to the evolution of receiving mechanisms: Individuals who respond appropriately to these displays tend to be favored, so that the attentional/perceptual systems of species members would eventually become preattuned to the pickup of these displays. The result of this evolutionary process is a biologically shared signal system involving both sending and receiving mechanisms.

Spontaneous Communication

In *Mind, Self and Society* (1934), George Herbert Mead argued that this kind of biologically shared signal system constitutes the primitive system from which human verbal communication originated. In doing so he distinguished between communication via "significant symbols" and the "conversation of gesture," referring to spontaneous emotional displays as gestures. Mead's example of a conversation of gesture was a dog fight, in which the antagonists circle one another, growling and snapping, and responding instantly to signs of advance or retreat on the part of the other animal. Mead noted that the gestures on which this conversation is based cannot be voluntary: "It is quite impossible to assume that animals do undertake to express their emotions. They certainly do not undertake to express for the benefit of other animals" (1934, p. 16). Thus one of the major qualities of the conversation of gesture is that it is spontaneous rather than voluntary and intentional.

A second major quality of spontaneous communication is that its elements are not "symbols" in that their relationships to their referents is not arbitrary. The relationship between a symbol (i.e., the word "tree" in a natural language, or the sign for tree in sign language or other artificial language) and its referent (the tree itself) is arbitrary and socially defined. This is the case even when the symbol is iconic, resembling the referent in some way (i.e., the English word "bark"). However, the elements of spontaneous communication are not in any sense arbitrary. In the language of semiotics they are *signs* which bear natural relationships with their referents. In fact, the sign (the gesture or facial expression) is an external manifestation of the referent (the animal's motivational/emotional state) in the same way that dark clouds are a sign of rain. The darkness of the clouds is an externally visible, and thus *accessible*, aspect of the referent (the rain). In exactly the same way, the growling and advancing of a dog are externally visible and accessible manifestations of internal states of anger and fear.

A third major quality of spontaneous communication flows from the above. Assuming that spontaneous gestures are an external manifestation of an internal state, it makes no sense to inquire whether they are true or false, for if the internal state did not exist, the gestures by definition would be absent. Since in Bertrand Russell's (1903) definition a proposition must be capable of being true or false, communication via gesture must be nonpropositional, in that the gesture is an external manifestation of the referent and cannot be false. If a gesture occurs in the absence of the appropriate motivational/emotional state—for example, if a person "puts on a happy face" while in fact feeling miserable, or if one intentionally looks angry without really feeling it—it is not spontaneous communication by this definition.

In summary, spontaneous communication is defined as having the following major qualities: (1) It is based upon a biologically shared signal system, (2) it is nonvoluntary, (3) the elements of the message are signs rather than symbols, and (4) it is nonpropositional, in that it is by definition not falsifiable. These qualities are summarized in Table 1.1, where they are contrasted with those of symbolic communication.

Symbolic Communication

In contrast to the nonvoluntary, nonsymbolic, and nonpropositional conversation of gesture is intentional communication via symbols, in which the communicative behavior has an arbitrary, socially defined relationship with its referent, knowledge of which is shared by sender and receiver. The most obvious examples of symbolic communication involve language behavior, but there are many nonverbal behaviors

Table 1.1 Summary of the Characteristics of Spontaneous and Symbolic Communication

Characteristics	Spontaneous communication	Symbolic communication
Basis of signal system	Biologically shared	Socially shared
Intentionality	Spontaneous: Communicative behavior is an automatic or reflex response	Voluntary: Sender intends to send a specific message
Elements	Signs: Natural externally visible aspects of referent	Symbols: Arbitrary relationship with referent
Content	Nonpropositional motivational/emotional states	Propositions: Expressions capable of logical analysis (test of truth or falsity)
Cerebral processing	Related to right hemisphere	Related to left hemisphere
Level of knowledge necessary	Knowledge by acquaintance	Knowledge by description

which are analogous to or directly related to language and which do not seem to involve the expression of internal motivational/emotional states. These include systems of sign language and pantomime, as well as body movements and facial expressions associated with language. The latter behaviors have been termed *emblems, illustrators,* and *regulators* in the useful typology of Ekman and Friesen (1969a), respectively involving (1) nonverbal gestures with a specific "dictionary" definition, (2) nonverbal behaviors which illustrate what is being stated verbally, and (3) nonverbal behaviors which regulate the give-and-take flow of interaction. Such behaviors are particularly emphasized in the pioneering work of Birdwhistell (1970) and his colleagues, which demonstrated close relationships between body movements and language behaviors, both within a single speaker and between speaker and listener (cf. Key, 1980; Siegman & Pope, 1972).

We shall further discuss the distinction between these symbolic gestures and emotional gestures, but it might be noted here that Ekman (1979) has discussed the differences between "conversational" and emotional facial expressions, defining the former as facial actions which are related to the process of speaking or listening, or facial emblems which may occur without speech. Such expressions may involve well-established habits which, like other aspects of language, may be learned so thoroughly that they operate virtually automatically and outside conscious awareness, but they are not signs of a presently existing internal motivational/emotional state. Also like language, the nature of such expressions differs from culture to culture, while the nature of spontaneous emotional expressions must be universal to the species.

THE RELATIONSHIP BETWEEN SPONTANEOUS AND SYMBOLIC COMMUNICATION

One might inquire at this point of the nature of the relationship between spontaneous and symbolic communication—whether, for example, they should be considered to be extreme points on a continuum or a dichotomy. In fact, the question of the relationship of spontaneous and symbolic communication is more complex: they may be supportive, contradictory, or relatively independent vis à vis one another, because they are based upon different processes that respond differently to events in the internal bodily milieu and in the external environment. Their relationship is an empirical rather than a logical matter, and it is as yet incompletely understood. We shall consider it at various points in this book; here we can only suggest the general nature of this relationship and the reasons for its complexity.

These may be best suggested by an analogy. Let us compare the evolving brain and its functioning with an evolving city in which new buildings are built, new transportation systems conceived and constructed, new centers of learning emerge which are based upon new conceptions of the world, new commercial enterprises develop, and so forth. At the same time, let us assume that *nothing is ever torn down*. The old buildings still remain, the old transportation systems continue to operate, old learning centers based upon the old conceptions still function, old commercial enterprises survive. The new structures tend to hide the functioning of the old, but they rarely replace them. The old structures continue to function much as they always had, hidden and yet constantly present, their effects now interacting with the functioning of the new structures in complex ways (cf. Sagan, 1980, pp. 276–279).

The relationship between the functioning of the old structure and the new is analogous to the relationship between spontaneous and symbolic communication. Spontaneous communication is associated with subcortical and paleocortical brain structures which, in the course of evolution, have been progressively relegated to "secondary" status by more recent, neocortical structures; while symbolic communication is based upon these neocortical structures. However, this does not mean that the old structures have ceased to function. Like the old structures in our hypothetical city, they remain and so influence all aspects of the functioning of the new structures.

Continuing with this analogy, let us assume that different types of cities emerge. Some are more developed than others, some are specialized as agricultural centers, ports, and centers of government, and some are less specialized. Thus like different species, different types of cities may reflect different levels of development and different patterns of functions. Also, individual cities may develop differently from other cities of the same type. Some may be starved, others may have plenty; some may live in peace and have good relationships with other cities, others may experience hostile relationships with other cities which interferes with orderly development. All of the cities, however, have the essential structure of old structures existing and functioning with the new.

Like the relationship between the functioning of the new and old structures of these cities, the relationship between spontaneous and symbolic communication is highly complex, varying with the species, the individual, and the particular situation. However, a few general features of this relationship may be discerned. These are symbolized in Figure 1.1. First, one can see that "pure" spontaneous communication is possible but that pure symbolic communication is not. Symbolic communication is always accompanied by tendencies toward spontaneous expression, however hidden and apparently inconsequential. Second, one can see that the relative degree of symbolic communication vis à vis spontaneous communication is variable. This dimension might be conceptualized in a number of ways. First, it is possible to regard this as a situational dimension, in which the relative impact of symbolic communication is greater in some situations than in others. Second, one could see this dimension as reflecting the phylogenetic scale, in which symbolic communication has greater relative importance as one goes "up" the scale. Third, this dimension could reflect the development of an individual, in which symbolic communication has greater relative importance with the course of cognitive development. These latter interpretations suggest the possibility that symbolic communication may be based upon spontaneous communication,

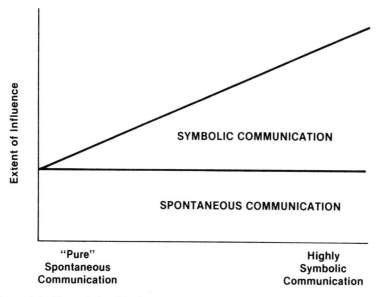

Figure 1.1. The relationship between spontaneous and symbolic communication.

both phylogenetically and ontogenetically. We shall discuss this possibility below, particularly in Chapter 4.

All in all, this analogy is meant to suggest that spontaneous and symbolic communication are not *logically* related to one another in any simple way, as in a continuum or dichotomy, but rather they are *biologically* related to one another in ways that cannot be precisely defined until the biological systems upon which they are based and their relationships with one another are more fully understood.

KNOWLEDGE BY ACQUAINTANCE VERSUS KNOWLEDGE BY DESCRIPTION

The significance of the distinction between spontaneous and symbolic communication may be further clarified by reference to a distinction that has long been made between knowledge by acquaintance, which involves direct sensory awareness, and knowledge by description, which involves the interpretation of sensory data. This distinction was made in clearly developed form as far back as the time of St. Augustine in *De Magistro* (Marsh, 1956), and it is reflected in many languages, as in the French *connaître* versus *savoir* and the German *kennen* versus *weisen* (James, 1890). More recently, it has occupied a central place in Bertrand Russell's (1912, 1948) epistemological theory.

Knowledge by Acquaintance

William James (1890) describes knowledge by acquaintance as follows: "I know the color blue when I see it, and the flavor of a pear when I taste it . . . but *about* the inner nature of these facts or what makes them what they are I can say nothing at all. I cannot impart acquaintance with them to any one who has not made it himself. . . . At most, I can say to my friends, 'Go to certain places and act in certain ways, and these objects will probably come'" (p. 221).

Russell states that knowledge by acquaintance involves "direct sensory awareness without the intermediary of any process of inference or any knowledge of truths" (1912, p. 73). Instead, it involves the presentational immediacy of experience and is therefore completely self-evident. "Thus in the presence of my table I am acquainted with the sense-data that make up the appearance of the table: its colour, shape, hardness, smoothness, etc.; all these are things of which I am immediately conscious when I am seeing and touching my table" (1912, p. 73). Knowledge by acquaintance includes not only our awareness of sense-data from the environment, but also the awareness of internal states. These include in particular the awareness of feelings and desires, for example, emotional and motivational states (Russell, 1912, 1948).

Knowledge by Description

In contrast, knowledge by description involves the *interpretation* of sense-data. As Russell (1912) puts it, "My knowledge of the table as a physical object . . . is not direct knowledge. Such as it is, it is obtained through acquaintance with the sense-data that make up the appearance of the table . . . the table is 'the physical object that causes such-and-such sense-data.' This *describes* the table by means of sense-data" (pp. 73–74).

Both James and Russell agree that knowledge by description depends upon, and follows in time, knowledge by acquaintance. As

James puts it, "feelings are the germ and starting point for cognition, thoughts the developed tree" (1890, p. 222). This conception is quite consistent with recent evidence presented by Zajonc (1980) that "affect and cognition are under the control of separate and partially independent systems" (p. 151), and that affective responses precede in time cognitive operations (cf. Kunst-Wilson & Zajonc, 1980; Wilson, 1979). We shall return to this issue in Chapter 4.

Implications for Communication

The distinction between knowledge by acquaintance versus description both clarifies the nature of, and emphasizes the fundamental importance of, the distinction between spontaneous and symbolic communication. Symbolic communication clearly requires knowledge by description, as it is necessary that sense-data be interpreted if they are to be encoded into conventional symbols. On the other hand, spontaneous communication requires only knowledge by acquaintance: the display in fact may be simply an externally accessible aspect of the process of knowing one's affective state. Thus when we see a tiger and are frightened, our spontaneous look of fear is an aspect of the internal motivational/emotional state just as is our subjective acquaintance with the feeling of fear. I shall argue below that the external expression and subjective experience of motivational/emotional states are not causally related to one another in either direction—instead, each has evolved independently of the other in accord with species requirements. Spontaneous expression is in this view a kind of running "progress report" which involves a direct reflection or "readout" of the affective aspects of the process of knowledge by acquaintance (cf. Buck, 1980).

It should be noted that I am in no way suggesting that cognitive knowledge by description has no influence upon the nature of our feelings. As Schachter (1964) and others have emphasized, cognitive factors influence the determination of the nature of motivational/emotional states. Thus if the tiger in the above example is in a cage at the zoo, it is less likely to evoke fearful affect than if it suddenly appeared in one's living room. However, whatever our affective response to the tiger might be, whether it is one of fear or mild interest, it is known to us by acquaintance and tends to be expressed to others via spontaneous nonverbal behavior.

SUMMARY

This section has suggested that there are two kinds of communication processes: a spontaneous and nonpropositional process based on the changing motivational/emotional state of the sender and the readiness of the receiver to attend and respond appropriately, and a symbolic process involving intentional messages or propositions. Thus far we have been concerned with distinguishing between spontaneous and symbolic communication processes, and have thus taken pains to isolate them and point out how they differ. However, it should be emphasized that, except perhaps in cases of serious brain damage, these systems are highly interactive. The precise nature of this interaction is not known at present, but its general nature was suggested by the cities analogy. "Pure" spontaneous communication is logically possible: It involves our tendency to express motivational/emotional states via sending mechanisms that have evolved specifically for this purpose. These states are always with us. The reader can recognize them easily, informing constantly about the state of the body. However, like the appearance of the color blue or the taste of a pear, one's personal knowledge by acquaintance of this state resists easy description. I suggest that these states are expressed outwardly just as constantly as they are experienced inwardly, and shall argue that both internal and external "readout" mechanisms have evolved for this purpose.

"Pure" symbolic communication on the other hand is not possible, except perhaps between computers. In any biological organism, symbolic communication is accompanied by spontaneous communication, because every biological organism carries with it the systems derived from its evolutionary past.

This view suggests that human communication occurs in two simultaneous streams: a spontaneous stream which involves an ongoing readout of the motivational/emotional state of the sender, and a symbolic stream which involves propositional messages. One of these streams is not more important than the other: The kinds of meanings communicated by the two streams is different, and in some situations the propositional message may be more important, in other situations the spontaneous message may take precedence. In any case, they interact and modify one another. However, it could be argued that the spontaneous stream is more important than heretofore realized (cf. Zajonc, 1980). It is not (as perhaps Mead considered) interesting only as a primitive form which preceded symbolic communication—it is still very much with us. The role of spontaneous communication and its relationship with symbolic communication is just beginning to be understood. It seems clear that the study of spontaneous communication will lead to greater understanding of symbolic communication: how it evolved in the human species, how it develops in the growing child, how it functions in adults. Symbolic communication has always formed a close partnership with spontaneous communication, and one cannot be fully understood without the other.

THE COMMUNICATION PROCESS

Despite the differences between spontaneous and symbolic communication, they have basic similarities in that they are both examples of communication processes. In this section we shall examine the basic features that are common to all communication processes, including purely mechanical systems, and then consider the particular qualities of human interpersonal communication.

THE SHANNON-WEAVER MODEL

The basic features of the communication process were outlined in 1948 by Claude Shannon in *The Mathematical Theory of Communication*, which was reprinted in Shannon and Weaver (1949) and is generally known as the Shannon–Weaver model of communication. The basis of the model originated during World War II with Shannon's work on secrecy codes and telecommunications, and the model was originally designed to describe a telecommunication network. However, the model proved very general; in fact, the definition of information developed by Shannon was independently developed by Norbert Weiner who was working on automated gunfire control systems. Since publication, the model has been applied in a wide variety of settings, including the definition of communication presented above. The information measure was widely adopted, so that the theory originally called communication theory by Shannon is now widely known as information theory. Dittman (1972) has described some of the adaptations of the model, and has discussed its relevance to our major topic: the communication of emotion.

The elements of the model as presented by Dittman (1972) are shown in the upper half of Figure 1.2. The model is in the form of a flow chart, with a *message* in the form of information passing from one element to another on the way from the source to the user. At this very general level, the information may consist of anything from the binary 0 or 1 provided by computer flip-flops to human speech, and the source and/or user may be human or machine. Dittman takes an example from the original telecommunications application: A message to be transmitted by telegraph (the *source*) is first transformed from the letters of the alphabet to dots, dashes, and the spaces between them by the *source encoder*. These are then transformed by the *channel encoder* into electrical impulses which are sent over a wire (the *channel*). These pulses are received at the end of the line and are transformed back into dots, dashes, and spaces by the *channel decoder*. Finally, these are translated by the *user decoder* into the original letters of the message which is read by the *user*.

The Shannon–Weaver model is particularly concerned with the quality of reproduction as the message is transformed from element to element. This is limited by two major factors: channel capacity and noise. *Channel capacity* refers to how much information can be transmitted over a given channel in a given time. It is thus measured in terms of rates of transmission: units of information per unit of time. If the channel capacity is limited, either less information can be sent over the channel or a given amount of information must be sent more slowly. In telecommuncations, the development of optical fiber is important because of its great channel capacity: A single optical fiber can carry more information than a large bundle of heavy cables.

The model regards *noise* as a random process which can be described in terms of statistical probabilities. The noise interferes directly with the signal being transmitted through the communication system. In the telecommunications application the noise might consist of thermal agitation of the molecules in the wire channel or in the components of the transmitting and receiving equipment. The theory is concerned with the development of practical ways to organize or code information so that it may be communicated over a given channel at maximum efficiency but with a vanishingly small probability of error induced by noise.

The version of the Shannon–Weaver model that we shall use to illustrate and define our terminology is presented in the lower half of Figure 1.2. It may be noted that, although there are significant similarities between our model and the original which make the analogy useful, there are also significant differences. For example, as Dittman (1972) has noted, applications of the Shannon–Weaver model to human face-to-face communication are limited by the fact that, whereas the source, source encoder, and channel encoder are independent components in the original model, they reside within one person—the *sender*—in the derived model. Similarly, the channel decoder, user decoder, and user all reside within the *receiver*. This is one of the problems that prevents us from using the Shannon–Weaver model too literally in dealing with the communication of emotion. The usefulness of the model lies in the fact that it illustrates the basic processes that must be present for communication to take place, and as such it alerts us to account for those processes when analyzing emotional communication.

THE EMOTION COMMUNICATION PROCESS

The Model

The source of the message in the spontaneous expression of emotion is the occurrence of a motivational/emotional state in the sender. We shall use facial expression in this illustrative example, although the message could as easily be transmitted via tone of voice, posture, and so forth. In some way, the motivational/emotional state must be

Figure 1.2. The Shannon–Weaver model applied to the spontaneous communication process.

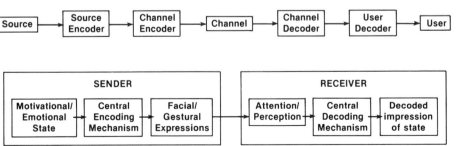

transformed into appropriate facial expressions, and this process must occur within a single person—the sender. We shall consider what is known about the process by which this is done in Chapter 3. For the present, we will posit the existence of a *central encoding mechanism* in the central nervous system which transforms the information that a given motivational/emotional state is present into motor neuron activity which influences the facial muscles. In other words, the presence of a motivational/emotional state is signaled via a pattern of neural activity within the central nervous system. This activity acts upon the central encoding mechanism (which in fact may be a series of mechanisms) which, performing a function analogous to the source encoder described above, transforms it into motor activity in the peripheral nervous system. This acts upon the facial muscles via the facial nerves, resulting in an altered facial configuration or display which is potentially informative of the sender's motivational/emotional state. The facial muscles, then, perform the function of channel encoder. This is an ongoing process, of course: As the sender's internal state changes, the information is passed down the line and the display is appropriately altered.

In order for communication to occur, the display must be transmitted to a receiver. The channel in this example consists of the visual relationship between sender and receiver. A number of factors might influence how well the facial display can be seen: that is, lighting, distance, angle, presence of intervening objects, and so forth. These factors could be considered analogous to the factors determining channel capacity and noise within channel in the original model.

Given the important assumption that the receiver is paying attention to the sender's face, the facial display is first apprehended by the receiver's sensory apparatus, in this case the visual apparatus, which performs the function of channel decoder. As with the sender, the processes that now occur within the receiver will be considered below, particularly in Chapters 2 and 6. In some way the visual representation of the sender's display must be perceived by the receiver and transformed into judgments or other responses appropriate to the sender's motivational/emotional state. The basic sensory information is transferred to the central nervous system via the sensory nerves, and is then transformed by what we shall term a *central decoding mechanism* (the user decoder) into a form that can be employed by the receiver in making a response.

Let us take, for example, a person who is angry. The anger is associated with central nervous system activity which is transformed into a facial display by a process or processes that we have termed the central encoding mechanism. This display is viewed by the receiver under given conditions of lighting, distance, and so forth. The visual information is transformed by a central decoding mechanism (or series of mechanisms) into a form useful to the receiver.

Display Rules

Reality, however, is clearly not this simple. An angry person does not simply display how he or she feels. Many factors act to inhibit or otherwise alter the direct expression of anger, and other motivational/emotional states as well. Ekman and Friesen (1975) have termed these factors *display rules*, which may be defined as cultural rules or expectations about the management of emotion displays. We learn within our culture that there are proper and improper ways to express emotion; for example, we do not laugh at funerals even if we feel happy, we do not look unhappy at parties even though we have a splitting headache, we keep a "stiff upper lip" in unpleasant situations. In general, we put on (or try to put on) emotion displays that are appropriate to the social situation and which may have little to do with how we actually feel.

In the terminology introduced above, the display rules represent symbolic communication processes, in that they emanate from sources other than the motivational/emotional state itself, and that they involve a more or less conscious intent to display a particular emotion state. If one is angry at a powerful person (i.e., the boss, a parent), he or she is unlikely to show a clear facial expression of anger. However, one's true feelings may "leak out" and be expressed in other ways: a change in the topic of discussion, an alteration of the tone of voice, a lowering of the eyes, a shuffling of the feet, a change of posture.

What we are suggesting is that there are two major sources in the emotion communication process: spontaneous sources (the motivational/emotional state itself) and symbolic sources (the state that the sender intends to convey). The latter may involve thoroughly learned habits which, like many linguistic phenomena, have become virtually automatic. These influences act simultaneously upon a variety of central encoding mechanisms involving a variety of effectors and channels—besides facial expression there is body movement, eye behavior, tone of voice, the content of speech, physiological responses, and so forth. The two sources will not act equally upon these different types of encoding mechanisms. We shall see in Chapter 6 that Ekman and Friesen (1969b, 1971) have suggested that senders may often attend to some channels (particularly the content of speech and facial expression) and ignore others (particularly body postures and movements) in their attempts to convey false impressions of emotion. Also, we shall see in Chapter 4 that some responses (i.e., physiological responses) may be relatively little affected by attempts at intentional display because of their relative inaccessibility.

It should be noted that the display rules do not always influence the process of spontaneous emotion expression. Under some circumstances, the influence of such rules must be relatively weak. When a sender is alone, for example, he or she should feel little pressure to present a proper image to others, and any emotion expression under such circumstances should be more likely to reflect an actual motivational/emotional state. Even under these circumstances, however, processes of "inhibition" may alter tendencies toward spontaneous expression. The whole question of *inhibition* and *deception* in the expression of emotion, how these are acquired, how spontaneous expression may *leak* and be discovered, and the ultimate emotional consequences of these processes to the responder, is a major focus of study in emotion communication, and we shall address it below in Chapters 4, 5, and particularly Chapter 6.

Decoding Rules

Like the display of emotion, the reception of affective information from others may be relatively direct, or it may be mediated by *decoding rules* that interact with such direct reception. Decoding rules may be defined as cultural rules or expectations about the attention to, and interpretation of, emotion displays. Thus when confronted with an emotion display, a receiver may be guided by cultural norms regarding what aspects of the display should be attended to, by expectations about what displays are deemed appropriate in that situation within that culture, by comparisons with previous displays from that sender, by relationships between different aspects of the sender's behavior (i.e., verbal vs. nonverbal behaviors), and so forth.

We shall see in Chapter 2 that, according to J. J. Gibson's (1979) analysis, the process of perception is direct and unmediated by cognitive processes. We shall thus speak of *emotion perception* as a direct process occurring without the mediation of decoding rules. It is analogous to knowledge by acquaintance as defined above. When decoding rules are in use, the receiver is by definition using cognitive processes involving memory and judgment. In such cases we shall speak of *emotion cognition* (cf. Baron, 1980; Baron & Buck, 1979).

Direct versus Mediated Encoding and Decoding Mechanisms

I have suggested that two kinds of processes are involved in both the central encoding mechanism and the central decoding mechanism. One is mediated by display or decoding rules, the other is relatively direct and unmediated by such rules. This distinction parallels the distinction between spontaneous and symbolic communication suggested above. Thus, an emotional display may either be a direct reflection of the motivational/emotional state—spontaneous expression—or it may be mediated by display rules involving the sender's expectations about what kind of display is appropriate in that situation—symbolic expression. Similarly, the decoding process may either be a direct apprehension of the emotional state of the other— emotion perception—or it may be mediated by decoding rules involving the receiver's knowledge about the situation, the sender, and so forth—emotion cognition. Thus there are direct encoding and decoding mechanisms that require no mediation versus mediated encoding and decoding mechanisms which involve the intervention of cognitive factors. We shall suggest in Chapter 3 that the differences in the direct or spontaneous and mediated or symbolic mechanisms parallel in important respects the differences in the functioning of the right and left hemispheres of the brain. There is convincing evidence that left- versus right-hemisphere processes are related to both emotional expression and sensitivity.

INTERACTIVE ASPECTS OF HUMAN COMMUNICATION

Thus far, the model of the communication process that we have proposed is essentially linear, with the message passing from sender to receiver. The application of such models to human communication has been rightly criticized, as they are unable to take interactive aspects of the communication process into account. In interpersonal verbal communication, for example, the receiver usually becomes a sender after the original sender's turn is over, and the resulting message is influenced by what went on before. Also, it is possible that a person who is a receiver on one channel of communication (i.e., a listener on verbal channels) may simultaneously be a sender on another channel (i.e., through eye contact, body posture, etc.). Thus a person listening to a verbal message may be signaling his or her response "on line" while that message is in the process of being delivered, and this may alter the verbal message by encouragement or discouragement, indicating understanding or a lack thereof. In fact, a listener may carry on a simultaneous nonverbal conversation with a third person who is not "officially" involved in the verbal conversation at all.

To deal with these complexities without losing the desirable features of the Shannon–Weaver model, we shall propose a nonlinear and multichannel version in which (1) the sender and receiver may exchange roles, and (2) different communicative relationships can exist simultaneously on different (or even the same) channels. Figure 1.3 illustrates that interactions exchange the sender and receiver roles in their verbal communication, showing the familiar pattern of *turn-taking*. While doing this, they may both simultaneously engage in interaction with others. For example, they might establish a brief relationship with person C (who is passing around hors d'oeuvres) which does little to interrupt their conversation. Also, person A may increasingly begin to indicate via body posture and frequent gaze a growing interest in another (person D).

Despite its complexity, this situation may be usefully analyzed using the Shannon–Weaver model. For example, person B may accurately decode person A's verbal message, but not the nonverbal behavior indicating A's interest in D. This would depend on such factors as the clarity of A's nonverbal behavior and B's attention patterns and decoding skills in this particular kind of situation. Also, if A's nonverbal behavior is accurately decoded, B may respond to this information in various ways: acknowledging it clearly and openly, acknowledging it in a disguised fashion, or ignoring it. In any case, the basic elements of the Shannon–Weaver model—the source, central encoding mechanism, display, channel decoder, central decoding mechanism, and user—are all present and their role in the communication process may be usefully analyzed.

A. Sender and receiver have a reciprocal relationship over time.

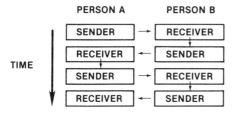

B. Different communicative relationships can exist simultaneously over different channels: i.e. a given individual may simultaneously be a sender on one channel and a receiver on another.

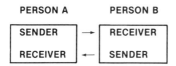

Figure 1.3. Adaptation of the Shannon–Weaver model to deal with nonlinear (A) and multichannel (B) processes.

THE PLAN OF THIS BOOK

This book examines the communication of emotion from a number of points of view. It first considers the general nature of emotion and how the communication of such states can be useful in the evolution of a species. It then considers the development of emotion communication within the individual, and how this relates to individual differences in emotion sending and receiving abilities. Finally, it examines the implications of all of this for the analysis of the process of human interaction.

The next section of the book, "The Nature of Motivation and Emotion," considers the role of the communication of motivational and emotional states in human nature and social organization, focusing upon the phylogenetic origins of such communication, the relationships between behaviors expressive of motivational/emotional states and the subjective experience of such states, and the physiological systems underlying motivation and emotion. Chapter 2 examines in detail Darwin's suggestions regarding the communication of emotion:

that mechanisms of emotion communication evolve and that there are universal features in human emotion expression. It examines the course of social evolution, taking examples from ethological studies of communication in the societies of several animal species and the process of the evolution of communicative displays. The implications of the animal findings for humans are discussed. Chapter 2 also considers the possible influence of expressive behavior upon emotion, including the "facial feedback hypothesis" of Darwin and others. Chapter 3 examines the brain mechanisms involved in the communication of motivation and emotion. The role of subcortical and paleocortical mechanisms underlying motivational/emotional states is discussed, as is the influence of higher brain centers, particularly the role of the left versus the right cerebral hemispheres.

The third section, "Individual Differences in Emotion Communication," examines the development and functioning of emotion communication within the individual. Chapter 4 covers the development of emotion communication, stressing the roles of learning and experience (particularly early experience) in the development of appropriate patterns of response. Chapter 5 focuses upon individual differences in emotion sending accuracy: the tendency to accurately convey one's emotion state to others via spontaneous nonverbal behavior. Chapter 6 explores the issues of the inhibition of the expression of spontaneous motivational/emotional states, and the related question of deception. Chapter 7 focuses upon individual differences in nonverbal receiving ability: the ability to make accurate judgments about others based upon their nonverbal behavior. The chapters in this section draw upon the literature in developmental and social psychology and psychosomatic medicine which, until recently, have largely been divorced from the nonverbal communication literature and from each other, including studies of stress-related disease, coping styles, infant–caretaker interaction, social perception and inference, and attribution theory.

The fourth section, "Emotion Communication and Social Interaction," relates the phenomena discussed above on an individual level to social behavior, considering the role of emotion communication in the regulation of human interaction in interpersonal exchanges. Chapter 8 examines how both spontaneous and symbolic nonverbal behaviors give structure to informal interpersonal transactions in much the same way that a printed program gives structure to a formal transaction: telling participants whether and when to begin the interaction, how to take appropriate speaking turns, how intimate the interaction should be, whether and when to end the transaction, and so forth. It also argues that innate emotional factors involving sex and aggression, intimacy and dominance, form the foundation of human social interaction.

PART TWO

THE NATURE OF
MOTIVATION AND EMOTION

2

THE EVOLUTION
OF EMOTION COMMUNICATION

Some approaches to motivation and emotion have emphasized the close relationship between the two concepts, while others have pointed out the differences. The latter approaches have typically defined motivation as the process by which behavior is activated and directed, while emotion has been associated with subjective feelings and expressive behaviors. We shall follow the former approach, considering motivation and emotion to be two aspects of the same underlying process which involves all of these qualities—two sides of the same coin. In this chapter we shall briefly introduce this concept of motivation and emotion, and then outline its relevance to the notion of spontaneous communication above, and how it relates to the evolution of communication.

THE NATURE OF MOTIVATION AND EMOTION

We shall consider motivation and emotion to have three aspects. The most fundamental of these is that motivation and emotion are basically concerned with bodily *adaptation* and the maintenance of *homeostasis*. The second aspect involves the *external expression* of motivational/emotional states, which is most relevant when the communication of a given motivational/emotional state is useful for social coordination in a particular species. The third aspect involves the *direct subjective experience* of motivational/emotional states, which may be useful for self-regulation in species with significant cognitive capacities.

ADAPTATION AND HOMEOSTASIS

It is possible to consider every species that has evolved on the earth as containing a means of "packaging" the primordial environment in which life arose. This environment contained certain chemical balances, temperature ranges, and so forth, and the basic life processes involving DNA and other chemical substances are still tied to this environment to some extent. Thus one of the central life functions involves maintaining this internal environment in the face of changes in the external environment.

Originally, these functions could be served with relative ease. The promordial environment was structured so that the chemical reactions basic to life were natural occurrences. We can still see that in the simplest species, essential nutrients are provided continuously and almost automatically, as oxygen is provided to us. If the supply is cut off, the organism must die or perhaps revert to a state where nutrients are not necessary, as with simple creatures that dry up when a pond evaporates, only to resume their lives when water is restored.

As species evolved and became more complex, systems became necessary that would maintain the vital flow of nutrients—homeostasis—and adjust the organism as circumstances in the environment changed—adaptation. The autonomic nervous system and endocrine system have evolved in mammals to serve such functions as respiration, digestion, circulation, and temperature regulation, as well as basic "fight-or-flight" responses to threat, stress, and injury. The particular kinds of systems that evolved within a given species are tuned to the specific requirements of that species.

Because of general similarities in species requirements within the Earth's ecosystem and relationships between species during the course of evolution, some motivational/emotional systems are relatively universal, such as the needs for food, water and oxygen in animals. However, even within a single kind of biological need, there can be great differences in the specific systems employed by different species. Thus the respiration systems of fish, flies, and frogs are quite different. Other motivational/emotional systems reveal relatively subtle differences from species to species that reflect special requirements, such as the tendencies to gnaw, burrow, and hoard in small rodents, or the long period of infant attachment in the primates.

SOCIAL COORDINATION

In the simplest of organisms there is no real need to consider other organisms. Many creatures are able to survive and reproduce without any social contact at all. Perhaps the most basic motivational/emotional system that went beyond a solitary, virtually automatic process involved sexual reproduction. Successful sexual reproduction ordinarily requires some kind of coordination of behavior with at least one other organism, and it therefore cannot be an entirely internal affair. There must be some way in which potential mates are identified, attracted to each other, and encouraged to court and mate. This must involve mechanisms which, in the most general sense, are mechanisms of communication with all of the basic characteristics of communication systems defined in Chapter 1.

In highly social species, it became important for individuals to signal the state of certain motivational/emotional systems to each other beyond purely sexual signals. This led to the evolution of the chemical communication systems in ants, termites, and other insects; gestures of dominance and submission in a wide variety of species; and the wide variety of communicative postures, facial expressions, and calls in primates. We shall discuss below such biologically based communication systems and how they evolve.

SUBJECTIVE EXPERIENCE

Neither the processes of adaptation and homeostasis via the autonomic and endocrine systems, nor the communication of motivational/emotional states in the service of social coordination necessarily require much in the way of cognitive mediation and involvement, and they do not require any consideration of intention or planning. Both kinds of processes can be seen at work in the very simplest of creatures. At the same time, it is possible that both of these kinds of systems can be the source of a kind of subjective experience. The James–Lange theory argues that our perception of feedback from our visceral and skeletal muscle responses to motivational and emotional states is responsible for the subjective experience of such states.

However, I suggest that the most important source of such experience does not involve bodily feedback. Instead, emotional experience is largely a direct function of neurochemical activity in relevant brain regions; that is, one of the consequences of activity in the neurochemical systems underlying motivational/emotional states is a direct *readout* of motivation and emotion into conscious experience. I suggest that this kind of readout evolved in a way analogous to the evolution of expressive displays in social species—that it is useful for a creature with significant cognitive capacities to have direct knowledge of the state of certain of its own neurochemical systems associated with motivational/emotional states, just as it is useful for a social animal to have knowledge of certain of the motivational/emotional states of its fellows. The next chapter shall consider how neurochemical activity in relevant brain areas might translate into conscious experience.

TERMINOLOGY

Now that our general conception of the nature of motivation and emotion has been introduced, I shall drop the use of the term "motivation" in favor of "emotion," simply because the phrase "motivation and emotion" is cumbersome and repetitive, and the range of connotative meanings of "emotion" is more pertinent to the present book. However, it should be stressed that the term "emotion" is meant in a broad sense that includes the traditional concept of motivation and is identical to the phrase "motivation and emotion" as used above. This usage is not meant to suggest or imply that the concept of motivation should be subsumed under the concept of emotion.

THE EVOLUTION OF EMOTION

THE PROCESS OF EVOLUTION

Darwin's theory of evolution, published in *The Origin of Species* (1859), flows from several basic premises. From Malthus, Darwin took the notion that living things multiply faster than nature can provide, so that some will die before reproducing. Further, Darwin posited that there are individual differences in animals, and that the properties of some individuals are better adapted to the environment than are those of others. The better adapted individuals have a slightly higher probability of surviving and reproducing. Thus the fittest will tend to survive—the fittest being those who are best adapted to the particular environment. In doing so, the fittest will be more likely to pass their characteristics on to the next generation. This is the process of *natural selection*. Through it, attributes which are adaptive and useful to the survival of the species will naturally tend to increase, or be selected, over the generations. To the extent that a given attribute is useful to species survival, there is *selection pressure* for the increase of that attribute within that species.

Darwin referred to natural selection as the struggle for existence. However, it should be noted that this need not involve an active rivalry between creatures of the same species. The fittest animal tends naturally to survive because of its better adaptation to the environment. In a subsidiary doctrine of sexual selection, Darwin suggested that some species characteristics may evolve because they directly encourage the selection of a given individual as a mate. This doctrine, and other hypotheses about the precise nature of the methods of evolution, remain controversial, but the basic fact of evolution is firmly established in contemporary scientific thought.

THE EVOLUTION OF BEHAVIOR

It is relatively easy to see the process of evolution at work for the physical features of animals—how the turtle's shell evolved as a means of defense, how the neck of the giraffe evolved to allow the eating of vegetation which is out of the reach of other animals, and how the hoof of the deer evolved to maximize running speed and efficiency. It is perhaps less obvious that the behavior patterns of animals also evolve, including behavior patterns relating to emotional states. Glickman and Schiff (1967) have analyzed how each species has evolved behavior patterns that are adaptive to that particular species. For example, animals which must search for their food and who are not threatened by predators tend to show more evidence of curiosity and exploratory behavior than do species which have an easily obtained food supply and which are threatened by predators. Curiosity is less likely to kill a cat than a mouse. According to Glickman and Schiff, each species has evolved behavior patterns that "bring the animal into contact with stimuli which are relevant to its survival (approach) and . . . which remove it from stimuli which are threatening to its survival (withdrawal)" (p. 68).

It is interesting to note that some extremely threatening and dangerous stimuli cause no emotional reaction in humans. For example, as Tomkins (1962, 1963) has pointed out, a lack of air leads to severe emotional responses in humans whereas a lack of oxygen does not. In fact, anoxia can lead to euphoria, and for this reason can be extremely dangerous for high-altitude pilots. Similarly, unlike burns from thermal radiation, dangerously high doses of nuclear radiation are not experienced as painful. Perhaps during the course of evolution anoxia and nuclear radiation did not constitute dangerous problems for our species, and thus there was no selection pressure favoring individuals who removed themselves from such dangers. Therefore, the appropriate emotional systems never evolved.

THE EVOLUTION OF SOCIAL STRUCTURES

If it is difficult at first glance to see how behavior tendencies evolve, it is even more difficult to imagine the evolution of social structures, since evolution would seem to be able to affect only the properties of individuals, and social structure is a property of groups of individuals. However, it is clear that some social structures do indeed evolve, such as the social structures of the insects—bees, ants, termites, and so forth. The answer to this paradox lies in the fact that: (1) social structures can be based upon communication systems, and (2) communication systems can evolve within the individual just as can other kinds of behavior.

The communication systems that so evolve must include all of the characteristics of the communication process that we outlined in Chapter 1. They must involve both *sending accuracy*, defined as the encoding of relevant information into a form that can be accurately decoded by others, and *receiving ability*, defined as the ability to accurately decode this information. Sending accuracy must involve a central encoding mechanism, and receiving ability a central decoding mechanism.

The evolution of social structures via communication systems can be seen most clearly in the insects. In his pioneering study, von Frisch (1968) described the biological signal system by which bees communicate the location of food to their fellows. Similar observational studies by ethologists have disclosed much about the functioning of the societies of termites and ants, where communication occurs via chemical signals. Such communication must be strictly spontaneous in the sense of the term introduced in Chapter 1; that is, it must be reflexive and nonpropositional in both its sending and receiving aspects. Information in the environment must activate the sender's behavior in a way strictly dictated by evolution, and this behavior must influence the behavior of the receiver in a way strictly dictated by evolution. The resulting communication is extremely rigid and can go wildly astray, as is illustrated by the observation that ants normally give off an odorous substance when dead, whereupon their fellows typically carry them to a graveyard within the colony. This normally works well and has all the outward appearance of purposive behavior. However, if a live ant is daubed with the substance, it is carried kicking and struggling to the graveyard and unceremoniously dumped. It may then try to escape, only to be captured and dumped again. This process will continue until the substance finally wears off or the unfortunate creature really does die.

There is abundant evidence that analogous kinds of communication systems, involving the communication of emotion, support the much more complex social structures of vertebrates, including human and nonhuman primates. We saw in Chapter 1 that Darwin (1872) argued that emotion communication has adaptive value in social animals because it functions to aid in the coordination of social behavior. That this behavior is innate is demonstrated by the observation that squirrel monkeys who have been isolated from species-specific vocalizations by having been deafened from birth, and/or raised with surgically muted mothers, produce in adulthood vocalizations that are virtually identical to those produced by monkeys reared under normal conditions (Riggs, Winter, Ploog, & Mayer, 1972; Winter, Handley, Ploog, & Schott, 1973). Such a phenomenon would require a "prewired" genetically determined mechanism for call production.

Andrew (1963, 1965) has analyzed the vocal and facial displays of primates in detail. He notes, for example, that in baboons, the nature of their societies was such as to greatly favor any change making the transfer of information "more explicit and less ambiguous" (1963, p. 91). Within the baboon species, the displays of the highly social plains-dwelling baboon are more complex than those of the mandrill or drill baboons which lead a more solitary existence in the forest (1965).

In other words, it is useful for social animals to be able to communicate their internal states of anger, fear, interest, sexual excitement, and so forth, to their fellows without actually having to engage in the overt behaviors associated with those states. The more highly social the species, the stronger are the selection pressures favoring the evolution of such communication systems. At the same time, we shall see in Chapter 4 that the more complex the animal and the social system, the more the animal must *learn how to use* these communication systems in the course of individual social development. In effect, the animal must learn to effectively employ display and decoding rules. For the present, we shall consider how emotion communication systems evolve in social species.

THE EVOLUTION OF EMOTIONAL EXPRESSION

RITUALIZATION

Behavior patterns that have evolved as signals in the service of social coordination are termed "displays," and the process by which displays evolve is termed "ritualization" (Blest, 1961; Tinbergen, 1959). The source or precursor of a display is a behavior on the part of the sender which is (1) potentially informative about the emotion state to be expressed, and (2) visible or otherwise accessible to the receiver via sensory cues (Buck, 1981a, 1981b). Thus the display most likely evolves from some behavior associated with the emotion state which is visible to others via such modes as visual, auditory, and olfactory cues.

As an example, Eibl-Eibesfeldt (1972) has analyzed the ritualization of the eyebrow-raise into a display associated with surprise or interest in humans. He notes that a widening of the eyes in primates is naturally associated with an increase in visual acuity, thus it tends to occur in situations where the animal is attempting to see more clearly what is happening. This commonly occurs in situations associated with the emotions of surprise or interest; thus, widening of the eyes is potentially informative of surprise or interest, but is not in itself very accessible (visible) to others. However, the widening of the eyes is naturally accompanied by a raising of the skin above the eyes, which is potentially visible to others. Eibl-Eibesfeldt suggests that the eyebrow has evolved in primates in part to make the raising of this skin more visible, and that the eyebrow-raise thus constitutes a ritualized display associated with surprise or interest. In humans, he notes that the eyebrow-raise has acquired different meanings in different cultures; thus it means "yes" in Samoa and "no" in Greece. Eibl-Eibesfeldt suggests that this indicates the role of social and cultural learning in determining the exact communicative role of the display. In our terms this indicates that the eyebrow-raise and other ritualized displays can take on symbolic meaning which may differ from culture to culture. However, it may be argued that each of these symbolic meanings may have ultimately derived from the original message concerning the state of the sender's visual attention associated with surprise and interest.

As the above example attests, the ritualization of displays is often accompanied by the evolution of physical characteristics that serve to increase the accessibility of the display. Examples include the eyebrow in primates (including humans), which emphasizes the raising and lowering of the skin above the eyes; the colorful tail feathers of the male peacock, used in courtship displays; and the tympanum of the grasshopper, used to produce acoustical signals (cf. Eibl-Eibesfeldt, 1970; Wilson, 1975). Andrew (1963, 1965) has suggested that the complex facial masculature of primates, particularly humans, has evolved in part to serve the functions of emotion communication.

HUMAN FACIAL EXPRESSIONS OF EMOTION

If human facial expression evolved for this reason, it implies that the basic facial expressions of emotion must be universal to the human species. Much of the debate over the implications of Darwin's analysis of the evolution of emotion expression to human beings has revolved around this implication. The debate over whether human facial expressions of emotion are universal and thus innate versus culturally variable and thus learned has been long and, at times heated. Darwin set out the former position in *The Expression of the Emotions in Man and Animals* (1872). Like other explanations of human behavior that posited innate determinants, this position was challenged by those who argued that human behavior is wholly learned. This view has been challenged in turn by more sophisticated analyses of the biological bases of behavior which, like that of Eibl-Eibesfeldt (1972), take both innate mechanisms and learning into account (cf. Ekman, 1973; Ekman, Friesen, & Ellsworth, 1972a).

A major landmark in this process was the publication of Sylvan Tomkins's *Affect, Cognition, and Personality* (1962, 1963), in which Tomkins argued that there are eight *primary affects*: happiness, sadness, anger, fear, disgust/contempt, surprise, interest, and shame. Each of the primary affects was said to be innately based upon a physiological program in the central nervous system, and each was associated with a specific and universal facial display. Tomkins's theory influenced the work of both Paul Ekman and Carroll Izard, who found support for the theory using photographs of posed facial expressions in cross-cultural studies (Ekman *et al.*, 1972a; Izard, 1977). For example, Ekman and his colleagues found that the posed expressions of certain of the primary affects by Westerners could be accurately decoded even by persons from preliterate tribes who had had little or no contact with Western culture, and that videotapes of their posed expressions could be accurately decoded by Americans (Ekman & Friesen, 1975; Ekman, Sorenson, & Friesen, 1969).

Ekman and Friesen (1975) discuss in detail the general facial configurations associated with certain of the primary affects. However, they also stress that the facial expression is not a simple and automatic function of the emotion state, being influenced by the learned display rules about what facial displays are appropriate under what circumstances. Thus a person might *qualify* a display by adding a further expression as a comment on the felt expression, as when one smiles following a display of a negative emotion (anger, fear, sadness) to instruct others that "I won't go too far," or "I'll go through with it anyway," or "I can take it." Also, one can *modulate* the expression of emotion, increasing or decreasing its intensity relative to what one actually feels. Finally, there are a number of ways in which one can falsify emotion: *masking* what one actually feels or *simulating* an unfelt emotion.

The model of the facial expression of emotion that is suggested by Ekman and Friesen's (1969a, 1975) analysis is illustrated in Figure 2.1. An emotional stimulus sets off a response in one or more of the physiological systems underlying the primary affects. These initiate spontaneous tendencies toward the facial expressions innately as-

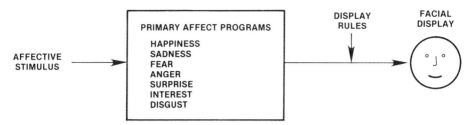

Figure 2.1. The Ekman and Friesen (1969a) model of the sending process. Adapted with permission from Figure 2 in "The Repertoire of Nonverbal Behavior: Categories, Origins, Usage, and Coding" by P. Ekman and W. Friesen, *Semiotica*, 1969, *1*, 49–98.

sociated with the primary affect(s) involved, but the actual expressions are also influenced by the (symbolic) display rules that the sender has learned in such situations. Thus the ultimate facial expression is a joint function of the spontaneous, innate, and universal mechanism; and the symbolic, learned, and culturally variable mechanism.

SUMMARY

We may summarize the evolution of emotion displays as follows: If the communication of a given emotion state is adaptive to a species, individuals who show evidence of this state in their visible or otherwise accessible behavior will tend to be favored. The more clearly the state is displayed, the more the individual is favored, so that over the generations, the display becomes ritualized. However, although the tendencies to display have an innate basis, the nature of the actual display is also influenced by learned factors which are sensitive to the situation: the display rules.

THE EVOLUTION OF RECEIVING ABILITY

INNATE FACTORS IN RECEIVING ABILITY

The display would be of little evolutionary value for the species if other animals fail to respond appropriately to it. It is often not recognized that what is evolving must not simply be a display, but must involve a communication system, and that as we have seen involves a receiver as well as a sender. Thus individuals who respond appropriately to the displays of others must also be favored, so that over the generations the attentional and perceptual systems of species members must become "preattuned" to the pickup of important emotion displays.

The notion of innate systems underlying receiving ability has not been emphasized in most analyses of nonverbal receiving ability. Like most theorizing about the process of person perception in general, most have assumed that the receiving process is largely learned. In other words, it is typically assumed that the sender's behavior has little or no meaning in itself as unelaborated stimulus input. The emphasis instead is on how the receiver learns through experience, imitation, or reinforcement to structure or process the raw data provided by the sender's behavior. The basis of this view is the notion that one must learn to construct meaning from a chaotic perceptual field—the "booming, buzzing confusion" supposedly experienced by the infant. In effect, such a view emphasizes knowledge by description, as we have defined it, to the virtual exclusion of knowledge by acquaintance in analyzing the process of person perception.

This kind of view has been challenged in recent years, particularly by the theory and research on perception generated by J. J. Gibson (1966, 1979), which emphasizes the importance of information present in the environment, suggesting that perception involves the direct "pickup" of this information with no need for its conversion, transformation, or processing. Gibson's view emphasizes the richness of the information given "as is" in the stimulus array, and this tends to underscore the role of knowledge by acquaintance.

We shall present a brief account of Gibson's theory, which emphasizes the role of the evolution of perceptual systems, and shall consider the implications of this view to the analysis of person perception in general and emotion receiving ability in particular.

GIBSON'S ECOLOGICAL THEORY OF PERCEPTION

The Evolution of Perception

The notion of an evolution of receiving ability is consistent with Gibson's notion that perception must be determined by the nature of the ecological niche in which the species evolves. To Gibson, perception is made possible by compatibilities between the animal's qualities (e.g., the receptor apparatus) and the environment. These compatabilities involve the evolved qualities of the organism which may be "tuned" by experience. Gibson argues that the nature of the human species—that is, a terrestrial, bipedal, social animal with efficient binocular vision, and so forth—has evolved hand in hand with a certain way of knowing the world. This is true of all species—each has evolved a way of knowing which is compatible with what it *must* know in order to survive in its environment. Thus, the organism is seen to be biologically prepared or "attuned" to properties of it's environment that are objectively present, accurately specified, and veridically perceived (Neisser, 1976, p. 19).

In other words, perceptual systems have evolved to "pick up" or extract certain information from the environment that is relevant to survival. For example, human visual perception begins from the pattern of ambient light reflected from surfaces in the environment:

> The complex structural properties of this *optic array* are determined by the actual nature and position of the objects. This structure *specifies* those objects; the information about them is in the light. When the observer or an object moves, certain higher-order characteristics of the optic array remain invariant while others change, and these invariants over time specify the layout of the environment still more precisely. The observer perceives by simply "picking up" these invariances. He may have to search for information but he need not process it, because it is all in the light already. (Neisser, 1976, pp. 18–19; emphasis in original)

An interesting example of the evolution of communication, including the possible evolution of emotion communication in an ecological context very different from our own, involves the dolphin. Dolphins have no sense of smell, and their sense of sight is of limited use in their undersea environment. It has been suggested, however, that they are capable of forming sonic "images" by sensing the echoes of trains of high-frequency clicks that they emit, which may be focused by a "lens" of fat in the forehead. These sonic images may be highly refined: Dolphins appear capable of making discriminations between degrees of "hollowness" in metal balls that equal the capabilities of human visual discrimination. It is clear that dolphins "can 'hear' the composition and texture of objects around them," and may be able to "look *into* each other in eerie ways, inspecting the contours of internal air spaces" (K. S. Norris, in Linehan, 1979, pp. 515–516). This sonic "X-ray vision" may provide the highly social dolphin with information about the emotional state of its fellows which is analogous to that obtained via spontaneous facial/gestural expression in primates such as ourselves, and which may serve a similar function: social coordination. That is, the contours of internal air spaces in dolphins may conceivably vary with emotional states, and receiver dolphins may be able to "pick up" such information to assess states analogous to fear, anger, excitement, and so forth, in the sender.

Affordances and Social Affordances

Gibson (1979) deals with the perception of meaning through the concept of *affordance*. Affordances involve conjunctions between the properties of the organism and the environment—all of the potential uses of the objects constitute the activities they afford, and according to Gibson these are directly perceived (Baron & Buck, 1979; Neisser, 1976). Thus what makes an object afford "graspability" involves a conjunction between the physical properties of the object and the characteristics of the organism.

The adequacy of the affordance concept in dealing with the perception of meaning is the subject of controversy that is beyond the realm of the present discussion (cf. Heil, 1979; Neisser, 1976, pp. 72–75). However, both Neisser and Gibson have suggested that affordances may involve the characteristics of other persons as well as physical objects in the environment. Thus Gibson proposed that sexual behavior, nurturant behavior, cooperative behavior, and so forth, can be treated as affordances in which the sender provides possibilities for interaction that can be directly perceived by the receiver. It could be argued that the process of spontaneous communication may be viewed in terms of such "social affordances."

There is some experimental evidence supporting the notion that perceptual systems are preattuned to environmental information important to the species. For example, infant rhesus monkeys who have been isolated from other monkeys since birth react with appropriate fearful behavior when confronted with a photograph of a large male monkey making a threat display (Sackett, 1966). Also, it has been demonstrated that human facial expressions of fear and anger are more readily associated with aversive events than are happy or neutral expressions in classical conditioning studies (Lanzetta & Orr, 1980; Ohman & Dimberg, 1978).

Finally, Dimberg and Ohman (1983; Dimberg, 1983) have demonstrated that happy versus angry faces affect conditioning only when they are directed *toward* the subject. The differential effects of the expressions are reduced or lost when the faces are directed away from the responder.

The Education of Attention

In a sense, Gibson's viewpoint stresses the importance of the stimulus more than the processes going on within the receiver. If the stimulus is "veridically perceived," one should theoretically know what is perceived by describing the stimulus. However, it is clear that perceivers differ from one another in the information they extract from a given stimulus, and several authors have suggested that Gibson's theory is not entirely satisfactory in dealing with such differences (Heil, 1979). Neisser (1976) has suggested that Eleanor J. Gibson's (1969) work on cognitive development addresses some of these issues. For example, she suggests that the difference between a skilled and naïve perceiver lies in the fact that the former can extract more information from the stimulus, detecting features and higher order structures to which the naïve perceiver is not sensitive. Thus the perceiver's skill involves the ability to extract information efficiently, rather than the ability to process information differently. An older child may learn to note information that a younger child ignores (Neisser, 1976).

Gibson (1966) has referred to the perceptual selection of good information as the *education of attention*. This notion suggests that the perceptual organization of an event is an important aspect of observer skill, because it determines the information an observer may draw upon in making judgments and inferences. Thus a person skilled in nonverbal receiving ability may differ from a less skilled receiver not only in the ability to decode an emotion display once it is perceived, but in the tendency to attend to emotion displays at all. A "poor receiver" may be a person who simply ignores the emotion displays of others, and such a person may be a successful decoder when attending to such displays. We shall see that the notion of an education of attention is extremely useful at several points in our discussion, and shall return to it particularly in Chatpers 4, 6, and 7.

LEARNING AND COGNITIVE FACTORS IN RECEIVING ABILITY

Many who are essentially sympathetic to the Gibsonian view of direct perception have argued that it cannot be a complete account of the process (Heil, 1979). Neisser (1976), for example, argues that one must also understand how cognitive structures internal to the perceiver are modified by information in the environment. These cognitive structures, or schemas, are involved in a perceptual cycle: They are modified by environmental information and then, in turn, direct the process of perceptual exploration and attention, leading to the sampling of new environmental information. Neisser's concept of perceptual cycles has similarities with Piaget's (1971) process of equilibration through assimilation and accommodation, and Elkind's (1971) cognitive growth cycles. All of these attempt to describe how the cognitive system "constructs its own structure" in the course of adaptation to the external world. We shall discuss this sort of cognitive development, and how it relates to emotional development, in Chapter 4.

From our present point of view, this implies that emotion receiving ability must involve more than the spontaneous response to emotion displays: it involves knowledge by description as well as knowledge by acquaintance. This is clearly seen in the phenomenon of decoding rules. This shall be considered in detail in Chapters 4, 6, and 7. Here, we next consider how the spontaneous and symbolic processes relate to one another in emotion receiving ability.

THE SOCIAL KNOWING CONTINUUM

Hochberg (1956) has suggested that this relationship might best be represented as a continuum, one extreme of which involves the case where knowledge of the stimulus is both necessary and sufficient to completely predict the receiver's response, and the other extreme of which involves the case where the receiver's response is independent of the stimulus, knowledge of which is neither necessary nor sufficient for the prediction of the response. In between lies a domain in which the stimulus accounts for some but not all of the variance in the response. The upper part of Figure 2.2 illustrates this dimension.

Baron (1980; Baron & Buck, 1979; Baron & Harvey, 1980) has suggested an analogous distinction which is relevant to this relationship. This "social knowing continuum" is presented in the middle part of Figure 2.2. At one extreme is perception-based knowing, where meaning is entirely given by information in environmental events, requiring no additional cognitive processing. At the other extreme is cognition-based knowing, where meaning is purely a function of cognitive operations without regard to the stimuli. When the object of knowledge is a person, Baron speaks of *person perception* at one end of the continuum and *person cognition* at the other.

Both of these continua can be regarded as analogous to a continuum between "pure" knowledge by acquaintance, involved as we have suggested in spontaneous communication, and "pure" knowledge by description. However, as suggested in the last chapter, the relationship between phenomena associated with spontaneous and symbolic communication in biological organisms is probably too complex to be described by a continuum. Instead, it may be useful to describe it in terms of a variant of the relationship shown earlier in Figure 1.2.

Figure 2.2. The social knowing continuum and alternative formulation.

Hochberg (1956)
Stimulus predicts response ——————— Response independent of stimulus

Baron (1980) social knowing continuum
Direct knowing via perception ——————— Indirect knowing via cognition
Person perception ——————————————— Person cognition

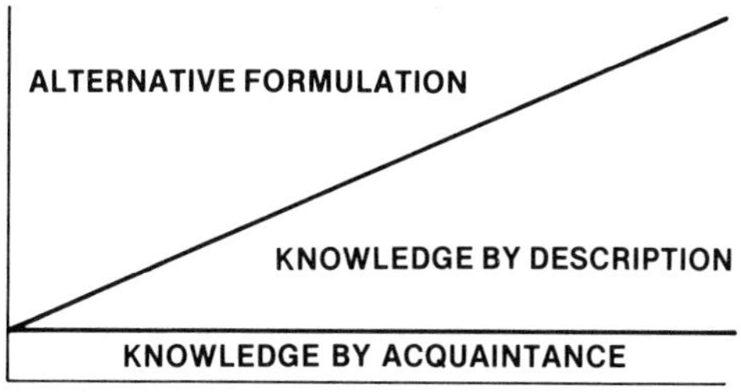

ALTERNATIVE FORMULATION

KNOWLEDGE BY DESCRIPTION

KNOWLEDGE BY ACQUAINTANCE

The lower part of Figure 2.2 presents this relationship stated in these terms. It suggests that person cognition is always accompanied by person perception, and cannot exist in "pure form."

SUMMARY

It may be seen that this account of the evolution of receiving ability is analogous to the model of sending accuracy presented in Figure 2.1 in that spontaneous, biologically based, nonpropositional processes occur simultaneously with symbolic, socially based, and propositional processes. The former are associated with direct perception, the latter with mediated perception. The former processes involve knowledge by acquaintance, the latter, knowledge by description. Thus emotion communication in both its sending and receiving aspects is conceptualized here as involving two simultaneous "streams" in humans, one spontaneous and the other symbolic. The evolutionary origins of both kinds of communication involve the need for the coordination of behavior in social animals.

In the next chapter we shall examine the biological systems underlying spontaneous and symbolic emotion communication. We shall now turn to the evolution of a third major aspect of emotion: subjective experience.

THE EVOLUTION OF EMOTIONAL EXPERIENCE

Subjective emotional experience may be seen as having evolved in a process analogous to the evolution of emotion communication. Awareness of one's own emotion state can be seen to be useful in the regulation and coordination of one's own behavior, just as the communication of emotional information is useful in the regulation and coordination of social behavior. This could provide selection pressures for the evolution of "readout" mechanisms, which provide emotional information directly to the cognitive system.

It is also possible that, as the James–Lange theory suggests, some aspects of emotional experience involve feedback from peripheral visceral and skeletal muscle responses associated with bodily homeostasis and adaptation, and emotional expression. This section reviews this theory, and the evidence for the role of each of these peripheral systems in determining subjective experience. It then considers the evidence for a direct "cognitive readout," and its implications.

THE JAMES-LANGE THEORY

The central notion of the James–Lange theory, proposed independently by William James (1884) and Carl Lange (1887), is that somatic and visceral changes occur when an emotional stimulus is perceived and that "our feeling of these same changes as they occur *is* the emotion. . . . Without the bodily states following on the perception, the latter would be purely cognitive in form, pale, colorless, destitute of emotional warmth" (James, 1968, p. 19; emphasis in original). Thus, we do not cry because we feel sorry; we feel sorry because we cry.

James clearly felt that skeletal muscle activity, including facial expression, was involved in these bodily changes:

> Can one fancy the state of rage and picture no ebullition of it in the chest, no flushing of the face, no dilation of the nostrils, no clenching of the teeth, no impulse to vigorous action, but in their stead limp muscles, calm breathing, and a placid face? (1968, p. 23)

Thus, James felt that without somatic and visceral changes, the perception of an emotional stimulus would be purely cognitive and "unemotional": We might see a bear, and judge it best to run, but we could not actually *feel* afraid (1968, p. 19). Thus he considers peripheral somatic and visceral responses to be necessary to add a subjective emotional quality to the perception of an event. James noted that the ultimate test of his theory would be to study persons deprived of their peripheral sensation. If such a person "recognized explicitly the same mood of feeling known . . . in his former state, my theory of course would fall. It is, however, to me incredible that the patient should have an *identical* feeling, for the dropping out of the organic sounding board would necessarily diminish its volume in some way" (1968, p. 36; emphasis in original).

In 1927, W. B. Cannon reviewed the clinical and experimental work relevant to the James–Lange theory, and found several basic objections to it. In particular, Cannon argued (1) that visceral sensation is too diffuse and insensitive to account for the wide range of human emotion experience, and (2) that the autonomic nervous system acts too slowly to account for the speed and lability of human emotion experience (Cannon, 1927, 1932). However, these points were more relevant to the role of visceral feedback, and they did not apply to skeletal muscle activity. In fact, it could be argued that the skeletal muscle activity involved in emotional expression, and particularly facial expression, is both fast enough and differentiated enough to account for human emotional experience. This view is, in fact, highly consistent with Darwin's position as presented in *The Expression of the Emotions in Man and Animals*:

> Most of our emotions are so closely connected with their expression, that they hardly exist if the body remains passive. . . . The free expression of outward signs of an emotion intensifies it. On the other hand, the repression, as far as this is possible, of all outward signs, softens our emotions. (1872, p. 365)

From the combination of the James–Lange theory and Darwin's position has developed the notion that the skeletal muscle activity associated with emotional expression plays a direct role in regulating emotional processes. Thus Ekman *et al.* (1972a) argued that the facial muscles in particular might underly emotion experience: "The face might . . . fill the information gap left by a solely visceral theory of emotion, distinguishing one emotion from another, changing rapidly and providing feedback about what is occurring to the person" (p. 173). This "facial feedback hypothesis" has been adopted by a number of recent theories of emotion which, in other respects, are quite different from one another. These include the theories of Plutchik (1962, 1980), Tomkins (1962, 1963), Gellhorn (1964, 1967), Mandler (1975), and Izard (1971, 1977). In the following paragraphs, we shall consider the evidence for the role of visceral and skeletal muscle feedback in the subjective experience of emotion, the evidence for a direct cognitive "readout" in subjective experience, and the role of the interaction between physiological mechanisms and cognition in subjective experience.

VISCERAL FEEDBACK

There is convincing evidence for the importance of visceral feedback in emotional experience, but, as we shall see, visceral feedback does not appear to be either necessary or sufficient for all kinds of emotion experience.

One of the most important studies of visceral feedback is that of Hohmann (1966), who studied the reported emotion experience of veterans with spinal cord injuries. In asking them to compare their experience of emotion before and after the injury, Hohmann found that most reported decreased emotion experience which was related to the height of the spinal lesion. The higher the lesion, and thus the greater the loss of visceral/bodily sensation, the greater was the reported decrease in subjective experience. Some of the patients reported that they acted emotional without really feeling it: One said "I get thinking mad instead of shaking mad, and that's a lot different" (p. 151). Another reported acting out a kind of cold anger: "Sometimes I act angry when I see some injustice. I yell and cuss and raise hell, because if you don't do it sometimes, I've learned that people take advantage of you, but it just doesn't have the heat that it used to. It's a mental kind of anger" (p. 151).

An observation by Delgado (1969) also suggests that visceral feedback contributes to subjective experience. A patient who underwent a unilateral sympathectomy for cancer "found that his previous and customary sensation of shivering while listening to a stirring passage of music occurred in only one side and he could not be thrilled on the sympathectomized half of his body" (pp. 134–135).

On the other hand, other observations from the clinical literature on the effects of spinal injuries in humans suggests that many aspects of emotional behavior are preserved. Cannon cited Dana's (1921) description of a number of such cases, including that of a woman who suffered a complete loss of sensation from the neck down after breaking her neck in a fall. Despite her injuries, she reported having apparently normal emotions of affection, joy, annoyance, and grief, and she showed no change in personality.

Mandler and his colleagues developed a self-report scale of visceral perception, the Autonomic Perception Questionnaire (APQ; Mandler, Mandler, & Unviller, 1958), but attempts to relate scores on the scale to objective abilities at heart rate detection have not been successful (Whitehead, Dresher, & Blackwell, 1976). More recent studies of visceral perception have stemmed from research in autonomic self-regulation associated with biofeedback. Brener (1977) has suggested that the success of biofeedback training in facilitating the voluntary control of visceral responses depends upon the learning of the ability to discriminate such responses. This has led to a variety of attempts to assess the accuracy of visceral perception, most of them studying the perception of heart rate (Brener & Jones, 1974; Brener &

Ross, 1980; Katkin, Blascovich, & Goldbrand, 1981; Whitehead, Drescher, Heiman, & Blackwell, 1977). This is an emerging area of study, and different methods of assessing visceral perception do not always agree with one another (Pennebaker, 1982). However, it is interesting that several studies using a signal detection technique have found that males are better able to discriminate heart beats than females (Katkin, Morell, Goldbrand, & Bernstein, 1980; Katkin *et al.*, 1981; Whitehead *et al.*, 1977). Katkin *et al.* (1981) note that a proper explanation for this gender difference is not yet apparent, but that it may relate to other gender differences in the pattern of emotional expression.

SOMATIC FEEDBACK: THE FACIAL FEEDBACK HYPOTHESIS

Studies Employing Posed Expression

Whereas there is considerable evidence for the role of visceral feedback in at least some kinds of emotion experience, the evidence for the role of somatic feedback is less clear and more susceptible to alternative interpretation (Buck, 1980). The studies demonstrating the role of visceral feedback have shown that individuals with differing amounts of visceral sensation have differing overall levels of emotion experience. This has not been demonstrated by studies on facial or somatic feedback. Instead, most of the relevant studies have used repeated measures designs which suggest that a given person will report different experiences when he or she is posing different facial expressions than when he or she is not. For example, Laird (1974) found that subjects induced to "frown" or "smile" reported feeling more angry or more happy, respectively, as they viewed affective slides. Similarly, Lanzetta, Cartwright-Smith, and Kleck (1976) showed that subjects induced to pose strong reactions to shock had larger skin conductance responses and reported more severe pain than they did when induced to pose no reactions to the same shock levels.

More recent studies have not always supported the notion that posing facial expressions leads to corresponding changes in emotion experience. Tourangeau and Ellsworth (1979) asked subjects to hold their faces in a fearful expression, sad expression, or effortful non-emotional expression while viewing sad, fear-arousing, or emotionally neutral films. They found no evidence that facial expression had any effect upon reported emotion, and found evidence that physiological responses may have been affected by the effort involved in making an expression, rather than the emotional nature of the expression.

The latter conclusion has been supported in a recent study by McCaul, Holmes, and Solomon (1982). These authors asked subjects to pose fearful versus calm versus "normal" expressions. Posing fear led to skin-conductance and heart-rate increases, but had no significant effect upon the subjective report of anxiety. In a second study, subjects listened to loud or soft noise while portraying either fear, happiness, or calmness. Portraying either fear or happiness led to increased heart-rate responding, but had no effect upon self-reports of noise loudness. The authors conclude that changes in facial expression may influence physiological responses through the movement involved in posing, but they suggest that they do not influence self-reports of emotion.

Criticisms of Posed Studies

In a series of responses to the Tourangeau and Ellsworth (1979) results, several investigators who have been identified with some version of the facial feedback hypothesis have questioned the relevance of studies employing experimenter-induced facial movement (Hagar & Ekman, 1981; Izard, 1981; Tomkins, 1981). Izard, for example, noted that in an unpublished study (Kotsch, Izard, & Walker, 1978), he found an increase in anger ratings using non-emotion-related facial contractions, and suggested that facial muscle movements play a role in emotion regulation only when self-directed, that is, when "subjects initiate the facial patterns for reasons of their own, the reasons consonant with the desired effect" (Izard, 1977b). Similarly, Tomkins (1981) argued that the voluntary simulation of facial responses would not generate appropriate sensory feedback for emotion experience, and he also noted that he has recently altered his theory to assign a more secondary role to the facial musculature in generating such feedback, emphasizing instead blood flow, temperature, and altered sensory thresholds (Tomkins, 1979). Hagar and Ekman (1981) dismissed the Tourangeau and Ellsworth results on methodological grounds, arguing among other things that the study did not employ "valid analogues" of emotional expressions, and could not assure that spontaneous expressions did not occur.

Ellsworth and Tourangeau (1981) responded in turn by pointing out that these authors had made strongly worded statements that, even though they may have been qualified in other parts of their writings, had nevertheless been widely interpreted as supporting the notion that facial expression is a necessary and sufficient cause of emotional experience. They also suggested that these authors had been indefinite regarding their predictions about the effects of voluntary expressions. Ellsworth and Tourangeau defended their methodology, and concluded that their results at the least indicate that the facial feedback hypothesis must be highly qualified to state that only a "valid" facial expression, congruent with eliciting stimuli, will affect emotional experience.

Izard's Position

More insight can be gained into the important theoretical questions involved in this issue by considering Izard's position more closely. Although he has argued that the facial feedback hypothesis cannot be properly evaluated by studies which manipulate expression, he does clearly feel that the subjective experience of emotion is based upon facial expression. He has stated that "facial feedback plays its role in emotion activation in a rapid reflexive fashion, and awareness of facial activity or facial feedback is actually our awareness of the subjective experience of a specific emotion" (1977a, p. 60). He goes on to point out that "one does not ordinarily become aware of the proprioceptive and cutaneous impulses (as such) created by frowning or smiling; rather, one becomes aware of experiential anger or joy" (p. 60). In a 1981 paper, he suggests that emotional experience is a result of "cortical–limbic interactions and cortical integrative processes" (1981, p. 352), implying that it is mediated by cortical–limbic pathways that integrate the sensory data provided by feedback from the face.

The problem of evaluating this position is made more complex when it is stated that there are a number of ways in which emotion experience may occur *without perceptible facial expression* (cf. Izard, 1977a, pp. 60–61). First, rapid "micromomentary expressions" that cannot be easily perceived by an observer may be sufficient to provide the feedback required for subjective experience. Izard cites Haggard and Isaccs's (1966) demonstrations of such expressions and the Schwartz *et al.* studies of "covert expressions" in which electromyographic recordings reveal muscle movements not visible on the face (Schwartz, Fair, Greenberg, Freedman, & Klerman, 1974; Schwartz, Fair, Salt, Mandel, & Klerman, 1976). Second, one may learn to simulate facial feedback by means of an inner or "reafferent loop" in which the motor messages to the face trigger sensory feedback messages without actually stimulating the facial muscles. Related to this, the "memory" of what facial feedback "feels" like could elicit subjective experience via processes analogous to classical conditioning.

Izard's position is thus more subtle and sophisticated than a simple statement of the facial feedback hypothesis might suggest. It is not clearly disconfirmed by the Tourangeau and Ellsworth (1979) result, but on the other hand it is not clearly supported by studies such as those of Laird (1974) or Lanzetta et al. (1976). Tourangeau and Ellsworth (1979) in fact suggest that the hypothesis might not be testable at all: "If the only influential facial expression is one that results from an involuntary natural response and if the facial muscles can be bypassed intracranially, the causal role of the face becomes inaccessible to any sort of definitive empirical test" (p. 1522).

Relationships between Facial Expression and Other Measures

Whether or not one accepts the notion that the highly qualified version of the facial feedback hypothesis is testable, there does not appear to be any convincing evidence in favor of it at the present time. Also, there is negative evidence from another quarter. All statements of the facial feedback hypothesis imply that the degree of facial expression should be positively related to other indices of emotion. These statements have not been sufficiently explicit on this point, but the strongest versions of the hypothesis would imply that this should be true of both between-subjects and within-subjects relationships (cf. Buck, 1980). The hypothesized between-subjects relationship would be that persons who show much facial expression should have greater responses on other emotional indices than persons who show little expression; the hypothesized within-subjects relationship would be that a person should tend to show larger emotional responses on occasions on which *that same person* shows much facial expression.

The evidence suggests that the within-subjects relationship between facial expressiveness and other emotional responses may be positive as predicted by the facial feedback hypothesis. However, there are potential explanations for this that do not require a causal relationship between facial expression and the other indices: perhaps the emotional stimulus is simply more effective on occasions where the person responds strongly on both facial and other measures. One would clearly expect that a given person would show more facial expression, self-reported experience, and physiological responding to a strong emotional stimulus than to a weak one. The demonstrations of a positive within-subjects relationship between facial expression and other indices could easily be due to this trivial cause.

The between-subjects relationship is thus more important for the evaluation of the facial feedback hypothesis, and here the weight of the evidence is contrary: A number of studies have shown, for example, that spontaneously expressive persons have *smaller* physiological responses to emotional stimuli than do nonexpressive persons (cf. Buck, 1979a, 1980, 1981b; Notarius & Levenson, 1979; Notarius, Wemple, Ingraham, Burns, & Kollar, 1982). These studies and their implications shall be discussed in Chapter 5. The fact that they involved spontaneous facial expression appears to be particularly damaging to the most recent, qualified versions of the facial feedback hypothesis, since it cannot be argued that they involved "invalid" expressions.

Undoubtedly this conclusion will be challenged, and the role of facial feedback in the emotion process eventually clarified, although it may be that animal experiments or studies of brain-damaged patients will be necessary to accomplish this. At present, however, there does not appear to be evidence that facial feedback is as effective as visceral feedback has been demonstrated to be in affecting emotional experience (Buck, 1980).

Bodily Feedback and Emotion

Although there are many studies of facial feedback, there are very few studies of the effects of bodily feedback—movement or posture—upon emotional responding. The lack of such studies is surprising. It is apparently due to the fact that facial feedback has been accorded special status in emotion theory, even though there is no evidence that such status is warranted. Studies showing that bodily feedback also influences emotional responding would tend to cast doubt upon this special status. In fact, one could suggest that, if bodily cues are less controlled and more "leaky" than facial cues, as suggested by

Ekman and Friesen (1969b; see Chapter 6), they should be more reliably linked to actual emotion than are facial cues (Buck, 1980). We shall see in Chapter 4 that studies of interoceptive conditioning suggest that bodily events which are reliably associated with emotional states or stimuli could be expected to come to influence emotional responding.

In one recent study, which paid commendable attention to the possibility of demand factors and experimental bias, Riskind and Gotay (1982) investigated the effects of physical posture (slumped vs. erect; hunched vs. relaxed) upon emotional behavior and reports of experience. They found that a slumped, "depressed" posture led to more "helpless" behavior in a standard learned helplessness task, although interestingly verbal reports of confidence versus depression were not significantly affected. Another study showed that subjects placed in a hunched and tensed ("threatened") posture reported higher stress ratings and more physiological symptoms of stress (e.g., a knotted feeling in the stomach). These results indicate that facial feedback is not the only kind of somatic feedback that can affect emotional responding. More study of the influence of bodily feedback, and the relationship between bodily posture and physiological responding, is clearly warranted.

DIRECT EMOTIONAL EXPERIENCE

Brain Stimulation Studies

Although there is evidence that visceral feedback contributes to emotional experience, and suggestions that facial/bodily feedback may do so as well, it is virtually certain that neither of these is either necessary or sufficient for all kinds of emotional experience. There is another kind of data which is relevant to any discussion of the subjective experience of emotion, but which is rarely mentioned in such discussions: the emotional impact in humans of direct brain stimulation. The importance of such observations is that they do not involve any external stimulus or releaser which normally elicits either a posed or spontaneous emotional response. The emotional stimulus is entirely internal.

Such studies have established beyond doubt that stimulation to certain portions of the brain, particularly in the limbic system, elicit apparently irresistible and uncontrollable feeling states which bear little relationship to the external situation. For example, Mark and Ervin (1970) report the case of a young woman who had viciously attacked other persons during psychomotor epileptic seizures which involved abnormal electroencephalograph activity in the vicinity of the amygdala. This brain region was stimulated via telemetery while the patient was quietly playing a guitar—she suddenly and violently smashed the guitar against the wall. King (1961, pp. 484–485) reports a similar case of a woman stimulated in the same general region during an interview. She suddenly appeared and sounded angry, saying "I don't want to be mean! . . . I just want to hit something. I want to get something and tear it up. . . . I don't like to feel like this!"

Charles Whitman suffered from a tumor in the same brain region. He wrote a letter which movingly and frighteningly described his state of mind:

> I don't understand what it is that compels me to type this letter. . . . I don't really understand myself these days. . . . I have been a victim of many unusual and irrational thoughts. These thoughts constantly recur, and it requires a tremendous mental effort to concentrate on useful and progressive tasks. . . . After my death I wish that an autopsy would be performed on me to see if there is any visible physical disorder. . . .
>
> It was after much thought that I decided to kill my wife, Kathy, tonight after I pick her up from work. . . . I love her dearly, and she has been a fine wife to me as any man could ever hope to have. I cannot rationally pinpoint any specific reason for doing this. . . . At this time though, the most prominent reason in my mind is that I truly do not consider this world worth living in, and am prepared to die, and I do not want to leave her to suffer alone in it. I intend to kill her as painlessly as possible. (quoted in Johnson, 1972, p. 78)

Later that night, Whitman killed his wife and his mother. The next morning he shot 38 people from a tower at the University of Texas, killing 14. Autopsy revealed a malignant tumor the size of a walnut near the amygdala (Sweet, Ervin, & Mark, 1969).

Not only aggressive feelings, but also feelings of pleasure and sexual arousal have been evoked in humans with brain stimulation. Heath and his colleagues have found such responses to be associated with stimulation in the septal area (Heath, 1964a, 1964b). One depressed patient immediately terminated a self-condemning account of his father's illness when the septal region was stimulated and "within 15 seconds exhibited a broad grin as he discussed plans to date and seduce a girl friend. When asked why he had changed the conversation so abruptly, he replied that the plans concerning the girl suddenly came to him" (Heath, 1964a, p. 225).

These and many other observations demonstrate that apparently complete emotional states, involving self-reported experience, expressive behavior, and instrumental responses, can be elicited via disease processes which affect certain brain centers and via brain stimulation (cf. Buck, 1976a, pp. 77–108, 182–190). We shall see in the next chapter that, in general, "positive" states such as pleasure and sexuality often occur with septal stimulation, while "negative" fearful and aggressive responses are often associated with the amygdala, while stimulation of the hypothalamus in humans often is *not* associated with strong subjective experiences, even though substantial autonomic/visceral responses may occur (cf. Sem-Jacobsen, 1968; White, 1940).

Implications

These observations are consistent with the notion that emotional experience must to some extent be a direct function of neurochemical activity in certain brain regions: that a "readout" of emotion into conscious experience occurs as one of the consequences of this activity. The mechanism by which this experiential readout occurs is, of course, not clear, but it can be argued that the reason the mechanism is present is analogous to the reason that emotion expression constitutes a readout of emotion in social behavior. Specifically, I am suggesting that it is useful for a species with significant cognitive capacities to have direct knowledge of the state of certain of its own neurochemical systems associated with emotion, just as Darwin argued that it is useful for a social animal to have direct knowledge of certain of the emotions of its fellows.

The direct subjective experience of the state of certain motivational/emotional systems may thus have evolved in a way analogous to the evolution of the external display of certain motivational/emotional systems. If it was useful to the species, selection pressures could favor the evolution of direct subjective experience just as they could favor the evolution of external expression.

Note that the reasoning about both external expression and subjective experience does not apply to *all* motivational/emotional states; only to those displays which confer a selection advantage will evolve. Thus as noted above, dangerous stimuli which did not constitute a

threat during human evolution, such as anoxia, do not produce emotional responses in humans. Also, there are no specific facial displays
associated with hunger or thirst in most adult animals because there
is no evolutionary requirement for such a display as there might be
for anger, fear, interest, and so forth. However, it might be noted that
in many species (e.g., birds) infants *do* have specific hunger and thirst
displays, for obvious reasons (cf. Koenig, 1951).

THE COGNITIVE-PHYSIOLOGICAL INTERACTION

The argument that emotional experience involves a direct cognitive
readout implies a close interconnection between emotion and cognition, and in fact the existence and importance of this interconnection
is well documented. The clear interrelationship of emotion and cognition, particularly in humans, has led many to suggest that emotion is
simply an aspect of basic cognitive processes—that emotion results,
for example, when the process of goal attainment is interfered with,
or when the environment is appraised as being threatening. However,
recent evidence from a variety of sources suggests that it is useful to
regard emotion and cognition as based upon separate systems (cf.
Tucker, 1981; Zajonc, 1980), and that of the two it is emotion which
is the more "basic."

Russell's Observations

One of the most useful insights into the nature of subjective emotional
experience can be traced to a suggestion by Bertrand Russell in 1927
that cognitions arising from the responder's understanding of the
emotional situation accounts for the quality and speed of emotional
experience. In reflecting upon the experience induced by an injection
of epinephrine given by a dentist, Russell noted that he felt the same
bodily reactions he would experience during strong emotion, but that
he did not really feel any emotion. Instead, he reported that he felt *as
if* he was excited, or afraid, or angry, but that he did not really
experience these emotions because there was no *reason* to feel emotional. The epinephrine caused a visceral response similar to that
which occurs during strong emotion, but the epinephrine by itself
was insufficient to cause a full-blown emotion because the cognitive
element was lacking. Russell suggested from this that there are two

determinants of emotion: visceral changes and appropriate cognitions. "In normal life, there is already a cognitive element present . . . but when [epinephrine] is artificially administered, the cognitive element is absent, and the emotion in its entirety fails to arise" (Russell, 1961, pp. 226–227).

This evaluation of the effects of epinephrine injections is supported by Maranon's observations of 210 patients (1924). When asked about their experiences, 71% reported only physical symptoms, such as tightness in the chest, heart palpitation, and muscle tension. The rest reported emotion, but it had the same detached "as if" quality noted by Russell: They reported feeling "as if afraid," or "as if moved," or "as if awaiting a great joy." A few subjects did seem to experience genuine emotion, but only when a self-supplied cognitive element was present. Thus, two patients with epinephrine showed responses of grief when describing the loss of a loved one.

The Schachter and Singer Study

The notion that a complete emotional experience involves both physiological and cognitive elements is a basic premise of Schachter's theory and experiments on emotion. Schachter and Singer (1962) in their famous experiment studied the effects of manipulating different cognitions in persons who had received an injection of epinephrine. Some subjects were correctly informed of the drug's physical effects, while others were given incorrect information, being led to expect numbness and a slight headache. A third group was told nothing about the effects of the drug. It was reasoned that the subjects who were injected with epinephrine, but who were not informed or were misinformed about its physical effects, would be in a state of physiological arousal but would have no appropriate cognitions to explain that state of arousal. Schachter and Singer suggested that they would therefore tend to scan the environment for appropriate explanations for their arousal. To determine this, they provided differing environments which would provide different explanations for the arousal state. In both environments, the subject waited with another person who had also supposedly received the injection. In one of the conditions, the other person (actually another experimenter) acted angry, in the other condition he acted euphoric. As expected, the uninformed subjects were more influenced by the other person's behavior than were the informed subjects: They acted more angry or euphoric, and also reported themselves as feeling more angry or euphoric, depending upon the other's behavior.

This result was complicated by the fact that subjects who received the placebo also were influenced by the model. This latter effect has been explained as being due to the effects of the general arousal elicited by the experimental situation, and has contributed to a number of studies of the effects of cognition on "natural arousal" (cf. London & Nisbett, 1974).

Emotional Experience and Social Influence

The Schachter and Singer study and theory continue to arouse considerable discussion and controversy (cf. Marshall & Zimbardo, 1979; Maslach, 1979; Schachter & Singer, 1979). In a recent review, Manstead and Wagner (1981) argue that the most distinctive proposition of the theory—that unexplained arousal can be experienced as different emotions according to cognitive circumstances—has received only very limited support. However, it seems reasonable to suggest that such effects *can* occur, but that they are relatively rare and difficult to demonstrate experimentally. Such a phenomenon could explain the extent to which human emotion may be swayed by social influences into constructive or destructive paths: Humans have been known to act with courage and self-sacrifice to save others, and they have been known to encourage a potential suicide to jump. It would be difficult to account for this great diversity of response as being the result of "built in" emotional systems. Perhaps what is built in is our strong tendency to be influenced by others, particularly in ambiguous or novel situations (cf. Milgram, 1963, 1974). Thus the high physiological arousal elicited by the novel situation of witnessing a potential suicide may be labeled as amusement for one group because of the influence of a few sociopathic individuals, and as concern and self-sacrifice by another group because of the influence of a few concerned and courageous persons (cf. Buck, 1976a, pp. 400–413).

Limits of the Theory

Schachter's theory has been useful in organizing many of the findings pertaining to the James–Lange theory of emotion. Thus, Schachter (1964) has argued persuasively that cognitive factors can account for the speed and range of emotional experience that is missing from a purely visceral version of the James–Lange theory. Also, the theory has stimulated much research under the rubric of "self-attribution theory" (cf. Buck, 1976a, pp. 350–379). However, the theory cannot easily explain the observations on brain disorder and intracranial stimulation in humans cited above, as in those cases apparently complete emotion experience and behavior arises with no cognitive "reason" for the state. Indeed, many report feeling strong emotions *despite* the fact that they recognize that they are inappropriate.

Another interesting albeit anecdotal example which seems incompatible with a strict interpretation of Schachter's viewpoint comes from studies of "split-brain" patients whose cerebral hemispheres are surgically separated for the treatment of epilepsy. As we shall discuss in the next chapter, tests have shown that such patients can verbally report information received by the left hemisphere, but not the right hemisphere. However, the right hemisphere seems to be able to generate emotion on its own. In one study, a picture of a nude was occasionally presented to one hemisphere or the other amid pictures of ordinary objects. The nude produced an amused reaction regardless of the hemisphere:

> When the picture was flashed to the left hemisphere of a female patient, she laughed and verbally identified the picture as a nude. When it was later presented to the right hemisphere, she said in reply to a question that she saw nothing, but almost immediately a sly smile spread over her face and she began to chuckle. Asked what she was laughing at, she said: "I don't know . . . nothing—that funny machine." Although the right hemisphere could not describe what it had seen, the sight nevertheless elicited an emotional response like the one evoked from the left hemisphere. (Gazzaniga, 1972, p. 124)

Conclusions

Schachter's theory that a cognitive–physiological interaction accounts for the subjective experience of emotion is appealing in many respects, and undoubtedly cognitive factors often do contribute to the determination of emotional experience, particularly when the eliciting situation is ambiguous or unclear. Also, we shall suggest in Chapter 6 that persons may at times label their feelings incorrectly—make misattributions about their feelings—in a kind of "self-deception" process. However, it is apparent that there are neurochemical systems in humans whose activation can generate emotional experience independently of cognitive factors. I suggest that this constitutes an internal cognitive readout mechanism analogous to the external readout that can be seen in expressive behavior.

EMOTION AS READOUT

TYPES OF EMOTION

I have suggested that there are three major aspects of emotion: (1) it is concerned with bodily adaptation and the maintenance of homeostasis, (2) it is expressed in externally accessible behaviors, and (3) it is experienced subjectively. Each of these aspects can be seen as a kind of running progress report or "readout" of the state of certain neurochemical systems within the central nervous system. We shall discuss the nature of these systems in the next chapter.

There are three kinds of readout corresponding to these three aspects of emotion. The most basic kind of readout involves adaptation and homeostasis and takes place via the autonomic nervous system and endocrine system. The state of the central neurochemical systems is "read out" in adaptive and homeostatic peripheral bodily responses. We shall term this *Emotion I*. In the case of anoxia, only these kinds of responses occur—there is no signal either to others or to the cognitive system that something is wrong. The second kind of readout, *Emotion II*, is the external display of the state of neurochemical systems via ritualized signs which are accessible to others— odors, color changes, postures, facial expressions, and so forth. These displays evolve only when information about the state of certain neurochemical systems is useful for the coordination of behavior in a species. It should be stressed that Emotion II involves spontaneous rather than symbolic expression, which, as we shall see in Chapter 3, involves quite different neural systems. *Emotion III*, the third kind of readout, involves the direct subjective experience of the state of certain neurochemical systems. We suggest that it functions to allow the cognitive system fast and easy access to the state of those systems in which cognitive processes may be instrumental in the process of satiation. Thus if an individual is directly aware of its need for food, drink, or air, and the state of its tendencies toward fight, flight, and courtship, it may constitute a "feedforward" mechanism which allows the creature to anticipate homeostatic deficits before they actually occur (cf. Mogenson & Phillips, 1976).

TYPES OF EMOTION RESPONSES

Different kinds of emotional behavior are differentially involved in Emotions I, II, and III as defined above. Autonomic and endocrine responses reflect most closely the processes of homeostasis and adaptation, and they should be most relevant to Emotion I. Expressive behaviors such as facial expressions and postural responses should be most relevant to Emotion II, but only to the extent that they are spontaneous. They obviously may also be "goal-directed behaviors," which are influenced by display rules which reflect learning and cognitive functioning. Self-reports of subjective experience are most relevant to Emotion III, as are instrumental goal-directed behaviors, but they may of course be influenced by display rules as well.

A GENERAL MODEL OF EMOTION

A general model of emotion, which includes these four kinds of emotion responses and their suggested relationships with Emotion I, II, and III processes, is presented in Figure 2.3. We shall use the term "primary motivational/emotional systems," abbreviated as in Figure 2.3 as PRIMES, to refer to the motivational/emotional states associated with subcortical and paleocortical neurochemical systems.

The model assumes that internal or external affective stimuli impinge directly on these neurochemical systems without cognitive mediation (cf. Wilson, 1979; Zajonc, 1980), and that the impact of a given affective stimulus for a particular person in a particular situation is determined by (1) the responsiveness of the relevant neurochemical systems, and (2) the individual's relevant learning experiences with that affective stimulus.

The response of a particular neurochemical system depends upon its current state of *arousal* and also upon its *arousability*, or capacity to become aroused (cf. Whalen, 1966). "Arousal" refers to the current state of activation; "arousability" is a longer term phenomenon which is dependent upon a number of factors, including

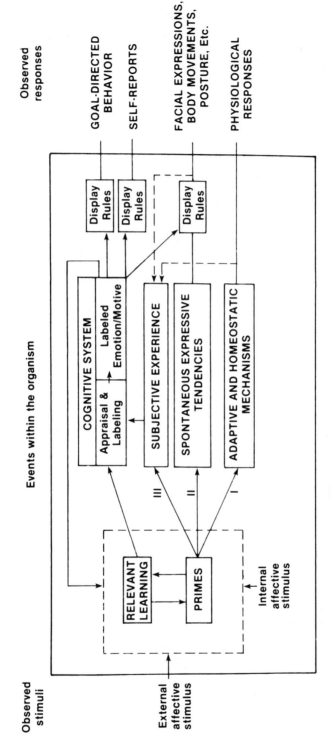

Figure 2.3. A general model of emotion.

short-term influences such as the effects of drugs, neurotransmitter levels, or blood chemistry; long-term influences such as heredity, early experience, or disease; and interactions with other neurochemical systems (cf. Buck, 1976a, pp. 207–226). Variations in arousability and arousal function in part to increase or decrease the range of stimuli which will release or trigger an emotional response. For example, high arousability in neurochemical circuits associated with aggression creates a high readiness to respond with subjective feelings of anger and overt aggression, even to inappropriate stimuli (Moyer, 1971). Von Holst and von Saint Paul (1962) demonstrated that electrical stimulation in "aggression circuits" in roosters caused them to attack a stuffed polecat which they had previously ignored. The cases of violence noted above associated with temporal lobe disease and intra-cranial stimulation were presumably due to hyperreactivity to mild stimuli caused by abnormal electrochemical activity in aggressive circuits (cf. Mark & Ervin, 1970).

The impact of affective stimuli is also in part a function of learning experiences, which may involve classically conditioned associations as well as direct or vicarious learning experiences about the affective stimuli (cf. Buck, 1976a, pp. 112–124). For example, a negative experience in high places might cause a mild fear of heights. Because of this experience, the individual might experience a fear of high places, which may be particularly strong when the particular neurochemical systems are aroused or in a state of high arousability (i.e., due to fatigue).

Thus affective stimuli are, in effect, "filtered" by relevant learning experiences and the arousal/arousability of the relevant neurochemical systems, and this filtering determines their impact. This impact occurs at both cognitive and emotional levels. On the emotional level, adaptive and homeostatic processes are activated (Emotion I), tendencies toward spontaneous expression occur (Emotion II), and subjective experiences occur, both directly from the activation of the neurochemical systems (Emotion III) and indirectly via feedback from visceral and skeletal muscle systems (Figure 2.3, dashed lines). On the cognitive level, the cognitive–physiological interaction occurs in which the individual "labels" or "appraises" the affective stimuli on the basis of past experience, the emotional experience, and the present situation (Schachter, 1964, 1970; Lazarus, 1966). Once the affective situation is appraised/labeled, the individual has a basis for making appropriate goal-directed instrumental "coping" responses and self-reports describing his or her subjective response. The labeled emotional state may itself become an internal affective stimulus, beginning another cycle of response. At the same time, these overt responses and the spontaneous tendencies toward emotional expression (Emotion II) will be influenced by display rules, in that the individual may only make overt responses appropriate to the situation rather than revealing his or her "true feelings."

THE EVOLUTION OF SYMBOLIC COMMUNICATION

This chapter has been concerned with the evolution of emotion and emotion communication, and although the influence of display rules, person cognition, the cognitive–physiological interaction, and so forth, has been noted, it has stressed the evolution of the bases of spontaneous communication. We are too early in our examination of the nature of and relationships between spontaneous and symbolic communication to deal with the evolution of the latter at this point, but shall return to this issue in Chapter 4.

CONCLUSIONS

This chapter has presented a view of emotion in which its three commonly recognized aspects—that it involves homeostasis and adaptation, that it involves external expressive behavior, and that it involves subjective experience—are seen as having evolved separately, albeit by analogous mechanisms. The resulting system seems well suited to participate with cognitive mechanisms in the activation and direction of behavior—the commonly recognized function of motivation.

This chapter outlined the process of evolution, and particularly the evolution of the three aspects of emotion. In regard to the evolution of emotion expression, it argued that both sending and receiving mechanisms must be based upon biological factors to some extent, although in both cases learned factors normally play a part as well. Thus human communication is seen as simultaneously involving spontaneous and symbolic processes, as defined in Chapter 1. In regard to the evolution of emotion experience, I argued that bodily feedback plays a secondary role in such experience, and that the most compelling aspects of emotional experience involve a direct readout of the neurochemical systems underlying emotion.

The formulation of emotion as "readout" applies to all three aspects of emotion. Emotion I is the readout of the neurochemical systems to the mechanisms of bodily adaptation and homeostasis; Emotion II is the readout of the neurochemical systems in accessible expressive behaviors; Emotion III is the readout of the neurochemical systems to the cognitive system. The former two mechanisms can be seen at work in the simplest of creatures, the latter perhaps evolves with complex cognitive systems. In the next chapter, we shall consider what is known about the nature of these neurochemical systems.

3

NEUROCHEMICAL MECHANISMS
OF EMOTION
AND EMOTIONAL EXPRESSION

NEUROCHEMICAL MECHANISMS
AND EMOTION COMMUNICATION

We have suggested that motivation and emotion are based upon neurochemical mechanisms in the central nervous system which have three kinds of effects involving three kinds of "readout" processes: adaptive/homeostatic processes, external expression, and subjective experience (Emotion I, II, and III, respectively). Given the important relationships between emotional processes and their external expression, it is rather surprising that investigations in the area of the nonverbal expression of emotion and investigations in the areas of the neurophysiology of the emotions have generally proceeded largely independently of one another. A major exception in this regard has been the studies of the neurological basis of vocalizations, which are quite relevant to both areas, as we shall see. Also, a few recent studies have related emotional expression to left- versus right-hemisphere processing, but there is still very little work specifically relating the very extensive knowledge of limbic and subcortical mechanisms of emotion to their nonverbal expression.

This is even more surprising when one considers that many, if not most, of the classical animal studies on brain mechanisms of emotion are, in a sense, studies of "nonverbal communication," as the investigators have often relied upon the animal's expressive displays as major dependent variables for inferring the presence of emotion. Thus Hess's early (1928) studies of intracranial stimulation, and

Cannon and Britton's (1925) studies of lesioning used expressive displays to study the "rage response": They observed attack and flight behaviors, hissing, spitting, clawing, and erection of the hair. They did not closely analyze how it was possible that a human being should be able to make such inferences on the basis of the behaviors of cats. More recent studies have continued to rely upon such expressive displays, but not the analysis of such displays *per se*.

This chapter briefly reviews what is known about the nature of the neurochemical systems underlying emotion, beginning with an examination of peripheral mechanisms: the autonomic nervous system and endocrine system underlying adaptive/homeostatic processes (Emotion I), and the somatic nervous system serving the skeletal muscles. It then reviews the subcortical and paleocortical mechanisms—those in the spinal cord, brain stem, hypothalamus, and limbic system—and their interrelationships. In doing so, it examines the physiological mechanisms underlying the major measures of emotion: both the peripheral psychophysiological measures and measures of the facial/bodily expression of emotion. It then reviews studies on the central nervous system mechanisms of emotional expression, both facial and vocal expression. From this, a model of central nervous system mechanisms of emotional expression (Emotion II) is suggested. Finally, this chapter reviews recent evidence on neocortical mechanisms and emotion, including evidence relating the right cerebral hemisphere to emotional processing. Suggestions that the right hemisphere may be associated with spontaneous communication, and the left hemisphere with symbolic communication, are also discussed, and a provisional model is presented of the central nervous system mechanisms underlying emotional experience (Emotion III).

PERIPHERAL SYSTEMS AND EMOTION

The peripheral nervous system includes the nerve fibers entering and leaving the brain and spinal cord: the sensory nerves carrying information from the various sense organs and the motor nerves leaving to various effectors, such as the muscles and glands. The peripheral nervous system is divided into the *autonomic nervous system* serving the heart, glands, and smooth muscles of the viscera; and the *somatic nervous system* serving the striated, or skeletal muscles responsible for facial expression and body movement. The autonomic nervous system and the *endocrine system* of ductless glands and hormones are the systems most directly concerned with the Emotion I process of homeostasis and adaptation. The somatic nervous system is less directly involved in the Emotion I process, but it is basic to the Emotion II process of external emotional expression.

THE AUTONOMIC NERVOUS SYSTEM

The Sympathetic and Parasympathetic Nervous Systems

The autonomic nervous system functions, along with the endocrine system, in the process of bodily adaptation and the maintenance of homeostasis. Most of these functions are nonconscious and involuntary. The central nervous system controls the autonomic nervous system largely through the hypothalamus. The autonomic nervous system has two branches—the *sympathetic* and *parasympathetic* branches. Most structures innervated by the systems have inputs from both branches, and the actions of the two branches are usually antagonistic. This antagonism is at the basis of the emergency theory of emotion, which was proposed by the physiologist W. B. Cannon (1915, 1932).

The Emergency Theory of Emotion

In general, the parasympathetic branch serves vegetative functions, such as digestion and the "anabolic" buildup of energy reserves, while the sympathetic branch serves emergency functions, which Cannon called the "fight-or-flight reaction." When the sympathetic system is dominant, a number of bodily reactions occur which Cannon argued were useful in facing danger. First, breathing is faster and deeper, there is less secretion of mucus in the air passages, and the bronchioles of the lungs dilate, which may function to increase the amount of oxygen coming into the body to fuel metabolism. At the same time, heart rate and blood pressure increase, arteries in the viscera constrict, while arteries in the skeletal muscles and brain dilate, which may function to increase the blood supply to the latter organs. A number of other actions also occur: The eyes dilate, increasing visual acuity, the sweat glands in the palms of the hands and soles of the feet are activated, stores of sugar are released into the bloodstream, and so forth. According to Cannon, "all of these changes are directly service-able in rendering the organism more effective in the violent display of energy with fear or rage may involve" (1932, p. 228).

The functioning of the sympathetic branch is catabolic, in that it tends to deplete the energy reserves stored within the organism, and for this reason among others, the long-term effects of sympathetic activation are stressful and detrimental to the body. The opposite functions are ascribed to the parasympathetic branch—the anabolic restoration of stored supplies. Such a buildup of energy stores takes place when the parasympathetic branch is dominant, as during sleep. Heart rate and blood pressure decrease, the blood is diverted to the viscera, digestion and the buildup of sugar reserves is increased, and so forth (cf. Sternbach, 1966).

It should be noted that, if the sympathetic response is too strong, the organism may be enervated rather than invigorated (Arnold, 1960). Many arousal theorists have suggested that the relationship between sympathetic arousal and behavioral efficiency is best ex-pressed as an inverted U, with the most efficient behavior being associated with moderate levels of arousal (cf. Hebb, 1955).

THE ENDOCRINE SYSTEM

The endocrine glands are ductless glands that release chemical sub-stances called hormones directly into the bloodstream. Like the auto-nomic nervous system, the endocrine system serves functions of bodily adaptation and the maintenance of homeostasis. However, whereas the response of the autonomic nervous system is faster and relatively short-lived, the bodily changes wrought by endocrine re-sponding are slower and longer lasting.

As with autonomic nervous system functioning, long-term acti-vation of the endocrine system's mechanisms of adaptation have deleterious effects. These have been described by Hans Selye in his analysis of the *stress syndrome*. In many respects, Selye's analysis is an extension of Cannon's emergency theory to the functioning of the endocrine system. Selye (1950, 1978) defines stress in terms of the failure of normal homeostatic mechanisms to adapt the body to a situation. Thus any situation may be stressful if the body cannot adapt to it. Selye has shown how chronic activation of the bodily mecha-nisms of adaptation can lead to disease, debilitation, and death.

A MODEL OF THE EMOTION I PROCESS

The autonomic and endocrine responses underlying Emotion I processes are summarized in Figure 3.1. It can be seen that both systems are under the direct control of the hypothalamus. The two systems tend to reinforce each other. For example, in emergencies the autonomic nervous system provides a fast but relatively brief response, while the response of the endocrine system is slower but also longer lasting (cf. Buck, 1976a, Chapter 2).

THE SOMATIC NERVOUS SYSTEM

The Pyramidal and Nonpyramidal Motor Systems

As noted above, the somatic nervous system is basic to the Emotion II process of spontaneous external emotional expression. This section will describe the general nature of the pyramidal and nonpyramidal motor systems, their roles in voluntary and nonvoluntary movement and expression, and the phenomenon of muscle tension.

Receptors exist throughout the skin, muscles, and tendons which are sensitive to stretch, pressure, pain, and temperature. Sensory nerves carrying information about these events enter the central nervous system via the spinal cord. This information is integrated with motor systems at a number of points, including the spinal cord, cerebellum, reticular formation, and cerebral cortex. The motor systems carry instructions for a wide variety of movements to the skeletal muscles. These include commands for gross voluntary movements, for precise and finely articulated skilled movements, and for largely unconscious postures, gestures, and facial expressions. This remarkable system allows us to walk without thinking about where our legs are, touch our forefingers together behind the back, and learn complex and intricate motor skills.

There are two major motor systems by which central nervous system influences are transmitted to the muscles. The *pyramidal system* connects the neocortical motor areas in the precentral gyrus with motor pathways in the cranial nerves (via *corticobulbar* pathways) and spinal cord (via *corticospinal* pathways). Like the sensory systems represented in the postcentral gyrus, most of the pryamidal fibers cross over to the opposite side of the body, so that, for example,

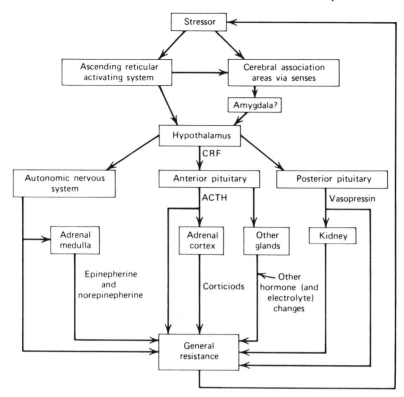

Figure 3.1. Summary of the bodily response to a stressor: the Emotion I process. From Figure 2.4 in *Human Motivation and Emotion* by R. Buck, New York: Wiley, 1976. Copyright 1976 by John Wiley & Sons. Reprinted by permission.

the left side of the brain controls the right side of the body. Also like the neocortical sensory system, the pyramidal system is characterized by a highly demarcated topological organization, so that specific areas of the body can be "mapped" on the precentral and postcentral gyri.

The pyramidal system is associated with the precise voluntary control of localized movements (Netter, 1962; Weil, 1974). Despite its sophistication, however, it does not appear to be necessary for all voluntary movement. Grossman (1967) points out that voluntary movements are possible even when the pyramidal tracts are completely transected, and he suggests that while they are important for the precise control of many muscles, the influence of the pyramidal tracts on basic postural and locomotor functions is expendable.

The *nonpyramidal* systems are phylogenetically older than the pyramidal system, and their functions are involved with the basic control of movement and expression. These systems are rather negatively conceptualized as comprising all central nervous system structures that affect motor activity via tracts other than the pyramidal tracts (Grossman, 1967). The precise fiber tracts involved are extremely complex and not well defined, but many originate in the *basal ganglia*.

The nonpyramidal systems are "nonspecific" systems involving complex servomechanisms for the control of general muscle tonus, posture, and diffuse repetitive motor patterns. These postures and movements involve both the musculature of the body (locomotion, rolling, turning, breathing) and the head/face (head/facial posturing and movement, eye movement, chewing, swallowing, speaking; Weil, 1974). This control is often but not always nonconscious and involuntary.

Different disorders affecting the nonpyramidal system are associated with a variety of movement disorders. One of the most common of these is the syndrome of parkinsonism, which is associated with the destruction of dopaminergic nonpyramidal pathways. One of the most consistent symptoms of parkinsonism is a "masklike" lack of facial expression and an absence of automatic movements such as swinging the arms while walking, resulting in an impression that the patient is rigid "like a statue" (Best & Taylor, 1966, p. 152).

Facial Expression, Gesture, and Posture

Spontaneous facial expressions, gestures, postures, and rhythmic movements expressive of emotion are also largely controlled via nonpyramidal fibers associated with motor nuclei in the brain stem (Weil, 1974). While there is evidence that some voluntary facial movements are dependent upon pyramidal pathways, spontaneous facial expressions are associated with nonpyramidal systems (Myers, 1976). This is clearly shown in clinical cases where pyramidal lesions impair voluntary facial movements but leave spontaneous expressions intact, while nonpyramidal lesions have the reverse pattern of effects. Also, as we shall see, electrical stimulation of the brain stem in both animals and humans has been shown to produce facial expressions and vocalizations closely resembling spontaneous responses. In some cases, these expressions appear to be dissociated from the emotional state *per se*.

Muscle Tension

Skeletal muscles are generally arranged in flexor–extensor pairs which maintain a state of dynamic balance or tension between themselves. Of course, this tension varies across different muscle groups according to the responder's activity. However, the muscle tension in irrelevant muscles—those not engaged in the task at hand—is sensitive to emotional processes. Like many autonomic and endocrine responses to emotion, this tension is lowest during sleep and relaxation, and increases with increasing alertness, particularly when stress and anxiety are involved. Also like the other peripheral responses, prolonged muscle tension can have deleterious effects. Symptoms caused by the abnormally prolonged contraction of particular muscle groups are common in anxious patients: For example, the prolonged and habitual contraction of the neck muscles can result in a type of tension headache (Lippold, 1967; Lachman, 1972).

The central nervous system controls generalized muscle tension by nonpyramidal systems, and specifically via numerous motor nuclei contained within the brain stem reticular formation. These nuclei have both facilitory and inhibitory influences on the rotation, flexion, and extension of the limbs and joints (House & Pansky, 1967).

Muscle tension is measured by the electromyograph (EMG), in which electrodes placed over a given muscle group, or needle electrodes placed within the muscle, pick up the electrical discharges associated with muscle activity. The EMG is one of the major psychophysiological measures used in the assessment of emotional responding. It varies, of course, according to the particular muscle group chosen for study. Muscle tension is particularly important in the study of emotional expression, because patterns of such activity across the body may suggest arrested or inhibited action. Thus muscle tension may increase in appropriate muscles with the intent to move even when there is no overt movement (Grossman, 1967; Jacobson, 1938, 1951). Malmo has reported interesting relationships between muscle tension and the content of psychiatric interviews, in which four patients (all women) showed muscle tension in the forearm during the discussion of hostile content, and muscle tension in the legs during the discussion of sexual content (Malmo, Kohlmeyer, & Smith, 1956). Also, Schwartz and his colleagues have detected EMG patterns on the face suggestive of emotional expression when no visible facial response occurs (Schwartz et al., 1974, 1976). We shall discuss the implications of the inhibition of the spontaneous expression of emotion in Chapters 5 and 6.

It should be noted that in some respects we should *not* expect muscle tension measures to behave as do autonomic and endocrine responses. We suggested in Chapter 2 that the latter are most closely associated with processes of homeostasis and adaptation (Emotion I), while muscle tension should be most closely associated with tendencies toward overt expressive behavior (Emotion II). There are situations in which these do not vary together (Buck, 1981b). For example, we shall see in Chapter 5 that adult females tend to be more facially expressive but *less* autonomically reactive compared with males in a variety of affective situations (Buck, Miller, & Caul, 1974; Buck, Savin, Miller, & Caul, 1972; Prokasy & Raskin, 1973). Also, Frankenhaeuser and her colleagues have demonstrated in a series of studies that males have greater psychoneuroendocrine responses than females in a variety of test situations (Frankenhaeuser, 1978; Frankenhaeuser, von Wright, Collins, von Wright, Sedvall, & Swahn, 1978). Thus these studies suggest that males have larger autonomic/endocrine responses. However, Schwartz, Brown, and Ahern (1980) have found that females have greater facial muscle tension than males when responding to emotional stimuli. Thus the muscle tension seems more related to the sex difference found in facial expressiveness than the opposite sex difference found in autonomic and endocrine responding (cf. Buck, 1981b).

CENTRAL NERVOUS SYSTEM MECHANISMS OF EMOTION: SUBCORTICAL AND PALEOCORTICAL STRUCTURES

The central nervous system includes the brain and spinal cord. It is divided into *subcortical* structures, which do not have the layered structure typical of the cortex; *paleocortical* or old cortical structures, which have a cortical structure but fewer than six layers; and *neocortical* or new cortical structures which have six layers. In this section we shall discuss the subcortical and paleocortical structures which contribute to emotion. The general location of these systems within the central nervous system is illustrated in Figure 3.2.

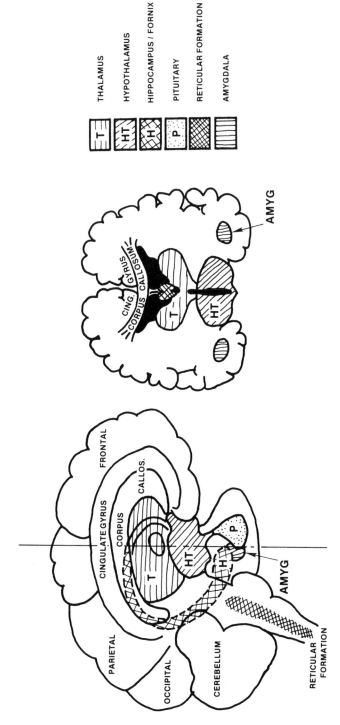

THALAMUS

HYPOTHALAMUS

HIPPOCAMPUS / FORNIX

PITUITARY

RETICULAR FORMATION

AMYGDALA

Figure 3.2. General location of subcortical and paleocortical structures within the brain.

PHYSIOLOGICAL MODELS OF MOTIVATION

The physiological models most relevant to the analysis of the central nervous system mechanisms of emotion have been stated in terms of motivation and have usually avoided the concept of emotion, with its taint of subjectivism. The major models include arousal theory (Hebb, 1955; Lindsley, 1951, 1957) based upon the reticular formation; Stellar's (1954) model which posited specific "centers" for the drives of hunger, thirst, and sex based upon excitatory and inhibitory systems in the hypothalamus; the analyses of reward/punishment mechanisms beginning with Olds and Milner (1954); and the MacLean (1968, 1969, 1970) analyses of the limbic system. Each of these models has proved useful and has gained a share of empirical support, and indeed it appears that each may be substantially correct as far as it goes, but that each is incomplete. However, taken together they begin to provide a comprehensive view of the physiological bases of motivation and emotion. We shall thus consider each of them in the following paragraphs, along with the more recent models of Jeffrey Gray (1971, 1972, 1977) and Pribram and McGuiness (1975; McGuiness & Pribram, 1980), which suggest how the reticular formation, hypothalamus, and limbic system interact with each other.

THE RETICULAR ACTIVATING SYSTEM

The reticular formation is a diffuse collection of nuclei and scattered fiber tracts extending from the spinal cord through the brain stem to the hypothalamus and thalamus. Its importance in emotion was first recognized by Bremer (1935), who demonstrated that the cutting of the reticular system from the rest of the brain results in an often irreversible coma, manifested both in electroencephalograph (EEG) patterns associated with deep sleep, and a lack of behavioral arousal. This suggested that the reticular formation played a role in arousing the rest of the brain. This conclusion was supported in studies by Moruzzi and Magoun (1949) which showed that the electrical stimulation of the reticular formation produced sudden arousal of both behavior and the EEG.

D. B. Lindsley (1951, 1957) suggested from these and other findings that the reticular formation is the physiological basis of arousal and activation. He termed the portion of the reticular formation involved in arousal the *reticular activating system*, which has both ascending aspects (ARAS), arousing the rest of the brain, and descending aspects, arousing the body. Lindsley argued that the ARAS acts to arouse the brain in all kinds of situations, and that it is thus responsible for the "energizing" aspects of motivation and emotion.

THE HYPOTHALAMUS

The hypothalamus is a collection of nuclei and fiber tracts located above the brain-stem reticular formation and below the thalamus. It plays a central role in the regulation of emotional processes, as is demonstrated by its control over the autonomic nervous system and endocrine system and the fact that lesions and stimulation of the hypothalamus have dramatic effects upon eating, drinking, sexual behavior, and a variety of emotional behaviors. The hypothalamus appears to gather and integrate information relevant to emotional processes from many peripheral and central sources, using it to appropriately alter autonomic and endocrine functioning.

Two kinds of hypothalamic mechanisms are important in this control of emotion. One type involves the excitation and inhibition of specific behaviors, such as eating, drinking, and sexual behaviors. Some of these mechanisms involve behaviors that are quite species specific. The other mechanism involves more general functions of reward and punishment. The former kind of mechanism is considered most directly in Stellar's (1954) theory of motivation; the latter is particularly associated with the work of Olds and his colleagues (Olds & Milner, 1954). We shall consider each in turn.

Hypothalamic Centers

Interest in the role of the hypothalamus in motivation was stimulated by evidence beginning in the 1940s that the ventromedial nucleus (VMN) acts as a "satiety center," in which lesioning increases the eating of palatable food, and that the lateral nucleus (LN) acts as a "hunger center," in which lesioning results in starvation and stimulation in voracious eating (cf. Brobeck, Tepperman, & Long, 1943; Brugger, 1943; Hetherington & Ranson, 1942; Teitelbaum, 1961). Other studies found evidence that hypothalamic "centers" are implicated in the regulation of drinking, sexual behavior, and aggressive behavior (Grossman, 1967).

These studies formed the basis of Stellar's (1954) theory of motivation, which suggested that behavior is motivated via the activity of excitatory centers in the hypothalamus, which is regulated by the activity of inhibitory centers, also in the hypothalamus. Stellar suggested that both kinds of hypothalamic centers are influenced by chemical and physical information from the internal environment of the body (i.e., hormones, blood temperature, osmotic pressure, etc.), by learned and unlearned sensory stimuli, and by higher brain centers. Stellar regarded the hypothalamus as the "final common path for behavior," in that the influence of higher centers upon behavior is mediated by the hypothalamus.

Recent studies have suggested many complications to the attractively simple picture presented by Stellar. Grossman (1979) reviewed the evidence concerning hunger and thirst, and concluded that there do seem to be neural mechanisms in or near the LN and VMN specifically related to eating and drinking. However, some of the functions originally attributed to nuclei within the hypothalamus may instead be caused by manipulations of "fibers of passage" which course through the hypothalamus (McGuiness & Pribram, 1980). Also, other investigators have suggested that, beyond the "classic" drives of hunger, thirst, sex, and so forth, there seem to be a variety of behavior mechanisms represented in or near the hypothalamus which are specific to each species. Thus when the hypothalamus is stimulated, rats may gnaw or hoard, roosters may crow, gerbils may thump their feet. Valenstein, Cox, and Kakolewski (1970) demonstrated that brain stimulation that normally elicits feeding can eventually elicit gnawing in rats if food is withheld for a time. Also, Glickman and Schiff (1967) have suggested that particular behavior patterns unique to each species are represented within the brain stem and hypothalamus. They argue that the appropriate expression of these behavior patterns when the associated neurochemical substrate has been activated is in itself reinforcing. Thus they regard reinforcement as being tied to these species-specific circuits.

Reward/Punishment Systems

Others regard reinforcement as involving a general mechanism which is independent of these species-specific circuits. Olds and his colleagues in particular view reinforcement and motivation in general as involving reward/punishment systems which pass through the hypothalamus. Rather than attempting to localize and characterize "centers" associated with specific motivational systems, these investigators have focused on this more general motivational mechanism, using the technique of intracranial self-stimulation.

Olds and Fobes (1981) and Routtenberg (1978) have reviewed the research in this area. The strongest reward effects are found in the medial forebrain bundle (MFB) which courses through the LN of the hypothalamus. However, reward effects are also found outside the hypothalamus, as in the septal area of the limbic system and in parts of the brain stem. Punishment effects are less common than reward effects, at least in the brain of the rat. Olds (1961) found that, of 200 electrode sites, 60% produced neither reward nor punishing effects (most in the thalamus and cortex), 35% produced reward effects, and only 5% produced punishing effects. There is evidence that punishing effects may be more common in other species, such as the cat.

Olds conceived of two discrete but interacting pathways mediating rewarding and punishing effects spanning the length of the brain but coursing through and particularly concentrated in the hypothalamus. The reward system, excitation of which produced self-stimulation and other positive effects, is centered in the MFB and thus the LN of the hypothalamus. The punishment system, excitation of which produces escape and other negative responses, runs parallel to and medial to the reward system in the periventricular system (PVS) running through the medial hypothalamus (Olds & Olds, 1963, 1964, 1965; Stein, 1968). Routtenberg (1978) adapted this view to include the reticular activating system, suggesting that three systems mediate motivation: the reticular system mediates general arousal and attention, while the reward and punishment systems mediate positive and negative effects upon behavior.

The reward and punishment systems have been associated with different neurotransmitters, with considerable evidence that self-stimulation is based upon neural systems with catecholaminergic transmitters, particularly *norepinephrine* (NE) and *dopamine* (DA) (cf. Olds & Fobes, 1981). The neural systems underlying self-stimulation are associated with these neurotransmitters, and drugs that enhance synaptic transmission via NE and DA tend to increase self-stimulation, while blocking drugs tend to inhibit it (cf. Routtenberg, 1978, p. 164). This is compatible with the catecholamine hypothesis of affective disorders in humans, which suggests from the actions of various drugs upon mood that "depression may be associated with a relative deficiency of NE . . . whereas elation may be associated with an excess of such amines" (Schildkraut & Kety, 1967, p. 28). There is also evidence that the morphine-like substance *enkephalin* found in certain parts of the brain may support reward effects (cf. McGeer & McGeer, 1980). On the other hand, Stein (1968) has suggested that the effects of punishment may be mediated by a cholinergic system, that is, a system in which *acetylcholine* (ACh) is the neurotransmitter.

In summary, there is considerable agreement about the presence of neural systems associated with reward and punishment coursing through the hypothalamus, and the nature of these systems is under active investigation. The nature of the relationship between these systems and the specific hypothalamic "centers" described above is not understood and indeed it is one of the major issues in the field (Olds & Fobes, 1981).

We have seen that some regard reinforcement as being associated with the appropriate response to activation in species-specific "centers" in the hypothalamus and brain stem, while others regard reinforcement as a general process associated with the activation of reward and punishment systems, also associated with the hypothalamus. It may be that both views are correct—that both mechanisms in fact exist, with the more general mechanism perhaps being a more recent evolutionary addition. As the "city" analogy presented in Chapter 1 suggests, when a new system evolves, it does not necessarily replace the original system. Unless the functioning of the original system is directly contrary to the survival of the species, it persists beside the new system. As Crider (1980) puts it, the brain during the course of evolution has "integrated and carried forward elements of previous function into new and more complex structures" (p. 328). Thus it is not surprising that there may be different systems responsible for the reinforcement of behavior existing side by side within the brain.

The Subjective Experience of Hypothalamic Events

We have seen that the hypothalamus is intimately involved with a wide variety of emotional and motivational processes, and one might expect that because of this, the stimulation of the hypothalamus must be accompanied by vivid subjective experiences. This does not appear to be the case. Even in animals, the emotional reactions resulting from hypothalamic and brain-stem stimulation often seem to require integration with higher structures if they are not to appear "pseudo-affective" and incomplete (Grossman, 1967). In humans, we noted in the last chapter that hypothalamic stimulation rarely produces strong subjective experiences of emotion. White (1940) reported that although hypothalamic stimulation produced pronounced autonomic changes, it did not elicit reports of unusual sensations or emotional changes. Sem-Jacobsen (1968), in a report of 2651 electrode placements in 82 patients, similarly found relatively little changes of mood or emotion when the hypothalamus was stimulated. Heath (1964a, 1964b) reports that, consistent with animal findings, stimulation of the MFB in the lateral hypothalamus yields positive responses: "This is a good feeling." "Drunk feeling." "Happy button." Also, stimulation of the PVS induces "discomfort." However, these feelings presumably require cortical integration (cf. Grossman, 1967, p. 324). Self-stimulation has proved to be a difficult technique to apply in humans. Patients report stimulating their brains for reasons other than for pleasure or reward: that is, to capture an elusive memory, to explore an unusual, possibly unpleasant, sensation, or simply because they assume that since they are given a button they are expected to push it (cf. Buck, 1976a, pp. 98–102).

Taken as a whole, the evidence suggests that the phenomenon of subjective experience is based upon structures other than the hypothalamus. It appears that it requires the involvement of higher structures, particularly structures within the limbic system.

THE LIMBIC SYSTEM

The limbic system encompasses the paleocortical structures in the brain which as noted above are cortical, or layered, in organization, but have five or fewer such layers. They are distinguished from the neocortex in that the latter has six definable layers. Besides the paleocortical structures, a structure typically included within the limbic system is the amygdala, which is not layered but which has many reciprocal connections with paleocortical structures (Grossman, 1967).

The importance of the limbic system in emotion was first suggested by the anatomist James Papez (1937), largely on anatomical grounds. He noted that while the neocortex tends to be reciprocally connected with the thalamus, the paleocortical structures are connected with the hypothalamus. Papez suggested that this hypothalamic–paleocortical system constitutes the "anatomical basis for emotion," and suggested that while emotional *expression* is mediated by the hypothalamus, subjective emotional *experience* is mediated by the paleocortical structures.

MacLean's Conceptualization of the Limbic System

One of the major attempts to conceptualize the functioning of the limbic system is contained in the model of Paul D. MacLean (1968, 1969, 1970), which suggests that the limbic system contains three major circuits. The first is identified particularly with the amygdala, and involves emotions concerned with self-preservation, such as aggression and fear. The second system is identified with the septal area, and involves emotional systems particularly concerned with the preservation of the species, such as sociability and sexuality. Both of these systems are present in lower animals and receive much input from the olfactory apparatus. The third system is virtually absent in reptiles and develops greatly during evolution, reaching its greatest size in humans. It includes the mammillothalamic tract connecting the mammillary bodies with the anterior thalamus and fibers continuing to the cingulate gyrus. MacLean suggests that this circuit may serve social and sexual functions like the septal circuit, and that its growth during evolution may reflect the shift from the olfactory to the visual regulation of behavior (MacLean, 1970).

Although the limbic system is enormously complex and is only beginning to be understood, on balance there does appear to be evidence that the system involving the amygdala is concerned with aggression and fear, while the septal system is involved with sex and sociability.

Circuits Involving Aggression and Fear

Not long after Papez suggested the importance of the limbic system in emotion, Kluver and Bucy (1937, 1938, 1939) found the first evidence that bilateral destruction of the amygdala can result in a dramatic loss of fear and aggression. Subsequent studies demonstrated that stimulation of the amygdala often produces rage-like attack and fear-like defensive behaviors. These effects have been observed in humans as well as in animals. Although it has been highly controversial, amygdalectomy has often been performed on humans whose aggressive behavior resists conventional kinds of therapy (cf. Heimburger, Whitlock, & Kalsbeck, 1966; Narabayashi & Uno, 1966; Mark & Ervin, 1970; Valenstein, 1973). Similarly, stimulation of the amygdala can produce uncontrollable feelings of rage in humans. We discussed the letter written by Charles Whitman in Chapter 2, whose aggressive behavior was likely associated with a malignant tumor located near the amygdala, and the observations of uncontrolled rage manifested by patients upon stimulation of the amygdala (King, 1961; Mark & Ervin, 1970).

Circuits Underlying Positive States

Stimulation and lesioning of the septal area produces effects that are markedly different from the effects produced by stimulation and lesioning of the amygdala. Septal lesions can produce transitory viciousness and increased evidence of fear, while septal stimulation is often positively reinforcing. In a project exploring the potential of septal stimulation in the relief of chronic pain and the treatment of schizophrenia, Heath and his colleagues have found that septal stimulation in humans usually produces subjective reports of pleasure, often with sexual overtones (Heath, 1964a, 1964b; Heath & Mickle, 1960). We saw an example in Chapter 2 where septal stimulation produced a striking positive change in the content of an interview with a depressed man, which the patient could not explain.

SUMMARY

We have seen that there are a variety of neurochemical systems at different levels of the central nervous system that underlie motivation and emotion. It will be recalled that in Chapter 2 we termed these the *primary motivational/emotional systems*, or PRIMES. These systems are summarized in Figure 3.3. The brain stem contains the arousal systems emphasized in Lindsley's view of motivation and emotion; along with the hypothalamus, it also contains species-specific systems responsible for the excitation and inhibition of a wide variety of specific behaviors important to individual and species survival, as is emphasized in Stellar's view. This region also contains the reward and punishment systems emphasized by Olds and his colleagues. The

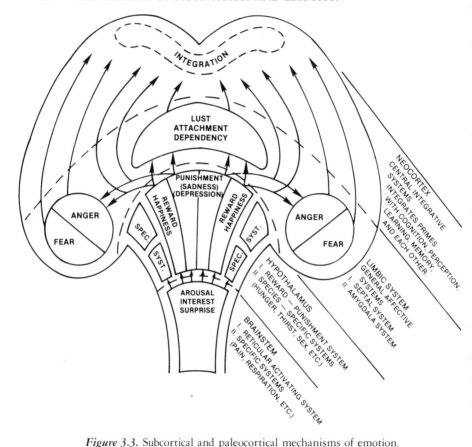

Figure 3.3. Subcortical and paleocortical mechanisms of emotion.

limbic system contains more general affective systems, including the
septal system associated by MacLean with sociable and sexual affects
underlying the preservation of the species, and the amygdala system
associated with fearful and aggressive affects underlying the preservation of the individual.

This view is relevant to the long-standing controversy between
typological approaches to the classification of emotions, such as those
by Tomkins, Ekman, Izard, and others, which assume fundamentally
different emotion types (surprise, fear, anger, happiness, sadness,
etc.), versus dimensional approaches which assume that emotions
vary quantitatively along bipolar dimensions (strong–weak, dominant–submissive, pleasant–unpleasant) (cf. Russell, 1979; Russell &

Mehrabian, 1977; Schlosberg, 1952). A consideration of the structure of the neurochemical systems underlying emotion suggests that both kinds of structure occur. The reticular activating system varies along an intensity or arousal dimension (strong–weak), and the reward/ punishment system could be conceptualized as varying along a pleasant–unpleasant dimension. At the same time, the hypothalamus and limbic system contain centers that are associated with relatively distinct types of motivational/emotional states, ranging from highly species-specific systems to more general affective systems (sex, fear, anger, etc.). Thus it is not surprising that emotional behavior reflects both kinds of structure.

THEORIES OF CENTRAL NERVOUS SYSTEM FUNCTIONING IN EMOTION

Although much is known about each of the elements of the limbic system, the hypothalamus, and the reticular formation considered in isolation, it is much less certain how they interact with each other. It is known that there are rich interconnections between these systems, and that they must interact with one another in emotional functioning. This section considers two viewpoints that are particularly relevant to the topics in this book: the views of Jeffrey Gray and Pribram and McGuiness.

GRAY'S THEORY

The Behavioral Activation System

Gray's (1971, 1977) model is based upon the notion of reward and punishment systems in the brain. The organism is motivated to increase activity in the reward system, and any behavior or stimulus that becomes associated with reward serves to increase that activity. The result is a *behavioral activation system* (BAS), a positive feedback control system in which the animal performs behaviors which "home-in" on reward. Gray identifies the BAS with the adrenergic medial forebrain bundle coursing through the lateral hypothalamus to the septal area, which produces the highest levels of response in self-stimulation research.

The Behavioral Inhibition System

The organism is motivated to minimize activation in the punishment system, leading to a *behavioral inhibition system* (BIS), a negative feedback system which puts a brake on any behavior which increases such activity. The operation of the BIS is particularly associated with the occurrence of the 4–8-Hz *theta rhythm* from the hippocampus. Gray presents evidence that the theta rhythm is driven from the medial septal area and that in higher animals the medial frontal cortex (*orbitofrontal cortex*) exerts executive control over the system. He thus terms this system the *septal–hippocampal–frontal* (SHF) *system*.

The Arousal System

Gray also posits an *arousal* mechanism which receives facilitatory influences from both the BIS and BAS. The arousal system increases the intensity of behavior, and Gray notes that when a previously rewarded stimulus is met with punishment or frustration (nonreward), the *vigor* of the animal's approach to that stimulus often increases even while the *probability* of the approach decreases. He argues that this increased vigor of response is due to arousal, which is associated with the reticular formation.

The Fight-or-Flight System

Gray (1971) argues that the above model can account for the phenomenon of passive avoidance, where the animal responds to threatening stimuli associated with punishment with a "tense, silent immobility." However, it does not account for the unconditioned response to punishment itself, which involves great activity which—according to the stimulus—may take the form of flight or defensive attack: the *fight-or-flight response*. Gray suggests that a separate mechanism must account for the fight-or-flight response. He posits three levels to this system: the amygdala, the VMH, and the central gray of the midbrain. The "final common pathway" for flight or defensive attack involves the PVS descending into the midbrain central gray. This is normally inhibited by the VMH. This inhibitory influence is itself inhibited by the amygdala via the stria terminalis, so that activation of the amygdala releases the fight-or-flight mechanism. Gray also suggests that the VMH inhibition may be intensified by

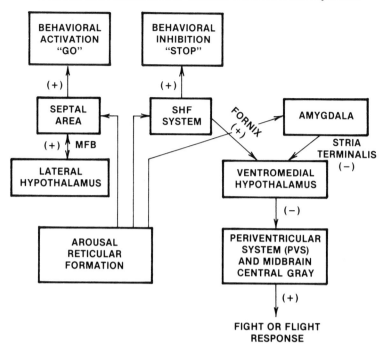

Figure 3.4. A summary of Gray's theory of central nervous system functioning in emotion.

influences from the BIS, which proceeds from the SHF via the fornix. A simplified summary of the interactions of these systems are summarized in Figure 3.4.

PRIBRAM AND MCGUINESS

A model of the interactions between the cortex, limbic system, hypothalamus, and reticular formation in the control of attention has been proposed by Pribram and McGuiness (1975; McGuiness & Pribram, 1980), providing an interesting comparison with Gray's model. Pribram and McGuiness argue that two major systems interact in the control of attention: an *arousal system* associated with orienting to external stimuli, and *activation system* associated with the vigilent readiness to respond. In addition, they posit an *effort–comfort system* involving the hippocampus, which coordinates arousal and activation.

Essentially, the arousal system is concerned with answering the question "What is it?," the activation system answers "What is to be done?," and the effort–comfort system coordinates the other two.

The Arousal System

The basic function of the arousal system is to *orient* the organism to new input. It extends from the spinal cord, through the reticular formation, and into the "defense region" of the hypothalamus. In the latter, low levels of stimulation produce orienting, while higher levels produce "defensive reactions" of hissing, snarling, piloerection, and running.

Pribram and McGuiness suggest that two systems, one facilitatory and one inhibitory, allow the sensitive control or "tuning" of the arousal system. The facilitatory system involves the lateral frontal cortex, where lesions abolish orienting responses. The inhibitory system involves the orbitofrontal cortex. Both of these systems act on arousal through the amygdala. As noted above, stimulation of the amygdala often leads to aggression, while lesions have "taming" effects, suggesting that a facilitatory effect on arousal is being manipulated. However, carefully restricted lesions and electrical stimulation have found evidence of inhibitory as well as facilitatory effects on arousal from the amygdala (Rosvold, Mirsky, & Pribram, 1954; Ursin & Kaada, 1960). Pribram and McGuiness suggest that the facilitatory mechanism acts upon lateral portions of the hypothalamus, and the inhibitory mechanisms upon medial portions. This model is illustrated in Figure 3.5. McGuiness and Pribram suggest that NE and serotonin (also termed 5-hydroxytryptamine or 5-HT) are particularly important neurotransmitters in the arousal system, with 5-HT fibers being influenced or modulated by a system of NE fibers.

The Activation System

While arousal involves attention to input, activation involves *what is to be done* about the input. Activation occurs when there is a delay between the input and the actual performance of overt behavior, when the organism "expects" or "intends" to do something about the input but prior to the actual performance. This state is associated with a slowly developing negative shift in brain electrical potential termed *contingent negative variations* (CNVs). CNVs are associated with intended behavior–expectations or sets that demand postural

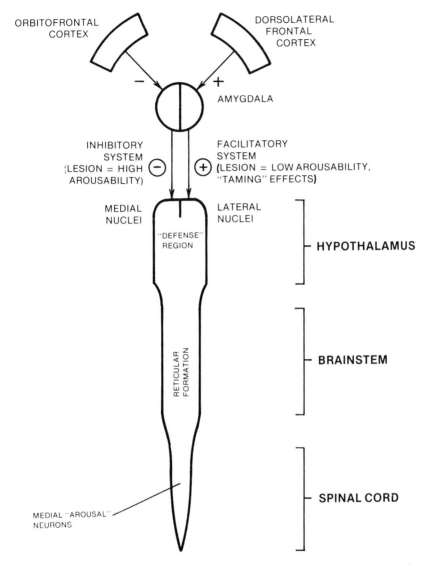

Figure 3.5. Systems involved in the Pribram and McGuiness model of arousal.

readiness. The negative potential abruptly becomes positive when a response occurs.

Pribram and McGuiness suggest that CNV develops whenever a portion of the brain is maintaining a readiness of processing, and they note that there is preliminary evidence that CNVs indicative of activation are controlled by the basal ganglia. The basal ganglia are involved in the extrapyramidal maintenance of postural sets, and they are the origin of many fiber tracts which go through the far-lateral hypothalamus to link with brain-stem mechanisms. The largest of these is the *nigrostriatal* pathway which is the prime dopaminergic system in the brain. McGuiness and Pribram (1980) suggest that the brain stem and hypothalamic systems associated with activation are cholinergic, with ACh as the neurotransmitter, so that activation involves an Ach system acted upon by DA influences.

The Effort–Comfort System

Pribram and McGuiness suggest that a system involving the hippocampus serves to coordinate and regulate arousal and activation. They argue that without such regulation the behavior of the organism becomes "captured" by primitive stimulus–response relationships. The hippocampal mechanism serves to couple or uncouple stimulus and response, and this demands *effort*, which is defined as an expenditure of energy due to the actions of central control systems. Effort is the basis of the "voluntary" control of behavior.

Pribram and McGuiness also suggest that effort is related to the hippocampal theta rhythm. They suggest that arousal is associated with an increase in the power (amplitude in millivolts) of theta, that activation is associated with a decrease in the power of theta, and that effort is associated with changes (narrowing or broadening) in the range of power around the peak theta frequency. McGuiness and Pribram (1980) suggest that ACTH-related neuropeptides are involved in the hippocampal mechanism, and function there to modulate an "effort–comfort" dimension of experience and behavior.

CONCLUSIONS

The Pribram and McGuiness model explains major features of the neural systems underlying attentional control. It is particularly useful in pointing out how the neural mechanisms controlling the brain's receptivity to input are distinct from those regulating motor readiness (cf. Tucker & Williamson, 1984). The analysis of effort also suggests the nature of the neural systems underlying voluntary as opposed to nonvoluntary behavior, and it seems quite compatible with other descriptions of the mechanisms of voluntary and nonvoluntary attention (cf. Schneider & Shiffrin, 1977). However, many questions remain unanswered. For example, the relationships between the arousal, activation, and effort–comfort systems on the one hand, and the reward/punishment systems analyzed by Gray on the other, are far from clear. The two models are oriented toward different phenomena, with the Gray model concerned with reward and punishment and the Pribram and McGuiness model concerned with attention. However, there are significant overlaps in the mechanisms they are discussing. One wonders, for example, whether the arousal and activation systems could be two sorts of "behavioral activation systems" in Gray's terms. Certainly both NE and DA support "reward" effects in self-stimulation studies, and thus the organism appears to be motivated to increase activity in those systems. Also, the notion of a BIS in which the organism is motivated to minimize activation is absent in the Pribram and McGuiness model. It may well be that both of these models contain substantial elements of truth, and that the eventual model of the relationships between neocortex, limbic system, hypothalamus, and brain stem will contain major elements of both.

CENTRAL NERVOUS SYSTEM MECHANISMS OF EMOTIONAL EXPRESSION

This section discusses the central nervous system mechanisms involved in the external expression of emotion. It focuses upon the differences in the control of spontaneous expression—Emotion II—and voluntary expression, which in the terms introduced in Chapter 1 is "symbolic" in nature. We have seen above that there is clear evidence that different neurochemical systems underlie spontaneous and symbolic expression, with those underlying symbolic expression involving neocortical motor mechanisms discharging via the pyramidal motor system. Spontaneous expression, in contrast, involves the "built in" expression via nonpyramidal systems of the primary motivational/emotional states mediated by subcortical and paleocortical structures.

Central nervous system structures underlying spontaneous emotional expression may be of two types: sites eliciting the expression directly, and sites eliciting the expression as a secondary result of activating a primary motivational/emotional state (Jurgens, 1979; Ploog, 1981). In animals these must often be distinguished by the degree of integration of the animal's behavior. If stimulation of a site leads to a complete, well-integrated response (e.g., a cat hissing, spitting, laying back the ears, showing piloerection, and striking out with the claws), it is usually assumed to involve a complete motivational/emotional state, while if different aspects of this pattern are seen in isolation, the response is said to be "pseudoaffective," involving the excitation of an isolated expression.

FACIAL EXPRESSION

Many of the studies that we have considered on the neurochemical bases of emotion have used facial/bodily expression in their measurement of emotion. Unfortunately, few have analyzed facial or bodily expression *per se*, but have instead reported on these responses as an aspect of the expression of emotion. However, it does seem clear that there are two kinds of central nervous system input to the nuclei in the brain stem involved in facial expression—corticobulbar fibers from the precentral motor cortex involved with voluntary facial movement, and nonpyramidal fibers involved with spontaneous emotion expression (Courville, 1966; Monrad-Krohn, 1924, 1939; Steklis & Raleigh, 1979). It also seems clear that the motor control of facial expression is organized and integrated in brain-stem mechanisms, some of which contain "hard-wired" systems of facial/autonomic response.

The functioning of brain-stem mechanisms in facial expression is illustrated in an early study by Weinstein and Bender (1943). These authors explored the expressions elicited in cats by stimulation of the brain stem, finding some areas where facial movements are apparently fairly simple reflex acts—one-sided, tetanoid, and isolated—and other areas where bilateral, smooth, "life-like" expressions occurred in conjunction with appropriate autonomic changes. The latter often had "recognizably purposive" functions associated with nursing, swallowing, coughing, defecation, and so forth.

There is evidence that facial expressions also occur in humans with stimulation of the brain stem. Wilson and Nachold (1972) report the results of the stimulation of the reticular formation in 12 patients being treated for intractable pain. They observed facial expressions of fear and depression that seemed to be isolated "fragments of emotions," as well as more integrated expressions associated with pain and in one case with "a desire to cry." Also, the bilateral interruption of corticobulbar tracts within the brain stem, between the internal capsule and pons, can result in unrestrained outbursts of laughing and crying without the appropriate affect (Truex, 1959). This symptom complex, designated *pseudobulbar palsy*, has been characterized as a "pure disorder of emotional expression" involving the excitation or disinhibition of "hard-wired" mechanisms of expression in the brain stem (Bear, 1980).

The distinction between neural systems involved in spontaneous and volitional movements in humans has long been recognized by neurologists, and there is evidence that analogous systems control facial expression in nonhuman primates. In a review of the literature on facial expression in humans and other primates, Steklis and Raleigh (1979) note that limbic system lesions that impair emotional and motivational processes also result in less frequent and/or appropriate facial expressions. They conclude that the neurochemical bases for affectively based spontaneous facial expression is similar in humans and other primates. Also, they note that there is clear evidence in humans that lesions in the precentral motor neocortex can impair voluntary expression while leaving spontaneous expression intact (Kolb & Milner, 1981b), and that an early study by Green and Walker (1938) suggests a similar phenomenon in the rhesus macaque and baboon. Steklis and Raleigh conclude that present evidence suggests that the neocortical motor areas may contribute "more to volitional than to involuntary (spontaneous) expression" in nonhuman primates as well as humans, and they suggest that the nature and extent of the volitional control of communicative displays (both facial expressions and vocalizations) should be more systematically investigated in nonhuman primates (p. 274).

EXPRESSIVE VOCALIZATIONS

In contrast to the relatively sparse literature on facial expression, there are many studies that have specifically examined the neurochemical systems underlying spontaneous vocalizations expressive of emotion (cf. MacLean, 1978; Ploog, 1966, 1981). This may partly be due to the fact that it is possible, by means of the sound spectrograph, to explicitly specify the nature of spontaneous vocalizations, while efforts to objectively specify facial expression are more recent, more complex, and procedurally more difficult.

Motor Coordination

The literature on the neural control of expressive vocalizations has been comprehensively reviewed by Jurgens (1979) and Ploog (1981). From extensive studies of nonhuman primates, these investigators conclude that this control is organized in a hierarchical manner. The lowest level involves the brain-stem reticular formation at the level of the pons and medulla, including the nuclei directly involved in facial movement and respiratory control and the mechanisms for integrating their actions. The motor coordination of the specific behaviors necessary for phonation occurs at this level, but it is doubtful that the specific neural patterns characterizing specific calls is generated at this level, and it seems unlikely that this integration system can produce calls on its own, without the influence of higher structures.

Spontaneous Vocalization

The next hierarchical level involves midbrain mechanisms (specifically the caudal periaqueductal gray and laterally adjacent tegmentum between the inferior colliculus and brachium conjunctivum) in which Jurgens and Ploog suggest that motivation is coupled with vocal expression. The vocalization-eliciting areas which simultaneously elicit motivational/emotional responses (and which thus presumably cause vocalizations secondary to those states) project directly into this area. They suggest that this area selects and triggers vocal patterns according to influences from the motivational/emotional systems, and that the motor integration of these patterns takes place in the pons–medulla area.

This midbrain mechanism would seem to serve the functions of spontaneous external expression—Emotion II—in that the expression is a nonvoluntary "readout" of the emotional/motivational state. It is noteworthy in this regard that this vocalization-eliciting system has a great phylogenetic age. Jurgens and Ploog point out that this area has been related to call production in birds, reptiles, amphibians, and even fish, despite totally different sound-producing systems in these different vertebrate classes.

Voluntary Call Initiation

The next two hierarchical levels involve the volitional control of vocalization, and have been investigated only in monkeys and humans. The third integration level is associated with voluntary call *initiation*, and involves the area of the cingulate gyrus, comprising the anterior limbic cortex in the squirrel monkey and the supplemental motor area and anterior cingulate cortex in humans. The importance of these areas in human vocalization was suggested by Penfield and Roberts's (1959) observations of the effects of brain stimulation in conscious patients during brain surgery, and has recently been discussed by Jurgens and von Cramon (1982). Whereas the midbrain mechanism controls calls that are direct "readouts" of motivational/emotional states, the cingular vocalization area controls vocalizations independently of such states, apparently via facilitatory or inhibitory influences upon the midbrain mechanism. It thus does not form new calls, but rather initiates the expression of calls that are already hard wired in the midbrain mechanism..

Voluntary Call Formation

The fourth integration level involves the voluntary *formation* of calls. This function is particularly associated with the area of the precentral gyrus concerned with the larynx. This area gains increasing importance in the control of vocalization as one moves from lower mammals to monkeys to humans. It appears to be dispensible in animals with a wholly innate vocal repitoire, where voluntary call formation is not necessary, but its damage in humans causes severe disturbances, as we shall see below. It is noteworthy that emotional vocal utterances and highly stereotyped verbal utterances such as curses and salutations often survive destruction of this area in humans, possibly because the voluntary control of call formation is relatively unimportant for such vocalizations (cf. Jurgens, 1979).

Ploog (1981) suggests that these systems follow a distinct maturational sequence in the infant, with the spontaneous expression mechanism functioning from birth. The voluntary call initiation system may become operational at about 3 months of age, when the infant's vocal behavior becomes conditionable. The neocortical call formation system may begin to influence vocal patterns by the end of the first year.

A MODEL OF THE EMOTION II PROCESS

A model of the central nervous system mechanisms underlying the facial/vocal expression of emotion, based upon the Jurgens and Ploog analysis, is presented in Figure 3.6. The model assumes that the mechanisms underlying facial expression are similar in general ways to those underlying vocal expression. Such an assumption seems reasonable, as facial and vocal expression in this case serve similar functions via similar peripheral mechanisms—the expression of primary motivational/emotional states via the facial musculature. Also, the literature on the neurological bases of facial expression, while not as extensive as that for vocal expression, seems generally consistent with this assumption. For example, we have seen that, as with vocal expression, some facial expressions appear to be "hard wired" into brain-stem mechanisms, that they can occur without affect, and that voluntary and nonvoluntary systems underlying facial expression can be distinguished.

The model in Figure 3.6 assumes that the motor control of facial/vocal expression is controlled in the lower brain stem (1). This may be influenced via the hard-wired programs of expression based upon upper brain-stem mechanisms (2), or by voluntary expressions initiated via corticobulbar pyramidal fibers (dashed lines) from the precentral motor cortex (4). The latter constitutes a system of *voluntary expression formation* analogous to voluntary call formation. The upper brain-stem mechanisms (2) may be activated by motivational/emotional systems in the limbic system/hypothalamus (cross-hatched areas). This is the Emotion II process: the spontaneous readout of motivational/emotional responses in externally accessible behaviors. Alternatively, the upper brain-stem mechanism may be activated via voluntary influences, constituting a system of *voluntary expression initiation* corresponding to voluntary call initiation. Jurgens and von Cramon (1982) have noted that a patient damaged in the anterior cingulate cortex and left supplemental motor area showed an apparently permanent general flattening of emotional expression.

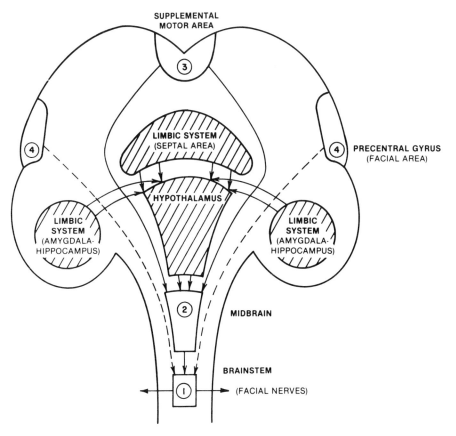

Figure 3.6. Neural bases of emotional expression: the Emotion II process.

We shall thus follow the vocalization literature and suggest tentatively that the voluntary expression initiation mechanism is associated with the anterior cingulate cortex and/or the supplemental motor area above the cingulate gyrus (3).

It might be observed that this analysis of an expression initiation mechanism implies that universally recognizable emotional expressions can be employed in the flow of symbolic communication: An individual can "call up" the prewired expressions at will, so to speak. Related to this, such a mechanism implies that the process of initiating or posing emotional expression is different from the process of voluntary expression formation, since the former has the "assist" of the hard-wired upper brain-stem systems while the latter does not. The existence of such a mechanism would account for the otherwise unexplained ability of humans to pose emotional facial expressions, what Tomkins (1981) has called "an assumed and generally true consensus about what an innate facial response is" (p. 356). This ability is related to spontaneous facial expressiveness (Buck et al., 1974), and is sufficiently powerful that posed facial expressions are universally recognizable in widely different cultures (Ekman et al., 1969). This implies in turn that it is particularly important to distinguish spontaneous emotional expression, posed emotional expression, and requested facial movement, a point which has been recently made by Ekman (1980).

SUMMARY

The analogies between facial expression and expressive vocalizations suggest the possibility that the Jurgens and Ploog notion of a hierarchical structure in the neural control of expressive vocalization may be applicable to the analysis of facial expression. Thus, "prewired" expressions associated with spontaneous displays may be initiated either by the activation of motivational/emotional states or via voluntary expression initiation. The latter mechanism would explain the human facility at posing universally recognizable facial expressions. This would allow the use of such expressions in the service of the flow of symbolic communication. In addition, a voluntary expression formation mechanism based upon pyramidal corticobulbar fibers is suggested.

Thus far, we have been primarily concerned with the role of subcortical and paleocortical systems in emotional expression. In the next section we shall consider neocortical mechanisms contained in the right versus the left cerebral hemispheres.

CEREBRAL LATERALIZATION AND EMOTIONAL EXPRESSION

Recent studies of the different functions of the left and right hemispheres of the brain have suggested that the two hemispheres play different roles in emotion and emotional expression. This research has proceeded along several fronts—among patients with brain lesions, epileptic foci, or psychopathological symptoms, and in normal persons. Initially, much of the research was designed to examine whether there is a differential representation of emotional processes in the two cerebral hemispheres, and these studies have found substantial evidence for such hemispheric specialization (cf. Tucker, 1981). However, the exact nature and meaning of this specialization is only beginning to be understood and its implications appreciated. In this section we shall review this evidence and some of the initial attempts at conceptualization.

LEFT-HEMISPHERE FUNCTIONS

Cognitive Capacities

Left-hemisphere processing is associated with an analytic ideation and a linear, sequential mode of processing that leads to the articulation and differentiation of concepts (Tucker, 1981). It is particularly important in verbal and linguistic abilities, as is made tragically clear when the left hemisphere is damaged in humans.

Aphasia

Damage to the left cerebral hemisphere in humans is often associated with a variety of communication deficits collectively termed "aphasia." These deficits particularly involve problems in verbal communication, such as speaking and writing. However, symbolic "nonverbal" behaviors are also affected. Deaf mutes who suffer left-hemisphere damage have been found to lose their abilities at signing and finger spelling (Kimura, 1979). Also, a number of studies have demonstrated deficits of gesture and pantomime recognition and/or expression in aphasic patients (Duffy & Duffy, 1981; Duffy, Duffy, & Pearson, 1975; Gainotti & Lemmo, 1976; Goodglass & Kaplan, 1963; Pickett, 1974; Varney, 1978). These studies have found that the degree of verbal impairment is closely related to the degree of pantomimic/gestural impairment, wirh r's ranging between $+.48$ and $+.89$. Moreover, Kimura and her colleagues in a series of studies have demonstrated difficulties in the copying of nonrepresentational patterns of movement in aphasic patients: that is, in copying hand and arm movements (Kimura & Archibald, 1974), producing oral movements such as extending the tongue (Mateer & Kimura, 1977), and moving to new hand postures (Kimura, 1977, 1979).

The meaning of these findings has been the subject of some controversy. On the one hand, it has been suggested that left-hemisphere damage results in a general inability to express symbols in any modality. This explanation is consistent with Finklnberg's (1870) characterization of aphasia as "asymbolia" (cf. Duffy & Liles, 1979). Others have suggested that these findings do not represent a general communication deficit *per se*, but instead are the result of apraxia, which involves the inability to perform voluntary movement (Goodglass & Kaplan, 1963; Kimura, 1979).

Apraxia

Apraxia involves disorders of learned pyramidal movements which cannot be ascribed to weakness, incoordination, sensory loss, inattention, or a lack of comprehension of commands (Geschwind, 1975). For example, a patient may be completely unable to *pretend* to blow out a match, but may perform correctly when an actual match is provided. Geschwind (1975) suggests that such effects are due to the presence of nonpyramidal movements which are not cued by the request to pretend but which are cued by the actual presence of the match. For similar reasons, axial movements involving midline structures such as the eyes, trunk, shoulders, and hips (but not including the lips, tongue, or larynx) are generally better preserved than movements of lateral structures such as the hands and feet. The latter are more dependent upon pyramidal innervation, while axial movements involve much nonpyramidal influence. Geschwind cites a case in which a patient could correctly assume the stance of a boxer, but was utterly unable to respond to requests to punch, jab, or uppercut: "He simply looked with great perplexity at his fists, without making any response" (1975, p. 192).

The Control of Gesture and Pantomime

Like aphasic disorders, apraxic disorders are often associated with left-hemisphere brain damage, and it is unclear whether the deficits in gesture and pantomime are due to a general disorder of symbolic communication, whether they are aspects of an apraxic disorder, or perhaps both. To the extent that they involve pyramidal motor movements, one would expect that they would be disrupted in apraxia, while on the other hand since they are involved so intimately with language, one might expect that they would be disrupted in aphasia. There are adherents for both positions. Thus Kimura (1979) points out that aphasic patients had difficulty with "meaningless" movements which were nonrepresentational and unrelated to communicative movements. On the other hand, Duffy and his colleagues have performed multiple regression and path analyses of the relationships between pantomime recognition/expression, verbal aphasic deficit, intelligence impairment, and limb apraxia, and find that the most parsimonious models are those that treat the aphasic deficit as the determinant of the other measures (Duffy & Duffy, 1981; Duffy, Watt, & Duffy, 1981). Also, Cicone, Wapner, Foldi, Zurif, and Gardner (1979) found similarities in the gestural patterns and patterns of speech output in qualitative analyses of the behavior of four aphasic patients, and interpret their findings in terms of a "central organizer" that controls both verbal and gestural behavior.

These explanations may not be as different as they first appear. One could argue that *any movement which is explicitly called for or which is to be explicitly copied* is representational in that sense, and thus not wholly "meaningless." This view would suggest that *any* specific voluntary movement, such as those involved in tests of apraxia, may be considered "symbolic" in our sense of the term. This would in turn be consistent with the notion that symbolic processing, as we have defined it in Chapter 1, can be considered to be based upon the left hemisphere.

On the other hand, there is clinical evidence that the systems involving the language functions underlying aphasia and the motor functions underlying apraxia can reside in different hemispheres. Heilman, Coyle, Gonyea, and Geschwind (1973) describe a case in which a left-handed patient with a right-hemisphere lesion demonstrated apraxia with his unparalyzed right arm without manifesting any language disorder. This suggests that the motor programs in this patient were based in the right hemisphere, while language was based in the left. It would be most interesting to know the extent to which gesture and pantomime were disrupted or intact in this particular patient. It seems clear that the final resolution of this complex issue must await more research, but the question has considerable theoretical and practical importance.

Spontaneous Expression and Aphasia

While there is evidence that symbolic communication, as we have defined it, is based upon left-hemisphere processing, there is evidence that spontaneous communication is not, and that it may instead involve right-hemisphere processing. It has long been noted that many aphasic patients are able to use words for the expression of a *presently existing* motivational/emotional state. Thus they may swear when frustrated or say "hello" when greeting a friend, but be utterly unable to repeat those words a few moments later when asked to do so after the immediate motivational/emotional state which elicited the words has passed. We noted above that, because such phrases are so overlearned, they may bypass the call formation mechanism analyzed by Jurgens (1979) and Ploog (1981).

Also, there is evidence that the ability of aphasic patients to communicate via spontaneous facial expression is not impaired by their condition, even though significant facial paralysis may be present. Buck and Duffy (1980) showed left-hemisphere-damaged aphasic patients a series of emotionally loaded color slides while videotaping their spontaneous facial–gestural responses. Later, judges viewed the videotape and attempted to guess on each trial what kind of slide had been viewed. Results indicated that observers could determine the category of slide viewed by the left-hemisphere-damaged patients as well as they could from the expressions of non-brain-damaged controls. Also, Duffy and Buck (1979) showed that the spontaneous sending accuracy of the left-hemisphere-damaged patients was essentially unrelated to the extent of verbal ability ($r = .00$), while pantomime expression and recognition were both strongly related to verbal ability ($r = .99$ and $.90$, respectively). The lack of relationship between spontaneous expressiveness and verbal ability stands in sharp contrast with the strong relationships that are typically found between verbal ability and intentional gesture, pantomime, and movement.

Buck and Duffy (1980) also found that patients with right-hemisphere brain damage were significantly lower in spontaneous expressiveness when compared with left-hemisphere-damaged patients and controls, and that in fact right-hemisphere-damaged patients were not significantly more expressive than were patients with Parkinson's disease, a disorder which as noted above has long been associated with a "mask-like" dearth of facial expression. The general pattern of the Buck and Duffy results has been replicated (Borod & Koff, 1982).

RIGHT-HEMISPHERE FUNCTIONS

Cognitive Capacities

In contrast to the left hemisphere, the right hemisphere is associated with what has been termed a "syncretic" conceptualization, in which sensory and cognitive elements are fused or synthesized into a global experience (Werner, 1957). Instead of digital data being organized in a linear and sequential manner, the right hemisphere organizes analogue data in a holistic manner. Thus the human brain appears to involve two functionally different information-processing subsystems, with enormous implications for the understanding of every aspect of human nature which are only beginning to be appreciated (cf. Tucker, 1981).

Emotional Expression

We have seen that there is evidence that left-hemisphere damage leads to deficits in symbolic communication abilities, while emotional speech and spontaneous communication still occur. Right-hemisphere damage in contrast does not typically lead to deficits in verbal behavior or in intentional gesture, pantomime, or movement (Duffy et al., 1975; Duffy & Duffy, 1981), while spontaneous expressiveness appears to be reduced.

Other evidence has implicated the right hemisphere in a variety of processes associated with emotion (cf. Tucker, 1981). For example, Graves and Natale (1979) found that spontaneous facial expressiveness is greater in subjects who show evidence of right-hemisphere dominance. Also, there is evidence that right-hemisphere processing is involved in the recognition of emotion in others. In normal right-handed subjects, several studies have found that the left ear better recognizes emotion expression in speech—*how* the statement is expressed as opposed to *what* is expressed (Carmon & Nachshon, 1973; Haggard & Parkinson, 1971; Safer & Leventhal, 1977)—and the emotional quality of tonal sequences (Bryden, Ley, & Sugarman, 1982). Furthermore, there is a left-visual-field superiority for the processing of faces, *particularly if the face is expressing emotion* (Heller & Levy, 1981; Landis, Assal, & Perret, 1979; Ley & Bryden, 1979; Suberi & McKeever, 1977). These left-sided advantages both suggest that the right hemisphere is particularly responsible for the processing of these responses.

Studies of brain-damaged patients have suggested a similar conclusion, in that right-hemisphere-damaged patients have particular difficulty comprehending and discriminating affective tones in speech (Heilman, Scholes, & Watson, 1974; Tucker, Watson, & Heilman, 1977), and with the recognition and discrimination of emotional faces and pictures (Cicone, Wapner, & Gardner, 1980; DeKosky, Heilman, Bowers, & Valenstein, 1980; DeRenzi & Spinnler, 1966; Katz, 1980). Also, they do poorly on the Rosenthal, Hall, DiMatteo, Rogers, and Archer (1979) Profile of Nonverbal Sensitivity (PONS; Benowitz, Bear, Rosenthal, & Mesulam, 1980).

There is also evidence that facial asymmetry or "facedness" is significantly left-sided during the posing of emotional expressions: that is, the expression is stronger on the left side of the face than it is on the right (cf. Borod & Caron, 1980; Borod, Caron, & Koff, in press; Campbell, 1978; Koff, Borod, & White, 1981; Sackeim, Gur, & Saucy, 1978). Moscovitch and Olds (1982) found analogous left-facedness in the expressions associated with relating emotional experiences. These data have been interpreted as being consistent with the notion of relative right-hemisphere activation during emotion: Since the right hemisphere is connected more directly with the left side of the face than the right, the left side of the face more directly reflects the emotional processes mediated by the right hemisphere. Also, Sackeim *et al.* (1978) suggest that negative emotions may be more "faced" than are positive emotions.

The question of whether spontaneous expressions are also "faced" is unresolved. Ekman (1980) has criticized Sackeim *et al.* for failing to distinguish between requested facial movements, posed expression, and spontaneous expression in their study. Ekman, Hagar, and Friesen (1981) report that, in a sample of children, both posed smiles and negative expressions were often asymmetrical and left sided. However, in a study of the children and a sample of women viewing affective films, they found that spontaneous smiles are rarely asymmetrical, and when they are they are evenly divided between left-

and right-sided asymmetry. Although they caution that they found relatively few spontaneous negative expressions, they observed that they were often asymmetrical, but were evenly divided between right- and left-sided asymmetry. They also cite unpublished observations that the nonemotional facial actions involved in the punctuation of speech and the concealment of felt emotion are asymmetrical and left sided. We shall return to a consideration of these findings below.

General Emotional Processes

The right hemisphere has also been implicated in more general emotional processing. In brain-damaged patients, left-hemisphere damage has been associated with a reaction of anxiety, hostility, and depression called a "catastrophic reaction," while right-hemisphere damage has been associated with an "indifference reaction" characterized by indifference, denial of illness, disinhibition, and euphoria (Gainotti, 1972; Geschwind, 1979a, 1979b). These clinical findings were reinforced by the finding of similar symptoms in healthy persons whose cerebral hemispheres are temporarily inactivated (Terzian, 1964; Terzian & Ceccotto, 1959). The latter was accomplished by the Wada sodium amobarbital test, which involves the injection of the barbiturate sodium amobarbital into either the right or left carotid artery (Wada & Rasmussen, 1960).

   In normal right-handed subjects, it has been found that left-sided conjugate lateral eye movements suggestive of right-hemisphere activation occur during stress (Tucker, Roth, Arneson, & Buckingham, 1977), and when answering affectively loaded questions (Schwartz, Davidson, & Maer, 1975). Also, college students who show evidence of a hysteric cognitive style tend to look to the left when answering reflective questions, suggesting a preference for right-hemisphere processing (Gur & Gur, 1975; Smokler & Shevrin, 1979).

Spontaneous versus Symbolic Expression and the Right Hemisphere

It is particularly important to distinguish between spontaneous and symbolic expression when discussing right-hemisphere functioning, because there is evidence that small differences in laboratory procedures can result in dramatically different results and potential confusion. This is illustrated in the Ekman *et al.* (1981) demonstration of facedness in conversational and posed expressions, but not spontaneous expressions. Another example is a study by Kolb and Milner (1981a) which found no difference in facial expression following right- versus left-hemisphere damage, a finding apparently contrary to that of Buck and Duffy (1980). However, in the Kolb and Milner study, facial expression was assessed during a testing session involving face-to-face contact, so that symbolic conversational expressions could have occurred. Since the left-damaged patients could probably not converse easily, their output of such expressions should be markedly reduced. The technique used by Moscovitch and Olds (1982) also involved conversational expression. To encouarge the occurrence of spontaneous expression, as defined here, affective stimuli must be employed to evoke emotional states, and social contact should be minimized or routinized to minimize conversational expression (cf. Buck, 1978).

HEMISPHERIC SPECIALIZATION AND PSYCHOPATHOLOGY

The evidence relating the right hemisphere to emotional processing has been reviewed by Tucker (1981). He suggests that a variety of psychopathological symptoms may be related to different forms of hemispheric processing. For example, there is considerable evidence relating schizophrenia to left-hemisphere dysfunctions and affective disorders to right-hemisphere dysfunctions (cf. Flor-Henry, 1974, 1979). Also, there are suggestions that lateralized brain processes may be involved in personality disorders; Flor-Henry (1974), for example, suggests that left-hemisphere dysfunctions may be involved in psychopathic behavior in males and hysteric personality patterns in females. Related to this are observations that conversion reactions and hypochondrial symptoms tend to occur on the left side of the body, suggesting right-hemisphere influence. Tucker suggests that psychopathy and hysteria may both involve a relatively low level of left-hemisphere cognitive functioning, and constrasts this with obsessive–compulsive disorders in which there is evidence that left-hemisphere influences are particularly strong. He feels that the lack of anxiety in the former disorders compared with the high level of anxiety in the latter is an important clue that anxiety involves left-hemisphere functioning.

HEMISPHERIC SPECIALIZATION AND EMOTIONAL VALENCE

One of the areas of greatest confusion and controversy in the current literature on hemispheric specialization involves the question of whether the positive or negative valence of the emotional states is differentially associated with the two hemispheres. The research relating to this issue is complex and not yet resolved (cf. Tucker, 1981). Some investigators suggest that the left hemisphere is concerned with positive affect while the right hemisphere is associated with negative affect (Reuter-Lorenz & Davidson, 1981). These authors stress the finding noted above that posed negative expressions appear to be more "faced," suggesting greater right-hemisphere activation. Also, Sackeim, Greenberg, Weiman, Gur, Hungerbuhler, and Geschwind (1982) have shown that involuntary laughing and crying is associated with right- and left-sided lesions, respectively. On the other hand, other investigators suggest the opposite: that the right hemisphere is associated with positive emotion and the left hemisphere with negative (Bear & Fedio, 1977). Part of this confusion may involve the ambiguity of the terms used to describe emotion. Thus the term "euphoria" may be used to refer to elation, denial, or indifference, "negative emotion" may mean fear, disgust, anger, anxiety, depression, or pain. For example, Geschwind (1979b) has noted that the "euphoria" manifested by some right-hemisphere-damaged patients resembles a gross unconcern and indifference, and that some left-hemisphere-damaged patients (with Wernicke's aphasia) often show a "much more truly euphoric" reaction.

THEORIES OF CEREBRAL LATERALIZATION AND EMOTION

Galin

The theories concerning the emotional capacities of the two hemispheres have often viewed the left hemisphere as exerting control, usually inhibitory control, over the right hemisphere. Thus Galin (1974) compared right-hemisphere processing with the "primary process" in psychoanalytic theory, in that both depend upon nonverbal imaginal representations, use holistic modes of association rather than logic, and lack a perception of time and sequence. In classical psychoanalytic theory, the primary process is identified with the *id*, which contains tendencies to spontaneously and impulsively reflect "primitive" drives and desires. In contrast, Galin viewed the left-hemisphere processing as analogous to the "secondary process" associated in the classical theory with the *ego*, which functions as a "censor" to control and inhibit these impulsive action tendencies.

Galin suggests that the right hemisphere–left hemisphere interaction may be the neurophysiological basis for at least some forms of *repression*, and that the right hemisphere may be the anatomical locus for some kinds of unconscious mental processes, in that due to an inhibition of neural transmission between the two hemispheres, events in the right hemisphere may become functionally disconnected from the left hemisphere and "continue a life of their own" (p. 581). As an example, Galin suggests a paradoxical communication situation resembling a "double bind," in which a parent gives a child one message verbally—"I love you"—and another, contradictory and negative message via facial/bodily expression and tone of voice. Because of their different skills, the two hemispheres will extract different information from the experience: "Each hemisphere is exposed to the same sensory input, but because of their relative specializations, they each emphasize only one of the messages. The left will attend to the verbal cues because it cannot extract information from the facial gestalt effectively; the right will attend to the non-verbal cues because it cannot easily understand the words" (p. 576). Because of the different information, the response tendencies of the hemispheres might be different: "In this situation, the two hemispheres might decide upon opposite courses of action; the left to approach, and the right to flee . . . the left hemisphere seems to win control of the output channels most of the time, but if the left is not able to 'turn off' the right completely, it may settle for disconnecting the transfer of conflicting information from the other side" (p. 576).

In this situation, the information in the right hemisphere may be "repressed" and become "unconscious": "The mental processes in the right hemisphere, cut off in this way from the left hemisphere consciousness that is directing overt behavior, may nevertheless continue a life of its own. The memory of the situation, the emotional concomitants, and the frustrated plan of action all may persist, affecting subsequent perception and forming the basis for expectations and evaluations of future input" (p. 576). Galin suggests in addition that the right hemisphere might "seize the opportunity to express itself" during daydreams, night dreams, and other periods when, presumably, the "censoring" functions of the left hemisphere are temporarily relaxed (p. 577).

While Galin's view is valuable in reestablishing contact between the fields of neurology and psychodynamics, it should be emphasized that many aspects of this analysis have yet to be tested, and thus must be viewed with caution.

Tucker

Tucker (1981) argues that the different kinds of cognitive processing in the two hemispheres is central to the understanding of their functioning in emotion, stating that "emotional processes are at one level dependent on basic neurophysiological activation processes and at another level intrinsic to the differential forms of conceptualization of the two cerebral hemispheres" (p. 19). He suggests that the syncretic conceptualization of the right hemisphere provides a "kind of perception and behavioral organization necessary for adequate emotional functioning" (p. 22), in which information from visceral and other sensory channels is integrated into a superordinate conceptualization.

Thus the right hemisphere seems to have a special capacity to facilitate certain kinds of emotional experience. In our terms, the right hemisphere may play a central role in the Emotion III process, the internal cognitive readout of the state of the motivational/ emotional systems.

It should be noted that Tucker uses the term "cognitive" in a different way than we have been using it. "Cognition" is usually defined in terms of knowledge by description, and the analytic, conceptual, and linear kind of processing associated with the left hemisphere. This usage is implied, for example, in Baron's (1980) distinction between direct "person perception" and mediated "person cognition," and in Zajonc's (1980) argument that "emotion" and "cognition" are based upon separate systems. However, Tucker's position on "cognition" encompasses knowledge by acquaintance as well: From this point of view, the kind of knowledge involved in "pure" spontaneous emotion—knowledge by acquaintance—is a kind of "cognition." This kind of knowledge is the subjective experience that we have called Emotion III.

Tucker's position implies that it is necessary to distinguish two kinds of cognition: *syncretic cognition* involving knowledge by acquaintance, and *analytic cognition* involving knowledge by description. We shall continue to use the term "cognition" in the latter, more usual sense to avoid confusion, unless stated otherwise. However, Tucker's usage has a number of interesting implications. For example, if there are two kinds of cognition, there must be two kinds of cognitive development. We shall explore this in the next chapter.

Tucker also considers that question of emotional valence, for example, whether positive versus negative emotions are differentially represented in the two hemispheres. Unlike some earlier theorists, he suggests that the left hemisphere is not "unemotional," but has emotional functions of its own. While the last word on this issue undoubtedly has yet to be written, Tucker suggests on the basis of his review and his own recent studies that the left hemisphere is associated with anxiety and that it exerts a kind of verbally mediated control over the emotionality of the right hemisphere. Thus, "the two hemispheres seem to exist in some sort of mutually balancing, dialectical relationship, each hemisphere's affective tendency opposing and complementing that of the other" (p. 21; cf. Shearer & Tucker, 1981; Tucker & Newman, 1981; Tucker, Stenslie, Roth, & Shearer, 1981). A recent study employing measures of regional blood flow is consistent with the notion of a special left-hemisphere involvement with anxiety, in that it found evidence of increased blood flow in the frontotemporal region of the left hemisphere during anxiety (Johanson, Risberg, Silfverskiold, Hagstadius, & Smith, 1982).

Tucker considers the frontal region of the brain to be the link between the cognitive operations of the hemispheres and the primary motivational/emotional systems in the subcortical/paleocortical regions. The right hemisphere may be more closely connected with the latter. There is evidence for example that NE and 5-HT fiber tracts thought to mediate mood levels are lateralized on the right side.

Tucker and Williamson

Tucker and Williamson (1984) have recently extended Tucker's (1981) views and combined them with the Pribram and McGuiness

(1975) model of arousal and activation. They agree with the basic distinction between neural systems involved in orienting to input (arousal) versus those involved with motor readiness (activation), and they agree that the hippocampus mediates between the arousal and activation systems. However, they argue that the "effortful" (voluntary) attention control that Pribram and McGuiness attribute to the hippocampal system can be more parsimoniously ascribed to higher order features of activation. They suggest that arousal and activation involve different information-handling features of noradrenergic and dopaminergic systems that are controlled by the right and left hemispheres, respectively. They suggest that the two forms of information processing associated with the two hemispheres are analogous to arousal and activation.

Tucker and Williamson (1984) argue that arousal functions to orient the brain to novel stimuli, so that the content of the information stored in short-term memory (STM) is determined by external sources. Attention is caught up by the perceptual qualities of the input, and this is directed in a reflex, automatic, and "nonvoluntary" fashion. In effect, attention is saturated by unique data, which is best handled by the global, holistic, syncretic mode of cognition associated with the right hemisphere. In contrast, activation restricts the flow of information from the outside, constricting the information in STM and focusing on that information that is essential for making a response. This restriction in the range of information allows for precise sequential control: Since there is a bias against any change of information in STM, any such change must be highly determined. The result is a tightly controlled mode of processing, with attention being directed in an orderly, deliberate, "voluntary" fashion. Tucker and Williamson suggest that this processing is handled by the sequential and analytic mode of cognition associated with the left hemisphere.

Tucker and Williamson also agree with Pribram and McGuiness that the arousal and activation systems are associated respectively with NE and DA, and they note that whereas the NE and 5-HT tracts are lateralized on the right side of the brain, the DA tracts are lateralized on the left. They relate this with drug effects and different kinds of psychopathology which may be associated with right- versus left-sided disturbances in the brain, and with personality differences which may be based upon individual differences in lateralized brain processes. These are considered further in Chapter 6.

Buck and Duffy

It is interesting to note that the results and interpretations of the Buck and Duffy (1980) study are quite consistent with Tucker's (1981) analysis. Based upon the high degree of facial expressiveness in the left-hemisphere-damaged patients, Buck and Duffy suggested that "the left cerebral hemisphere may normally exert an inhibitory influence over spontaneous nonverbal expression. Damage to the left hemisphere, in this view, would decrease this inhibition and allow for greater nonverbal expression. The low expressiveness of the right hemisphere-damaged patients suggests that this expression may be mediated in part by the right cerebral hemisphere" (p. 357).

A consideration of the pattern of sending accuracy across the four kinds of emotionally loaded slides used in this study support and extend this interpretation (see Figure 3.7). The communication accuracy of most of the subjects viewing the slides was significantly

Figure 3.7. Percent of slides correctly categorized across slide categories. From Figure 1 in "Nonverbal Communication of Affect in Brain-Damaged Patients" by R. Buck and R. Duffy, *Cortex*, 1980, *16*, 351–362. Copyright 1980 by Masson Italia Editori. Reprinted by permission.

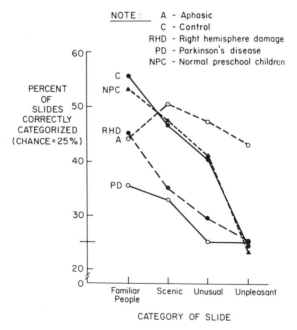

related to the type of slide involved. "Familiar people" slides, showing pictures of persons known to the subject, produced the highest communication accuracy scores in all of the patient groups except the left-hemisphere-damaged aphasic patients. The slides also produced this pattern of communication accuracy in preschool children. As shown in Figure 3.6, data taken from an earlier study (Buck, 1977) show that normal preschool children exhibit a pattern of accuracy across the slide categories that is remarkably similar to that exhibited by the elderly hospitalized men who constituted the control group in the Buck and Duffy study. This pattern may be associated with the action of display rules which, as we have seen, facilitate some kinds of emotional expressions and inhibit others. Thus our display of positive affect when we see friends may be facilitated and our display of negative affect may be inhibited. This pattern occurs in all of the groups except the left-hemisphere-damaged aphasic patients. They tend to be *less* expressive than controls on the familiar people slides and *more* expressive on the unpleasant slides. This suggests the possibility that the action of both inhibitory *and facilitatory* display rules may be disrupted with left-hemisphere damage, and that the level of expression is thus a true reflection of the actual motivational/ emotional state.

FACEDNESS AND EMOTIONAL VALENCE: AN INTERPRETATION

We saw above that there is some controversy about the relationship between hemispheric lateralization and positive versus negative emotional valence. We also saw that there is evidence that posed facial expressions are more "left faced" than spontaneous facial expressions, and that posed negative expressions may be more left faced than posed positive expressions. It may be that all of these observations can be organized into a coherent picture that is consistent with the analyses by Jurgens and Ploog, Tucker, and Buck and Duffy (Buck, 1982a). Let us first assume that facial expressions would only be "left faced" to the extent that they involve expression formation based upon the precentral gyrus. This is consistent with the lack of asymmetry in spontaneous expressions, which are based upon nonlateralized subcortical systems. Further, let us suggest that the expression is left faced, not because the expression is based upon the right hemisphere and thus appears relatively stronger on the left, but instead it is left faced because the expression tends to be *inhibited by the left hemisphere* and thus appears relatively *weaker on the right.* If this is the case, the evidence that negative expressions are more left faced would be readily explained by the fact that negative expressions are inhibited more than positive expressions (cf. Buck, 1975; Odom & Lemond, 1972).

In other words, this analysis would assume with Tucker (1981) and Buck and Duffy (1980) that the right hemisphere is associated with general affective processes (both positive and negative), and the left hemisphere with anxiety and the inhibition of these processes. Posing of affect expression would involve the precentral pyramidal mechanisms which are highly lateralized, so that those on the left (controlling the right face) most strongly reflect that inhibition, resulting in a "left-faced" expression. This phenomenon might be expected to be more apparent on expressions which have been subjected to the greatest inhibition, such as negative emotional expressions and also perhaps expressions to sexual or other taboo stimuli.

COGNITIVE MOTIVATION

In the terms of the readout view of motivation and emotion which we have been developing, the Tucker (1981) and Buck and Duffy (1980) analyses suggest that the Emotion III process—the readout of the motivational/emotional state into consciousness—may take place in both the right hemisphere and left hemisphere, with the right hemisphere particularly involving the experience of the primary motivational/emotional systems discussed above, and the left hemisphere particularly involving the experience of anxiety, which perhaps involves central inhibitory mechanisms. It may be suggested that the experience of other "higher order" motives/emotions may also be particularly associated with the left hemisphere. There are a variety of affect-like states which seem to be actively involved in the development and maintenance of the cognitive system. These "cognitive motives" include the intrinsic rewards provided by behaviors and experiences that enrich the cognitive system, termed "aliments" by Piaget (1971) and "effectance motivation" by White (1959). They also include the perhaps related and very little understood motivational forces behind the learning of language, and the motivational force behind the efforts to evaluate the accuracy and consistency of one's knowledge about the world and about oneself (cf. Buck, 1976a, Chapters 8 and 9). Although it was once thought that these motives must be derived from more "primitive" motivational/emotional systems, this does not seem to be the case: It appears that they are autonomous and have evolved as systems in their own right. From what we know about the nature of the functioning of the left hemisphere, it seems reasonable to suggest that the experience of these states may be particularly associated with left-hemisphere functioning.

A MODEL OF THE EMOTION III PROCESS

A provisional model of the Emotion III process, adapted largely from the Tucker (1981) and Buck and Duffy (1980) analyses, is presented in Figure 3.8. Affective information from the primary motivational/emotional systems in the subcortical/paleocortical regions is passed via the frontal lobes more directly to the right hemisphere (solid line) than the left hemisphere (dashed line).

The left hemisphere on the other hand may typically receive information from the classical sensory systems (including external

Figure 3.8. A model of the Emotion III process.

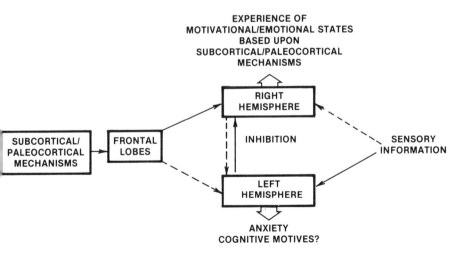

information from the environment and somatic information from the body) more directly than does the right hemisphere. It is noteworthy in this regard that Galaburda (1980) has suggested that there are two primordial origins in the evolution of the neocortex: a hippocampal origin associated with spontaneous innate activity which tends to be particularly responsive to internal stimuli, and an insular origin associated with olfaction which tends to be particularly responsive to external stimuli. In general, the right parietal neocortex originated from the former system, while the left parietal neocortex originated from the latter (cf. Galaburda & Geschwind, 1981). Whether these different origins relate to the present functioning of the two hemispheres is open to question, but the possibility is indeed intriguing.

The two hemispheres also interact, tending often (but not always) to inhibit the functioning of the other, with the left hemisphere usually (but not always) dominating the right hemisphere. The Emotion III process of the readout of emotional states into consciousness takes place in both cerebral hemispheres, with the experience of those states based upon primary motivational/emotional systems particularly involving the right hemisphere, and the experience of anxiety and also perhaps other "higher order" cognitive motives particularly involving the left hemisphere.

CONCLUSIONS

This chapter has reviewed the neurochemical mechanisms underlying emotion and emotional expression, including the mechanisms involved in homeostasis and adaptation (Emotion I), external expression (Emotion II), and subjective emotional experience (Emotion III). Models have been suggested summarizing the present knowledge relating to each of these mechanisms.

These models must of course be considered provisional, as these neurochemical systems are far from being understood. Nevertheless, our present knowledge of these systems, incomplete as it is, has important implications for the analysis of emotional expression and communication. Also, the analysis of emotional expression and communication may hopefully contribute to furthering our understanding of these neurochemical systems and their functioning.

PART THREE

INDIVIDUAL DIFFERENCES IN EMOTION COMMUNICATION

4

THE DEVELOPMENT OF EMOTION AND EMOTION COMMUNICATION

In the last section we presented a general view of motivation and emotion, considered how emotion communication evolves within the species, and outlined the nature of the neurochemical mechanisms underlying emotion and emotional expression. This section considers how emotion and emotion communication is unique to each individual. The present chapter suggests how emotion and emotion communication develops within the individual, taking into account the role of experiences unique to a given person. In doing so we shall see that the importance of these experiences is not confined to human beings, and that the provision of social experience is crucial to the emotion communication ability of many animal species as well. It also considers the relationship between emotion and cognitive processes, particularly cognitive processes involving language, and the implication of this relationship for the analysis of emotion in animal versus humans, and the role of language and cognitive development in the development of emotion and emotion communication.

This chapter first considers the role of the maturation of the neurochemical systems underlying emotion presented in Chapter 3. It then examines the relationship of social experiences to this maturational sequence, showing that normal emotional development involves a coordination between social experience and maturation. It then examines the particular problems posed by the social learning of emotional responses. These considerations result in an "animal model" of emotion and emotional development that encompasses processes shared by animals and humans. Finally, this chapter considers language and its special implications for the analysis of aspects of emotional development that are unique to humans.

MATURATION OF THE EMOTION SYSTEMS

One reason that some kinds of emotion-related behaviors are present at birth, while others appear later, involves the physical maturation of the neurochemical central nervous system mechanisms underlying emotional states. Studies of the social and emotional development of rhesus monkeys conducted by H. F. Harlow and his colleagues suggest that this maturational sequence is related to the social learning environment which the infant is likely to experience.

SOCIAL DEVELOPMENT IN RHESUS MONKEYS

Harlow and his colleagues initially studied the effects of "contact comfort," involving infant contact with soft, skin-like surfaces, in rhesus monkeys (cf. Harlow, 1971). They noted that isolated infant monkeys raised in bare wire cages often sickened and died, but that the survival rate increased significantly if a piece of cheesecloth were provided to the infant. The infants seemed to develop an intense attachment to the scrap of cloth: They protested loudly when it was removed for cleaning, hugging it closely upon its return. This observation suggested the possibility that contact with a soft surface is involved in the formation of infant attachment to the mother. This position was contrary to the contemporary explanations for attachment stemming from psychoanalytic and learning theory which held that attachment arises from the association of the mother with the satisfaction of the infant's hunger.

This led to Harlow's studies of cloth and wire "surrogate mothers," in which infants were raised with various combinations of cloth-covered versus wire surrogates which could be "lactating" (i.e., equipped with a nipple and bottle) or not (Harlow & Zimmerman, 1958). The studies demonstrated that contact with a soft skin-like surface was more important than feeding in the formation of attachment. For example, they showed that the infant spent much time clinging to the cloth surrogate whether or not it was associated with feeding, and that the mere presence of the cloth object served to calm the infant in the presence of novel and frightening stimuli. Thus an older infant placed alone in an unfamiliar playroom would huddle fearfully in a corner. If its cloth surrogate were present, however, it would rush through the feared room to the surrogate. It would cling to the surrogate for some time, but would begin to explore the room visually, and eventually the infant would make forays away from the surrogate, exploring the novel objects. These forays might be increasingly extended, eventually leading to adaptation to the playroom. These observations suggested that the cloth surrogate somehow imparted a feeling of trust which was necessary for the infant to overcome its fear and gain confidence necessary for exploring the environment. The wire mother could not instill such confidence even if it had been the source of milk to the infant.

The infants in these initial studies had been isolated from other monkeys to assure experimental control. The isolation *per se* was not the object of investigation. However, it became of central interest when the initial studies were over and the isolation ended. As the surrogate-reared animals came of age they were placed in a breeding program, the results of which were, in Harlow's words, "frighteningly unsuccessful." The isolated animals were incapable of normal sexual behaviors. Some animals, particularly those that had been reared only on wire surrogates, were wildly fearful and aggressive, and could not even be housed with other monkeys. Some of these were self-destructive, tearing at their own flesh, so that their canine teeth had to be pulled to prevent serious and even fatal injury (Figure 4.1). The cloth-surrogate-reared animals could generally be housed together, but breeding was unsuccessful. Some seemed to be willing enough, but the animals could not find the way: They exhibited immature sexual postures characteristic of younger animals and could not complete coitus. Some of the isolated females were successfully impregnated by normal males, but then were neglectful and often abusive when their first infants were born, which is most uncharacteristic of normal monkey maternal behavior (Figure 4.2). Interestingly, these females mothered their later-born offspring adequately. These effects of isolation were quite resistant to early attempts at "treatment" and in most cases were apparent throughout the animals' lives, although more recent investigations have had some success in pairing isolates with younger juveniles (Suomi & Harlow, 1972).

These studies showed that isolation from conspecifics during the first year of life has devastating and lasting effects upon social behavior in rhesus monkeys. It is noteworthy from our point of view

Figure 4.1. Self-destructive behavior in an isolated male rhesus monkey. Photograph courtesy H. F. Harlow, University of Wisconsin Primate Laboratory. From Figure 5.1 in *Psychology* by H. Harlow, J. McGaugh, and R. F. Thompson, San Francisco: Albion, 1971. Reprinted by permission.

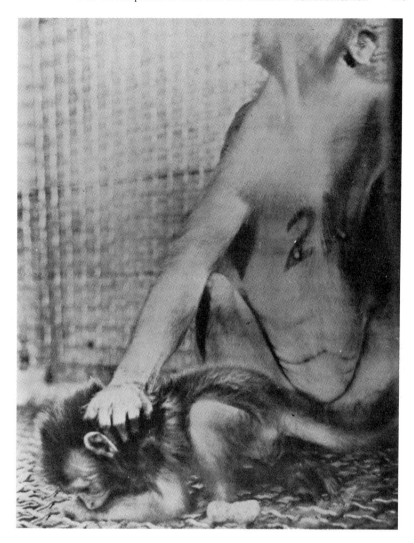

Figure 4.2. Punitive behavior toward an infant in an isolated female rhesus monkey. Photograph courtesy H. F. Harlow, University of Wisconsin Primate Laboratory. From Figure 5.3 in *Psychology* by H. Harlow, J. McGaugh, and R. F. Thompson, San Francisco: Albion, 1971. Reprinted by permission.

that, although the isolated animals were raised in an environment which provided little or no opportunity to learn fearful and aggressive behaviors from other monkeys, their levels of fearful and aggressive behaviors toward other monkeys were much greater than normal. Harlow had not expected this; indeed, at one point he suggested that the cloth surrogates were "good mothers" in that they never got angry or rejected the infant (Harlow, 1959). However, it turned out that the social isolation—even from the experience of rejection—constituted a deprivation experiment strongly suggesting that rhesus monkeys' fearful, aggressive, and affectionate reactions are based upon innate mechanisms which develop in a certain maturational sequence.

EMOTION COMMUNICATION IN RHESUS MONKEYS

A Model of Emotion Maturation

Harlow next turned to the study of the normal process of social development in rhesus monkeys, and particularly the development of affection, fear, and aggression. Observation of normal infants and their mothers suggested that, although affectionate behavior is normally present in the infant monkey virtually from birth, there is little evidence of aggression or fear. The young animal shows curiosity about everything and fear of nothing, so that the mothers' protective presence is essential for survival. After a few weeks, fearful responses to some stimuli begin to appear, and by 6 months they are well established. Harlow suggests that the neural mechanisms underlying fear gradually mature during this time, becoming fully mature by 6 months of age. However, aggression has not yet fully appeared. The 6-month-old monkey shows some isolated aspects of aggressive behavior during play, such as biting, grimacing, gesturing threat, and submission, but it is not until the end of the first year that play occasionally becomes seriously violent and abusive. At this point, the neural circuits underlying aggressive behavior are presumably mature. A dominance ordering gradually emerges from these bouts, and open fighting subsequently declines and is largely replaced by gestures of threat and submission (cf. Deets & Harlow, 1971).

Harlow's data suggest that the systems underlying affection, fear, and aggression develop in a fixed maturational sequence, but that the animal learns to deal with these emotions through social experiences that normally are coordinated with this maturational sequence. The neurochemical substrate underlying fearful and aggressive behaviors (i.e., the amygdala circuit in MacLean's model) fully matures only after the youngster normally has had much experience in social relationships with other monkeys. The infants are, however, capable of experiencing affection, and their initial social experiences allow them to become familiar with, learn to trust, and form strong affectional bonds with other monkeys in their group. Fear appears only after such affectionate social ties have had much time to become established so that the young animal does not fear other familiar monkeys. Aggressive feelings are even later to emerge, after much experience in interacting with other monkeys has been gained. However, if the infant is isolated from other monkeys while the neural substrates underlying fear and aggression mature, its relationships with other animals may be forever colored by these negative emotions.

Deprivation Studies

A series of deprivation studies was conducted to test this model (Deets & Harlow, 1971). One group was isolated for the first 3 months of life, a second group for the first 6 months, a third for the first 12 months, a fourth from 6 to 12 months, and a fifth control group was isolated from 18 to 26 months.

The results are summarized in Table 4.1. The first group made a good eventual adjustment after some initial "autistic-like" behavior—lying while clutching the head and body with the arms and legs. The second group was isolated from birth to the time the maturation of fear should have been completed. It was expected that the infants' adjustment with other monkeys would be affected by strong fear responses. As anticipated, the isolates in this condition rarely approached other monkeys, and autistic behavior and other fearful responses were common. Play was virtually nonexistent, and the threats and occasional attacks that are normally seen in 6-month-old monkeys were absent. This kind of reaction was seen even more strongly in the third group of isolates, who showed the "social devastation" seen in the wire-reared isolates in the original studies. The animals engaged in almost continuous self-clutching and other bizarre behaviors and showed almost no social interaction. In later years, they showed heightened aggression that was often directed at inappropriate targets —they attacked younger juveniles brutally and made suicidal attacks on large, fully grown adult males. Sexual behavior also was inap-

Table 4.1. Summary of Experiments Illustrating the Effects of Social Deprivation on Fearful and Aggressive Behaviors

Period of isolation	Social behavior at end of isolation period	Later social behavior
0–3 months	Initial autistic behavior, gradually make good adjustment	Essentially normal
0–6 months	Low affiliation, high fear, low aggression	High fear, high aggression directed at inappropriate targets (young and adult monkeys)
0–12 months	Very high fear, autistic behavior, almost no social behavior	Very high fear, low levels of aggression developing to high levels
6–12 months	Normal levels of fear, high aggression	Some affiliative behavior, normal fear, high aggression
18–26 months	Initial high levels of social behavior, gradually make normal adjustment	Essentially normal

Note. Adapted with permission from Deets and Harlow (1971). From Table 7.1 in *Human Motivation and Emotion* by R. Buck, New York: Wiley, 1976. Copyright 1976 by John Wiley & Sons. Reprinted by permission.

propriate in adult years, largely because the isolates tended to attack or flee from potential mates.

The fourth group was run to determine whether animals isolated after fear had matured, but before aggression had matured, would show disturbances of aggression but not fear. As predicted, these animals were not unduly fearful but they did show high aggression which continued into adolescence. The fifth group demonstrated that if isolation is delayed until the emotion systems are mature and emotional behavior is well established, the isolation does not have pronounced permanent effects. The study revealed that the late isolates showed after isolation transitory increase in all social behavior—sex, play, threat, submission, and so forth—but that within a week social behavior had returned to normal.

EMOTIONAL MATURATION IN HUMANS

As Deets and Harlow (1971) point out, human infants show a similar absence of fearful and aggressive responses during the early months of life, while active affectionate behavior—smiling, clinging, laughing, responding to others—is shown with both familiar and unfamiliar adults. Also, the very young infant does not show prolonged protest at separation. By 6 months, a "fear of strangers" and distress at separation often appears. Deets and Harlow conclude that "social affiliation and attachments are established in the human infant before fear of unfamiliar stimuli becomes manifest" (p. 22). Although less is known about the aggressive behavior of infants and toddlers, the "terrible twos" are well known to parents for revealing the impressive aggressive capacities of their offspring.

Beginning with Bridges's classic (1932) study, a number of investigations have attempted to trace the course of the appearance of emotion in human infants. These have been hampered by problems of eliciting emotion and of precisely specifying the nature of the infant's emotional responses. The possibilities of experimentally inducing emotion in children are clearly restricted by ethical constraints, and even with controlled emotional stimuli it is difficult to assess the emotional state of the infant and very young child because subjective reports and judgments of the intentionality of their behavior are suspect.

It is possible, however, to develop precise criteria of emotion responding in very young children based on their nonverbal displays, and particularly upon facial expressions; this fact has opened new possibilities for the study of emotion maturation and development in humans (cf. Parisi, 1977; Hiatt, Campos, & Emde, 1979; Izard, Huebner, Risser, McGinnes, & Dougherty, 1980). For example, Parisi (1977) has studied infant facial expressions to a variety of affective stimuli, such as a jack-in-the-box, a halloween mask, a stranger's approach, and Field and her colleagues have recently completed a number of studies of infant emotional responding, which we shall examine in more detail in the next chapter (Field, 1982; Field & Walden, 1982). Similarly, Izard (1979a) conducted a naturalistic and longitudinal study of the facial expressions of infants and young children to a necessary series of immunization injections. These injections begin at 2 months of age and continue until 2 years of age, so that changes in expression as the child grows can be assessed.

In Izard's (1979a) study, the child is videotaped as an unfamiliar nurse takes the child, and then returns the child to its mother. A painful injection is then performed on the child, the child is briefly comforted, and the nurse takes the child again. The initial results suggest that the painful stimulus does not evoke facial expressions of fear or anger in infants younger than 6 months, although components of those expressions may appear. Izard reports that the typical facial response to pain in younger infants is similar to the adult anger expression, with the mouth open and squared and the eyebrows down and together at the midline. Unlike the adult anger expression, however, the eyes are squeezed tightly shut (see Figure 4.3a). This is associated with a scream which may function in alerting the caregiver. This expression is often followed by a classic "sad" expression (see Figure 4.3b). The latter is regarded by adults as cute and lovable, and Izard suggests that this may function to reinforce the bond between the caregiver (summoned by the scream) and the injured infant. It is only later that complete expressions of fear and anger appear (see Figures 4.3c and 4.3d). Thus, these initial data seem consistent with Harlow's model regarding the course of the maturation of emotional systems.

SUMMARY

The physical maturation of the neurochemical systems underlying motivation and emotion is an important consideration in the analysis of the development of emotion and emotion communication. Harlow's studies suggest that rhesus monkeys deprived of early social experience suffer lasting damage to their social behavior. One reason for this may be that the maturation of the systems underlying fear and aggression is delayed, creating a "critical period" in the early months in which social attachment can easily occur. The pattern of social experience in rhesus monkeys is normally coordinated with this maturational sequence, so that much social experience occurs during this period. There is evidence suggesting that analogous phenomena occur in humans.

SOCIAL EXPERIENCE AND EMOTION COMMUNICATION

THE AFFECTIONAL SYSTEMS

From the observation of the interactions of young rhesus monkeys with their mothers, siblings, and peers, Harlow and his colleagues have attempted to characterize in general terms the kinds of social

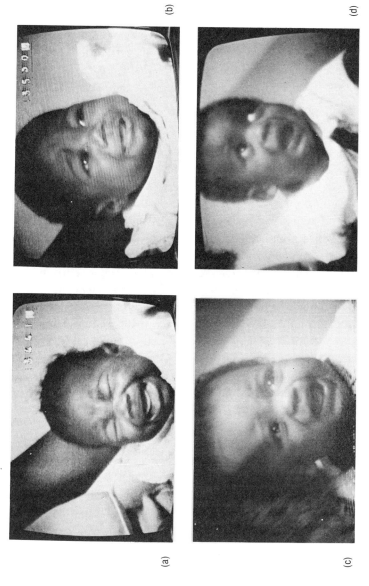

Figure 4.3. (a) Physical distress expression in a 2-month, 2-day-old girl immediately after inoculation. (b) Sad expression about 11 seconds after inoculation. (c) Anger expression directed toward nurse in an 8-month, 28-day-old boy after inoculation. (d) Fear expression as nurse approaches after inoculation. Photographs courtesy C. Izard, University of Delaware.

experiences that tend normally to occur as the monkey grows. From this, they speculated about the possible role that experience in these social relationships plays in social and emotional development, culminating in the pattern of adult relationships that Harlow terms the "heterosexual affectional system" (see Table 4.2). The general outlines that emerged from this analysis have been consistent with the findings of observational studies carried out with other species of monkeys and apes, such as Jane Goodall's (1971, 1979) as well as recent analyses of early human development (Sroufe, 1979).

The Maternal Affectional System

The maternal affectional system occurs during the first year in the life of the infant rhesus monkey. Harlow (1971) suggests that, at birth, the infant monkey has the capacity to experience (and signal to others) affectionate emotions, and perhaps also curiosity and pain, but that fearful and aggressive behaviors are absent. The infant monkey comes into a world populated by other monkeys who literally cannot elicit fearful and angry emotions. Instead, they can elicit only affection, and thus the helpless infant comes to know, trust, and love his or her irascible conspecifics. We have seen that there is evidence that the maturation of the neurochemical systems underlying fear and aggression does not normally take place until affectional social ties have had much time to become established; the system has thus evolved so that the maturation of motivational/emotional systems is synchronized with the normal social experiences of the infant. The maternal affectional system provides a basic sense of trust in other monkeys that is essential to later social and emotional development.

Table 4.2. Summary of the Affectional Systems

Affectional system	Necessary conditions	Functions
Maternal affectional system	Contact comfort	Establishes basic sense of trust
Peer affectional system	Basic sense of trust; relative independence from mother	Social experience, with associated learning of emotion communication[a]
Heterosexual affectional system	Social experience; accurate emotion communication	Basis of social life and group organization

Note. Adapted with permission from *Learning to Love* by H. Harlow, San Francisco: Albion, 1971.

[a]Accurate emotion communication involves the abilities to send and receive gestures of courting, threat, submission, and so forth, associated with sex, anger, or fear.

The maternal affectional system begins with a period in which the infant experiences "unconditional positive regard." This is the "stage of contact," involving relatively unrestricted contact with the mother, which lasts for the first few months while the infant is most vulnerable. However, there is evidence that excessive maternal attention may be socially damaging if it restricts contact with age mates. Maternal attention decreases during the "stage of rejection," in which the mother begins to increasingly punish unrestricted contact. Such punishment grows in frequency and intensity as the infant grows. This is consistent with the infant's high level of curiosity and improving locomotor skills, and it encourages the infant to become more independent, resulting at about 5–6 months of age in the "state of relative separation" from the mother. Since similar-age peers are normally present in the environment, this separation from the mother tends to naturally encourage increased interaction with peers, leading to the peer affectional system.

The infant's separation from the mother is often exacerbated by the birth of a new sibling, which takes up much of the mother's time and which may be quite traumatic to the older infant. However, this "cutting of the apron strings" may be essential for normal social development. Harlow (1971) has found evidence that contact with peers may be more important than contact with the mother in the development of normal social behavior, and Goodall (1979) has described the development of Flint, a young wild chimpanzee who remained dependent upon his elderly mother and died at a young age shortly following her death.

The Peer Affectional System

The maternal experience lays an emotional groundwork in that it establishes a basic sense of trust in other monkeys that persists in the face of the fearful and aggressive emotions that mature during the second half of the first year of life. The peer affectional system begins with the relative separation of mother and infant. It is characterized by much "rough and tumble" play, during which elements of adult social behavior can often be discerned. For example, there is much immature sexual gesturing and playing at aggression with immature threat and submissive gestures. These are the kinds of experiences that are sorely missed by the infants raised in isolation. Harlow (1971) suggests that during the frequent sessions of play, the young monkey acquires the social skills necessary for adult functioning. One of these skills involves the practical use of the rhesus' system of emotion communication. Experience with emotion communication is naturally provided to the young monkey during the affectional systems, and the peer affectional system is particularly important in this regard. The youngster "learns how to use" the communication system during these bouts, which naturally leads to the development of monkey social behavior which is considered "normal."

The Heterosexual Affectional System

The heterosexual affectional system encompasses normal adult social behavior, including a dominance order which is maintained largely by signals of threat and submission rather than fights, a process of courting and sexual behavior, proper maternal behavior, and a variety of behaviors signaling greeting, grooming, warning, and so forth. Together, these behaviors transform these irascible creatures into social animals. It is apparent that animals isolated in infancy cannot function effectively in this system, both because the presence of other monkeys may be emotionally overwhelming due to a failure to experience others under the proper emotional conditions, and because the normal rhesus emotion communication system cannot be used effectively due to a lack of social experience.

SOCIAL EXPERIENCE AND EMOTION COMMUNICATION IN MONKEYS

One of the major lessons that must be learned by the infant in the affectional systems is how to use the system of emotion communication that has evolved in the species. We saw in Chapter 2 that systems of spontaneous emotion communication, involving both sending and receiving mechanisms, have evolved in social species. However, the behavior of the isolated animals suggests that, at least in rhesus monkeys, these are rather elementary forms of communication which require learning to function effectively (Mason, 1961). This kind of learning is normally provided to the developing monkey during the course of the affectional systems, but the isolated animals have no opportunity to acquire these social skills.

This was illustrated in a series of studies by Robert E. Miller and his colleagues, who developed the "cooperative conditioning" technique to measure emotion communication in rhesus monkeys. They taught two monkeys to press a bar within a few seconds after a light came on in order to avoid a painful electric shock. After both animals had thoroughly learned this avoidance task, they were paired in different rooms so that one, the "sender," could see the light but had no access to the bar, while the other "receiver" could use the bar but could not see the light. The receiver could see the televised image of the head and a facial region of the sender. It was reasoned that if the sender made a facial reaction when the light came on, and if the observer could perceive and accurately interpret this reaction, the observer could press the bar which would avoid the shock for both of them. Miller found in several studies that normal rhesus monkeys could solve this task with little difficulty (Miller, Banks, & Kuwahara, 1966; Miller, Banks, & Ogawa, 1962, 1963; Miller, Murphy, & Mirsky, 1959).

To determine how isolated monkeys would do at this task, Miller, Caul, and Mirsky (1967) put three 12-month isolates from Harlow's laboratory in the communication task in all possible combinations with three normal monkeys. In the initial training phase, the isolate monkeys learned the avoidance task as quickly as did the normals, so their ability to learn did not seem to be impaired. However, when paired with other monkeys, the isolates were deficient both as senders and as receivers. As receivers they were completely incapable of using the facial expressions of other monkeys to perform the appropriate response. When isolate senders were paired with normal receivers, the normals showed a number of avoidance responses at the appropriate time when the light was on. However, the normals also made many responses at inappropriate times: They pressed the bar between trials when the light stimulus was not on, perhaps because the isolate senders made many fearful facial expressions throughout the testing session whether the light was on or not. The number of such intertrial responses was weighed in computing whether significant communication occurred for each session, and the resulting data showed a large number of significant sessions only when normal senders were paired with normal receivers. Miller *et al.* concluded that their study supports the hypothesis that the lack of opportunity to acquire communication skills is a major factor in the social deficit of isolate monkeys. "It was strikingly apparent from this experiment that the monkeys deprived of social relationships during the first year of life do not utilize social information as do normals even after 3–4 years of social opportunities following the isolation period" (Miller *et al.*, 1967, p. 239).

The studies we have considered illustrate nicely the interaction between innate factors and learning: Both the maturation of innate neurochemical mechanisms and social experience are apparently required for the normal development of emotional expression and communication in rhesus monkeys. There is evidence in humans also of the importance of this interaction.

SOCIAL EXPERIENCE AND EMOTION COMMUNICATION IN HUMANS

The relationships with the developing child and its caregivers and peers provide social experiences which apparently serve functions similar to those served by analogous relationships in monkeys and apes: creating an emotional basis for later social behavior and enabling the use of the human version of the emotion communication system (see Sroufe, 1979). In addition, experiences during this time undoubtedly lay the groundwork for the learning of language.

Infant–Caregiver Interaction

It is clear that the early interaction between human infants and their caregivers helps to form the emotional and communicative basis for later social behavior. Much of the traditional work in infant development has been one sided, in that it has been concerned with identifying how the caregiver influences the infant. Thus the traditional approach of social learning theory regards the caregiver as the model who is imitated by the infant or child. More recently, studies have been directed at the influence of the infant on the caregiver (e.g., Lewis & Rosenblum, 1974). Thoman (1975) has noted that the caregiver's behavior is in large part a function of the infant's characteristics, both the nature of the infant's precipitating behavior and the infant's response to the caregiver's response. She has argued that "communication of the newborn with the (caregiver) is biologically determined, is based on the interactive capabilities of the infant organism that have derived from the evolutionary process, and is a critical form of early adaptation that assures the infant's survival" (Thoman, 1981, pp. 3–4).

In her observation of the response to blind infants, Fraiberg (1974) has contributed a compelling example of the reciprocal effects of infant and caregiver, and how these can go awry to the detriment of the infant's development. Fraiberg noted in the course of her studies that she did not *talk* to blind infants as she did to sighted infants, and suggests that this occurred because talking does not evoke the responses (eye responses, smiles, etc.) in blind infants that it evokes in sighted children. She suggests that there is a "sense of something vital missing in the social exchange" with blind infants. Fraiberg notes that this is often reflected in observers' faces as they watch films of children: "With sighted children it is always interesting to see the resonance of response on the viewer's face. We smile when the baby on the film smiles; we are sober when he is distressed. . . . But the blind baby on the screen does not elicit these spontaneous moods. . . . There is a large vocabulary of expressive behavior that one does not see in a blind baby at all. The absence of differentiated facial signs on the baby's face is mirrored on the face of the observer" (Fraiberg, 1974, p. 217).

Other studies have suggested that certain characteristics of premature infants, and particularly an aversive quality to their cry, may trigger aggressive abuse in the caregiver (Frodi, 1981; Frodi & Lamb, 1978; Zeskind & Lester, 1978). Such abuse appears to involve impulsive aggression which is "pulled out" from the responder by the characteristics of the stimulation (cf. Berkowitz, 1964). It is perhaps particularly striking and troubling, as are Fraiberg's observations, because it illustrates the powerful effects of a disruption of the infant–caregiver relationship which is not expected from our more usual—cognitive—view of human relationships. It illustrates that people can and do, in fact, act like animals, with minimal cognitive controls.

Emotion Communication and Language Learning

It may be significant that Fraiberg notes that the blind infant's lack of expression leads to less of a tendency to talk to the infant. There is increasing evidence that the emotion communication process is involved in important ways in language learning and processing (cf. Key, 1980). Thus Bruner (1979) has noted that an interactional process is basic to language development, and Key has stated that "the development of nonverbal behavior . . . is crucial in the acquisition of language; there is evidence that disruptions of nonverbal behaviors may result in disruptions of acquisition of language" (quoted in Friedman, 1980, p. 79).

One of the areas of great interest in this regard is the study of rhythmic patterns in the interaction of infant and caregiver. Friedman (1980) has studied "protorhythms," which she defines as primary rhythms of physiological origin, which are manifested in infant vocalizations from the earliest cries. She considers them to be "formal constitutive elements for the development of any language" (p. 89).

Condon and his colleagues have emphasized the phenomenon of interactional synchrony, in which speaker and listener "move in precise synchrony with the articulatory structure of the speaker's speech" (Condon, 1979, p. 161). Condon suggests that these body movements are peripheral reflections of the central neurological processing of speech: When the listener is *really* listening, his or her body movements are in rhythm with the speaker's articulation; when the listener's "mind wanders," it is reflected in a decrease in synchrony. The result is in effect an external "readout" of the listener's state of involvement in the speaker's articulation, which may play an important role in the establishment and maintenance of the interactional relationship.

Condon (1979, 1980) argues that interactional synchrony plays an important role in language acquisition, and reports that marked synchronization of body movement with speech in different languages (Chinese and American English) has been observed in a study of the movements of one to 4-day-old infants in response to both live and tape recorded human voices (Condon, 1973; Condon & Sander, 1974). He also reports that the analysis of films of dysfunctional children (autistic, aphasic, dyslexic, etc.) reveal distorted forms of synchrony. Kendon (1980) has emphasized the rhythmic basis of interactional synchrony, suggesting that it reveals "a view of human communicative activity as a shared rhythmic process, with listeners participating simultaneously with the speaker" (p. 74).

Interactional synchrony, and particularly the early synchrony of infants with speech in different languages, must reflect an innate, spontaneous communication process which may well play an essential role in language acquisition. The details of how this occurs are just beginning to be discovered, but the implications are of fundamental importance to the study of language development, suggesting that the understanding of the roots of language development requires the understanding of spontaneous communication. We shall discuss the phenomenon of interactional synchrony further in Chapter 8.

Temperament and Social Experience

The phenomenon of the infant's influence upon the caregiver increases the potential importance of the role of temperament in the process of social and emotional development, since it emphasizes the importance of the infant's characteristics. Temperament refers to general emotional–behavioral dispositions based in part upon individual differences in neurochemical mechanisms underlying emotion (Buck, 1976a, p. 242). Thomas, Chess, and Burch (1970) have demonstrated in a longitudinal study that many (although not all) children show a basic constancy of behavioral disposition from birth to the teenage years. The effects of the environment in general, and of the behavior of caregivers and other socialization agents in particular, depend in part upon the temperament of the individual child. As we shall see in the next chapters, individual differences in temperament may be reflected in individual differences in emotional expressiveness that have important implications for social and emotional behavior.

SUMMARY

Harlow has described the general social experiences that normally tend to occur as the infant rhesus monkey grows as a series of "affectional systems," beginning with the maternal, continuing with the peer, and culminating in the heterosexual affectional system. There is evidence that learning experiences occur during each period that help to "set the stage" for the next, and that during these periods the animal learns how to efficiently and appropriately use the emotion communication system that has evolved within the species. This implies that some degree of what we have termed "symbolic" communication is necessary for normal monkey social behavior. Together with the above discussion on the maturation of the emotion systems, this illustrates how innately determined emotions and expressive tendencies are coordinated with patterns of social experience, so that these emotions may be handled in social animals. Again, there are suggestions that analogous processes occur in humans, and that disruptions in these processes can have serious consequences for social and emotional development and language learning.

SOCIAL LEARNING AND
EMOTION COMMUNICATION

One way in which the youngster learns about emotion and emotion expression is via social learning processes, involving imitation and social reinforcement (Bandura, 1977; Bandura & Walters, 1963). However, the social learning of emotion is complicated by the fact that there are multiple aspects of emotion, some public and other private. We saw above that the candidacy of a motivational/ emotional response for the evolutionary process of ritualization was partly a function of the degree to which it is perceivable, or available via sensory cues, which we shall refer to as the *accessibility* of the response. Just as the accessibility of a response is important in the process of ritualization, it must also be important in the process of social learning. Here it is not only the accessibility of the response to others that is important, but also the accessibility of a response to the responder (cf. Buck, 1981a).

THE ACCESSIBILITY DIMENSION

Accessibility shall be defined as the degree to which a response is normally apparent to the responder and to others around the responder via sensory cues. A response may be apparent to others via visual, tactual, auditory, or olfactory cues; and it may be apparent to the responder from these cues and via proprioceptive, cutaneous, or interoceptive cues as well. In human social learning the visual channel is undoubtedly highly important relative to other channels, although other channels should not be ignored.

Social learning theory implies that responses with different degrees of accessibility *must* be associated with different patterns of social learning. Highly accessible responses, which are easily available to the responder and to others, can undergo thorough training via imitation and social reinforcement. Responses that are not accessible to the responder or to others must not be susceptible to this kind of direct social learning; social influences must affect them indirectly, outside the awareness of everyone involved. Responses that are accessible to the responder but not others, and responses accessible to others but not the responder, must be subject to still different kinds of social learning and influence. Let us consider the types of response to emotion outlined in Chapter 2 from this point of view.

Instrumental Behavior

Goal-directed instrumental behavior can be seen both by the responder in other persons and by others in the responder, so that it may undergo thorough training through imitation and social reinforcement. For example, others can "shape" the overt behaviors of the child through social reinforcement, and the child can see and learn directly from the overt emotional behaviors of his or her parents and other models. Goal-directed instrumental behavior is generally thought to be voluntary or intentional, because it involves a contingency between the responder's behavior and reinforcement—the reinforcement (reward or escape/avoidance of punishment) occurs only if a correct instrumental response occurs (Miller, 1969). Therefore it presumably must be accessible to the responder in his or her own behavior.

Goal-directed instrumental behavior is thus normally the most accessible type of emotional response. The child is at least potentially conscious of his or her own instrumental emotional behavior, and can learn to make many discriminations both from personal and from vicarious experience about how one is supposed to respond in different sorts of emotional situations. In our culture a young boy will find that male models often respond to anger-inducing situations with overt aggression, and they will probably be less likely to experience punishment when expressing overt aggression than will a young girl. The boy will be likely to learn to "take his own part," while the girl might well learn that "young ladies don't fight."

Subjective Experience

This kind of fine discrimination learning cannot apply to the subjective feelings associated with emotion. Several theorists, including Skinner (1953) and Schachter (1964), have discussed the process by which such learning is achieved, pointing out that the child has no direct access to the subjective emotion experiences of others, and they have no direct access to those of the child. Learning about subjective events must take place indirectly, via the reports and descriptions of subjective experience that the child gains from others, and the reports that he or she gives to others.

It may be that through the process of associating one's private experiences with interpretations provided by the community, the child develops a set of "labels" by which to identify and categorize his or her subjective experience. A child might learn to "correctly" identify and label the subjective experience associated with activation of nuerochemical systems of anger by repeated direct and vicarious experience with situations which arouse such feelings and label them appropriately. When a child is overtly expressing felt anger, a parent might say, "I see that you are angry," or the child may see others overtly angry and/or in a situation that would commonly evoke anger and hear them describe their feelings as "anger." It should be noted that this process depends upon overt emotion responding: If there is no overt response, such learning cannot occur. Also, the labeling process may be erroneous. Conceivably a child might learn to mislabel the subjective experience associated with anger as "fear" or "guilt."

Expressive Behavior

It will be recalled that in the model of emotion presented in Chapter 2, emotional expression is a joint function of spontaneous expressive tendencies which are innate, and symbolic display rules which are learned. To the extent that expressive behavior is intentional, it should be similar to instrumental behavior—accessible to both the responder and to others. To the extent that it is spontaneous, it is still accessible to others, but the responder should be relatively unaware of it.

The notion that people are unaware of their spontaneous expression is supported by the observation that people are generally unaware of how they appear to others, and are often surprised when viewing themselves on film, or hearing themselves on audio tape, and frequently they report learning more about themselves when they view their own behavior from the perspective of others (Storms, 1973). A number of studies have suggested that people are more aware of some of their own expressive behaviors than they are of others. Ekman and Friesen (1969b) suggest that people are most aware of the actions of the face, less aware of the hands, and least aware of the legs and feet, and they present evidence that "nonverbal leakage" occurs with the latter behaviors. The behaviors that are more "leaky" are in our terms more spontaneously expressive of the actual emotion state and less accessed by the responder. We shall return to this point in Chapter 6.

Although the responder is relatively unaware of his or her spontaneous expressive behavior, it is accessible to others and thus is subject to shaping via social reinforcement. Similarly, the expressive behavior of others is accessible to the child and is thus available for modeling and imitation. Thus a young boy in our culture is likely to find relatively few male models for the open expression of many emotions, and is likely to experience punishment when openly expressing them; as girls learn that they must not hit, boys learn that they must not cry.

Relationships between Measures

Social pressures that encourage or discourage the kinds of emotion responses we have considered thus far would tend to have similar effects on the others. If instrumental behavior is discouraged in a given kind of emotion situation, it is likely that spontaneous expressive behavior will be inhibited in that situation as well, and it is less likely that the subjective experience will be correctly labeled or openly admitted in self-reports if it is labeled. For example, if women are discouraged from expressing aggressive behavior, it is likely that they will also be discouraged from looking angry and admitting angry feelings. For this reason, it is likely that measures of spontaneous expressive behavior, instrumental behavior, and self-reports will be positively correlated with one another.

Psychophysiological Responding

Psychophysiological responses must be associated with a quite different kind of social learning process. Most autonomic, endocrine, and muscle tension responses normally take place outside conscious awareness, so that a child would not ordinarily learn to identify or label them. For example, since there are relatively few interoceptive afferent neurons carrying feedback from the viscera, it is difficult if not impossible to determine the position of food in one's digestive tract, while in contrast knowing the position of one's arm with the eyes closed from proprioceptive/cutaneous feedback is relatively easy (cf. Markov, 1950). Also, most psychophysiological events are inaccessible to others, although a careful observer might detect changes in coloration, sweating, and so forth, that are associated with such events.

Since normally physiological events are relatively inaccessible, they are not greatly affected by the social pressures that influence other emotion responses. However, they can be modified by learning experiences, as demonstrated by Russian studies of interoceptive conditioning and studies of biofeedback (cf. Orne, 1979; Razran, 1961). Indeed, Razran (1961) has suggested that interoceptive conditioning involving psychophysiological responses is "an almost built-in function that is constantly regenerated in the very process of living and action" (p. 97), and that a unique and largely unconscious system of conditioned physiological reactions must be built up within the life of each organism. These findings suggest that a given person's psychophysiological response in a given situation must be determined in great part by his or her conditioning history in similar kinds of situations (cf. Buck, 1976a, pp. 112–124).

For example, one might expect that the more stimuli that have been conditioned to cause autonomic arousal in the past, the higher that arousal will be. If a child has intensely arousing experiences in situations involving anger, it is likely that he or she will show strong arousal in situations involving anger as an adult. This explanation has been used to account for the finding that the spontaneous emotion expression is often negatively correlated with autonomic responses in between-subjects analyses: Situations which result in the inhibition of overt responding may tend to be stressful and associated with arousal; thus persons who have experienced much inhibition will tend to be high in autonomic arousal but low on other measures of emotion (cf. Buck, 1979a, 1980, Buck *et al.*, 1974).

Summary

Emotional responses which differ in accessibility tend to be associated with different kinds of social learning, and different kinds of emotional responses are related to different features of an emotion-arousing situation. This analysis may be clarified with reference to Figure 2.3. Goal-directed instrumental responses should be closely related to the responder's expectations about what behavior is appropriate and expected by the community, since they are highly salient to the responder and have been subjected to much discrimination learning via imitation and social reinforcement. This should also be true of expressive behavior to the extent that it is intentional, but to the extent that it is spontaneous, expressive behavior should be less alien to the responder and more closely related to the actual emotional state. Subjective experience should be related to the actual emotional state, but reports of that experience should reflect the labels and interpretations that the responder has associated with that state, and also expectations about what experiences are appropriate and socially acceptable. The responder's physiological responding should reflect among other things the intensity of the prior conditioning of arousal in similar situations for that particular person.

ACCESSIBILITY AND THE EDUCATION OF ATTENTION

We have argued thus far that the accessibility of a response is largely a function of the nature of the response, and indeed it seems clear that some responses are more accessible than others. However, it should be noted that response accessibility is not an invariant property of these response systems. It is clearly possible for an individual to learn to attend to responses which to others remain "inaccessible," a process which is analogous to the concept of an "education of attention" presented in Chapter 2.

For example, it may be that certain Eastern traditions encourage a greater attention to internal cues than do most Western cultures. In 1933, Wenger noted that the muscle relaxation ability of a student from India trained in Yogic exercises was far superior to the performance of American students. In subsequent studies in India, Wenger and his colleagues found that students of Yoga could demonstrate impressive control of autonomic functions, including changes in heart action, blood pressure, and skin temperature (Wenger & Bagchi, 1961; Wenger, Bagchi, & Anand, 1961). Possibly such control involves learning to attend to bodily cues that are ignored by most Westerners. We noted above that one of the goals of biofeedback training is to teach control of normally automatic bodily functions by making them artificially "accessible" via the feedback (cf. Katkin *et al.*, 1981; Miller, 1978).

Regarding expressive behavior, we have noted that expressive behavior is composed of both spontaneous and symbolic aspects. It is clear that individuals learn a variety of "expression management techniques" to intensify or mask their spontaneous emotion displays (Ekman & Friesen, 1975). We shall see in Chapter 6 that this process may involve the education of attention to particular kinds of expressions. In our culture, we have noted that people learn to be more aware of the face than the body (Ekman & Friesen, 1969b). Conceivably, in another culture this learning might be different, and the face may be relatively more spontaneously expressive and the body relatively more controlled.

This reasoning should apply to the decoding of expressive behavior as well as to sending accuracy. There undoubtedly are both individual and situational differences in the tendency to attend to emotional expression in others. Some persons may learn to attend to expressive nonverbal cues more than others, and for that reason may be more "empathic" with the feelings of others. As we shall see in Chapter 7, many tests of nonverbal decoding ability instruct the subject to attend to nonverbal cues, thus missing possible individual differences in the spontaneous tendency to attend to such cues. Also, persons may learn to attend to expressive cues in some situations more than others. It is probable that a therapist learns to use quite different patterns of attention to expressive cues when with a friend than when with a patient (Buck & Lerman, 1979). In fact, if a therapist "reads" friends like patients, he or she may well end up with few friends. Finally, persons may learn to attend to some expressive cues and ignore others. In this regard, DePaulo and Rosenthal (1979b) have suggested that although females are superior to males in decoding most expressive cues, they may not learn (or *learn not*) to attend to "leakier" cues that reveal emotional states that others would rather hide (cf. Rosenthal & DePaulo, 1979a, 1979b). We shall explore this issue in more detail in Chapter 7.

THE ANIMAL MODEL OF EMOTION AND EMOTIONAL DEVELOPMENT

THE ANIMAL MODEL

This chapter has considered a number of animal studies that have clear relevance to the study of human emotion and emotional development. Indeed, some of the most important work in the study of the development of emotion and emotional expression has been done with animals, and there has emerged what might be termed an "animal model" of emotion and emotional development.

The animal model involves those aspects of emotion and emotional development that are common to animals and humans. It includes the essential insight that neurochemical systems of emotion that are relevant to social relations have evolved hand in hand with spontaneous communication mechanisms (Emotion II) and patterns of social experience. Indeed, as we have seen, the physical maturation of the neurochemical systems appears to be articulated with social experience, allowing the communication mechanisms to function.

Spontaneous communication, as we have defined it, is clearly included in the animal model of emotion, but this model also allows us to see the importance of the role of social learning, intention, and symbolic communication. It is noteworthy in this context that, whereas a monkey stimulated in an aggression-eliciting area of the brain in the presence of submissive animals generally attacks them, if the same animal is stimulated in the same area in the presence of animals dominant to itself, it may become the recipient rather than the originator of aggressive abuse (Delgado, 1969). Apparently the stimulation causes an increase in aggressive tendencies in both cases, but the animal retains enough "intentional" control to refrain from suicidal attacks on stronger animals. However, the stimulation apparently causes the unfortunate animals to "unintentionally" give threatening signals, or to fail to give submissive signals, and it leads to punishment regardless.

HUMANS VERSUS ANIMALS

Although it is clear that the animal model is useful in understanding some aspects of human motivational/emotional development and expression, it is also clear that some aspects of human behavior, including emotional behavior, are qualitatively or quantitatively different from animal behavior. It is interesting to note that, from the time of the Greeks, Western thought has distinguished between "rational" processes unique to humans and the processes governing animal behavior (cf. Cofer & Appley, 1964). Both Plato and Aristotle denied "rational souls" to animals, but they granted them lesser souls capable of caring for basic bodily functions. Following them, St. Thomas Aquinas equipped animals with a "sensitive soul" and humans, in addition, with a rational soul. Decartes's dualism was similarly grounded in the distinction between animal behavior, which could be accounted for by mechanical forces, and human behavior which was partly mechanical but partly influenced (via the pineal gland) by a nonmechanical soul. Gilbert Ryle (1949) has termed this theory the "dogma of the ghost in the machine." Related to this view is the notion that "right conduct" involves the control of the animal passions through knowledge and reason (although through Western history there has consistently been a group who glorify the passions, including Schopenhauer, Rousseau, and others).

Part of the revolutionary impact of Darwin's theory was that it challenged the long-standing conviction that humans have a rational soul that is absent in animals. Most psychologists have accepted this notion, and regard humans as complicated animals, and that is perhaps accurate. However, there is one thing that all groups of human animals have that no other animals have, and that is language. Human motivation and emotion are based upon biological systems, as they are in all animals. In both humans and animals, learning and cognitive factors influence these motives and emotions. This kind of cognitive–emotional interaction is not unique to humans. What *is* unique to humans is language, which results in a culturally patterned system of behavior control that is functionally independent of biology, and fundamentally different from anything seen in animals.

Although the roots of language learning may be found in spontaneous communication, as suggested above, once learned, language becomes functionally independent of those roots, and begins to organize behavior according to its own structure. Only in humans does behavior come so completely under the influence of principles of logic, reason, and social rules, which are mediated by language. The result might be termed *"emotional education,"* defined as linguistic influences upon emotion in humans which go beyond the animal model of emotional development (Buck, 1982a, 1982b, 1983b). Unfortunately, theories of cognitive development which take such processes into account have not been widely applied to the analysis of human emotion, despite the widely held view and ample evidence that cognitive processes play an essential role in emotion.

COGNITIVE DEVELOPMENT, LANGUAGE, AND EMOTIONAL EDUCATION

Clearly, the detailed integration of theories of cognitive development with the analysis of emotional development would be a major undertaking. This book can only suggest some of the implications and possible results of such an application. The next paragraphs briefly summarize some of the major features of Piaget's theory of cognitive development, and suggest how they might be relevant to the analysis of emotional development and education. The implications of the cerebral lateralization data to such an application shall then be discussed.

THE COGNITIVE BIAS

Studies of human development in recent decades have had a strong cognitive bias which has often excluded the consideration of emotional phenomena. A striking example of this bias has been pointed out by Gottman and Parkhurst (1978) in a discussion of Piaget's highly influential *Language and Thought of the Child* (1930). Piaget was interested in questions of children that concerned physical causality, but he explicitly excluded questions about "psychological explanation," such as "Why was he crying?" or "Why has he gone away?" In fact, they note that one of Piaget's tables (p. 54) indicates that 56% of children's questions concerned such intentions or actions, but this passes without comment. Gottman and Parkhurst conclude:

> Clearly, for the children in Piaget's sample, questions about psychological explanation are highly salient. Piaget uses the infrequency of nonsocial causal questions as evidence that the children are not functioning cognitively at a high level. Since throughout his monograph he assumes low-level cognitive functioning to be equivalent to socially non-adapted functioning, he ends by using the children's social orientation as a negation of its own existence. (p. 10)

This example suggests that a consideration of emotional phenomena may clarify our understanding of cognitive as well as emotional development.

PIAGET'S THEORY OF COGNITIVE DEVELOPMENT

Piaget's theory embodies perhaps the most widely accepted and influential analysis of the process of cognitive development. He argues that cognitive development results from the interaction of the child and the world. In order to know the world, the child must act on it—"In order to know objects, the subject must act upon them, and therefore transform them; he must displace, connect, combine, take apart, and reassemble them" (Piaget, 1971, p. 704).

Assimilation and Accommodation

The major concepts used to analyze this process, *assimilation* and *accommodation*, involve how information about the world is integrated into the existing cognitive structure, thus altering that structure. Piaget and Inhelder (1969) suggest that reality data are transformed into the cognitive structure much as food undergoes a chemical transformation when it is integrated into the substance of the organism. Just as food must undergo the process of digestion, reality data must be assimilable 'by the child. The degree to which reality data are assimilable is determined by the preexisting cognitive structure: Data are assimilable if they are not too discrepant from the existing structure. Once assimilated, they modify and enrich the existing structure. This modification of the assimilating structure to fit what is assimilated is termed "accommodation." In essence, the child must be able to assimilate a new experience before accommodation is possible, and the accommodation involves an alteration and enrichment of the assimilatory structure.

Piaget feels that a situation which is partially but not completely assimilated is intrinsically motivating because it demands more accommodation—it constitutes a challenge. Experience with that situation is like a food or *aliment* for the cognitive structure. Elkind (1971) has described this process in terms of "cognitive growth cycles." He believes that the first state of such a cycle is characterized by stimulus-seeking behavior, that moderately novel stimuli serve as an aliment for further growth, and that the child is intrinsically attracted to such stimuli. The motivational state involved in such attraction is analogous to White's (1959) "effectance motivation," and similar constructs play central roles in analyses of stimulus-seeking, exploratory behavior, personal causation, and achievement motivation (cf. Buck, 1976a, pp. 278–290). These are among the "cognitive motives" that were tentatively associated with the left hemisphere in the last chapter.

Stages of Cognitive Development

Piaget analyzes the process of cognitive development as a series of stages which involve qualitative changes in the style of mental functioning. The *sensory–motor period* (birth to 18 months) is the first stage. Piaget feels that the newborn is aware of his or her sensory experiences—what we have called knowledge by acquaintance—but that these are relatively unorganized. Recent research suggests that the newborn "knows" more than one might imagine via this process, and that the behaviorists' convention that the infant is a "blank slate," experiencing only a "booming, buzzing confusion," is likely incorrect. We have seen that the infant comes with certain emotional proclivities, perceptual preattunements, and spontaneous sending tendencies which lay the groundwork for social and emotional development. However, there is no doubt that the infant's experiences with reality serve additional organizing functions. As the infant experiences the world, consistencies occur, beginning the processes of assimilation and accommodation which are the basis for cognitive development.

One of the major accomplishments of the sensory–motor period is the development of the object concept. According to Piaget, the infant acts at first as if the existence of an object depends upon the infant perceiving it: "The universe of the young baby is a world without objects, consisting only of shifting and unsubstantial "tableaux" which appear and are then totally reabsorbed" (Piaget & Inhelder, 1969, p. 14). However, as the infant acquires experience with the reappearance of objects, he or she gradually begins to act as if objects are stable and permanent. Thus an older infant will attempt to retrieve a toy that is hidden under a blanket by an investigator in view of the infant, while a younger infant will not. The stages of cognitive development are defined by tests such as this "hidden toy" procedure. Some suggest that they underestimate the true abilities of the infant and child, but this will be demonstrated conclusively only when better tests are devised.

Many other developments take place in the sensory–motor period; in general, the infant acquires the basic sensory and motor skills needed for exploring the environment (cf. Baldwin, 1967; Piaget & Inhelder, 1969). The second of Piaget's stages is the *preoperational period* (18 months to 6–8 years), which begins with positive evidence of the "semiotic function": the ability to internally store symbolic representations of the external world. In this period the child acquires the ability to use logical operations in guiding his or her behavior. The internal cognitive representations of reality become organized according to such logical principles as the conservation of volume and number, as is revealed by the well-known conservation tests.

The process of using logical operations to guide behavior requires "decentering": The child must come to understand that the world appears different to other persons and to other points of view. This loss of "egocentrism" involves, in effect, a "Copernican revolution" in the child's thinking. Piaget points out that it has implications for the development of moral judgment, making it possible for the child to judge intention in the behavior of others (Piaget, 1932).

The third stage is the *concrete operational period* (6–8 years to 12–14 years) in which the child has the ability to reason about concrete logical operations centered on real objects. The ability to use abstract or formal propositions which are removed from the actual observation of real objects (i.e., to consider alternatives and non-present possibilities) must await the fourth stage, or *formal operational period* (12–14 years to adulthood).

APPLICATIONS TO THE THEORY OF EMOTION: EMOTIONAL EDUCATION

Piaget's theory has been used to study a variety of phenomena in which cognitive development plays a major role, including the analysis of moral development (Kohlberg, 1963; Piaget, 1932), where the theory was employed to study the development of moral judgment. Another example is Selman's analysis of role-taking ability: the ability to view the world and oneself from the perspective of another person (Selman, 1973; Selman & Byrne, 1972). It can be argued that the theory can be applied as well to the study of emotional development. Although it is widely accepted that cognitive factors influence emotion, the implication that cognitive development must influence emotional development has not been clearly spelled out. We have seen that such an analysis must involve the child's adaptation to the internal world of subjective experience as well as the external world. Such an analysis seems essential to the eventual understanding of the uniquely human aspects of emotional development and expression.

Emotional Aliments

One potential application of Piaget's theory to emotion involves the concept of aliments. We have seen that aliments involve situations that intrinsically motivate attempts at cognitive understanding and mastery. There may also be situations which intrinsically call forth attempts at emotional understanding and mastery: A child who experiences for the first time feelings associated with activity in a neurochemical system (i.e., when first feeling fear toward a stranger, or at puberty when sexual systems become active) may be seen to be in a situation analogous in many respects to that of a child who experiences a novel external event. Indeed, the emotional situation may be even more compelling, for unlike an external event, the child cannot physically run away from or avoid his or her own feelings.

If the experience is beyond the child's capacity to assimilate, the child might soon forget it, but it is possible that such an experience might leave a lasting impression of some kind. One could reasonably suggest a variety of ways in which "unconscious" influences could persist and affect later behavior in processes perhaps analogous to repression and fixation (e.g., via interoceptive conditioning; cf. Buck, 1976a, pp. 115–122; Razran, 1961). Unfortunately, there is little empirical data in this area upon which to base discussion or speculation. It will be recalled that we noted in the last chapter Galin's (1974) suggestion that one type of repression may involve the inhibition by the left hemisphere of input from the right hemisphere. In effect, the child could conceivably alter the conscious experience of its own feelings by blocking transmission of the feelings (mediated by the right hemisphere) to labeling and verbalization (mediated by the left hemisphere).

If the experience is within the capacity of the child to assimilate, Piaget's theory would predict that the situation might be intrinsically attractive to the individual, even if the emotions involved might not necessarily be pleasant. A study which may be interpreted as supporting this notion was conducted following the murder of a woman student at a large university (Boyanowski, Newtson, & Walster, 1972). The investigators called women students randomly selected from the victim's dormitory and a comparable "control" dormitory, giving them a telephone interview unrelated to the murder. For their cooperation, the students were given a choice of tickets for two movies playing locally at the time: *The Fox*, a story of a lesbian relationship, and *In Cold Blood*, based upon the brutal murder of a family. A week following the murder, students from the victim's dormitory showed a significant preference for *In Cold Blood*. The authors interpret this preference as involving an attempt to reduce fear and anxiety via desensitization, that is, subjecting oneself to a mild form of the feared stimulus while relaxing. However, one could also interpret the preference as indicating an attempt to cognitively accommodate feelings evoked by the murder.

Such a process might account for the human fascination which depictions of emotion of many kinds and in many forms, from novels and stories to mass media programing. We suggested above that important aspects of emotion usually remain "inaccessible" to the outside observer. Perhaps an important determinant of the "assimilability" of an emotional situation is the degree to which the emotion is made "accessible" in all of its aspects. The situation which teaches something about one's feelings, and helps one to understand emotions more completely, may constitute an emotional "aliment" regardless of the quality of the emotion. The depiction of emotion via various media may acquire much of its attraction from its ability to make accessible the normally inaccessible aspects of emotion.

Stages of Emotional Development

The child's readiness to comprehend such lessons will naturally depend upon the child's level of cognitive development. Many predictions about the child's response to depictions of emotional situations can be made on the basis of Piaget's theory and what is known about the process of cognitive development. For example, the "egocentric" preoperational child should have difficulty understanding that others have different feelings, while the concrete operational child should be able to comprehend the emotional response of a specific other in a given situation, but might have difficulty generalizing this to classes of persons or classes of situations. The investigation of such questions will undoubtedly contribute to the understanding not only of emotional development, but of cognitive development as well and how the two relate to one another.

An interesting example of this kind of study has been provided by Barden, Zelko, Duncan, and Masters (1980). These authors asked children of various ages (4–5, 9–10, and 12–13 years) about the probable affective reactions to events described in brief vignettes ("If you played hide-and-seek so well that no one could find you, would you feel . . . ?" "If a classmate walked up to you and hit you in the stomach, would you feel . . . ?"). The vignettes were categorized in terms of eight types of experience: success, failure, dishonesty–caught, dishonesty—not caught, nurturance, aggression, justified punishment, and unjustified punishment. The potential affects that the children chose included happiness, sadness, fear, anger, and neutral affect.

The results are summarized in Figure 4.4. They indicated that there was a high degree of consensus across age about some vignettes: that is, being happy at success, and sad and angry about aggression and unjustified punishment. However, other vignettes showed age changes suggestive of developmental trends in children's under-standing of emotion. For example, younger children consistently expected a happy response to "dishonest—not caught," while older children predicted a fearful response; older children became somewhat less likely to expect a "happy" response to nurturance in favor of a neutral reaction; older children moved toward a consensus of ex-pecting a neutral reaction to failure rather than sadness. The authors discuss each of these changes in terms of socialization and the cogni-tive complexity of the experiences involved.

In a related study, Carolyn Saarni (1979, 1982) has investigated the development of display rule usage in children in Grades 1, 3, and 5. Subjects were presented with four interpersonal conflict situations in comic-book style (i.e., showing a child being bullied by another child in front of an onlooker, or a child receiving a disappointing gift). In the final frame, the child's face was averted. Subjects were asked to select the facial expression that the child probably revealed and to justify their choices. Results indicated that display rule usage, where affect and expression were dissociated, increased with age. Saarni analyzed four reasons used to justify such dissociation: (1) trouble avoidance ("If he shows he's scared, they'll really beat him up"); (2) maintenance of self-esteem ("He doesn't want to be a coward"); (3) qualifying factors in the relationship ("He doesn't want to hurt his aunt's feelings"); and (4) maintenance of norms ("It's impolite to show you feel that way"). She found that the trouble-avoiding account was given most frequently (44%) followed by pre-serving self-esteem (30%), qualifying relationship factors (19%), and norm maintenance (8%). The norm-maintenance account was given only by the oldest children. In a review of this and related studies, Saarni (1982) suggests that the trouble-avoiding account involves direct deception in a relatively simple process to gain reward and/or avoid punishment, that the preserving self-esteem account involves the emergence of personal display rules, and that the norm

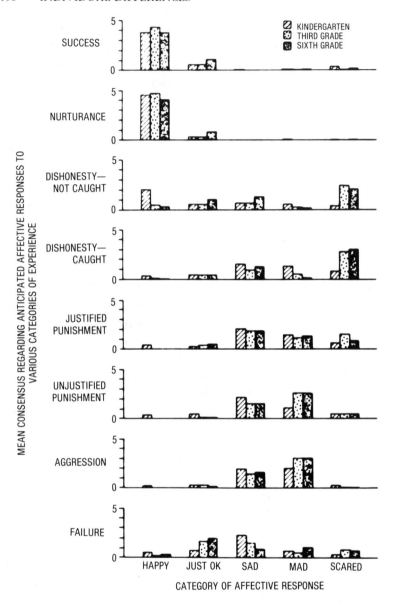

Figure 4.4. Mean consensuses regarding various anticipated affective responses to different categories of experiences by children at three different ages. From Figure 1 in "Children's Consensual Knowledge about the Experiential Determinants of Emotion" by R. C. Barden, F. A. Zelco, S. W. Duncan, and J. C. Masters, *Journal of Personality and Social Psychology*, 1980, 39(5), 968–976. Copyright 1980 by the American Psychological Association. Reprinted by permission.

maintenance involves cultural display rule usage. The latter requires cognitive appraisal of a system of norms and it is based upon both direct deception and personal display rule usage.

In another relevant study, Sommers (1981) has demonstrated a relationship between tests of social cognition and a measure of "emotional range," with persons high in role-taking ability and complexity in their descriptions of other persons mentioning a wider variety of affect states in a story completion task than persons low on those measures. It is noteworthy that neither Barden *et al.* (1980), Saarni (1979), nor Sommers (1981) found evidence of sex differences, in contrast to the common finding of sex differences in less cognitively based studies of emotion. It may be that sex differences are smaller or less important in the area of the cognitive determinants of emotion.

Emotional Education and the Coping Process

The interaction between biologically based motivational/emotional systems and the cognitive system is basic to the process by which humans deal with, or "cope" with emotion. Studies of the coping process have long been concerned with the interaction of cognitive and emotional factors. For example, in an influential series of studies Lazarus and his colleagues have demonstrated that cognitive manipulations can modify the affective impact of unpleasant films. One film depicted the gruesome circumcision-like ritual performed on adolescent boys in an Australian aboriginal culture. Viewing the film normally produced large increases in skin conductance. Spiesman, Lazarus, Mordkoff, and Davison (1964) created sound tracks that denied the harmful features of the rite, stating that the event was actually a happy one (denial commentary); that described the scene technically (intellectualization commentary); or that emphasized the horror and pain experienced by the boys (trauma commentary). The first two tracks significantly reduced autonomic arousal relative to the silent film, while the third track increased arousal. Subsequent studies showed that denial information presented before the film "short circuited" the threat, in that it was more effective than the same information presented on the sound track (Lazarus & Alfert, 1964).

Such studies demonstrate without doubt that the cognitive appraisal of the emotional significance of a stimulus is an important factor in the emotional response to that stimulus. Whether such appraisal is prior to, and necessary for, that emotional response is a subject of some controversy. Averill's view of emotion holds that cognitive processes create the emotional response (cf. Averill, 1974, 1980; Averill, Opton, & Lazarus, 1969). However, we have seen that studies by Zajonc (1980) and others suggest that some kinds of emotional response can occur prior to the cognitive registration of a stimulus. In any case, it is clear that cognitive factors normally contribute to the emotional response.

The notion that cognitive development is associated with a process of emotional education provides a useful perspective from which to analyze the developmental aspects of the coping process. This book has presented the view that motivational/emotional systems occur at various levels—for example, instincts, drives, and affects—but at base they are special-purpose processing systems concerned with bodily adaptation and the maintenance of homeostasis. Different aspects of emotional states can be made relatively accessible or inaccessible via the education of attention, so that the child may learn a variety of lessons about the meaning of emotional behaviors. Such learning is incorporated in the cognitive system, which is a general-purpose processor that has evolved to make sense out of the external (and internal) milieu, and to construct a representation of reality from experience in the milieu. In humans, the powerful principles of organization associated with language dominate cognition, and thereby influence the biological processes associated with emotional reactions. Processes of logic and reasoning mediated by language are used to monitor emotion, and this results in the development of *rules* concerning emotional phenomena. *Coping* may be defined as the application of linguistically structured rules to emotional phenomena. Thus, coping involves *reasoning about emotion* (Buck & Reardon, 1983). We shall return to this view of the coping process in Chapter 6.

Emotional Education and the Mass Media

Another area of potential application for a theory of emotional education concerns the role of drama, literature, and, in modern society, the mass media in the emotional education of children. Most research on the social impact of the media has focused upon depictions of sex and violence. It may be that the depictions of many other kinds of emotion are equally or even more important. For example, McClelland (1961; McClelland & Winter, 1969) argued that achievement motivation can be fostered or discouraged by a society through its teaching to its children. He reasoned that literature and children's stories play a part in this process of socialization, and that they thus should reflect these cultural values. He found that the level of achievement imagery in children's stories published in 1923 in a number of societies was positively correlated with the growth in economic development in those societies as measured by per capita growth in electrical production between 1929 and 1950. Similarly, periods of growth and decline of achievement imagery in Spanish literature (1350–1700 A.D.) and English literature (1550–1800 A.D.) preceded periods of growth and decline of economic activity.

If these kinds of analyses are applied to other motivational/emotional systems, the implications are considerable, suggesting that much of what is unique about the flavor and ambience of a culture may reflect the emotional education of its young. It also testifies both to the importance of the animal model of emotion to human beings, and to the ultimate freedom of humans from its influence. The processes that we see in animals lays the foundation for the emotional life of human beings, but the family and culture provide variations and detail that make the human emotional life unique.

SUMMARY

It is suggested that the boundary between the animal model of emotion versus emotional processes unique to humans involves the learning of language, which constitutes a system which becomes functionally independent of its roots in spontaneous communication. Much human behavior is mediated by principles of logic and reasoning which are mediated by language. The analysis of this kind of cognitive development has rarely been applied to the study of emotion. However it is argued that theories of cognitive development, such as that of Piaget, have important implications for the study of human emotion, and *vice versa*. Emotional education was defined as the general development of linguistically mediated influences upon emotion. Some of the major points in Piaget's theory were summarized and it was suggested how they might be applied to the analysis of emotional education, including the analysis of emotional aliments, stages of emotional development, the coping process, and the influence of literature, drama, and the media.

CEREBRAL LATERALIZATION AND EMOTIONAL DEVELOPMENT

This chapter has suggested that an animal model of emotion may be useful in analyzing the foundations of human emotional development, but that a full understanding of the latter requires a consideration of how emotion is influenced by principles of logic and reasoning that are mediated by language. This section relates this analysis to the phenomenon of cerebral lateralization and the modes of cognition associated with the cerebral hemispheres.

CEREBRAL LATERALIZATION AND COGNITION

As noted in the last chapter, Tucker's (1981) analysis suggests that there are two sorts of cognition: syncretic cognition associated with right-hemisphere functioning and analytic cognition associated with left-hemisphere functioning. This implies that there must be two sorts of cognitive development as well. In other words, the suggestions by Tucker (1981) and others in the area of cerebral lateralization that right-hemisphere functioning is associated with a syncretic and holistic type of cognition that is distinct from the sequential and analytic cognition of the left hemisphere implies that any analysis of emotional development must be concerned with both types of cognition, and their interactions. At first glance, one might associate syncretic cognition with the animal model of emotion, and analytic cognition with humans, who have lateralized brains. However, there are suggestions that cerebral lateralization may not be unique to humans.

Hemispheric Laterality in Animals

There is evidence that cerebral lateralization occurs in animals as well as humans, and that analytic and synthetic cognition occur in both animals and humans. Denenberg (1981) has reviewed evidence of hemispheric laterality in lower animals, including birds, rats, and monkeys. For example, left-hemisphere dominance for song production has been demonstrated in some (but not all) songbirds, such as the canary (Nottebohm, 1970, 1977, 1979). Also, Denenberg and his colleagues have shown evidence of laterality in rats. (Denenberg, Garbanti, Sherman, Yutzey, & Kaplan, 1978). Rats with left-hemisphere lesions show greater emotional reactivity (as measured by mouse killing) than rats with right-hemisphere lesions or intact controls (Garbanti, Sherman, Rosen, Hofmann, Yutzey, & Denenberg, 1980). Current evidence suggests that auditory and visual learning and "symbolic" communicative behavior involve the left hemisphere, and that spatial performance and emotional behavior involve the right hemisphere, in at least some animal species. This suggests in turn that the differences between the cerebral hemispheres that we have been discussing are not unique to humans, but play a part in the "animal model" of emotion and emotional development as well.

Early Experience and Laterality

Denenberg (1981) has advanced an interesting hypothesis with important implications for the possible developmental antecedants of individual differences in cerebral lateralization. In earlier work, Denenberg and his colleagues investigated the effects of early experiences in rats, and particularly the effects of early handling and being raised in enriched sensory environments. These studies demonstrated that early handling has a wide range of effects on rats, making them less emotionally responsive and more exploratory, and modifying the hypothalamic–pituitary–adrenal response to stress (cf. Denenberg, 1964, 1969; Levine, 1969). Being raised in an enriched environment also decreases emotionality, increases abilities on problem-solving and perceptual tasks, and alters the weight, thickness, and chemistry of the brain (cf. Denenberg, 1981; Rosenzweig, Bennett, & Diamond, 1972).

Recent studies by Denenberg and his colleagues have suggested that such early experiences can facilitate the development of brain laterality (Denenberg et al., 1978). Handled rats show evidence of laterality on a variety of measures that is not apparent in nonhandled rats. Denenberg (1981) suggests that stimulation during early life stimulates the development of the corpus callosum, which transmits much information between the two hemispheres. He suggests that asymmetry is the initial condition of brains, with the left hemisphere being preferentially biased to deal with analytic functions—discrimination and symbolic communication—and the right hemisphere with syncretic—spatial and affective—matters. Each hemisphere is set to maximize its own special abilities (*specialization*), but each also has an initial plasticity (*redundancy*) as a "fail-safe" backup in case the other hemisphere is injured. Specialization requires influences from the homologous brain region—the corresponding brain region in the other hemisphere—which are mediated via corpus callosum. If these influences do not occur, either because of injury to the homologous region or the corpus callosum, redundancy will occur and the specialized abilities will not develop. As specialization develops, the potential for redundancy declines accordingly. Denenberg suggests that early stimulation leads to greater hemispheric lateralization by enhancing the development of the corpus callosum.

THE EVOLUTION OF LANGUAGE

Cerebral Asymmetry

It thus appears that cerebral lateralization, with its attendant modes of syncretic versus analytic cognition, may not be unique to humans. What *is* unique to humans is language, and there is evidence that particular structures in the left hemisphere have evolved to serve as the basis for language. There are asymmetries in the anatomical structure of the human brain, with the Sylvian fissure being longer on the left than the right, and the left hemisphere being larger than the right in most right-handed persons (Geschwind, 1979a). These anatomical asymmetries are also found in the apes—chimpanzees, gorillas, and orangutans—but monkeys such as the rhesus macaque do not show these asymmetries (Geschwind, 1980). This may well be relevant to the findings in the apes of significant capacities for the production of symbolic communication with close similarities to language, using sign language, computer keyboards, and other systems of symbolic manual language adapted to their manual abilities (e.g., Gardner & Gardner, 1969).

Thus, it seems possible that the ability to produce or send the complex symbolic messages associated with language may be associated with the evolution of left-hemisphere mechanisms whose presence is indicated by anatomical asymmetries. There are intriguing indications that the ability to receive and respond appropriately to messages from others may also involve left-hemisphere mechanisms in animals, which may be phylogenetically older than those associated with the production of messages.

Intention in Sending versus Receiving Processes

There are logical grounds for believing that the role of intention must be different in receiving as opposed to sending communicative messages. We noted above that the spontaneous expression of emotion is not voluntary. However, the same cannot be said for the process of receiving information from such spontaneous behaviors in others. Although there may be innate preattunements to "pick up" spontaneous cues, any overt behavior resulting from that pickup of information is goal-directed instrumental behavior which must involve voluntary responses.

If this is the case, it follows that social learning should be more important to the receiving process than it is to the sending process, as symbolic communication evolved. There is evidence for this in the Miller *et al.* (1967) study considered above. Animals who had been isolated in early life could not use the facial expressions of other animals to avoid shock, even though they had learned the original avoidance task of using a light as a cue to avoid the shock. Significantly, when normal monkeys viewed the isolates, there were too many false positives: The normal animals pressed the bar too often during the interstimulus interval, apparently because the isolates made many fearful expressions even when the light associated with shock was off. In other words, both isolate and normal animals expressed fear spontaneously, although the normals expressed it only in the presence of the appropriate external cue. The isolation thus did not alter the nature of the spontaneous expression of fear *per se*. The receiving process on the other hand was disrupted in the isolates: They could not respond appropriately to the facial cues of the senders even though they had responded appropriately to the light.

It is interesting in this regard that there is evidence that receiving processes are lateralized in the left hemisphere in monkeys. Beecher, Peterson, Zoloth, Moody, and Stebbins (1979) presented Japanese macaques with tape recordings of macaque vocalizations, training them to discriminate between two classes of sounds which differed either according to a communication-relevant dimension—"smooth early high coos" (SE) versus "smooth late high coos" (SL)—or a communication-irrelevant dimension—high pitched versus low pitched. The animals learned the SE–SL discrimination more readily than the pitch discrimination. Also, they showed a right-ear (left-hemisphere) advantage for the SE–SL discrimination but not the pitch discrimination, suggesting left-hemisphere processing for the communication-relevant discrimination. Both findings—of a selective attention to communication-relevant events, and left-hemisphere processing of such events—parallel similar findings in human speech perception (Beecher et al., p. 443).

Spontaneous Communication, Symbolic Communication, and Language

This chapter has suggested a fundamental distinction between an animal model of emotion and emotional development, which is associated with both spontaneous and symbolic communication processes, and emotional education, which is associated with language and is thus uniquely human. This is not meant to suggest that there is a great biological gap between animals and humans. On the contrary, the evidence reviewed above suggests just the opposite—a gradual and orderly evolution of the biological mechanisms underlying language. It is also not meant to suggest that animals cannot learn language. The evidence suggests that some animals have previously unsuspected linguistic abilities, and there is no indication that the full range of these abilities has yet been explored. It *is* meant to suggest that if an animal did learn language, it would cause a fundamental change in the animal's behavior, for its behavior would now be controlled by a system having a different sort of structure, with different principles of organization, *in addition to* the systems which had previously controlled its behavior. Specifically, behavior would now come partially under the control of linguistically organized rules.

SUMMARY

The notion that there are two sorts of cognition—syncretic cognition associated with spontaneous communication and the right cerebral hemisphere, and analytic cognition associated with symbolic communication and the left hemisphere—was discussed in Chapter 3 in terms of the notion of knowledge by acquaintance versus knowledge by description. In this chapter it was discussed in terms of the animal model of emotion, suggesting that the gradual evolution of symbolic communication is seen in the requirement that animals must "learn how to use" the innately given spontaneous communication system. This chapter also discussed the evolution of hemispheric lateralization, suggesting that lateralization is a feature of lower animals as well as apes and humans. In addition, it discussed hemispheric differences in brain anatomy which may be associated with the uniquely human attribute of language. These differences, which are characteristic of humans, can also be seen in the apes, and there are suggestions that, given training, apes have significant linguistic abilities. These phenomena have not been identified in monkeys, but lateralization of the reception of species-specific vocalizations has been demonstrated in monkeys (macaques). The overall picture suggests a graduate evolution of mechanisms serving symbolic communication abilities, culminating in mechanisms complex enough to support language. However, the existence of these mechanisms *per se* apparently did not guarantee the emergence of language, or apes in the wild would manifest the linguistic abilities that have been demonstrated in the laboratory. In any case, the invention of language provided for humans a new and powerful vehicle for the control of behavior which is functionally independent of its biological roots.

CONCLUSIONS

This chapter has attempted to develop a coherent framework for relating emotion and cognition in the development of the individual, and to account for the uniquely human attribute of language. In the first sections an "animal model" of emotion and emotional development was outlined, which takes into account the interacting effects of the maturation of the neurochemical systems underlying emotion and the provision of appropriate social learning experiences in the development of emotion communication. It was suggested that this animal model represents an incomplete view of human emotion, due to the important role of language. This view implied that theories of cognitive development in humans should be relevant to a uniquely human view of emotional development, involving the process of *emotional education.* Piaget's theory and some of its implications were examined from that point of view. The implications of the research on cerebral lateralization were also examined, suggesting that the animal model of emotion encompasses both spontaneous and symbolic communication, and both right- and left-cerebral processing, but that it misses the role of language. Language makes possible a new system of behavior control, a new set of principles or rules for the organization of behavior, which is functionally independent of the biological systems upon which it is based. This system was identified with the *coping process*.

It is instructive at this point to return to the model of the relationship between spontaneous and symbolic communication presented in Figure 1.1, which showed the importance of symbolic communication increasing over a constant level of spontaneous communication. It was noted then that the horizontal axis of that figure could refer also to phylogenetic scale or individual state of development, in that the relative importance of symbolic communication generally increases with those variables while spontaneous communication remains relatively constant. We are now in the position to suggest other features of these relationships. Figure 4.5 gives the

Figure 4.5. Hypothetical relationship between the importance of spontaneous and symbolic communication across the phylogenetic scale.

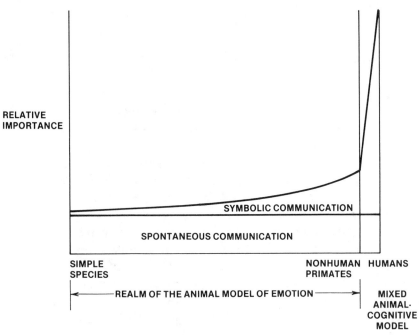

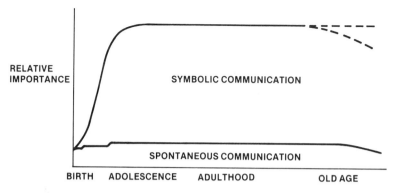

Figure 4.6. Hypothetical relationship between the relative importance of spontaneous and symbolic communication in the development of an individual human.

hypothetical distribution between the relative importance of spontaneous and symbolic communication across the phylogenetic scale, assuming (1) that spontaneous and symbolic communication are based respectively upon subcortical/paleocortical versus neocortical mechanisms, and (2) that there is a discontinuity in this relationship as one moves from nonhuman primates to humans, indicating the role of language in humans and the limit of the animal model of emotional development. Figure 4.6 illustrates the hypothetical relationship between the role of spontaneous and symbolic behavior in the development of an individual human. It shows changes as motivational/emotional mechanisms underlying spontaneous communication go "on line" and "off line" with maturation and aging, and changes in symbolic communication with cognitive development and experience, plus possible decline as a result of aging and/or disease. The latter figure is meant to be general, of course, and actual figures would vary with the individual and situation.

One additional observation seems appropriate here. This chapter has argued that language makes humans different in fundamental ways from animals, because it allows behavior to come under the control of principles of logic and reasoning that are mediated by language and functionally independent of biology. With language also comes the conformity and obedience to culturally patterned social rules. Perhaps all this is what Plato, Aristotle, and others meant by the human "rational soul." There is irony here, for most of these philosophers assumed that the rational soul is the source of good and the animal passions the source of evil. However, it is reason, logic, and conformity to social rules that enables humans to claim justification for the planning and execution of a holocaust, the use of nerve gas, or the dropping of an atomic bomb. The animal passions really play little part in the most monstrous of human acts.

5

NONVERBAL
SENDING ACCURACY

The last chapter considered the development of emotion and emotion communication, suggesting a fundamental difference between the "animal model" of emotion and models that include the consideration of uniquely human linguistic processing. The next three chapters involve the study of nonverbal communication in humans, with the understanding that this must consider how spontaneous and symbolic communication based upon the animal model interacts with language. The present chapter deals with nonverbal sending accuracy, Chapter 6 will explore inhibition and deception, and Chapter 7 will analyze nonverbal receiving ability.

Nonverbal sending accuracy is defined as the tendency for an individual to reveal his or her internal motivational/emotional states via nonverbal behavior. This chapter first reviews the methods of studying spontaneous sending accuracy, and of analyzing the often complex data that result. It then outlines the evidence relating to individual differences in spontaneous facial expressiveness, including sex and personality differences in expressiveness and the relationship of expressiveness to autonomic/endocrine responding. It examines developmental studies which suggest the relative roles of temperament and social learning in the development of sending accuracy. Finally, it considers psychometric measures which have been developed to measure tendencies toward spontaneous expression.

DEFINITIONS

Our definition of sending accuracy is guided by the view of nonverbal communication established above. Specifically, spontaneous expression is distinguished from intentional expression, which in our terms must be a kind of symbolic communication. However, as noted in Chapter 3, intentional expression *initiation* may differ in important ways from intentional expression *formation* (see Figure 3.5). Expression initiation, or "posing" a specific emotional expression, involves the voluntary acting out of an expression which is already organized at some level within the nervous system. There is thus relatively less need to voluntarily construct the expression, only to act it out. Expression initiation may take place in two ways. The person might attempt to create the expression by attempting to experience the relevant motivational/emotional state, as in Stanislavski acting. Alternatively, the person might be able to voluntarily initiate the expression directly, without the experience of the motivational/emotional state.

In intentional expression formation, in contrast, the individual must "put the expression together" much as one must construct a sentence or other verbal expression. This must involve elements of praxis (the ability to perform voluntary movements; see Chapter 3) which are different from those involved in expression initiation. Thus the abilities involved in expression initiation and expression formation may be quite different, and both differ from spontaneous expressiveness, where there is no intentional expression.

This leaves us then with spontaneous expression and three kinds of voluntary expression: (1) voluntary expression initiation based on the activation of midbrain mechanisms by a motivational/emotional state; (2) voluntary expression initiation based on direct influences upon midbrain mechanisms; and (3) voluntary expression formation analogous to the construction of verbal expression.

METHODS OF STUDYING
SPONTANEOUS SENDING ACCURACY

The communication process requires both a sender and receiver, and any measure of communication accuracy involves both sending and receiving accuracy. The measurement of sending accuracy and receiving ability both involve the assessment of communication accuracy, but the data are handled in different ways. Suppose the expressions of 20 senders to pleasant or unpleasant events are shown to 20 receivers, who guess whether the sender is responding to something pleasant or unpleasant. The accuracy scores of the 20 receivers may be averaged for each sender, resulting in "sending accuracy" scores reflecting the relative ease at which each sender's expressions were decoded. Alternately, the accuracy scores of the 20 senders may be averaged for each receiver, resulting in "receiving ability" scores reflecting the decoding ability of each receiver for that sample of senders.

This section reviews methods of studying spontaneous sending accuracy, involving the viewing and analysis by receivers of the spontaneous and unposed emotional expressions of senders. Any technique attempting to study spontaneous expression must study the sender under conditions where emotion is evoked, either naturally or via artificial emotionally loaded stimuli. A variety of procedures has been adopted for this purpose, each of which has its own strengths and weaknesses. They should thus be considered alternative, rather than competing, techniques. Often results gathered by one technique can be significantly amplified and extended by the use of others.

ARTIFICIAL EMOTIONAL STIMULI

The Cooperative Conditioning Technique

One of the most widely used and useful paradigms for investigating spontaneous expression originated in the cooperative conditioning technique developed by Robert E. Miller to study emotion communication in rhesus monkeys. It will be recalled from Chapter 4 that Miller first trained two monkeys in a standard avoidance situation. Both animals learned to press a bar when a light came on to avoid receiving an electric shock. He then paired the animals so that the sender could see the light but not press the bar, while the receiver could press the bar but not see the light. However, the receiver was provided with the televised image of the head and facial region of the sender, so that if the sender made an appropriate expression when the light came on, *and* if the receiver perceived and correctly interpreted the sender's expression, then the receiver could press the bar and avoid the shock for both. In a series of studies, Miller and his colleagues demonstrated significant communication using both the avoidance paradigm and a reward paradigm (in which the light signaled food rather than shock), and, as related in the last chapter, they showed that monkeys isolated as infants manifested disrupted patterns of communication. They also investigated the effects of psychoactive drugs on communication and social behavior (Miller, 1971, 1974; Miller *et al.*, 1962, 1963, 1966, 1967).

The Slide-Viewing Technique

The Miller paradigm was employed on humans directly by several investigators, who videotaped the facial expressions of male subjects while they anticipated receiving electric shock (Gubar, 1966; Lanzetta & Kleck, 1970). It was used in modified form by others, who sought other means to elicit emotion in the laboratory. The problem was to find a way to arouse a variety of motivational/emotional states in a laboratory setting. The slide-viewing paradigm represents one way to approach this problem. In this technique, senders watch and discuss their reactions to a series of emotionally loaded color slides while, unknown to them, their facial/gestural responses are viewed by receivers, who make judgments about them. For example, the receivers might be asked to guess what type of slide the sender viewed, and how pleasant or unpleasant the sender's response was to the slide. These ratings are compared with the actual type of slide viewed and with the sender's rating of his or her own emotional experience (cf. Buck, 1978).

Photographs of the kinds of slides viewed by children, the experimental situation, and samples of expressions are shown in Figure 5.1. The slides include *familiar people* pictures of the child and his or her friends, *unfamiliar people* pictures of persons unknown to the child, *unpleasant* pictures found to be mildly unpleasant to children, and *unusual* pictures of strange photographic effects. Adults have also viewed *sexual* slides showing nude males and females, *scenic* pictures of pleasant landscapes, and more unpleasant slides of burns and facial injuries (cf. Buck, 1978, 1979a, 1979b).

Motion-Picture-Viewing Techniques

Another variant of Miller's procedure employs emotionally loaded motion pictures rather than slides. This has been used by Zuckerman and his associates (Zuckerman, DeFrank, Hall, Larrance, & Rosenthal,

1979a; Zuckerman, Hall, DeFrank, & Rosenthal, 1976; Zuckerman, Larrance, Hall, DeFrank, & Rosenthal, 1979b), who employed unpleasant and pleasant videotapes of automobile accidents, comedy shows, and so forth. It has also been used by Ekman, Friesen, and Ancoli (1980a), who employed brief (1-minute) scenes with pleasant or unpleasant content. In addition, the facial responses to television programs have been employed in studies whose primary focus was on the effects of television rather than emotion expression *per se* (Ekman, Liebert, Friesen, Harrison, Zlatchin, Malmstrom, & Baron, 1972b; Lagerspetz & Engblom, 1979; Lagerspetz, Wahlroos, & Wendelin, 1978). Thus Ekman *et al.* (1972b) demonstrated that boys who showed positive facial expressions while viewing televised violence were more likely to respond aggressively after viewing such violence.

NATURAL EMOTIONAL STIMULI

The other general kind of technique that has been used to study spontaneous expression involves the ethological approach of analyzing expressive behavior in natural settings where emotionally relevant events occur. This approach was employed by Eibl-Eibesfeldt and his colleagues (1970, 1972; Hass, 1970) in their extensive observations of expressive behaviors occurring in natural settings in a wide variety of cultures. These investigators employed a camera fitted with a lens which filmed events occurring at an angle 90° away from where the camera appeared to be pointing, so that the subjects were unaware of being filmed. They filmed similar situations, involving greeting, flirting, begging, praying, and so forth, in a variety of cultures, including cultures in India, Africa, New Guinea, and the Brazilian jungle. Important cross-cultural similarities were found and illustrated in many of these situations, such as the occurrence of an "eyebrow flash" during greeting (see Figure 5.2). Some of these observations have involved "naturalistic experiments" in which an artificial element is introduced into a natural situation. Thus, Eibl-Eibesfeldt and his associates introduced such elements as a box containing a jumping snake to elicit surprise, and a bank note left on the ground to elicit curiosity and conflict (Eibl-Eibesfeldt, 1972; Hass, 1970).

Kraut and Johnston (1979) have demonstrated that in a variety of situations smiling seems to be more strongly related to social interaction than to assumed emotional experience. They filmed

Figure 5.1a–5.1d. Examples of stimuli used to evoke facial responses in young children: (a) familiar; (b) unfamiliar; (c) unusual; (d) unpleasant. Photographs a–c by R. Buck; d, S. Shelton/Monkmeyer. From Figure 7.12 in *Human Motivation and Emotion* by R. Buck, New York: Wiley, 1976. Copyright 1976 by John Wiley & Sons. Reprinted by permission.

Figure 5.1e–5.1j. (e) Child and experimenter view slide on back-lighted screen. (f) Mother views the televised expressions of the child in another room. (g) Typical facial response to a familiar-person slide. (h) Typical facial response to an unpleasant slide. (i) Typical facial response to an unusual slide. (j) Child rates emotional response by pointing to one of a series of facial drawings. From Figure 6.2 in "The Evolution and Development of Emotion Expression and Communication" by R. Buck, in S. Brehm, S. Kassin, and F. Gibbons (Eds.), *Developmental Social Psychology*, New York: Oxford University Press, 1981. Reprinted by permission.

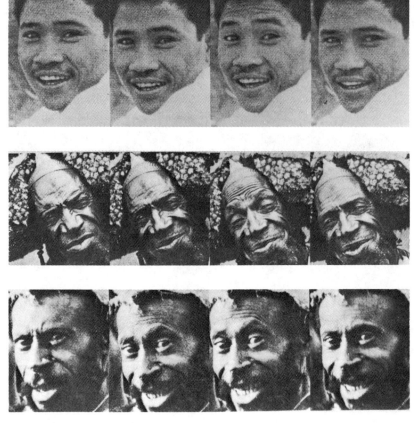

Figure 5.2. Eyebrow-flash during greeting. Upper row: Balinese of the island of Nusa Penida. Middle row: Papua, Huri tribe near Tari (New Guinea). Lower row: Papua, Woitapmin tribe near Bimin (New Guinea). Similar observations have been made of subjects from Samoa and France. Photographs courtesy I. Eibl-Eibesfeldt, Max Planck Institute for Behavioral Physiology. From Figure 265 in *Ethology: The Biology of Behavior* by I. Eibl-Eibesfeldt, New York: Holt, Rinehart & Winston, 1970. Reprinted by permission.

persons who were alone or with others while bowling, watching a hockey game, or walking on a pleasant day. They found that the occurrence of smiling was more closely associated with being part of a social interaction than it was with such presumably positive emotional stimuli as getting a strike in bowling, viewing an event favorable to the home hockey team, or being out on a pleasant day. These findings may reflect the extent to which the smile is a symbolic display associated with interaction, as opposed to a spontaneous expression of emotion.

The study by Izard *et al.* (1980) cited in the last chapter, in which the facial responses in infants to a series of immunization injections were analyzed, is another example of a "naturalistic experiment." Izard's study has the added advantage of being longitudinal, in that the same children may be studied as they grow.

EVALUATION

The comparison of the laboratory and experimental procedures which involve artificial emotional stimuli, with the naturalistic studies which involve natural emotional stimuli, offers a particularly good example of how different methodological techniques can be complementary to one another rather than competing. Each has its "blind spots," but each also has useful features, covering phenomena not addressed by the others. For example, the laboratory procedures allow more control over the nature of the emotional stimulus: The same stimulus can be used again and again, and the effects of different variables such as the age, sex, and personality of the sender, and the presence of others can be investigated systematically. Also, it is possible to obtain high-quality images of the sender's behavior in the laboratory which are difficult to obtain under natural conditions. On the other hand, the artificiality of the stimulus is a cause for concern. One wonders about the extent to which a "real" emotional state can in fact be created under laboratory conditions. It is particularly difficult to create certain expressions, such as angry or fearful expressions, by artificial stimuli. The natural situation involves a more realistic emotional state, but it is less controllable and the problems in obtaining high-quality images are greater.

METHODS OF ANALYSIS

Spontaneous expression involves an extremely complex stream of behavior in which different behaviors co-occur over time, at times related to one another and at other times not. In analyzing this behavior stream two problems stand out: (1) What happens? and

(2) When does it happen? A variety of methods have been employed to analyze this complex mass of data. In general, *notation systems* have been suggested to answer the question of what happens, in which there has been an attempt to identify "units" of behavior which are, in Scheflen's (1974) terms, "recognizable at a glance and recordable at a stroke." To address the question of the temporal organization of spontaneous behavior, a variety of *segmentation systems* have been proposed. Most transcription systems also contain information relevant to segmentation, that is, indications of when a given behavior occurs. The opposite is not necessarily the case: There are segmentation systems that do not involve specific transcription systems.

In contrast to the methods of studying spontaneous communication, which are best viewed as complementary rather than competing, one can make a case that different systems of analysis may well vary in their efficiency and usefulness, since often two different techniques of analysis can be applied to the same data, and one can inquire which is the more cost effective, that is, which gives the most useful information in the most efficient manner. Also, some techniques may be more suitable than others for analysis by highly efficient, automatic data-handling systems. This section reviews some of the more important techniques, noting their most prominent problems or useful features.

NOTATION SYSTEMS

Different notation systems share two common problems. First, most of them require carefully trained and skilled observers, and even then most are highly time consuming. Second, each notation system inevitably selects some features of behavior to study and ignores others. The kinds of information so laboriously obtained by different systems is thus different, and there is no way to determine *a priori* which system is most appropriate for a given application.

Context Analysis

The method of context analysis was formalized as a research method in 1956 at Palo Alto by Ray Birdwhistell, Gregory Bateson, and others (see the discussion of the structural approach in Chapter 8). It involves the observation of naturally occurring behaviors to discover "units" which occur in comparable contexts and whose presence or absence causes comparable shifts in contexts. Potential units are abstracted from the behavior stream by assigning symbols to them; they are then studied in additional contexts to determine whether they are truly unitary.

An interesting example of this process is the analysis of the head nod in a listener or "auditor," which is described by Birdwhistell in Chapters 22 and 23 of *Kinesics and Context* (1970). From films, Birdwhistell noted that nods occurred singly and in sequences of from two to nine consecutive nods, and context analysis revealed at least three "stem forms" which appeared to have similar effects upon the exchange: the single nod (symbolized $//n//$); the double nod ($//nn//$); and the multiple nod of three or more nods ($//nnn//$). All of these occur in the auditor listening to a speaker. The single nod, $//n//$, appears to sustain the interaction without altering the speaker's behavior. The double nod at times appears to be interchangeable with $//n//$, but at other times appears to be associated with a change in vocalization, such as an increase or decrease in the rate of vocalizing, or an elaboration of a previously established point. The multiple nod, $//nnn//$, is associated with a more dramatic change: It is usually accompanied or followed by a vocal hesitation, a change in subject, or a gradual fading away of phonation.

Thus context analysis suggests that $//n//$, $//nn//$, and $//nnn//$ play different roles in the communication process. However, more research suggested that the *speed* as well as the number of nods is important. A "fast nod" of less than .4 second ($//n - .4//$) appears to act as a strong affirmation of the speaker's behavior by the auditor. In contrast, a "slow nod" of more than .8 second ($//n + .8//$) often interrupts the flow of vocalization: After an $//n + .8//$, one speaker stopped talking, shifted his stance, and said "I was only joking." The clocking of $//nn//$ and $//nnn//$, and the possible significance of the length of time *between* $//n//$'s, had not been analyzed at the time of writing. Similarly, the possible importance of different *degrees* of nodding had not been fully analyzed, although Birdwhistell suggested that nods covering between 5° and 15° of arc appear to be equivalent.

Studies of patient interviews by inexperienced therapists suggested that still another aspect of nodding is important: its rhythmicity. Apparently the "understanding nod" (i.e., $//n - .4//$) is treated as encouraging only when it occurs *in synchrony with the speaker's behavior* (i.e., at points of primary stress). It then appears to emphasize the interdependence of patient and therapist. If it occurs out of synchrony, the same nod may betray a lack of attention and involvement on the part of auditors: "beating time to the pulse of their own anxiety rather than to the rhythm of the patient's story" (Birdwhistell, 1970, p. 162). Birdwhistell calls this the "sore thumb nod."

It can be seen from this example that the context analysis procedure requires an extremely detailed and exhaustive analysis of behavior. It requires observers who are trained in the use of an complex symbol system which is itself undergoing change. It has been estimated that at the beginning of Birdwhistell's research, approximately 100 hours were required to analyze 1 second of behavior. This was reduced to 1 hour per second after a decade of work, but it still represents a considerable expenditure of time. Scheflen's analysis of a group psychotherapy transaction, *Communicational Structure* (1973), took a team of skilled observers nearly a decade to complete (Weitz, 1979).

Dance Notation Systems

Very different ways of analyzing body movement have been developed in conjunction with the dance, although these too require careful analysis by trained observers. The Eshkol–Wachmann system (1958) analyzes movement much as music is scored, with different body parts on different lines and duration marked on a horizontal axis. Laban's notational system, Labanotation, with its associated effort–shape analysis, describes movement according to the factors of space, force, time, and effort (Davis, 1979; Weitz, 1979). Both of these systems, and others, have been found to be useful to investigators studying body movement, although the "picture" of movement that they present is quite different from that produced by context analysis.

Martha Davis (1979) has summarized some of the examples of the application of the Laban notational system to nonverbal communication. For example, Davis and Weitz (1977, 1978) have studied the repertoire of movement styles which distinguish males and females who are engaged in same-sex and opposite-sex interactions. They found that the women in their sample oriented more directly to their partners; they assumed "narrower" positions and moved with smaller, more peripheral body parts (head, hands, feet); and they used more within-limb movements with breaks at the elbow, wrists, knuckles, and so forth. Men, in contrast, assumed "wider and larger" positions; moved with larger, grosser body movements (i.e., the whole arm as a unit with no breaks); and showed more periods of complete stillness. Men showed fewer differences in how they moved with men versus women; women, in contrast, showed more "lower-status" behaviors when with men (assuming smaller positions, more palm presenting) and moved in freer, more expansive, and more mutual ways when with women.

In another interesting application of dance notation, Schallert, Whishaw, Ramirez, and Teitelbaum (1978) have used the Eshkol–Wachmann system for the analysis of the disordered movement patterns resulting from brain lesions in rats. They found evidence that lesions in the dopaminergic systems associated with Parkinson's disease in humans produce a gait in rats which the dance notation system reveals to be analogous to the shuffling gait of humans with Parkinson's disease. This is one of the few instances in which the behavior changes resulting from physiological manipulations has been precisely defined according to a notation system which can be applied to different species.

Facial Expressions of Emotion

The most recent notation systems specifically designed for the analysis of facial expression are of two types: systems designed to indicate the presence of facial configurations associated with particular emotional states, and the more general Facial Action Coding System (FACS) of Ekman and Friesen (1976, 1978), which is designed to handle *any* facial movement.

The systems associated with particular emotional states both evolved from Tomkins's (1962, 1963) notion of primary affects. Ekman, Friesen, and Tomkins (1971) developed the Facial Affect Scoring Technique (FAST), which involves scoring expression in three facial areas: the eyebrow/forehead, the eyes/lids, and the lower face. An atlas of photographic examples defines expressions in each area which are theoretically associated with each of six primary affects: happiness, sadness, fear, anger, surprise, and disgust. Coders view each of the areas of a stimulus face separately and classify the expression according to the atlas. There are 8 criterion photographs of the eyebrow/forehead, 17 of the eyes/lids, and 45 of the lower face.

Since the criterion photographs are linked with the different emotions, these classifications can be translated into frequency and duration scores for each of the emotions in each of the facial regions. Thus the output of FAST involves scores for each of the primary affects separately for the three facial areas (Ekman *et al.*, 1971).

A second, and in many ways similar, system derived from Tomkins's theory is Izard's (1979b; Izard *et al.*, 1980) Maximally Discriminable Facial Movement Coding System (Max). Max specifies the theoretically expected patterns of facial movement associated with each of 10 discrete affect expressions: interest, surprise, joy, sadness, anger, fear, disgust, contempt, shame, and pain. These include the 9 fundamental emotions defined by Izard's (1971, 1977a) Differential Emotions Theory, plus pain. Max describes and illustrates 27 appearance changes or facial movement units which, in certain specified combinations, are associated with these emotions. The emotion-related movement patterns for each of the emotions are described verbally and illustrated by standardized photographs of the brow, eye, and lower face regions. The application of Max requires coders to determine the presence or absence of each of these 27 units in one area of the face at a time. Thus, coders in the Izard *et al.* (1980) study worked through slow-motion videotapes of the spontaneous expressions of infants three times, once for each facial area. The movements observed were then compared with the theoretically expected pattern for each of the 10 discrete affect expressions. Izard *et al.* (1980) demonstrated that untrained judges could employ the procedure reliably, and that brief training resulted in significant increases in accuracy.

The Facial Action Coding System

Ekman and Friesen (1976, 1978) have pointed out that techniques such as FAST and Max are relevant only to a particular type of behavior, in this case the facial movement patterns associated with emotion. With the FACS, they have attempted to develop a more comprehensive system which can measure *any* visually distinguishable facial movement. FACS was derived from an analysis of the anatomical, muscular basis of facial movement. From long practice, Ekman and Friesen learned to control separately the muscles in their own faces, and photographed the resulting changes. This resulted in the definition of 24 action units (AUs) which could be distinguished accurately from the appearance changes associated with the firing of one to three muscles, and 19 more AUs which are less finely described and which may involve nonfacial muscles. Each AU is described in terms of its muscular basis, photographs of the associated appearance changes, and instructions to the user on how to produce the movement. All possible combinations of two AUs were similarly determined and described, and combinations of three and four AUs and more complex combinations were included if it seemed that they resulted in a distinctive facial movement. In total, between 4000 and 5000 facial patterns were produced and examined.

The user of FACS must become thoroughly familiar with the anatomical basis of the procedure. A self-instructional manual describes the single AUs, more than 43 combinations, and a variety of head- and eye-position descriptors. Photographs and films are available to illustrate each of these. Also, scoring systems and materials for dealing with more subtle combinations of AUs are provided, as are step-by-step instructions and practice materials. It reportedly requires approximately 40 hours to learn to score with satisfactory reliability.

Obviously, FACS is an elaborate, complex, and detailed system. Its great advantage is that it is designed to deal with any facial movement, and can thus handle the facial actions described by other systems as well as many that are not considered by others. Its major disadvantage involves this very complexity, requiring much time and training, and, therefore, cost.

THE SEGMENTATION TECHNIQUE

The segmentation technique derives from the work of Dickman (1963). It has recently been adapted to the study of perception and attribution by Newtson and his colleagues (Newtson, 1976; Newtson, Engquist, & Bois, 1977), and to the study of spontaneous emotional expression by Reuben Baron and myself (Buck, Baron, & Barrette, 1982; Buck, Baron, Goodman, & Shapiro, 1980).

The technique is deceptively simple. Observers are shown a film of a behavior sequence of some sort and instructed to press a button when, in their opinion, "something meaningful" occurs. The resulting data are illustrated in Figure 5.3. At the top of the figure are the "raw data" as they appear from an event recorder, with a one-impulse/ second timing track at the top which locates events on the film.

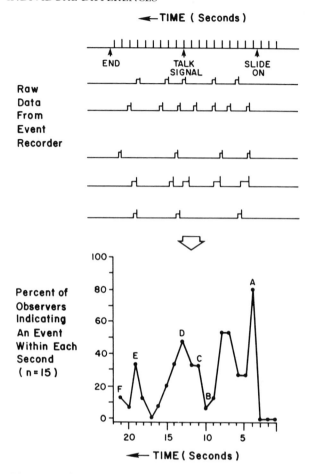

Figure 5.3. Segmentation record of reactions to an unpleasant slide.

Below is a representation of these data when they are averaged with the responses of other observers. One can see that there are "peaks" at points A, D, and E where observers agree that "something meaningful" has occurred.

The decision as to what is meaningful is largely left to the observer, although they can be instructed to break up behavior into large or small units by giving different examples of what is expected, and they can be oriented to attend to different kinds of events, for example, to actions versus emotions (Goodman, 1980). The important thing is that observers generally show a high degree of agreement about the location of "meaningful" points, however they may be defined. Newtson has shown that these consensually defined points of agreement correspond to "high information points" in the behavior stream that are particularly revealing of whatever it is that the observer has been instructed to attend to.

Buck *et al.* (1980, 1982) have applied the segmentation technique to the analysis of films of spontaneous facial behavior taken while subjects viewed emotionally loaded slides. In the first study, observers watching the films in large groups were asked to indicate by a pencil mark whenever a "meaningful" event occurred: "Mark off the behavior of the persons you'll be seeing into whatever units seem natural and meaningful to you. There are no right or wrong ways to do this: I just want to see how *you* do it" (Buck *et al.*, 1980, p. 524). With this procedure, it was impossible to tell exactly *when* the observer made the mark. Thus, it was possible only to count the number of marks, or *segmentation points*, associated with each of the videotaped sequences.

In the second study, observers viewed one of the same films viewed in the first study, but this time they were given buttons connected to an event recorder so that the temporal pattern of the segmentation points as well as their number could be assessed. This allowed the determination of a number of potentially useful measures of the temporal organization of spontaneous behavior: (1) the number of segmentation points, as in the first study; (2) the number of consensual segmentation points (CPs), where a CP is defined as a 1-second period which received more than 1 standard deviation over the mean number of segmentation points per second that is given to the sequence; (3) the percentage of CPs that are associated with facial expressions by a new group of observers who are shown the film and told where the CPs occur; the latter observers are asked, when told that a CP has occurred, to "judge whether it is based upon a facial expression on the part of the sender, or something else (e.g., a hand movement, shake of the head, change in posture)" (Buck *et al.*, 1982, p. 510); and (4) the consistency of which segmentation points are indicated within the sequence, defined in terms of the interrater reliability of the matrix of button presses to that sequence as indexed by coefficient alpha.

The conceptual variables associated with each of these variables are summarized in Table 5.1. The number of segmentation points should be a measure of the total amount of the behavior in question which is found in the stimulus; the number of CPs should correspond to the number of such behaviors that observers agree upon; the

Table 5.1. Conceptual Variables Associated with the Segmentation Measures

Measure and operational definition	Conceptual variable
1. Number of segmentation points (Number of button presses)	Total amount of the behavior in question
2. Number of consensual points (CPs) (Number of points that receive more than 1 standard deviation over the mean number of button presses)	The number of examples of the behavior in question that observers consensually agree upon
3. Percentage of facial expressions at CPs (Percentage of observers judging that a facial expression occurred at CPs)	The degree to which facial expressions are important in determining the occurrence of the behavior in question
4. Interrater reliability of segmentation points (Coefficient alpha of the matrix of button presses over time by observers)	The general degree to which observers agree on the location in the behavior stream of points showing the behavior in question (*Note:* in part a function of the number of such points)

percentage of CPs that are associated with facial expressions should give an indication of the extent to which such behavior is based upon facial expression as opposed to other expressive movements; the interrater reliability of the segmentation points is an index of the degree to which the observers agree on the location in the behavior stream of the behavior in question. These measures are not necessarily independent of one another, either mathematically or conceptually (cf. Buck *et al.*, 1980, 1982).

It might be noted that the measure involving the number of segmentation points showed a high level of reliability between the two studies. The average correlation between the number of points indicated for the different sequences in the two studies was $+.79$ ($p < .001$), which, considering the complexity of the behavior being segmented, seems highly satisfactory.

EVALUATION

The segmentation technique has a number of advantages. It is fast, it seems to be reliable, it can be used with untrained observers, and as we shall see in Chapter 7 it can be used to study the ways that observers perceptually organize spontaneous emotional displays. Also, it is readily amenable to analysis by efficient data-handling systems. The event indicators of the observers and a timing track on the film may be entered directly into a computer and processed on line. Also, the segmentation technique may be particularly valuable as a way to make the notation systems described above more efficient. By showing *where* observers indicate that important facial expressions and other behaviors occur, the segmentation technique can guide the analysis by the notation systems, so that only events at CPs might be subjected to analysis by the notation system.

SENDING ACCURACY

A number of studies have studied sending accuracy via spontaneous behavior, investigating among other things the relationships between spontaneous and posed expressiveness and between sending accuracy and receiving ability; sex and personality differences in sending accuracy, the relationships between sending accuracy and physiological responding, and the facilitating or inhibiting effects of the social context upon spontaneous sending accuracy.

SPONTANEOUS VERSUS POSED EXPRESSIVENESS

Studies have generally shown low but positive relationships between spontaneous expressiveness and posing ability, at least within a particular channel of expression. Thus, Buck (1975) found that spontaneously expressive preschoolers tended also to be rated as showing "more appropriate" expressions when asked to pose the facial expressions associated with the primary affects, and Zuckerman *et al.* (1976) and Cunningham (1977) found significant positive correlations between the ability to pose and spontaneous sending accuracy.

SENDING ACCURACY VERSUS RECEIVING ABILITY

Studies of the relationships between sending accuracy and receiving ability have been highly variable and inconclusive. This is in contrast to many of the relationships that we shall encounter between sending accuracy and other variables, which on the whole have shown remarkably consistent results from study to study.

Early studies on animals and humans found negative relationships between sending accuracy and receiving ability (Lanzetta &

Kleck, 1970; Miller *et al.*, 1966). However, the first attempts to systematically investigate this relationship in humans, carried out by Miron Zuckerman and his colleagues, found evidence of positive relationships (Zuckerman, Lipets, Koivumaki, & Rosenthal, 1975; Zuckerman *et al.*, 1976, 1979a, 1979b). Combining this result with the evidence of positive relationships between spontaneous and posed sending, Zuckerman *et al.* (1979b) suggested that the results support the notion of "general communication factors" which may "account for encoding and decoding in more than one communication mode. They also raise the possibility that posing and spontaneous behavior can be used interchangeably in experimental tasks (Zuckerman *et al.*, 1979b, p. 714)."

However, other studies did not confirm this finding of a positive relationship between sending accuracy and receiving ability. For example, Harper, Wiens, and Matarazzo (1979) found no significant relationship between sending accuracy and receiving ability, and suggested that "the process of nonverbal decoding and the encoding–decoding relationship is a phenomenon of much complexity which (studies) have only begun to address" (p. 190). Alper, Buck, and Dreyer (1978) found a positive relationship between sending accuracy and one measure of receiving ability (decoding posed photographs) and a negative relationship with another (decoding videotapes of spontaneous expressions). In a stem-and-leaf plot summarizing 17 studies relating sending and receiving abilities, DePaulo and Rosenthal (1979b) conclude that there is a median correlation between these variables of +.16, but that the range is from +.65 to −.80.

In general, the evidence suggests that nonverbal receiving ability is a more complex phenomenon than it first appears, and that its relationship with sending accuracy varies with a number of unknown factors. If "general communication factors" indeed exist, they must be influenced by a wide variety of other variables which are not yet understood. We shall discuss the issue and implications of the complexity of nonverbal receiving ability in Chapter 7.

SOCIAL FACTORS AND EXPRESSIVENESS

A new, but potentially rich and important area of investigation involves the impact of social factors on spontaneous expression. Most studies have attempted to avoid the "contamination" of spontaneous expression by social factors by using hidden cameras, making the subject feel that he or she was alone (Buck *et al.*, 1972, 1974). The importance of this procedure was demonstrated in a study by Kleck, Vaughan, Cartwright-Smith, Vaughan, Colby, and Lanzetta (1976) in which subjects were told that they were being observed in some conditions. Subjects who knew that they were being observed were significantly less expressive than subjects who did not.

Relatively few studies have been done in this area, but most have agreed that the known presence of an observer has a detrimental effect upon expressiveness. For example, Yarczower, Kilbride, and Hill (1979) found that, in the presence of an adult examiner, pre-school children were poorer in their posing of expressions, particularly "socially unacceptable" expressions such as anger and fear, than were children who posed alone. Kilbride and Yarczower (1980) found that such "social inhibition" increased with age in samples of U.S. children from ages 6-7 to ages 9-10, while there was no age change in a sample of Zambian children.

Regarding studies of spontaneous expressiveness, Yarczower and Daruns (1982) have reported social inhibition in groups of first and sixth graders. Children viewed affective slides either in the presence of a male and female experimenter or alone. They were rated as less expressive, and observers reported more uncertainty about their expressions, when they were with others. Also, Kraut (1982) has found evidence of the social inhibition of spontaneous expression in a study where pleasant and unpleasant smells constituted the affective stimuli. Senders in the presence of another naïve subject (who could not see them) tended to be lower in their spontaneous communication of whether smells were pleasant or unpleasant. Finally, Blumberg, Solomon, and Perloe (1981) have found that the presence of a male experimenter inhibited spontaneous expressions of "tenderness" in male but not female subjects. Male and female senders watched "cute" videotaped sequences of babies and puppies while alone versus while with a male experimenter. Judges viewing their facial expressions judged the reactions of male senders significantly less accurately in the latter condition, while the accuracy of their judgments of female senders was not affected by the experimenter's presence.

These studies have generally interpreted their results in terms of the influence of inhibitory display rules, suggesting that the presence of an observer causes the sender to suppress his or her spontaneous expression. However, it is theoretically possible for *facilitatory* display rules to increase expressiveness as well: Under some circumstances one is expected to show how one feels, even to overstate the extent of feelings (Ekman & Friesen, 1975). The studies done to date have used social settings which would seem to encourage masking. The "others" involved have been of different role and status in the situation compared to the subject, and they have not shared the emotional stimulus with the subject. It seems possible to construct a situation in which the presence of another would not interfere with spontaneous expressiveness. My studies of expressiveness in nursery-school-aged children employed an experimenter who sat beside the child, watching the slides. This proved more satisfactory than leaving these young children alone, and as discussed below the resulting measures of sending accuracy have encouraging evidence of validity (Buck, 1975, 1977). The experimenter involved was given specific training in (1) having an "icebreaking" conversation before the slides were shown; (2) watching the slide while it was on (rather than the child); (3) initiating interaction with the child in a strictly controlled way, but being free to respond naturally to any interaction initiated by the child; and (4) expecting and respecting individual differences in expressiveness between children (cf. Buck, 1978).

Losow (1981) has found possible evidence that the presence of others can have a facilitating effect upon spontaneous external expression. He ran females in the slide-viewing technique individually and in pairs, asking them both to discuss their feelings about the slides. Observers viewing the subjects (before they began to speak) were more accurate in judging the type of slide viewed by the groups than by the individuals. This was particularly true for sexual slides, a category in which previous studies showed that females exhibit relatively little expression. The analysis of the Losow study is as yet incomplete: Thus far the observers have seen both senders in the dyad, thus they have been exposed to two individuals rather than one. This could account for the greater sending accuracy of the dyads. However, inspection of the videotape suggests that the presence of the other can increase facial/gestural expressiveness in many cases, and additional observations are being planned to demonstrate this.

It should be noted that, in the Losow study, the "other" is a similar person to the subject (a female undergraduate), and is in a similar situation (watching affective slides in an experiment). Studies by Schachter (1959) and others have suggested that such similarity affects the tendencies to choose to affiliate with others under stress, and the stress-reducing power of the other (cf. Buck & Parke, 1972).

It would be interesting if such variables also mediate the effects of others' presence upon spontaneous emotional expression.

In general, it appears that measures of expressiveness in the presence of others may provide a sensitive indicator of important social processes. As one example, it may relate to the extensive literature in self-monitoring, in that individuals high in self-monitoring are presumed to be better able to manage their expressions relative to the social situation (Snyder, 1974, 1979).

GENDER DIFFERENCES IN EXPRESSIVENESS

One of the most interesting findings in the literature of spontaneous expressiveness is that adult women are generally more expressive than men in the slide-viewing technique. This result was found by Buck *et al.*, (1972, 1974), and has been replicated by Gallagher and Shuntich (1981), Fugita, Harper, and Wiens (1980), and Manstead, MacDonald, and Wagner (1982), although Zuckerman *et al.* (1976) found only a nonsignificant advantage for female senders.

Buck *et al.* (1980, 1982) subjected videotapes taken in previous studies to analysis via the segmentation technique, to determine more about the ways in which the facial/gestural behaviors of males and females differ. These studies suggest that, while the slide is on but before the subject discusses his or her feelings about it, (1) women show more facial/gestural behavior than men, (2) women show more CPs than observers agree is "meaningful," (3) CPs are more likely to involve facial expressions among females than males, and (4) receivers show greater consensus about the location of meaningful points in females than in males.

Data from the Buck *et al.* (1982) study are presented in Figure 5.4, which illustrates several relevant phenomena. First, it indicates that "peaks" of segmentation points were elicited about 3 to 4 seconds after slides onset, suggesting a latency of facial/gestural expression that is roughly similar to the latency of autonomic responding to a stimulus. Second, it shows that female senders elicited more segmentation points than males during the slide period but not the talk period, where there is no significant overall sex difference in the number of segmentation points. Third, it illustrates an interaction between the sex of the sender and the type of slide. Males tended to elicit more segmentation points on the sexual and unusual slides,

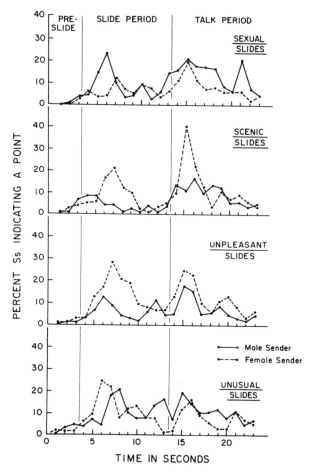

Figure 5.4. Segmentation patterns for male and female senders to different slide categories. From Figure 3 in "The Temporal Organization of Spontaneous Nonverbal Expression: A Segmentation Analysis" by R. Buck and D. Barrette, *Journal of Personality and Social Psychology*, 1982, *42*, 506–517. Copyright 1982 by the American Psychological Association. Reprinted by permission.

while females were segmented more finely on the scenic and unpleasant slides.

The Buck *et al.* (1980, 1982) studies also found interesting gender differences in the relationships between sending accuracy and the number of segmentation points elicited by the senders. The 1980 study found that sending accuracy was positively and significantly correlated with the number of segmentation points elicited from female senders, both with adults and (albeit at a marginal level of significance) with children. This was not the case with males (see Table 5.2). The later study found that events in the slide period, but not the talk period, were significantly correlated with sending accuracy, and that different segmentation measures were relevant in male and female senders. Among females, sending accuracy was related to both the number of segmentation points and the number of CPs elicited during the slide period. Among males, sending accuracy was related to the percent of CPs judged to involve facial expressions.

These results suggest that sending accuracy is based upon spontaneous behaviors occurring during the slide period as opposed to symbolic "conversational" behaviors associated with discussing the slides. They also suggest that sending accuracy is based upon different sorts of behavior in males and females. For females, the amount of facial/gestural activity that observers consider "meaningful" is related to sending accuracy. For males, this is not the case. Instead, the extent to which these "meaningful" behaviors involve facial expression is related to sending accuracy in males.

It thus appears that there are fundamental differences in sending accuracy in females and males, which involve qualitative as well as quantitative differences. It is not simply the amount of facial/gestural behavior that seems to be important, but the relationships between

Table 5.2. Correlations between Sending Accuracy and Segmentation Measures

	Female senders	Male senders
Data from Buck, Baron, Goodman, & Shapiro (1980)		
Adults (number of segmentation points)	$+.69^{***}$	$+.05$
Preschool children (number of segmentation points)	$+.54^{*}$	$+.09$
Data from Buck, Baron, & Barrette (1982)		
Slide period		
Number of segmentation points	$+.57^{**}$	$+.35$
Number of consensual points (CPs)	$+.57^{**}$	$+.26$
Percentage of CPs judged to be facial expressions	$-.40$	$+.68^{***}$
Talk period		
Number of segmentation points	$-.16$	$-.06$
Number of consensual points (CPs)	$+.02$	$-.28$
Percentage of CPs judged to be facial expressions	$+.01$	$+.36$

$^{*}p < .10.$
$^{**}p < .025.$
$^{***}p < .005.$

those behaviors and sending accuracy also differ. We shall see in Chapter 7 that this appears to be true of receiving ability as well. The explanation for this phenomenon is not yet clear, although as we shall see, there is evidence that sex-role-related social learning experiences play an important part in this difference.

PERSONALITY DIFFERENCES IN EXPRESSIVENESS

A variety of personality measures have been related to spontaneous sending accuracy. Due to the known gender difference discussed above, it is important that such relationships be assessed separately for male and female senders. In this section we shall review some of the most important of these personality differences.

Verbal Expressiveness

One factor that has reliably been related to sending accuracy is the expressiveness with which the sender verbally describes his or her emotional experience to the slide or film which elicits the expression. Buck *et al.* (1974) demonstrated that subjects who showed an "externalizing" mode of response (high sending accuracy and low electrodermal responding) also tended to describe their emotional response in a "personal" way, referring both to themselves and a feeling ("The picture makes me feel calm, pleasant, and happy inside."). In contrast, those showing an "internalizing" mode of response tends to describe their reaction more impersonally, not referring to themselves and often simply describing the content of the slide ("The picture doesn't make a strong impact. It's nice to look at, especially the lake."). This positive relationship between spontaneous sending accuracy and a personal description of the affective stimulus (termed "verbal involvement") has been replicated by Zuckerman and his colleagues in several studies (Zuckerman *et al.*, 1976, 1979a, 1979b).

Personality Correlates

The literature on personality correlates of spontaneous sending accuracy is somewhat scattered and inconclusive, which might be expected given the different techniques used to measure sending accuracy in various studies, and also the rather suspect nature of many of the personality measures, particularly those that are based on self-reports. However, some consistent results have emerged, enough at least to suggest areas of future investigation.

One of the most intriguing and potentially meaningful areas of research involves the relationship between sending accuracy and field dependence/independence. This is an important area because there is evidence that both sending accuracy and psychological differentiation may be related to cerebral lateralization: Thus field dependence has been linked to a lack of psychological differentiation, and, in turn, relatively low hemispheric specialization (cf. Witkin, Goodenough, & Oltman, 1979). Several studies have suggested that facially expressive males are more field dependent, but results for females have been contradictory. In male subjects, Harper *et al.* (1979) found facial expressiveness to be positively related to field dependence and also to the Wechsler Adult Intelligence Scale (WAIS) performance IQ, which has also been related to cerebral lateralization. Sabatelli, Dreyer, and Buck (1979) also found positive correlations between field dependence and facial expressiveness in both males and females, and Alper *et al.* (1978) found field dependence to be positively correlated with posing ability in preschool children, although the correlation with spontaneous sending accuracy did not attain significance. On the other hand, Shennum (1976) found evidence in adult females that spontaneously expressive subjects were more field independent. Also, Sabatelli, Dreyer, and Buck (1983b) have recently found field independence to be positively correlated with spontaneous expressions in females ($r = .35, p < .005$), with a zero-order correlation for males ($r = -.04$). Thus, it appears that the relationship between field dependence/independence and expressiveness varies with sex, but obviously more research is necessary before these relationships are fully understood.

Another measure that has been linked to spontaneous facial expressiveness is extraversion. Buck *et al.* (1972, 1974) found evidence that expressive subjects were higher on the Eysenck extraversion–introversion (E–I) scale. However, more recent studies employing male subjects have not found significant relationships between sending accuracy and the E–I scale (Harper *et al.*, 1979; Notarius & Levenson, 1979). Harper and his colleagues noted that several items of the Gough Adjective Check List, which were positively related to spontaneous sending accuracy, appear to describe qualities usually ascribed to extraverts (e.g., dominance, self-confidence, and heterosexual orientation). The reason for this disagreement in these findings is not clear, although one possibility to be considered is that the items of the E–I scale are becoming dated and therefore less reliable as indicators of extraversion.

Other personality variables which have been associated with spontaneous sending accuracy include depression, which has been associated with low sending accuracy (Gerson & Perlman, 1979; Prkachin, Craig, Papageorgis, & Reith, 1977); empathic tendencies, which have been related to high sending accuracy (Notarius & Levenson, 1979); and self-esteem, which has been positively related to sending accuracy in some studies (Buck *et al.*, 1974; Harper *et al.*, 1979), but not others (Notarius & Levenson, 1979).

Whereas attempts to relate spontaneous sending accuracy to existing personality measures have met with mixed success, attempts to construct psychometric measures of expressiveness have been more successful and have thus far shown remarkable consistency. These measures are considered below.

EXPRESSIVENESS AND PSYCHOPHYSIOLOGICAL MEASURES

The Externalizing–Internalizing Distinction

The question of the relationship between spontaneous sending accuracy and psychophysiological measures of autonomic responding has attracted considerable attention. A number of early studies using variants of the Miller paradigm found negative relationships between sending accuracy and physiological measures (skin-conductance responding and heart rate; cf. Buck, 1977, 1979a; Buck *et al.*, 1969, 1972, 1974; Lanzetta & Kleck, 1970; Miller, 1974). These findings were related to observations with a long history in the literature on electrodermal responding which suggested that "the greater the visible signs of emotion . . . the less the response on the galvanometer" (Prideaux, 1920, p. 66). The specific distinction between externalizing and internalizing patterns of emotional expression was first made by H. E. Jones in the course of his investigations of the development of electrodermal responding. The *externalizing* mode of response involves high overt expression but low electrodermal responding, while the *internalizing* response involves the opposite pattern (Jones, 1935). Figure 5.5 presents data from the Buck *et al.* (1972) study, labeled using Jones's terminology.

Jones's Theory

Studies of electrodermal responding in infants had found that few such response could be elicited, and many had concluded that some part of the sympathetic nervous system underlying the response was immature at this age. However, Jones (1930) found that such responses could be obtained from infants if disturbing or unpleasant stimuli were used. However, their threshold was higher and the response smaller than it was in older children. Also, Jones noted that electrodermal responding tended to decrease if the infant showed external signs of disturbance, such as crying. He hypothesized that

Figure 5.5. Relationship between communication accuracy and sender's skin-conductance response. From Figure 2 in "Nonverbal Communication of Affect in Humans" by R. Buck, V. Savin, R. E. Miller, and W. F. Caul, *Journal of Personality and Social Psychology*, 1972, 23, 362–371. Copyright 1972 by the American Psychological Association. Reprinted by permission.

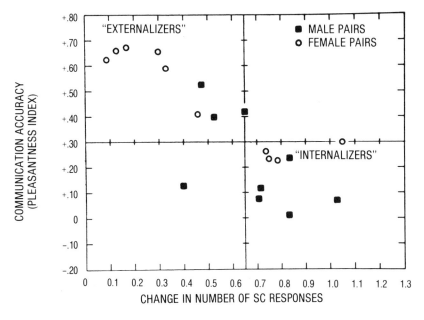

the increase in electrodermal responding with age may be related to the increased tendency to control the overt display of emotion as the child grows: "In older children, the increase in inhibition and apparent emotional control may not imply a diminished emotionality but merely a shift from outer to inner patterns of response" (Jones, 1950, p. 161). Unfortunately, Jones was not able to specify the mechanism by which this shift takes place.

Jones then studied preschool and nursery-school-aged children, presenting them with such stimuli as a buzzer, a live rat, and a dental examination, while electrodermal measures were taken and two observers rated the child's overt (vocal, facial, and bodily) response. The results indicated that, with some children, consistent patterns of physiological and overt responding could be demonstrated:

> These patterns are of at least three sorts, as represented by the "externalizer," who displays a somewhat infantile pattern of marked overt but reduced or infrequent galvanic responses; the "internalizer," who reverses this relationship; and the "generalizer," who tends to respond with a total discharge both overt and internal. There was also evidence in a few cases of what might be termed a compensating or reciprocal type of response. Such individuals exhibited marked overt and marked galvanic responses, but not on the same stimuli; their emotional expression tended to be selective, so that a heightened discharge in one direction was accompanied by a reduced discharge in the other. (Jones, 1950, p. 163)

Thus, for everyone except the generalizer, an overt response was associated with a reduced electrodermal response.

From the overall pattern of findings, Jones suggested that the infant naturally tends to show an externalizing mode of response, but that as the infant grows, "overt emotional expression tends to bring disapproval and punishment rather than succorance" (1960, p. 14), while the less accessible physiological responses are not disapproved or inhibited. Thus Jones feels that the negative relationship between overt and physiological responses are based upon inhibitory social learning experiences. He also suggests that the externalizing mode of response is "infantile" and less satisfactory than the internalizing mode of response.

The latter notion is based in part upon Jones's studies of high and low electrodermal reactors among adolescents aged 11 to 18. Of 100 subjects, Jones compared the 20 who showed the largest electrodermal responses with the 20 who showed the smallest on ratings made by classmates and by psychologists. He found that the high reactors were rated favorably on a variety of social characteristics: They were judged as being calm, poised, good natured, cooperative, and responsible. They also were rated as being emotionally controlled, quiet, reserved, and deliberative. In contrast, the low reactors were rated as having apparently maladaptive social characteristics (being assertive, attention-seeking, and bossy), and as showing an uninhibited expressiveness (being impulsive, active, talkative, and animated). Jones concluded that the pattern of response manifested by the low electrodermal reactors was infantile and maladaptive.

Jones's conclusion makes an interesting contrast with the evaluation of externalizing and internalizing modes of response made in a later study by Block (1957). Block studied psychologists' evaluations of 20 high and 20 low electrodermal reactors from a sample of 70 medical school applicants. In this study, it was the high electrodermal reactors who were judged as having "maladaptive" patterns of response—they were seen to be "withdrawing, worrying individuals who turn their anxieties toward inward routes of expression"—while low electrodermal reactors were seen to be "independent, aggressively direct, and relatively nonconforming" (Block, 1957, p. 13).

It can be seen that the actual behaviors exhibited by the high and low electrodermal reactors in the Jones and Block studies appear in fact to be quite similar: The high reactors were seen to be reserved and responsible, the low reactors to be impulsive and assertive. The difference is in the evaluation of these behaviors: Impulsive and assertive behavior was seen to be infantile and maladaptive when exhibited by an adolescent, but was seen as evidence of independence and "aggressive directness" when manifested by a medical school applicant; the cooperative and responsible behavior of the adolescent becomes in a medical school applicant evidence of a worrying submissiveness (cf. Buck, 1979a).

Recent Studies

Several investigators have reported difficulty in replicating the finding of a negative relationship between expressiveness and physiological responding (i.e., Winton, Putnam, & Krauss, 1979; Zuckerman, 1980), so that the relationship between these variables is not as robust as one might prefer, and it may be that there are moderating variables present which are not as yet understood. However, other studies have reported results consistent with the externalizing–internalizing distinction, and perhaps more importantly the externalizing–internalizing distinction allows us to make contact with an important and wide-ranging literature on general mechanisms of behavioral inhibition and expression.

Perhaps the most important of the recent studies which have found results consistent with the externalizing–internalizing distinction is the finding by Tiffany Field and her colleagues that facially expressive newborns show evidence of lower arousal on heart rate measures than do less expressive infants (Field, 1982; Field & Walden, 1982). Field and her colleagues have demonstrated that human neonates (average age, 36 hours) can discriminate happy, sad, and surprised expressions posed by a model, as evidenced by the infants' imitations of those expressions (Field, Woodson, Greenberg, & Cohen, 1982). Figure 5.6 shows sample photographs of a model's expressions and the corresponding expressions of an infant. Considerable individual variation was found in the expressiveness of neonates, and the more expressive infants showed lower mean heart rates and greater heart-rate variability during sleep and auditory stimulation, compared with less expressive infants (Field, 1982; Field & Walden, 1982). These results are particularly important because they bring into question the suggestion that the negative relationship between overt expression and physiological responding is based only upon social learning, and suggest that temperamental factors may be important as well. They constitute the first direct evidence that externalizing–internalizing modes of response can be detected before socialization has had a significant chance to operate.

Other recent studies relevant to the externalizing–internalizing distinction include a demonstration by Vaughan and Lanzetta (1980) of a negative relationship between unconditioned skin-conductance responding and measures of facial muscle activation presumed to reflect facial expressiveness. Also, Notarius and Levenson (1979) chose 23 "natural expressors" and 22 "natural inhibitors" on the basis of the spontaneous facial expressions of male subjects to a stressful film. They then exposed them to a shock threat, and demonstrated that the inhibitors were less expressive and more physiologically reactive on heart-rate and respiration measures than the expressor group. The result for the change in skin-conductance level, while in the same direction, did not attain significance. This study suggests

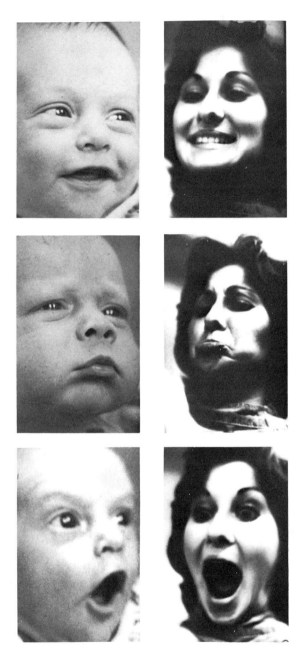

Figure 5.6. Sample photographs of model's happy, sad, and surprised expressions and infant's corresponding expression. From Figure 11-1 in "Individual Differences in the Expressivity of Neonates and Young Infants" by T. Field, in R. W. Feldman (Ed.), *Development of Nonverbal Behavior in Children*, New York: Springer Verlag, 1982. Reprinted by permission.

that the negative relationship between overt expression and physio-logical responses can be demonstrated across different situations. Interestingly, it also showed that the resting level of heart-rate was higher among expressors, while the resting level of skin-conductance was higher among inhibitors.

In another recent study, Notarius and his colleagues (1982) exposed female subjects to an interpersonal stressor (an experimenter angry at them for their work) while heart-rate measures were taken and facial expressions surreptitiously videotaped. After a 5-minute "stew" period but before the deception was revealed, the subjects rated their feelings, and after the study was fully explained they rated the degree of threat they experienced. Minimally expressive subjects displayed larger heart-rate responses and reported experiencing more guilt and threat, compared with expressive subjects. Notarius *et al.* (1982) suggest that the pattern of results is consistent with the externalizing–internalizing distinction and inconsistent with the facial feedback hypothesis (see Chapter 2).

It is instructive to compare these results with another recent study which, on first glance, seems contrary to the externalizing–internalizing distinction. Newlin (1981) studied a variety of autonomic nervous system responses to stressful tasks among right-handed male subjects. As in the Notarius *et al.* (1982) study, one of the tasks involved criticism by the experimenter: "Most people do it about twice that fast. Try to do it faster next time." Following the stressful tasks, questionnaires were administered orally by the experimenter. Subjects were categorized as "left or right movers" from observations of their lateral eye movements during the questionnaire—this would theoretically relate to "right hemisphericity" versus "left hemispheri-city," respectively. In addition, subjects were classified as facially expressive or not expressive during the administration of the ques-tionnaires. Results indicated that "right hemisphericity" subjects were marginally more expressive, and that "left hemisphericity" subjects showed larger autonomic responses to the stressful tasks. This is consistent with the notion developed in Chapter 3, that left-hemisphere functioning is associated with an inhibitory process involving low facial expressiveness and high autonomic activity.

However, Newlin also found a *positive* relationship between facial expressiveness and autonomic nervous system responding. Newlin interprets the latter finding as contrary to the externalizing–internalizing distinction, and suggests that procedural differences may account for the disagreement: His study measured facial expression during interaction, and no stressor was present during the actual assessment of facial expression. Both of these considerations would tend to insure that, in our terms, symbolic rather than spontaneous facial expressions occurred. To this it might be added that the fact that part of the stress involved criticism by the experimenter would surely confound the latter measure of facial expressiveness while later interacting with the same experimenter. Subjects who were particularly upset by the criticism might later try to ingratiate themselves, which might well involve greater facial expression. Also, it is conceivable that subjects who reacted with considerable facial expression *during the actual criticism* were relatively *unexpressive* during the interaction with the experimenter. Their lack of expression might reflect their *present* emotional state of shame and annoyance in the presence of the experimenter. The Notarius *et al.* (1982) study avoided such problems by assessing facial expression during the actual criticism, and by employing a different experimenter in the later phases of the study.

Inhibition versus Display Rules

The notion of externalizing versus internalizing modes of response implies the operation of an inhibitory influence upon spontaneous sending accuracy which is different from the influence of the display rules noted above. In Chapter 2 we presented Ekman and Friesen's (1969a) model of the sending process in which spontaneous tendencies toward expression are influenced by display rules, which are symbolic in nature (see Figure 2.1). The inhibitory process involved in internalizing and externalizing response modes do not, however, appear to be symbolic in the same sense, since they operate even in nonsocial situations when there would be no reason to employ display rules. We shall speak of these as processes of *inhibition*, as opposed to the alterations of the spontaneous display via display rules, which we shall call *deception*. These processes shall be examined in detail in the next chapter.

SUMMARY

We have considered a number of aspects of sending accuracy. In general it appears that evidence relating to sex and personality differences in expressiveness, and the relationship between expressiveness and psychophysiological measures, together suggest that spontaneous sending accuracy is a relatively stable individual characteristic of major importance. In addition, studies of social effects on expressiveness may provide a useful new paradigm for the study of the social determinants of display management.

We shall return to the notion of externalizing versus internalizing modes of response in the next chapter, when we consider the relationship of this distinction to other analyses of behavioral inhibition and expression, and consider the extensive literature on deception. For now, we shall consider studies relevant to the development of spontaneous sending accuracy, and attempts to develop paper-and-pencil measures of spontaneous expressiveness.

THE DEVELOPMENT OF SPONTANEOUS EXPRESSIVENESS

STUDIES IN CHILDREN

A number of studies have employed the slide-viewing technique to analyze facial/gestural expressiveness in young children, finding in general that slides elicit appropriate facial expressions in many children, although there are wide individual differences, with some children being quite expressive and others showing virtually no appropriate expression (cf. Buck, 1975, 1977). These studies have examined a variety of variables, including sex differences in expressiveness, differential tendencies to express different emotions, physiological responsiveness and overt expression in children, and the extent to which externalizing versus internalizing modes of response are based upon temperament or social learning.

Sex Differences

Several studies have analyzed sex differences in expressiveness in young children, with the hope that such studies will elucidate the basis of the female superiority in spontaneous expressiveness found in adults. Buck (1975, 1977) found evidence of a small sex difference in expressiveness in nursery-school-aged children which may increase with age: Undergraduate receivers were more accurate at guessing the type of slide viewed by girls as compared with boys, although there was no sex difference on another measure of sending accuracy. Neither study found a significant sex difference in sending accuracy when the child's mother was the receiver. This pattern of results was replicated in an unpublished study by Alper et al. (1978). Interestingly, Field (1982) did not find consistent sex differences in the expressiveness of neonates, and Yarczower and Daruns (1982) found no sex difference in a study of first- and sixth-grade children using the slide-viewing technique.

The Buck (1975, 1977) studies found evidence that sending accuracy may be negatively correlated with age among boys but not girls, suggesting that as boys get older they show less spontaneous facial/gestural expressiveness. This rather surprising finding has been replicated by Zuckerman and Przewuzman (1979), who report that in preschoolers, posing ability increases with age among girls but decreases among boys. Clearly the development of the sex difference in spontaneous expressiveness should be studied further, with effects due to factors such as the type of emotion and the social context systematically explored.

Type of Emotion

It was noted in the last chapter that Izard and his colleagues (1980), studying the spontaneous facial expressions of infants and young children to injections, found evidence that fearful and angry facial expressions do not appear in their youngest subjects. This may reflect the process of the maturation of the systems underlying these emotions.

There is evidence that older children are relatively less adept at posing negative emotions. A number of studies have found that children pose "socially acceptable" expressions such as happiness or surprise more easily than less acceptable expressions such as fear and anger (Buck, 1975; Field & Walden, 1982; Odom & Lemond, 1972; Yarczower et al., 1979). There is evidence that children (and adults) are more spontaneously expressive as well with more acceptable emotions (Buck & Duffy, 1980). It was noted above that Yarczower et al. (1979) found that this effect was particularly strong in the presence of an examiner who was requesting the expressions, suggesting that less acceptable expressions are particularly inhibited in the presence of an adult even when the adult is requesting the expressions. We noted above that the issue of the effects of the social context upon spontaneous expression is a potentially important new area of investigation, and it may be particularly interesting when applied to children.

Personality Measures

Buck (1975, 1977) constructed the Affect Expression Rating Scale (AERS) from the personality descriptions that Jones, Block, and others have found to distinguish high and low electrodermal reactors. The children were rated on this scale by their teachers in the nursery school, and these ratings were compared with the facial/gestural expressiveness of the children as measured in the laboratory. The results clearly showed that sending accuracy was positively related to characteristics previously found to distinguish low electrodermal reactors, such as activity level, the direct expression of hostility, having many friends, being impulsive, bossy, dominating, and "extraverted." Similarly, sending accuracy was negatively correlated with qualities previously associated with high electrodermal reactors, including being shy, emotionally inhibited, quiet and reserved, cooperative, and "introverted." The fact that the teachers' ratings correlated so highly with measures of facial/gestural expressiveness taken in the laboratory constitutes persuasive evidence of external validity for both of the measures.

The AERS has been used recently by Field and Walden (1982), who found that children scoring high on characteristics ascribed to low electrodermal reactors were better at posing expressions and also better at decoding posed expressions. Such children were also rated as being more spontaneously expressive during free play, and they were rated by their teachers as having more positive affect and being more popular among their peers.

Buck (1977) reported the results of a factor analysis of the AERS, which produced three easily interpreted factors in the varimax rotation. These were named as follows:

    I. *Expressive versus Inhibited:* involves items such as "Is an extravert," "Expresses feelings openly," and "Is quiet and reserved (−)."

    II. *Antagonistic versus Cooperative:* involves items such as "Is often difficult to get along with," "Is impulsive," "Is cooperative (−)," and "Often shows aggression."

III. *Independent versus Dependent:* involves items such as "Is independent of adults," and "Seeks reassurance from adults (—)."

These factors have been reproduced in the factor analysis of a version of the scale intended to be a self-report scale for adults (Buck, 1979a), and Hall and Halberstadt (1980) found the same factors in an application of part of the AERS scale.

Physiological Responding

Buck (1977) found evidence of a negative relationship between sending accuracy and skin-conductance responding in nursery-school-aged children that parallels the relationship found in adults. In addition, both sending accuracy and physiological responding were related in meaningful ways to the AERS measure. For example, among boys scores on the expressiveness factor were positively related to sending accuracy and negatively related to physiological responding, while among girls it was scores on the antagonism factor which were positively related to sending accuracy and negatively related to skin-conductance responding. Possibly this difference, like that between the Jones and Block studies, rests in the eye of the rater. Perhaps male and female children who are high in sending accuracy show similar behaviors in the nursery school, but the behaviors of the boys are seen as "expressive" while those of girls are seen as "antagonistic." In other words, for the same behavior a boy may be rated as "expressing himself openly" and a girl may be rated as being "hard to get along with."

Buck (1976a, 1977, 1979a) suggested that it is unlikely that the strong pattern of relationships between individual differences in sending accuracy, physiological responding, the teachers' ratings in such young children is based upon social learning experiences alone, and that innate temperamental factors may play a part as well. However, evidence for this proposition was based upon nursery-school-aged children, and it could be argued that early social learning experiences account for the results. However, as noted above, Field and Walden (1982) have recently demonstrated internalizing and externalizing response patterns in infants. These authors investigated the facial expressiveness and heart-rate responding of infants in a variety of situations (e.g., during sleep; during administration of the

Brazelton Neonatal Behavior Assessment Scale [Brazelton, 1973]; and during facial and auditory discrimination tasks). Infants who showed the greatest number of facial expressions showed a lessened cardiac responsiveness. The authors concluded that this pattern of individual differences in neonatal expression and responsivity parallels Jones's externalizing–internalizing distinction, and that it supports the notion of the importance of temperamental factors (Buck, 1977).

TEMPERAMENT VERSUS SOCIAL LEARNING

Based upon the pattern of results summarized above, Buck (1979a) suggested that sending accuracy is based upon both innate temperamental factors and social learning experiences, and that it may involve general neural mechanisms which are responsible for the inhibition versus the disinhibition or expression of a wide variety of behaviors. Specifically, it was suggested that a general mechanism could account for all of the findings we have considered if it had the following characteristics: (1) that early in life there are stable individual differences in the arousal and/or arousability of excitatory and inhibitory neural systems; (2) that learning experiences can result in situationally specific changes in these levels of activity; and (3) that activity in the inhibitory system relative to the excitatory system is associated with increased electrodermal responding and possibly other kinds of autonomic arousal (Buck, 1979a, p. 159).

This model is illustrated in Figure 5.7, which assumes four individuals, two male and two female. One female and male (A and B) show initial temperamental predispositions toward externalizing response patterns associated with high activity in the excitatory relative to the inhibitory response system. The other female and male (C and D) initially show internalizing response patterns. As they grow, these four individuals would tend to experience patterns of reward and punishment for overt emotional expression which, in our society, are sex linked. We assume that the occurrence of reward or punishment for emotional expression alters the relative balance of activity in the excitatory and inhibitory systems in similar situations in the future. Thus, being female, A and C tend to experience reward for general emotional expression, but are punished for being aggressive, while B and D experience the opposite patterns of reinforcement. The result is that, as adults, the females tend to show ex-

| NEURAL SYSTEM: | EXTERNALIZING TEMPERAMENT | | | | INTERNALIZING TEMPERAMENT | | | |
| | A (FEMALE) | | B (MALE) | | C (FEMALE) | | D (MALE) | |
	REW.	PUN.	REW.	PUN.	REW.	PUN.	REW.	PUN.
INITIAL STATE (AMOUNT OF AROUSAL/AROUSABILITY)	10	5	10	5	5	10	5	10
CHANGES IN GENERAL EMOTIONAL SITUATIONS	+5	−5	−5	+5	+5	−5	−5	+5
RESULTING ADULT PATTERN	15	0	5	10	10	5	0	15
CHANGES IN AGGRESSIVE SITUATIONS	−5	+5	+5	−5	−5	+5	+5	−5
RESULTING ADULT PATTERN	5	10	15	0	0	15	10	5

Figure 5.7. Example of the mutual role of innate temperamental factors and social learning in the determination of adult patterns of emotional expression. Hypothetical changes in the degree of initial arousal/arousability in "reward" and "punishment" systems caused by social learning.

ternalizing patterns of response in emotional situations, while males show externalizing patterns of response in aggressive situations, regardless of their initial temperament. However, it will be seen from Figure 5.7 that the initial temperament continues to affect adult behavior.

Field and Walden (1982) have proposed a "transactional" model in which the temperamental characteristics of the infant interact with the characteristics of the socializing environment to produce internalizing, externalizing, and generalizing modes of response in the child. The neural mechanism proposed here could serve as a physiological substrate for this model, and is also consistent with neurophysiological data concerning excitatory and inhibitory systems which we shall consider in the next chapter. As noted in the last chapter, such a mechanism may be considered to be a part of the "animal model" of emotion, as the mechanisms and phenomena involved may be seen in animals as well as humans.

SUMMARY

Studies of the development of spontaneous expression suggest that sex differences in adult expressiveness are based upon social learning, that the expression of negative emotions is more affected by inhibitory display rules than is the expression of positive emotions, and that stable relationships between spontaneous expressiveness and physiological responding can be demonstrated in very young children and even infants. The results are consistent with the notion that spontaneous expressiveness is based upon temperamental predispositions which can be altered by social learning.

PSYCHOMETRIC MEASURES OF SPONTANEOUS EXPRESSIVENESS

THE AFFECT EXPRESSION RATING SCALE

It will be recalled that the AERS was constructed from the attributes found by Jones, Block, and others to distinguish high versus low electrodermal reactors; it has successfully been related to spontaneous expressiveness in several studies employing nursery-school-aged children; it has been factor analyzed to reveal three independent factors (Expressiveness, Antagonism, and Independence); these factors have been revealed in an adult self-report version of the scale as well as the initial scale; and the Expressiveness and Antagonism factors have been related to sending accuracy and physiological responding.

It is instructive to compare the AERS with the concept of extraversion, in that they apparently involve similar dimensions of behavior. Several investigators have suggested that extraversion–introversion is not unidimensional (Carrigan, 1960; Mann, 1958). What has been termed the "American conception" of extraversion emphasizes sociability and ease in interpersonal relationships, while a "European conception" of extraversion emphasizes impulsiveness and a lack of self-control (Lester, 1974). These two conceptions of extraversion appear to correspond generally to the Expressiveness and Antagonism factors of the AERS. As we have seen, it is possible that observers may label the same behavior as having "expressive" versus "antagonistic" characteristics depending upon the age, sex, and status of the subject, and presumably other factors as well.

Independent evidence of the validity of the pattern of personality variables involved in expressiveness appears in a study by Ekman, Friesen, and Scherer (1976), in which observers exposed to various channels of nonverbal behavior (face, body, full speech, and filtered speech in which the content was rendered unintelligible) rated the sender on a variety of personality characteristics. The judgments of these observers were significantly correlated on only two of these characteristics: sociability (defined by scales of outgoing/inhibited, expressive/unexpressive, and sociable/withdrawn) and dominance (defined by a scale of dominant/submissive). Thus the different channels appeared to send consistent messages regarding the sender's placement on these dimensions. In contrast, ratings on scales such as honest/dishonest, relaxed/tense, and felt pleasant/unpleasant, were not as consistently correlated with one another across the different channels. This general pattern of results was also revealed in a subsequent study (Ekman, Friesen, O'Sullivan, & Scherer, 1980b).

Other independent evidence appears in the work of Howard Friedman and his colleagues (Friedman, DiMatteo, & Taranta, 1980a; Friedman, Riggio, & Segall, 1980c). These investigators have found that the ability to accurately pose emotion is related to ratings on a constellation of characteristics on the Jackson (1974) Personality

Research Form (PRF) which is strongly reminiscent of the characteristics appearing on the AERS. These include dominance, impulsivity, exhibition, and playfulness.

THE AFFECTIVE COMMUNICATION TEST

The Affective Communication Test (ACT) is a 13-item self-report scale designed to measure spontaneous emotional expressiveness (Friedman, Prince, Riggio, & DiMatteo, 1980b). Subjects high on the scale are rated as more expressive by friends; report having engaged in more activities hypothesized to involve expressive interpersonal skills (e.g., lecturing, political experience, acting, and sales); are high in affiliation and dominance on the PRF and in extraversion on the E–I scale; and high-scoring females tend to be high in the ability to pose emotion. Also, physicians who score high on the ACT are more popular (as measured by patient visits), and females score higher on the ACT than males.

EVALUATION

This general similarity in the traits related to both posed and spontaneous emotional expressiveness in a variety of subject populations and with a variety of methods of study is encouraging, suggesting that basic and stable relationships are being tapped. We have suggested that these may ultimately be based upon neural systems underlying behavioral inhibition and expression. In the next chapter, we shall review theories and recent research in this area.

CONCLUSIONS

A rich variety of techniques have been applied to study nonverbal sending accuracy. There has been a coherence of findings in this area which, taken together, suggests that spontaneous expressiveness is a relatively stable characteristic of an individual, that it is based upon innate predispositions of some kind, and that it can be altered in situationally specific ways by social learning. There appear to be similarities between animals and humans in the bases of this expressiveness, suggesting that general systems of expression and inhibition underlie nonverbal sending accuracy. We shall consider the nature of these systems further in the next chapter, along with symbolic influences upon sending accuracy which shall be conceptualized in terms of deception. We shall see that the literature on excitatory versus inhibitory systems is similar in many respects to a puzzle, many pieces of which are not yet in place, but in which an overall pattern or picture is beginning to emerge. The emergent picture is an exciting one, suggesting a major synthesis in which phenomena at greatly different levels of analysis, and areas of inquiry, which have long been separated from one another by differences in tradition, methodology, and focus of interest, may be brought into relationship with one another in a coherent focus.

6

INHIBITION AND DECEPTION

The model of sending accuracy presented in Chapter 2 posits two sources for nonverbal expression: innate emotional systems, which underlie spontaneous communication; and display rules, which are "symbolic" learned influences related to conversational rules and which are, at some level, intentional (see Figure 2.1). In Chapter 5 this model was altered somewhat, suggesting that there is a different process which, like display rules, can affect spontaneous expression (see Figure 5.6). This process was termed *inhibition*, which involves an attenuation of the display which is direct and in no way intentional or related to conversational rules. This chapter further considers the process of inhibition, and compares it with *deception*, which involves the intentional alteration of the display. Much work has been done in both of these areas, since they are potentially relevant to important applications in the analysis of psychotherapy, lie detection, and other situations in which the veracity of nonverbal communication is an issue. However, there has been relatively little contact between these areas.

This chapter first suggests initial definitions of "inhibition" and "deception," which will be supplemented as the literature is considered in more detail. It then outlines the remarkably diverse yet interrelated research relevant to inhibition, and the converging evidence that biologically based excitatory and inhibitory systems underlie an important dimension of both human and animal behavior. Following this, it reviews the many recent studies of deception, which has been an area of great interest to investigators of nonverbal communication. It then attempts to develop an integrated view of the control of emotional expression taking both inhibition and deception into account. Finally, it considers the concept of self-deception, and relates it to this view.

DEFINITIONS

In both inhibition and deception, the display initiated by the Emotion II process of spontaneous expression is altered. In the case of inhibition, there is always an attenuation of the spontaneous display. We have seen that this process may be the product of innate inhibitory systems, or acquired systems (see Figure 5.6). The inhibition process can be studied in animals and may be considered to be a part of the "animal model" of emotion presented in Chapter 4.

The concept of deception has been conceptualized in most recent research as involving highly intentional dissimulation, in which a sender consciously attempts to present a false "image" to a receiver who is attempting to detect this deception. However, we shall define deception in more general terms as involving the influence of symbolic display rules. Whereas in inhibition the display is always attenuated, deception may involve the full range of display rule effects noted by Ekman and Friesen (1975): modulation, qualification, or falsification (see Chapter 2). In keeping with the position presented in Chapter 4, it is suggested that animals can be deceptive in that they can learn to modulate, qualify, and falsify their spontaneous displays to fit situational requirements. However, in humans language makes possible both quantitative and qualitative increases in the possibilities of deception—both of others and oneself.

MECHANISMS OF EXPRESSION AND INHIBITION

There have been a variety of approaches to the phenomenon of behavioral expression and inhibition, many of which appear to have essential elements in common, both with each other and with the externalizing–internalizing distinction presented in the last chapter. These common features may reflect the influence of basic excitatory and inhibitory mechanisms. A remarkable convergence of findings from different areas of study is illustrated by the 1980 publication of review articles centered around the implications of the theories associated with Pavlov, Eysenck, and Gray—all of which are based upon notions of central nervous system inhibition—from the points of view of human psychophysiology (Fowles, 1980), the physiological bases of animal learning and performance (Gorenstein & Newman, 1980), and human psychometric studies (Zuckerman, Buchsbaum, & Murphy, 1980).

These approaches are reviewed in this section, including Pavlov's (1927) neurological typology, Eysenck's theory of extraversion–introversion, Gray's extension of Eysenck's theory, and the relationship of these theories to the externalizing–internalizing distinction. These approaches are then examined in the light of recent studies of subcortical and paleocortical mechanisms of excitation–inhibition, and cerebral lateralization. In particular, the implications are examined of the Tucker and Parkhurst extension of the Pribram and McGuiness arousal–activation model that was considered in Chapter 3.

PAVLOV'S NEUROLOGICAL TYPOLOGY

The Strength of the Nervous System

Pavlov's neurological typology was developed from his observation of individual differences in the behaviors of dogs in the classical conditioning situation. It is based upon the assumption that opposing forces of excitation and inhibition underlie all behavior, and it hypothesizes that there are three dimensions of the activity of these opposing forces within the central nervous system along which individuals may differ: mobility, equilibrium, and strength. The dimension of strength of the nervous system has been further studied in the Moscow laboratory of B. M. Teplov, and it has been of particular interest to Western psychologists (cf. Gray, 1972; Nebylitsyn, 1972; Nebylitsyn & Gray, 1972).

The notion of the strength of the nervous system is based upon the observation that a given stimulus seems to produce a greater response in some individual animals than it does in others. Pavlov (1927) suggested that the former animals had a "weak" nervous system, that is, one in which a given stimulus produces a greater excitatory effect. Animals with a stronger nervous system, in contrast, are relatively resistant to external stimulation because it produces a smaller excitatory effect. A strong nervous system thus is insensitive to weak stimuli, but it can deal with intense stimuli, while the weak nervous system cannot cope with strong external stimuli but it is effective in dealing with weak stimuli (Sales, 1971). Because of this, the strong nervous system is said to "need stimulation," while the weak nervous system is low in the need for stimulation.

The Need for Stimulation

Much of the interest of Western psychologists in the strength of the nervous system is centered around this implication that different levels of strength of the nervous system should be associated with different levels in the "need for stimulation." Theoretically, since a strong nervous system attenuates the effects of external stimulation, such an individual would tend to pursue highly stimulating activities in order to maintain an optimum level of stimulation. Conversely, a weak nervous system would encourage the avoidance of stimulation to maintain optimum levels.

Unfortunately, there are no generally accepted, easily applied measures of either the strength of the nervous system or the need for stimulation. Various methods of the strength of the nervous system, such as the measurement of sensory functions, reaction times, EEG responses, and so forth, do not always agree with one another (Ippolitov, 1972; Teplov, 1972). One of the most used measures of the need for stimulation has been Petrie's (1967) kinesthetic figural aftereffects (KFA) task, in which a blindfolded person feels an object between the fingers and then judges the size of the object on a wedge-shaped block. The "reducer" tends to underestimate the size of the object, while the "augmenter" tends toward overestimation. Thus the reducer acts as if the object has been reduced in size, while the augmenter does the reverse. In general, Petrie suggests that the reducer tends to subjectively "damp down" incoming stimulation, while the augmenter increases its intensity. Sales (1971, 1972) used this measure to demonstrate that reducers show behavioral evidence of being high in the need for stimulation, in that they show high activity when left alone in a room, report more exposure to complex and intense social situations, and respond favorably to complex stimuli, such as an experimentally created "psychedelic party."

Unfortunately, the measurement of augmenting–reducing in general and the use of the KFA task in particular has been the subject of considerable confusion in the literature. The KFA task has been criticized because of its low test–retest reliability and was abandoned by many investigators. However, Baker, Mishara, and their colleagues have argued that the test–retest procedure is inappropriate when applied to the KFA procedure, and they suggest that it may be a useful measure despite its low test–retest reliability (Baker, Mishara, Kostin, & Parker, 1976, 1979; Baker, Mishara, Parker, & Kostin, 1978; Mishara & Baker, 1978).

Buchsbaum and Silverman (1968) have used a technique for defining augmenting and reducing by the average evoked potential (AEP), which involves the direct measurement of cortical reactivity, and which correlates with their version of the KFA procedure. However, it is unclear whether the AEP measure reflects the same phenomenon as the KFA measure. Investigators using the KFA measure have identified characteristics such as high need for stimulation and "strong" nervous systems with "reducers" (e.g., Baker *et al.*, 1979; Sales & Throop, 1972), while investigators using the AEP have identified such characteristics with "augmenters" (e.g., Buchsbaum, 1976; Zuckerman, Buchsbaum, & Murphy, ·1980). Thus, the former investigators argue that reducers are high, and augmenters low, in the need for stimulation, while the latter investigators argue the reverse.

Davis, Cowles, and Kohn (1982) have suggested that the AEP actually measures "functional endurance," or the capacity to continue to respond to increasing stimulation, rather than the sensitivity to stimulation which is measured by the KFA. They criticize the Buchsbaum and Silverman (1968) version of the KFA, and suggest that the so-called AEP augmenters actually have strong nervous systems. Goldman, Kohn, and Hunt (1983) provide some support for this position, but they acknowledge the need for a single well-validated measure of augmenting–reducing. Clearly, more remains to be done on the definition and exploration of the implications of the augmenter–reducer distinction.

Marvin Zuckerman and his colleagues have suggested a questionnaire measure of the need for stimulation, termed the Sensation-Seeking Scale (SSS; Zuckerman, 1979a, 1979b, Zuckerman, Buchsbaum, & Murphy, 1980). The SSS involves four factors: thrill and adventure seeking, experience seeking, disinhibition, and high susceptibility to boredom. In general, the high sensation seeker is described as showing some traits that are similar to those of highly expressive persons as measured by the Affect Expression Rating Scale (AERS) and Affective Communication Test (ACT), such as being socially active and dominant, although the thrill-seeking aspects of the sensation seekers are not included in the latter scales. One of the major differences between the SSS and the expressiveness scales is that males tend to score higher on the SSS, while, as we have seen, females tend to be more expressive in many situations and score higher on the ACT. It may be that the items of the SSS concern situations in which males are taught to be overtly responsive in our culture, while the items of the expressiveness measures sample situations favoring female expressiveness. This is another area of interest where much remains to be learned.

The disinhibition scale is that part of the SSS which seems most directly analogous to the AERS and ACT. It shows evidence of a negative relationship with some autonomic measures, in that high "disinhibitors" show faster skin-conductance habituation and heart-rate deceleration rather than acceleration, when compared with "inhibitors" (Cox, 1978; Feij, Orlebeke, Gazendam, & van Zuilen, 1979). It is noteworthy that the disinhibition scale is the SSS factor which is most consistently related to the AEP measure of augmenting–reducing, and also to levels of gonadal hormones (Daitzman & Zuckerman, 1980; Daitzman, Zuckerman, Sammelwitz, & Ganjam, 1978).

Summary

In summary, the notions of strength of the nervous system and the need for stimulation are highly suggestive, but more remains to be done regarding the measurement of these variables. In particular, the notion of augmenting–reducing and its relationship to these variables needs to be clarified. The disinhibition scale of the SSS appears to be similar in some respects to the AERS and ACT measures of expressiveness, although unlike the latter scales its items may sample situations in which males are encouraged to be expressive.

EXTRAVERSION–INTROVERSION

Eysenck's Theory

Eysenck's (1967) theory of extraversion–introversion was stimulated in part by Pavlov's notion of the strength of the nervous system, and there are interesting theoretical parallels. Eysenck suggests that the introvert is more susceptible to influence from stimuli from the environment than the extravert; thus the introvert reveals a pattern of response resembling the reactive "weak" type of nervous system, while the extravert theoretically resembles the strong type who does not respond to stimulation. However, these theoretical parallels have not always been supported, and some regard the analogy between extraversion–introversion and the strength of the nervous system as more apparent than real (Blake, 1967; Nebylitsyn, 1972; Strelau, 1970; Zhorov & Yermolayeva-Tomina, 1972).

In his 1967 statement of his theory, Eysenck related extraversion–introversion to differences in the arousal threshold of the reticular formation, suggesting that this threshold is higher in extraverts than introverts, and that it is therefore easier for introverts to become conditioned by external events. Because introverts are more susceptible to the process of conditioning, they are also more susceptible to the process of socialization, and Eysenck argues that therefore the introvert tends to be "oversocialized" and the extravert "undersocialized." This difference is said to underlie the behavioral and psychological differences between introverts and extraverts. For example, Eysenck notes that when extraverts become neurotic, they tend to react with hysterical or psychopathic symptoms suggestive of undersocialization, while the introvert reacts with "dysthymic" disorders, such as high anxiety, phobias, and obsessive–compulsive disorders suggestive of oversocialization (Eysenck, 1967).

Gray's Theory

A basic implication of Eysenck's theory is that introverts should condition more readily than extraverts. This expectation has not been supported by relevant research, and this led to J. A. Gray's reformulation of Eysenck's theory. Gray (1971) suggests that, rather than being generally more conditionable, the introvert is more susceptible to punishment than the extravert, while the extravert is relatively insensitive to the threat of punishment.

Gray also extended Eysenck's theory regarding the physiological basis of extraversion–introversion, based upon the apparently "extraverting" effects of the barbiturate drug sodium amobarbital and the effects of septal lesions in animals. Some of the major elements of Gray's (1971) theory were summarized in Chapter 3. It will be recalled that Gray suggested that the hippocampal theta rhythm is associated with the functioning of a neural system which is activated by frustration or nonreward. The more the activitiy in the system, the greater is the animal's response to punishment, and the greater is the inhibition of whatever behavior has been associated with the punishment. Also, the more the natural level of arousal or arousability in this system, the more the individual is susceptible to punishment, and the more introverted he or she would be. It will also be recalled that Gray suggests that part of the septal area acts as a "pacemaker" for the hippocampal theta rhythm, that the system is represented at a higher level in the orbitofrontal cortex, and that the whole system is named the "septal–hippocampal–frontal (SHF) system." Gray also agrees with Eysenck that the reticular formation plays a role, in that it is involved in modulating the activity of the SHF system.

Gray (1977) has suggested that the SHF system constitutes a behavioral inhibition system (BIS) which interacts with a behavioral activation system (BAS) and the nonspecific reticular arousal system. The reticular system mediates diffuse general arousal, the BAS is associated with the initiation of behavior in response to cues associated with reward or the active avoidance of punishment, and the BIS is an "anxiety system" which inhibits behavior in response to cues associated with punishment (passive avoidance) and frustrative nonreward (extinction).

A diagram of Gray's theory is presented in Figure 6.1. Gray (1971) has argued that the relative insensitivity of extraverts for punishment can explain the development of dysthymic disorders in introverts, and impulsive disorders such as hysteria and psychopathy in extraverts, as well as the optimism and liking for other people in extraverts.

Gray's conception has much in common with the suggestions of such investigators as Stein (1968) and Routtenberg (1978) that a "reward system" and "punishment system" interact with the reticular formation in determining behavior. It is also consistent with evidence that drugs which deplete or inactivate certain catecholaminergic neurotransmitters, such as norepinepherine, have sedative or depressant effects, while drugs which potentiate these neurotransmitters have excitatory, antidepressant effects (Schildkraut & Kety, 1967). Thus, it is known that the brain areas that elicit the strongest self-stimulation effects have catecholaminergic neurotransmitters. Stein (1968) has suggested that these areas, particularly the medial forebrain bundle (MFB), constitute "reward" systems in which activity

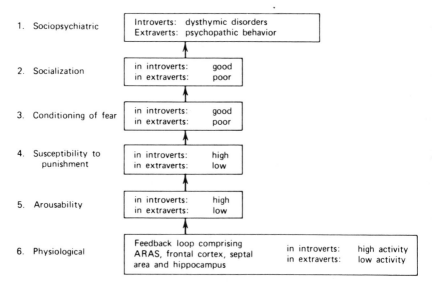

Figure 6.1. Gray's proposed modification of Eysenck's theory of introversion-extraversion. From "The Psychophysiological Nature of Introversion–Extraversion: A Modification of Eysenck's Theory" by J. A. Gray, in V. D. Nebylitsyn and J.A. Gray (Eds.), *Biological Basis of Individual Behavior*, New York: Academic Press, 1972. Copyright 1972 by Academic Press, Inc. Reprinted by permission.

tends to activate or disinhibit overt behavior. Conversely, the fiber tracts lying medial to the MFB, the periventricular system (PVS) which has cholinergic neurotransmissions, constitute a "punishment system" in which activity causes the inhibition of overt responding (see Chapter 3).

The Externalizing–Internalizing Distinction

The notion of extraversion–introversion is similar to that of externalizing–internalizing in that both involve the analysis of spontaneous expressiveness, and both suggest that overtly expressive persons may have smaller psychophysiological responses. However, the causal explanations given by the two positions are diametrically opposed: Jones (1950, 1960) suggested that inhibitory socialization experiences cause increased psychophysiological responding, while Eysenck and Gray suggest that a high level of psychophysiological responding is associated with innate physiological mechanisms that also cause socialization to be more effective (cf. Buck, 1976a). Interestingly, both of these theories imply that the negative intersubject relationship in overt behavior and psychophysiological responding is based upon socialization experiences: Jones suggests that socialization causes the inhibition of overt responding and the increase in psychophysiological responding; Eysenck and Gray suggest that the high psychophysiological arousal is associated with general physiological arousal, causing a high susceptibility to socialization which leads to inhibited overt responding. Neither of these theories can therefore account for Field and Walden's (1982) demonstration of a negative relationship between overt expression and psychophysiological responding in newborn infants.

Summary

Eysenck's theory of extraversion–introversion was based in part upon Pavlov's (1927) notion of strength of the nervous system, although the theoretical parallels have not always been borne out in empirical studies. Eysenck's theory has been altered and extended by Gray, who has suggested that specific physiological systems are associated with behavioral activation and inhibition. These suggestions are compatible with findings from animal research and psychopharmacology. The Eysenck and Gray theories have similarities with Jones's externalizing–internalizing notions, although neither theory predicts that extraversion–introversion (or externalizing–internalizing) effects should occur in the absence of socialization, as the Field and Walden (1982) result suggests.

RECENT DEVELOPMENTS

As noted above, several recent reviews have suggested the relevance of the Eysenck–Gray theory to a variety of areas of study that are traditionally separate, and there is converging evidence of a major synthesis. This section examines in particular (1) the phenomenon of psychopathy, (2) new developments in the analysis of the relationship of the traditional psychophysiological measures with excitatory and inhibitory neural systems, (3) the "septal syndrome" and general concept of disinhibitory psychopathology, and (4) the evidence of individual differences in the enzyme monoamine oxidase (MAO). It then considers the implications of the evidence on cerebral lateralization for this area of study.

Psychopathy and Socialization

Psychopathy (or sociopathy) has traditionally been associated with impulsive, acting-out behavior that has been attributed to a lack of normal mechanisms of inhibition. A number of studies have linked such behaviors to low electrodermal responding. Thus, Lykken (1957) demonstrated that psychopaths (or sociopaths) are less electrodermally reactive than nonpsychopaths. This result has been replicated and discussed by Hare and his colleagues (1965a, 1965b, 1965c, 1970, 1978; Hare & Craigen, 1974; Hare & Quinn, 1971). Waid and his colleagues have demonstrated that the relationship between a lack of socialization and low electrodermal responding is true in the range of normal subjects as well: Waid (1976) showed in college students that electrodermal responsiveness is positively related to scores on a socialization scale, and Waid, Orne, and Wilson (1979a, 1979b) found that less highly socialized students are more deceptive on polygraph examinations due to their low electrodermal responding. Conversely, highly socialized subjects have high electrodermal responding that may cause innocent subjects to be misclassified as deceptive. Also, Waid, Orne, Cook, and Orne (1981) have shown that a low dose (400 mg) of meprobamate, an "antianxiety" tranquilizer, reduces phasic skin-conductance responding on a polygraph examination so that deception cannot be detected.

In that these results show a negative relationship between overt and skin-conductance responding, they are consistent with the externalizing–internalizing distinction. Also, the effect of the meprobamate is particularly significant, as it suggests that the effects of socialization on electrodermal responding may be mediated via anxiety.

The Psychophysiology of Excitation and Inhibition

Fowles (1980) has reviewed the evidence concerning the relationship of two major psychophysiological measures—skin-conductance responding and heart-rate—to mechanisms of excitation and inhibition. Fowles reviews Gray's (1977) suggestion that there are three neural systems underlying extraversion: the BAS, BIS, and reticular activating system. He goes on to suggest that different psychophysiological responses differentially reflect responding in these three systems. Specifically, he suggests that activity in the BIS increases the number of nonspecific skin-conductance fluctuations and is associated with anxiety (Szpiler & Epstein, 1976). Activity in this system is decreased by antianxiety drugs, such as alcohol, barbiturates, and the minor tranquilizers. Conversely, Fowles suggests that activity in the BAS is associated with increased heart rate, and argues that such an interpretation would explain a variety of previous findings, including that of a "cardiac–somatic link" described by Obrist and his colleagues (Obrist, 1976; Obrist, Webb, Sutterer, & Howard, 1970a, 1970b) and Elliott (1969, 1972).

Platelet Monoamine Oxidase

A phenomenon which may be related to the role of the functioning of the BAS and BIS in mediating individual differences in expressiveness involves individual differences in the levels of MAO in the platelets of the bloodstream. MAO is an enzyme which participates in the breakdown of a variety of biogenic amines in the central nervous system, including catecholaminergic neurotransmitters such as norepinephrine, dopamine, and serotonin. We have seen that these neurotransmitters are associated with emotion: Drugs that increase the concentrations of amines in the brain tend to have antidepressant effects (i.e., amphetamine), while drugs such as chlorpromazine that decrease these concentrations have the opposite, calming or depressing, effects (Schildkraut & Kety, 1967). MAO-inhibiting drugs, which block the activity of the MAO enzyme, are widely used as antidepressant agents, presumably because they increase amine concentrations by reducing the amine breakdown by MAO.

MAO concentrations may be assayed from the platelets in humans (Murphy, 1973; Murphy et al., 1977). These concentrations vary widely, and reliable individual differences have been demonstrated over time. These differences have been related to behavior in both animals and humans. Thus, in rhesus monkeys, high MAO levels have been associated with passivity, inactivity, and a lack of social responsiveness, while low MAO levels are associated with high play behavior, activity, and social contact (Redmond & Murphy, 1975; Redmond, Murphy, & Baulu, 1979). In humans, low MAO subjects describe themselves as being more social, and they show greater interest in others and in social contacts on Minnesota Multiphasic Personality Inventory (MMPI) items (Coursey, Buchsbaum, & Murphy, 1979). Also, MAO levels are negatively correlated with SSS scores (Murphy *et al.*, 1977; Schooler, Zahn, Murphy, & Buchsbaum, 1978; Zuckerman, Buchsbaum, & Murphy, 1980), suggesting that low MAO subjects are sensation seekers and high in the need for stimulation.

The Septal Syndrome

We have seen that conceptions of the neural systems underlying excitation and inhibition have been applied to the analysis of individual differences in spontaneous expressiveness in humans, the effects of important psychoactive drugs, and the meaning of the responding of major psychophysiological measures. Gorenstein and Newman (1980) have pointed out that experimental procedures well known in animal research can also be illuminated by this analysis. Such studies have indicated that symptoms associated with lesions in the SHF system are remarkably similar to the symptoms of what they call "disinhibitory psychopathology" in humans. These include the disinclination to inhibit punished responses, a steep temporal gradient of fear arousal so that feared stimuli become effective in inhibiting behavior only when they are immediately at hand, poor impulse control in the face of rewards, and associated inability to delay gratification, and a high need for stimulation. Gorenstein and Newman term this the "septal syndrome," and suggest that it constitutes a functional animal research model which reveals a "basic manifestation of disinhibition uncontaminated by environmental influence" (p. 313). They suggest that this model may constitute the analogue of "disinhibitory psychopathology" in humans, which involves a genetically determined diathesis which is normally modified by environmental influences. (A *diathesis* is defined as a bodily condition which is predisposing to a disease.) They suggest that this diathesis is at the root of a wide variety of psychopathological disorders, including psychopathy, hysteria, hyperactivity, impulsivity, and alcoholism.

CEREBRAL LATERALIZATION AND EXPRESSION–INHIBITION

In Chapter 3, evidence was reviewed regarding the different cognitive capacities of the right hemisphere and left hemisphere, and that left-hemisphere damage is associated with deficits in symbolic communication, while right-hemisphere damage is associated with deficits in spontaneous communication. It will be recalled that Tucker (1981) and Buck and Duffy (1980) suggested that the left hemisphere is associated with a verbally mediated control of the emotionality of the right hemisphere. This control may involve anxiety and other "cognitive" motives. It also reviewed evidence that lateralized brain processes are differentially involved in psychopathology, with psychopathy and hysteria apparently involving a low level of left-hemisphere functioning, while obsessive–compulsive disorders involve evidence of particularly strong left-hemisphere cognitive functioning (Tucker, 1981).

There are striking parallels between this literature and the evidence we have been reviewing regarding mechanisms of inhibition and expression in this chapter, such as Gray's suggestion that neurotic extraverts tend to develop psychopathy and hysteria, while neurotic introverts develop "dysthymic" disorders including obsessive–compulsive disorders. If the former are labeled "disinhibitory psychopathology" by Gorenstein and Newman (1980), the latter might be termed "inhibitory psychopathology" (see also Seligman, 1975).

The view of right-hemisphere and left-hemisphere functioning presented in Chapter 3 is thus consistent with the evidence relating to subcortical and paleocortical expressive–inhibitory mechanisms, although the interactions between the latter and neocortical mechanisms, and the extent of lateralization of the subcortical and paleocortical systems, are far from being understood. Many pieces of the puzzle are still missing, but the overall outlines of a major synthesis seem unmistakable.

A MODEL OF INHIBITION

The research that we have been reviewing is consistent with the model of inhibition presented in the last chapter in Figure 5.7. That model involved a system based upon innate mechanisms—the genetically determined diathesis—which is modified by situation-specific learning. Beyond this, this research has suggested much about the nature of these excitatory and inhibitory systems. These suggestions are summarized in Table 6.1.

The content of Table 6.1 is tentative and meant only to summarize some of this evidence. For example, although there is no conclusive evidence that Stein's (1968) cholinergic "punishment system" in the periventricular region, Gray's BIS, and the inhibitory

Table 6.1. Tentative Characteristics of the BAS and BIS Suggested by the Literature

Characteristic	"Reward system" (BAS)	"Punishment system" (BIS)
Consequences of high relative activity		
Overt expression	High	Low
Psychophysiological responding	Low phasic skin-conductance responding	High phasic skin-conductance responding
Emotional consequences	Euphoria, excitement	Anxiety, depression
Emotional response mode	Externalizing	Internalizing
Personality/temperament	Extraverted	Introverted
Psychopharmacological properties		
Neurotransmitter	Noradrenergic and serotonergic	Cholinergic?
Activity increased by	Noradrenergic and serotonergic potentiators (amphetamine, MAO inhibitors)	Cholinergic potentiators? (i.e., physostigmine)
Activity decreased by	Noradrenergic and serotonergic blockers (reserpine, tetrabenazine)	Cholinergic blockers? (i.e., atropine) "Antianxiety" drugs Alcohol
Other characteristics		
Consequences of abnormal arousal	Disinhibitory psychopathology Psychopathy Hysteria	Inhibitory psychopathology "Dysthymic" disorders Obsessive–compulsive disorders Anxiety, phobias
Possible anatomical sites	MFB Septal area?	PVS? SHF system
Relationship with cerebral lateralization	Related to right-hemisphere functioning?	Related to left-hemisphere functioning?

processes ascribed to the left hemisphere are related to one another, such a suggestion seems reasonable. There is some evidence for the MFB–right hemisphere relationship: As noted in Chapter 3, noradrenergic and serotonergic pathways associated with the MFB and thought to mediate mood appear to be lateralized on the right.

INHIBITION AND ILLNESS:
THE SUPPRESSION HYPOTHESIS

A number of investigators have shown interest in the notion that emotional suppression may be related to physiological arousal, stress, and illness (Watson, 1981). This might be termed the "suppression hypothesis." Selye (1978) has shown how the body's attempts to cope stress can in time become stressful themselves, interfering with the actions of the immune system and thus contributing to a wide variety of disease processes.

One implication of the internalizing–externalizing phenomenon is that it suggests that if individuals do not show emotion spontaneously, they in effect "take it out" on their own physiological system, showing evidence of high autonomic arousal which could become a source of bodily stress and contribute to disease (Buck, 1976a, 1979a). McClelland (1982) has reported relationships between inhibited personality patterns, sympathetic activation, impaired immune system functioning, and cardiovascular disease. Similarly, Sifneos and his colleagues have found that patients with psychosomatic illnesses are similar to the internalizers in the Buck *et al.* (1974) study in that they have difficulty with the verbal description and expression of feelings (Nemiah & Sifneos, 1970). Sifneos (1973) coined the term *alexithymia* (literally, "no words for mood") to describe the inability to express feelings verbally. Several studies have found this quality in patients with a variety of psychosomatic complaints (Flannery, 1977; Pierloot & Vinck, 1977; Wolff, 1977), and Lesser (1981) has contributed a critical review of the historical, clinical, and theoretical setting of the alexithymia concept.

Anderson (1981) has suggested that impairment of emotional expression may be a necessary, if not sufficient, factor in the etiology of psychosomatic disease. She found a pattern of negative correlations between ratings of stress and a variety of physiological indices of arousal—in particular forearm EMG, skin conductance, and systolic blood pressure—in both psychosomatic patients and normal subjects. It is noteworthy that the only physiological measure to show a significant positive correlation with stress ratings in this study was forehead EMG, suggesting that subjects who openly admitted stress were also more facially expressive (cf. Buck, 1981b).

SUMMARY

Chapter 5 reviewed studies of spontaneous expressiveness, showing that there is evidence that individual differences in such expressiveness are related to basic modes of emotional responding, which following Jones were labeled "externalizing" and "internalizing" modes of response. Whether these are "personality traits" in the traditional sense of affecting behavior in all situations is doubtful, as there is evidence that the same person may, through a combination of temperament and social experience, come to manifest an externalizing mode of response in one situation and an internalizing mode in another.

Chapter 5 also suggested that these modes of response are based upon neural mechanisms associated with inhibition and expression, and outlined the theoretical requirements for such mechanisms. In the present chapter, we have seen that there is considerable evidence that such mechanisms exist, although their exact nature and the details of their functioning are far from being fully understood. Nevertheless, it appears that, besides spontaneous expressiveness, the following phenomena may be related to these mechanisms: (1) the strength of the nervous system; (2) the need for stimulation; (3) extraversion–introversion; (4) the socialization process and its relationship with temperament; (5) patterns of psychophysiological responding; (6) the role of the catecholamines and associated drug effects; (7) reward/punishment systems in the brain; (8) the "septal syndrome" in animals; (9) human "disinhibitory psychopathology," including psychopathy, hysteria, impulsivity, alcoholism, and hyperactivity; (10) human "inhibitory psychopathology," such as high anxiety, phobias, and obsessive–compulsive disorders; and (11) cerebral lateralization. This is an impressive list, and at first glance one might wonder why the omission of the kitchen sink. However, there appears to be both theoretical argument and direct evidence that these phenomena are related to one another, and the understanding of these relationships would constitute a giant step forward in our understanding of the nature of biological foundations of personality, communication, and social behavior.

DECEPTION

The mechanisms of inhibition considered above involve an attenuation of the spontaneous display which may be innate or acquired, but is still nonvoluntary. In contrast, deception involves the alteration of the spontaneous display by display rules which are symbolic in nature, and furthermore the term has been used to refer to situations in which this alteration is highly intentional. Deception has been the subject of much recent study by researchers in nonverbal communication, beginning with the analysis of nonverbal leakage and cues to deception by Ekman and Friesen (1969b).

LEAKAGE AND DECEPTION

In a highly influential paper, Ekman and Friesen (1969b) began by paraphrasing a statement by Darwin (1872, pp. 48–49) that:

> Some actions . . . may be partially repressed through the will, and in such cases the muscles which are least under the separate control of the will are the most liable still to act, causing movements we recognize as expressive. In certain other cases the checking of one habitual movement requires other slight movements; and these are likewise expressive.

This was followed by the classic quotation from Freud (1905) concerning nonverbal communication:

> He that has eyes to see and ears to hear may convince himself that no mortal can keep a secret. If his lips are silent, he chatters with his finger-tips; betrayal oozes out of him at every pore. (p. 94)

Ekman and Friesen go on to cite Goffman's (1959) writings regarding the dramatic performances which manage the impressions that one gives to others, noting that all social interactions may be considered to be "deceptive" in Goffman's sense. Ekman and Friesen, however, use the term in a more restricted sense, involving situations where there is a particular focus upon withholding information and dissimulating. Also, although they consider the phenomenon of self-deception, they are particularly concerned with situations where deceivers are aware of what they wish to conceal from others and plan their behavior accordingly. Furthermore, they emphasize situations in which there is antagonism, in which the deceiver wishes to maintain the deception, and the other wishes to uncover it. This is a more restricted view of the phenomenon of deception than is implied in the opening quotations.

Given these constraints in the definition of deception, which have tended to be carried on in this literature, Ekman and Friesen argue that it is important for deceivers to be aware of their actions so that they do not give away the secret, either by revealing their "true feelings" directly (*nonverbal leakage*), or by revealing that something is being suppressed via *cues to deception*.

Ekman and Friesen suggest that the deceiver's awareness of these actions depends upon *internal feedback*, which is defined in terms of the deceiver's conscious awareness of, and ability to recall, repeat, or enact, a sequence of motor behavior. They suggest that the availability of internal feedback varies for different nonverbal channels, and that the degree of internal feedback characteristic of a given channel is determined by the *sending capacity* of that channel, and also the degree of *external feedback* that is typically received from responses in that channel. Sending capacity is roughly analogous to the concept of channel capacity presented in Chapter 1: It involves the number of discriminable stimulus patterns which can be transmitted by a channel, their average transmission time, and the visibility of information in the channel. Channels with high sending capacity also tend to receive much external feedback from others: This is behavior by the other that the sender is likely to perceive as reactive to his or her own nonverbal behavior. Ekman and Friesen argue that people have the most internal feedback about channels from which they have received the most external feedback: One learns to pay attention to a channel when one learns that others pay attention to it. If others ignore a channel, the sender does not learn to attend to it. This concept, that external feedback from others determines the internal feedback from a response, can be viewed as part of the process of the education of attention, as presented in Chapters 2 and 4, in that the occurrence of external feedback would encourage the subject to attend to the behaviors associated with the feedback.

Ekman and Friesen (1969b) specifically consider the importance of the face, hands, and feet in deception. They argue that the face is highest in internal and external feedback and channel capacity, and that the feet are lowest, with the hands being intermediate. For this reason, it is likely that the face is the poorest source of deception and leakage cues, because (with the possible exception of micromomentary expressions) it is the most responded to by others and is therefore highest in internal feedback, awareness, and control by the deceiver. The feet on the other hand are ignored by others and by the responder, and they are therefore a good source of leakage and deception cues. The hands are again intermediate in being a source of such cues.

THE DECEPTION PARADIGM

This prediction was tested by Ekman and Friesen (1974a) in a study which introduced a paradigm that has often been employed in studies of deception. This "deception paradigm" often involves showing subjects affective stimuli, but asks them to show emotions that are different from, and often contrary to, those that tend to be spontaneously evoked. It is important to note that this generally occurs *after* the affective stimulus has been withdrawn. We shall return to this point below.

Ekman and Friesen (1974a) videotaped 16 female nursing students in each of two standard interviews after they had viewed affective films. In the "honest" interview, they had seen pleasant nature films and were asked in the interview to describe their true feelings. In the "deceptive" interview, they had seen a strongly unpleasant film showing burns and amputations, and were asked to conceal these negative feelings and convince the interviewer that they had seen a pleasant film. Videotapes of the subjects' facial or body behavior during the honest and deceptive interviews were shown to separate groups of observers, who judged whether the behavior was from an "honest" or "deceptive" interview. Results indicated that deception could be more accurately detected from the body than from the face, a result consistent with the suggestion that leakage and deception cues occur more in the body than on the face (Ekman & Friesen, 1969b).

The stimuli developed in the Ekman and Friesen (1974a) study were used later by Ekman et al. (1976) to further study the body movements occurring during the deceptive interview, and also to explore the contribution of voice pitch to judgments of deception. They found significantly fewer hand illustrators and a higher pitch during the deceptive interview. Voice pitch was negatively correlated with illustrators, and a low pitch was associated with judgments that the person was sociable and relaxed. Observers viewing the face rated the deceptive interviews as more positive, while those viewing the body rated the deceptive interview as more negative, a result consistent with the Ekman and Friesen (1974a) finding.

Ekman *et al.* (1980b) used this technique to further investigate the relative importance of cues from the face, body, and speech in mediating judgments of various personality characteristics during deceptive versus nondeceptive interviews. A new sample of 15 female nursing students were filmed in the honest and deceptive interview conditions and viewed by several groups of observers under varying conditions, including face only, body only, speech (audiotapes which included both speech content and voice quality), and the "whole person." The observers rated the stimulus person on a variety of attributes, including expressiveness, dominance, tension, and honesty. The study investigated the conditions under which the judgments of observers exposed to the single channels most closely correlated with the judgments of the observers exposed to the whole person, the assumption being that the most "informative" channel would most highly correlate with the whole person condition. It was found that these correlations depended upon the type of attribute being judged and the type of interview. In general, during the deceptive interview the judgments made by the observers exposed to speech were most similar to the judgments of those exposed to the whole person. However, the meaning of this result is open to question since both verbal content and voice quality were available to observers in both of those conditions, and the verbal content could have been the source of the similarity in ratings.

Other Studies

A number of other studies have employed variants of the deception paradigm. Senders have described persons they like as though they dislike them, and persons they dislike as though they like them (DePaulo & Rosenthal, 1979a); they have answered factual questions truthfully or falsely (Harrison, Hwalek, Raney, & Fritz, 1978; Streeter,

Krauss, Geller, Olson, & Apple, 1977); they have role-played being honest or dishonest in an interview (Kraut, 1978); they have role-played being "smugglers" in a mock customs inspection (Kraut & Poe, 1980); and so forth. DePaulo, Zuckerman, and Rosenthal (1981) have summarized the results of many of these studies, contrasting those employing verbal cues (combined audiovisual cues, audio cues, or verbal transcript) versus those with exclusively nonverbal cues (tone of voice, face, or body). The effect size of each study was estimated by the d statistic, which expresses the magnitude of the deception detection effect in standard deviation units (Cohen, 1977).

These studies provided only tenuous support for Ekman and Friesen's (1969b) prediction that the body is "leakier" than the face. However, it was clear that adding facial cues to verbal/vocal cues did not improve the ability to detect deception, and in fact there was evidence that the facial cues at times interfered with deception detection, as the Ekman and Friesen formulation would suggest.

Of major interest in the DePaulo *et al.* (1981) review was its demonstration that the effects of nonverbal cues on deception detection were highly variable. The three studies which obtained the largest effects employed only nonverbal cues: These included studies by Feldman (1976) and Zuckerman *et al.* (1979a) employing facial cues (effect sizes 1.82 and 1.98, respectively) and a study by Littlepage and Pineault employing body cues (effect size 2.51). On the other hand, the five studies that found below-chance deception detection also involved judgments of nonverbal cues. In contrast, the studies employing verbal cues revealed more moderate but consistent deception detection. Clearly, more remains to be learned about when nonverbal cues are and are not revealing of deception. We shall return to this point below.

Another noteworthy feature of the DePaulo *et al.* (1981) review is its demonstration that detecting the simple presence of deception (i.e., *deception detection accuracy*, regarding the ability to determine whether the other is lying or not) is different from, and relatively easier than, the accurate recognition of leakage (i.e., *leakage detection accuracy*, regarding the ability to judge how the other actually feels; De Paulo & Rosenthal, 1979a; Feldman, 1976). Two of the five below-chance findings involved the recognition of leakage as opposed to only 2 of the 22 above-chance results.

Related to both of these findings is the suggestion that nonverbal cues may be particularly important when the deception concerns affect (i.e., when the sender pretends to like someone who is actually disliked) as opposed to when it concerns an opinion (i.e., when senders accurately or inaccurately describe their living situation, college major, religion, etc.). DePaulo *et al.* (1981) suggest that when the sender lies about an opinion, there is little affect to be leaked, but there is detailed information which must make sense, so that the verbal content is likely to be particularly revealing and nonverbal cues relatively unimportant. However, to the extent that the lie involves strong emotion, nonverbal cues may be crucial both in the detection of deception and the recognition of leakage.

EMOTION AND DECEPTION

The DePaulo *et al.* (1981) analysis suggests that it is critical to specify the part that emotion plays in deception before one can predict the role that nonverbal cues may play in providing cues to leakage and deception. We have seen that deception *per se* has been conceptualized as a highly intentional process involving conscious dissimulation. Extending the DePaulo *et al.* analysis, one can see that there are at least three ways that emotion might be involved in this process. First, there may be no involvement of emotion at all, that is, *nonemotional deception.* Second, the process of deception may be associated with conflict and resulting stress that is not associated with the content of the deception but rather with the fact that deception is occurring at all. Such *stressful deception* is the basis of lie detection via polygraph. Third, the deception process may involve the alteration of an emotional display. This *emotional deception* is the construct involved in the notion of display rules, and it is the kind of deception most relevant to the Ekman and Friesen (1969b, 1974a) formulation. We shall consider each in turn.

Nonemotional Deception

Nonemotional deception is dissimulation involving little or no conflict or stress, in which the content of the deception is also nonemotional. Studies in which college students are asked to "lie" about comparatively inconsequential things, such as their major, religion, and so forth, and studies involving role playing, are all likely to involve nonemotional deception. Even studies employing what are apparently more involving issues, such as attitudes toward abortion or one's best friend, may not truly engender emotion in the artificial confines of the experimental situation.

There is no reason to expect that nonverbal behavior should be at all revealing of nonemotional deception. Some discussions of deception seem to imply the existence of nonverbal "deception cues" —signs of deception *per se* that are independent of emotional cues. However, there does not appear to be any theoretical or empirical rationale for the existence of such cues. It is implausible from an evolutionary point of view to suggest that there are special cues to deception *per se* (cf. Kraut, 1980). There may well be cues to the conflict, indecision, and stress that may often accompany deception, but not to deception *per se*, and if the deception does not happen to involve conflict, indecision, or stress, these cues should be absent.

In the absence of some coherent justification for the existence of special deception cues, we must assume that nonverbal cues to deception are important only to the extent that deception involves emotion. In contrast, observers exposed to the verbal channel might be expected to be successful in detecting deception even in a nonemotional situation, since, as DePaulo *et al.* (1981) pointed out, the verbal reasoning of dissimulating subjects may be faulty due to a lack of information and/or experience.

Stressful Deception

Stressful deception by definition involves conflict about dissimulation, the presence of which might be revealed by nonverbal cues. One of the major foci of interest in the deception literature has been the analysis of the nature of such cues, and the channels over which they are transmitted, with one implied purpose being to develop techniques to use "humans as lie detectors" for the nonverbal detection of deception analogous to the techniques based upon polygraph tests (cf. DePaulo & Rosenthal, 1980). Although one might wonder about the extent to which studies employing the deception paradigm can truly reflect stressful deception, since the subjects are complying with the wishes of the experimenter in dissimulating, laboratory deception studies employing the polygraph suffer the same problem.

The literature on the physiological detection of deception is, of course, relevant to the analysis of stressful deception. This literature has been associated with much controversy in recent years (cf. Lykken,

1974, 1979; Podlesny & Raskin, 1977; Raskin & Podlesny, 1979). Kraut (1980) has noted some of the problems endemic to this literature. In particular, there is large variability in the stimulus—in the behavior of the deceptive person—that is not taken into proper account in the nonverbal deception detection literature. Specifically, Kraut suggests that there are important differences in the responsiveness of potential liars to stress, in their behaviors in response to stress, in their abilities at using display rules to "cover" these behaviors, and in the display rules that they choose to use. We shall explore the possibilities of individual differences in "deceptiveness" below.

Emotional Deception

Emotional deception remains the kind of deception most relevant to the analysis of the display rules. It requires that some actual emotion be present, in order for it to be altered. This is a difficult requirement to satisfy, and few studies in the deception literature appear to unequivocally involve emotional deception. In fact, studies in the deception literature have tended to avoid using emotional stimuli during the deception itself, apparently because of a concern that emotional cues would interfere with "deception cues." However, we have seen that one could argue that there are no deception cues in the absence of emotional cues. From this point of view, the alteration of emotional cues is in itself a form of deception that is theoretically interesting and worthy of study in its own right.

Lanzetta et al. (1976) used a variant of the deception paradigm to study the effects of concealing facial expressions upon other kinds of emotional responses, which could also be used to study emotional deception. They asked subjects to pose anticipating receiving either no shock or extremely intense shock when they were being given a signal that they were actually about to receive a mild, moderate, or intense shock. One could use analogous procedures to study abilities to use display rules to modulate or falsify a felt emotion, that is, one evoked by a slide or film that is present at the time of attempted deception. The analysis of such abilities could be added to the many studies of the abilities to simulate or pose emotional expressions, and of spontaneous expressiveness, thus evaluating the suggestion that stable individual differences exist in the ability to deceive and relating them to other sending abilities. Such studies would be particularly interesting if combined and compared with studies of social context effects upon sending accuracy, such as those considered in the last chapter.

The next sections review three aspects of the deception literature: the analysis of the cues and channel effects involved in deception, the issue of individual differences in deceptiveness, and development of deceptiveness.

CUES AND CHANNELS OF DECEPTION

There appear to be a few behaviors that are often seen during deception. In a review, Kraut (1980) noted that deceivers often blinked frequently, hesitated longer before answering, used many grooming adaptors, and had more frequent errors and hesitations in speech. These may well be common nonverbal indicators of stress and conflict about what to say, as opposed to being cues of deception *per se*. Other behaviors, such as smiling, eye contact, change in voice pitch, and leg movements were not consistently related to deception, although they appeared to be important in some studies. All in all, it appears that there are no cues which are consistently revealing of deception across all deceivers and deception situations. In particular, there may be major differences between the cues revealing of emotional, stressful, and nonemotional deception (O'Hair, Cody, & McLaughlin, 1981).

Regarding the channels over which deceptive cues are transmitted, there appears to be considerable agreement about Ekman and Friesen's (1969b) point that channels which in ordinary circumstances are informative can become extremely misleading during deception. DePaulo and Rosenthal (1979a, 1979b; Rosenthal & DePaulo, 1979a, 1979b) have suggested an expanded continuum of "leakiness," with the face being the most controlled and least leaky, followed by the body, tone of voice, micromomentary facial expressions, and discrepancies between channels. They suggest the possibility that skilled "lie detectors" may alter their attention patterns to compensate for these channel effects, attending to the leakier channels with deception is expected (DePaulo, Rosenthal, Eisenstat, Rogers, & Finkelstein, 1978). This shall be discussed further in the next chapter.

INDIVIDUAL DIFFERENCES IN DECEPTIVENESS

It was noted above that Kraut (1978, 1980) suggested that there may be stable individual differences in the skillfulness at lying. This hypothesis is consistent with the material presented above on individual differences in sending accuracy, but is has not been widely investigated in regard to the nonverbal cues of deception. For example, as noted above, there are studies indicating that more socialized subjects have higher skin-conductance responses, and are thus more likely on polygraph tests to be classified (and misclassified) as deceptive compared with less socialized subjects. It would be interesting to compare the nonverbal behavior of more versus less socialized subjects during deception. One might expect that less socialized persons would experience less conflict and stress, so that they would be superior at stressful deception, but on the other hand they might be more nonverbally expressive, so that it is conceivable that they would be poorer at emotional deception.

Kraut (1980) goes on to argue that most deception judgments are stimulus driven, that the potential liar's behavior and the motivational context of the lie compel most observers to agree about whether a lie has occurred or not, and that individual differences among observers are relatively unimportant. He cites a study in which Kraut and Poe (1980) videotaped volunteer airline passengers going through a mock customs inspection after being instructed to role play being "truthful" or "lying" to the inspector about what they had to declare. The videotapes were viewed both by professional U.S. Customs Service inspectors and lay judges recruited through advertisements. The viewers were asked to guess whether or not the passenger carried mock contraband. Results indicated that both professional and lay groups showed low accuracy at distinguishing the "smugglers," as one might expect in such a basically nonemotional stimulus task where the subject is obeying instructions to lie and there is no emotional arousal connected with carrying the "contraband" *per se.* However, the viewers did tend to agree highly among themselves on whom to search. Generally, travelers ("smugglers" or not) were selected to be searched if they were young, appeared to be of "lower class," appeared nervous, hesitated before answering, avoided eye contact, and so forth. Individual differences among judges—successful inspectors versus less successful inspectors versus lay persons—had little effect upon the cues used to select "smugglers."

Other evidence of stable individual differences in deceptiveness was reported by DePaulo and Rosenthal (1979a) in a study in which male and female subjects first talked truthfully or falsely about liked versus disliked others, and also about others they were ambivalent about and others to whom they were indifferent. The same subjects later observed other subjects and attempted to detect both deception and leakage—whether the other subjects were lying and how the other subjects actually felt. Results indicated considerable homogeneity in "deceptiveness," in that persons whose deception was accurately depicted were also leakier about their feelings, and that deceptiveness was positively related to the personality dimension of Machiavellianism. On the other hand, there was no homogeneity in deception detection: The ability to detect deception was not significantly related to the ability to detect leakage.

We shall consider the abilities to detect leakage and deception further in the next chapter, in the context of the general discussion of nonverbal receiving ability. However, it might be noted that there is an important issue that is not considered in these studies. Individual differences in observers may well be relatively unimportant *only if one assumes that they are attending to the same general cues.* In the Kraut and Poe (1980) and DePaulo and Rosenthal (1979a) studies, the attention of the observers was specifically directed toward the detection of deception via nonverbal cues in a relatively simple, noninteractive situation where the observers were exposed to the same videotaped cues. However, in "real life," and particularly in an interactive situation, the task confronting the observer is much more complex, and there may well be individual differences in attention patterns than strongly influence the kinds of information that one extracts from a given situation, including information relevant to deception. It may be only in such situations that the differences between an expert customs inspector and a less expert inspector or a lay person become manifest. Thus the "education of attention" is again relevant to our analysis of nonverbal communication, this time from the point of view of the detection of deception.

THE DEVELOPMENT OF DECEPTIVENESS

Another area with considerable potential for the analysis of deception involves the development of the ability to deceive. Feldman and his colleagues have pointed out that many aspects of the deception literature have developmental implications. For example, one would expect that children should be more revealing than adults, and that revealingness should decrease with age, due to cognitive changes such as the loss of egocentrism, increased role-taking skills, and experience of "external feedback" from others, all of which should make the growing child more aware that his or her nonverbal behavior can be viewed and interpreted by others. Also, younger children should be relatively more revealing from the face than the body, since they are not yet attempting to control expression, while older children should become progressively less facially revealing. Thus the body should become progressively more revealing with age (cf. Feldman, Jenkins, & Popoola, 1979; Feldman & White, 1980).

The developmental studies done to date are generally in line with these predictions, although they have raised more questions than they have answered. Fortunately, the questions have been intriguing. Feldman and his colleagues (1979) asked children and adults to respond truthfully or deceptively in an interview following the tasting of sweetened versus unsweetened drinks; that is, they were asked to pretend to have liked both drinks in order to "fool" an interviewer in a game-like situation. They found that observers could detect deception in the facial expressions of first graders more successfully than in those of 7th graders or adults, which is consistent with the general expectation that deception should increase with age.

In a subsequent study, Feldman and White (1980) studied the responses of children ranging from 5 to 12 years of age in a similar situation, with different conditions showing the child's face or body as he or she responded truthfully, or attempted to convince an interviewer that a bad-tasting drink was good, or a good-tasting drink bad. The results suggested a markedly different pattern of results from boys and girls. In general, girls showed the expected pattern, in that the observers watching the face became less able to detect deception with increasing age. Observers watching the body, in contrast, became slightly more able to detect deception with age, so that in the older ages the body was more revealing than the face. On the other hand, for boys the face became *more* revealing with age, contrary to expectations, while the revealingness of body movements did not change significantly. Several explanations were proposed to explain the latter result, but it seems likely that final understanding of this finding must await further study.

SUMMARY

On the whole, the deception literature is somewhat disappointing, in that despite considerable study, a theoretically coherent point of view has not yet emerged, and potentially meaningful links with phenomena closely related to deception have not yet been exploited. This may be due in great part to the relative narrowness of focus of the research on deception, which contrasts sharply with the wide range of studies relevant to inhibition. First, the concept of deception has been narrowly defined to include only conscious dissimulation. Second, most studies have used the same paradigm—a variant of the deception paradigm—and in fact not all of the possible variations of that paradigm have been explored. Third, many studies have been concerned with the nature of the nonverbal cues that occur during deception, and the channels over which these cues are transmitted, with relatively less attention going to the study of such broader issues as individual differences in deceptiveness and in the ability to detect leakage and deception, and the development of deception. Fourth, there has been a tendency to regard deception as a process separate from emotion, when in fact deception may be profitably viewed as a special case of the control of emotional expression. Finally, although some mention has been made of the phenomenon of self-deception, the implications of such a notion have not yet been systematically pursued. These points, and particularly the latter two, shall be considered in the next section in an attempt to integrate the concepts of inhibition and deception in a broader context.

AN INTEGRATED VIEW OF INHIBITION AND DECEPTION

One of the first requirements in such an integration is to develop a broader view of deception as involving both more and less conscious influences upon the spontaneous display. We have seen that inhibition involves a direct attenuation of the spontaneous display and that it is apparently based upon subcortical and paleocortical systems in the brain. Although inhibition can be acquired, such acquisition does not involve instrumental learning (see Figure 5.6). Deception, on the other hand, involves the influence of symbolic display rules to modulate, qualify, or falsify a display (see Chapter 2). In humans, these rules involve linguistically structured processes of logic and reasoning. Like language, such rules are learned and culturally patterned, although, also like many aspects of language, their employment may become virtually "automatic." We saw above that Ekman and Friesen (1969b) noted that all social interaction may be considered "deceptive" in this sense, quoting Goffman's (1959) work on self-presentation as an example.

This more extended conception of deception is not considered when one considers only intentional dissimulation. However, it is clearly amenable to research, and in fact much of the research considered in the last chapter is relevant to this broader view of deception. For example, the learned sex differences and effects of the social context on expressiveness are both relevant to the analysis of how one learns to nonverbally "present oneself," that is, to express oneself to others in different situations.

The structuralist view of nonverbal communication, to be considered in more detail in Chapter 8, is relevant to this broader view of deception. The structuralists emphasize how nonverbal behaviors are learned and patterned within a culture, much as is language, and that each individual learns "rules" for using nonverbal behavior—display and decoding rules—that are normative in that culture. Each individual learns to use culturally approved patterns of self-presentation which, in effect, are patterns of deception. Likewise, the development of each dyadic relationship can be seen as involving the development of a system of rules or norms more or less unique to that relationship. In effect, these, too, are patterns of deception. This analysis is also consistent with the position of constructivists who emphasize how the individual comes to behave in terms of socially constructed rules (Kelly, 1955; Reardon, 1981), as we shall see below.

This broader view of deception may be related to the notions of nonemotional deception, stressful deception, and emotional deception developed above. Nonemotional deception is analogous to the knowledge of and ability to use the conventional rules of social behavior not involving emotion. Stressful deception is analogous to the following of such rules even when that involves conflict and stress (the stress associated with the fact that rules are being followed, rather than the specific content of the rules). Finally, emotional deception is analogous to following the rules of emotional presentation when that does not correspond to how one actually feels.

Regarding the relationship between inhibition and deception, it was suggested above that less inhibited persons may be more adept at stressful deception, since everything else being equal they should actually experience less anxiety. However, due to their expressiveness they may be less adept at emotional deception, and others may be more able to read their "true feelings."

In summary, the present conception of inhibition and deception views both as processes which alter the spontaneous display of emotion, but inhibition involves more "primitive" brain structures and processes, while deception is seen as a symbolic process involving the employment of learned display rules which may modulate, qualify, or falsify the spontaneous expressive tendencies. Highly conscious dissimulation, which has been the focus of so much research, is seen as an important albeit limited aspect of deception.

SELF-DECEPTION: REPRESSION AND COPING

The notions of inhibition and deception refer to the control of external expression—the Emotion II process—and there has been relatively little attention to the important concept of self-deception, in which the responder is the object of the altered or dampened emotional information. In our terms, self-deception may occur in two ways, via the direct alteration of the Emotion III process, and/or via the cognitive–emotional interaction (see Chapter 2, especially Figure 2.3). In the former, the altered information would involve a difference between the actual and the perceived emotional state; in the latter, the information would involve different potential explanations for a veridically perceived emotional state. It seems reasonable to suggest that the former sort of self-deception is based like inhibition upon relatively primitive structures and processes. Some forms of *repression* may fall into this category. The latter form of self-deception is cognitive in nature, involving the cognitive–emotional interaction and the processes of self-attribution, emotional education, and coping described in previous chapters.

REPRESSION

The Concept of Repression

Repression is a central concept in classical psychoanalytic theory, having played a particularly important role in Freud's early theorizing (Freud, 1904). It refers to the dissociation of a memory and/or feeling from consciousness. This would imply a direct interference with the Emotion III process of subjective readout. Some of the earliest interest by psychiatrists in the nonverbal communication process was based upon the common clinical experience that repressed material may often be expressed indirectly in nonverbal behavior.

Physiological Bases of Repression

Galin's (1974) intriguing view of a possible physiological basis for repression was discussed in Chapter 3: that it is possible that the right and left hemispheres may gain different information about a situation because of their different modes of cognition, that the response tendencies of the two hemispheres may differ, and that the left hemisphere may in some way block the response tendencies of the right hemisphere from verbalizable experience.

It is noteworthy that the "antianxiety" barbiturate drug sodium amobarbital has been found useful in the treatment of certain forms of repression. As noted above, Gray (1971) has associated this drug with "turning off" the SHF BIS, thus creating tendencies toward extraversion. This therefore suggests a relationship between repression and the mechanisms of expression and inhibition discussed above.

Anosognosia and Repression

Sackeim and Gur (1978; Gur & Sackeim, 1979) have discussed the phenomenon of repression as self-deception. Sackeim (1982) has speculated about the possible neurological substrate of repression and questioned the traditional psychoanalytic assumption that repression is an indication of psychopathology. He has noted that brain injury (and particularly right-sided brain injury) can lead to the phenomenon of *anosognosia* or denial of illness. This condition can be associated with truly bizarre symptoms. Patients may deny that they are paralyzed, that they are hospitalized, that they have had an operation, that they have urinary incontinence, yet except for this gross denial they may appear normally oriented to events around them. Geschwind (1980) has cited examples of patients who deny that they are blind, and who are so convinced and convincing that they pass for being sighted (albeit with poor eyesight). When examined, one such patient consistently answered queries about how many fingers were being held in front of his face. He was often incorrect, but his true blindness was revealed only when he continued to answer even though the examiner had moved and was no longer holding up any fingers.

Sackeim (1982) suggests that anosognosia is an extreme form of self-deception, which may be caused by damage to areas of the brain concerned with mood regulation—preventing the excessive depression or elevation of mood. He notes the common tendency to deny the negative and exaggerate the positive. For example, on hearing of a great loss, such as the death of a loved one, there is a common experience of almost reflex denial. Sackeim suggests that this may be based upon a neurally represented distortive mechanism. In some forms of depression, such self-deceptive strategies may fail, and in some cases the positive may be denied and the negative enhanced. Sackeim suggests the possibility that there may be two mechanisms—one tending to exaggerate the positive and the other to exaggerate the negative.

The Functions of Repression

In commenting upon the clinical implications of these observations, Sackeim (1982) suggests that self-deception—seen as pathological in traditional psychoanalytic theory—may at times be adaptive and healthy: "With at least some patients progress may occur only when they are encouraged to view themselves unrealistically, to exaggerate positive aspects of life, minimize the negative, and in general acquire and utilize the biases and distortions that characterize normal functioning" (1982, p. 89). Indeed, there is evidence that certain forms of what might be considered "self-deceptive" coping strategies are conducive to physical health. For example, several studies have suggested that denial of illness may be associated with decreased morbidity and mortality in cancer (Abrams, 1971; Greer, Morris, & Pettingale, 1979; Hackett & Weisman, 1969). However, there may be important differences between coping strategies which allow veridical access to feelings and those which alter the Emotion III process and actually deny access to feelings. This shall be further considered below.

COPING

Self-Attribution

Other forms of self-deception allow the subject veridical access to feelings and memories, but act to alter their interpretation in various ways. Many studies have shown that cognitive manipulations can markedly alter emotional responding (cf. Buck, 1976a, Chapter 10). Schachter's (1964, 1970) self-attribution theory of emotion is particularly relevant in this regard. This theory was discussed in Chapter 2, including the Schachter and Singer (1962) study suggesting that cognitive manipulations can alter emotional self-reports and behavior. It appears that cognitive factors contribute to emotional experience particularly when the eliciting stimulus is ambiguous or unclear, and that emotional experience can be generated by the Emotion III process independently of cognitive factors. However, it is also the case that even veridically and unambiguously experienced emotions can be cognitively altered.

Emotional Education and Coping

In Chapter 4, we discussed the process of emotional education, which involves general linguistic influences upon emotion which go beyond the animal model of emotion; and the process of coping, which was defined as the application of linguistically structured rules to emotional phenomena. The process of learning how to deal linguistically with biologically based motivational/emotional states—what we have termed "coping"—is thus viewed as one of the results of the process of emotional education.

Coping can be considered to be a process of self-deception, in the expanded view of deception presented above. Just as individuals learn culturally patterned rules of self-presentation which may modulate, qualify, or falsify their external display of emotion, they also learn culturally patterned rules relevant to self-attribution—how to deal with their own subjectively experienced feelings. Thus although their feelings may be veridically perceived, their reasoning and interpretations about those feelings may vary widely.

Coping as Rules about Emotion

In Chapter 4, coping was defined as "the application of rules about emotion," and this view should be considered further in the present context. In his theory of personal constructs, Kelly (1955) postulated that people construe the world and themselves by recognizing repeated themes. They develop systems of constructs which serve in the measurement of other persons, objects, and events, and facilitate predictions about the future. These constructs may be viewed as anticipatory sets involving rules which regulate for action. Reardon (1981) has suggested that such rules tend to specify behavior which is *appropriate* by the standards of significant others, *consistent* with the self-image of the actor, and *effective* in terms of meeting important goals.

Studies in this "constructivist" tradition have generally emphasized the self and the social environment in the construction of rules. However, this overlooks the fact that bodily events involving emotional and motivational states also become involved in the construction of rules. A person develops rules for coping with emotion which, like other rules for behavior, tend to be appropriate, consistent, and effective (Buck & Reardon, 1983; Reardon & Buck, 1983).

Coping can thus be seen broadly as involving three interacting sources of information: the self, the body, and the social and physical environment. Each of these is autonomous to some extent and governed by its own principles of internal organization. The self is governed by psychological principles, and in humans is dominated by principles of logic and reasoning mediated by language. The body is governed by biological principles. The environment may be broken down into the physical environment, governed by physical laws, and the social environment, governed by social rules.

The Effectiveness of Coping Styles

The appropriateness, consistency, and effectiveness of coping styles may be defined in terms of the environment, self, or body. From the point of view of the social environment, there may or may not be consensus among others regarding coping styles. This may vary for different groups; thus significant others may or may not agree about what coping styles are called for in a given situation. From the point of view of the self, some coping styles may seem more appropriate, consistent, and effective than others based upon past experience and personality patterns. This may or may not agree with the evaluations of others. From the point of view of the body, some coping styles may be generally more conducive to health (Reardon & Buck, 1983).

Coping and Defense

There are a number of ways in which the coping process might be conceptualized. One is in terms of the "ego defense mechanisms" which were added to the concept of repression during the evolution of Freud's psychoanalytic theory (Freud, 1926; A. Freud, 1966). For example, rationalization, projection, and displacement may all be considered to be processes in which the personal implications of a veridically experienced emotion may be cognitively altered. Rationalization is the reinterpretation of feelings in terms less threatening to the subject, projection involves the blaming of others for such feelings, displacement is the expression of such feelings toward neutral or less dangerous objects than the "real" source of the feelings, and so forth. In all cases, the subject is aware of the feelings, but "copes" with them by a variety of cognitive manipulations.

A different approach to the analysis of coping styles has been taken by Mullen and Suls (1982), who distinguish attention and rejection as general styles of coping. Attention involves focusing attention on the stressor and/or one's reaction to it; rejection involves focusing attention away from the stressor. They suggest that both attention and rejection have potential functional value, in that rejection provides surcease from the stressor, while attention may provide helpful information. In a meta-analysis of 26 studies, they found evidence that rejection is helpful in the immediate alleviation of stress, while attention is more adaptive in the long run. In fact, rejection may be dysfunctional over time because it uses energy that could be used in combatting the stressor. Mullen and Suls suggest that the most adaptive strategy may be to use rejection during exposure to the stressor, and then shift to attention. However, they note that this pattern may not obtain when emotional responses to stress are considered. Also, as noted above, denial of illness has been associated with positive effects in cancer. It may be that attention is useful only when the individual can do something about the stressor, and that otherwise rejection is a preferable style.

Health Implications

The analysis of the effectiveness of coping styles, and how they may vary for different individuals and social groups, can aid in the understanding of the role of psychological and social factors in the etiology and course of both physical and psychiatric disorders. The way that a person learns to cognitively cope with his or her emotions must have important bearings upon the type and severity of psychiatric disorders that are likely to become manifest (cf. Lazarus, 1966). Emotional education plays a similarly important role in physical disease. We saw above that emotional factors influence a wide variety of disease processes, and that a dearth of emotional expression may often be related to increased autonomic/endocrine responding which may in turn contribute to any of a number of stress-related physical disorders.

The study of the nature of patterns of coping that might contribute to, or ameliorate, disease processes is an important area of current research, but few firm conclusions have yet been drawn. Two alternative but not necessarily competing hypotheses may be derived concerning the effectiveness of coping styles in promoting health (Buck & Reardon, 1983). On one hand, it may be that there are certain coping styles that are effective across the board in protecting health, and one may hypothesize that *specific coping styles have specific effects on health*. The strong version of this hypothesis would state that the nature of the coping style is all important, and that social support and personal consistency are irrelevant.

On the other hand, it may be that the nature of healthy coping styles varies with the individual and social environment. If an individual has a strong preference for a given coping style, and receives support for that choice from others, it may promote health regardless of the specific nature of the coping style. This could work by reducing the sense of helplessness in the person, and by allowing a style of emotional expression that seems appropriate both to the individual and to others. However, if the individual encounters social opposition to a preferred style of coping, or if others disagree about what styles are called for, the sense of confusion, helplessness, and inability to express emotion could create stress and contribute to psychiatric or somatic disorder. Thus, one could hypothesize that *the social support for, and personal consistency of, a coping style determines its protective effect*. The strong version of this hypothesis would state that it is social support for a consistent style that is important, and that the nature of the style is irrelevant.

Obviously, both of these hypotheses may be correct. Some coping styles may be more health promoting than others, and the consistency of the style with the personality and its perceived social appropriateness may enhance the healthfulness of any style. However, it is possible that conflicts can occur which have destructive effects independent of the coping style *per se*. Coping styles inconsistent with a given person may be suggested by well-meaning others because of a perception that they are appropriate, resulting in confusion, guilt, and stress for that person. Alternatively, the person and others might choose a coping style that, unknown to them, is destructive to health.

HEALTH IMPLICATIONS OF SELF-DECEPTION

Repression versus Coping

This view of repression versus coping has implications for the design and application of treatment techniques relevant to these conditions, that is, to break the self-deception or to foster coping styles that may be beneficial. For example, it may be that interview methods are useful for changing attributions about veridically perceived feelings. However, to the extent that the feelings are actually not veridically perceived, special techniques involving drugs, hypnotism, or other emotional manipulations may be necessary. Hopefully, the increased understanding of emotional expression and experience will help to provide a coherent theoretical basis for the choice, design, and application of such techniques.

This distinction also has implications for Sackeim's (1982) argument that self-deception is in some cases adaptive. Sackeim defines self-deception as a state in which certain beliefs and feelings are not subject to awareness. It could be argued that such a state of affairs really is pathological, in that relevant information is not accessible to the individual. In contrast, his positive examples of self-deception (i.e., where depressed persons learn to "accentuate the positive") can be analyzed as manipulating self-attribution rather than encouraging repression.

Self-Deception and Inhibition

The health implications of inhibition versus self-deception also require comment. We saw above that the inhibition of spontaneous emotional expression (Emotion II) is considered to be potentially pathological, possibly contributing to bodily stress. We also saw that the same inhibitory neural system (the BIS) apparently involved in such inhibition may also be involved in repression. It may be suggested, in concert with early psychoanalytic theory, that high levels of such inhibition and such repression are inherently pathological, robbing the individual of information, and perhaps energy, that are needed for a full and healthy life.

One aspect of the information thus lost involves a direct loss of access to the individual's own feelings (repression). Another, perhaps equally important aspect of the information lost is social in nature. Since the expression of emotion is inhibited, others have difficulty in gauging the emotional state of the sender, and they thus cannot coordinate their own behavior appropriately, or give appropriate feedback. The social development of the sender would seem to be inevitably restricted under such circumstances.

The Placebo Effect

The manipulations of coping processes involving attributions about veridically perceived feelings, on the other hand, may well have therapeutic effects, even if such attributions are from some points of view "incorrect." One clear example is the placebo effect, where treatments considered ineffective have actual curative influences. There are many examples of cures by faith-healers and shamans, as well as cases of "voodoo death," which suggest that the individual has previously unrecognized abilities at self-persuasion which can affect health (Frank, 1961).

Such effects may well involve specifiable biological systems. Thus, studies have suggested that the endogenous opiates play a role in the placebo effect. One study employed a substance—naloxone—which binds to opium receptors in the brain and blocks effects due to opiates. Naloxone was compared with a placebo in a study of pain tolerance, and it was found that whereas the placebo led to the usual "placebo effect" of higher pain tolerance, there was no such effect in the naloxone condition. Apparently the naloxone blocked the placebo effect. This suggests that the placebo effect is mediated by a process in the brain involving the endogenous opiates. Such systems may underlie remarkable individual capacities for self-healing. The study of how such capacities can be "turned on" is only beginning, but it seems reasonable that coping styles involving self-attributions may be importantly involved in such effects.

CONCLUSIONS

This chapter has considered research on inhibition, which has been the object of investigation from many points of view over many years, so that there is now a rich diversity of relevant research which holds promise for a major synthesis; and deception, which has been the object of rather more narrowly focused research over a shorter period of time. Inhibition was seen as based upon subcortical and paleocortical brain structures, while deception has been studied in terms of a highly conscious dissimulation. It was suggested that the conception of deception be broadened to include the kind of "self-presentation" described by Goffman (1959) which is learned and culturally patterned but which nevertheless may become nonconscious and virtually "automatic."

It was suggested that one can distinguish two forms of self-deception which are analogous to inhibition and deception, respectively. The more "primitive" process involves repression, where there is a direct interference with the Emotion III readout into subjective experience. It was suggested that the neural systems underlying inhibition may also be involved in repression, and that high levels of these processes are pathological. The other process involves the cognitive labeling or attribution about the subjective readout, which underlies rules about emotion associated with coping styles and defense mechanisms such as rationalization, projection, and displacement. Careful manipulations of such self-attributions may produce therapeutic effects even if the attributions are incorrect, that is, are "misattributions." The placebo effect is but one example of such a manipulation.

7

NONVERBAL RECEIVING ABILITY

Studies of nonverbal sending accuracy form a relatively coherent package. Different approaches to the study of sending accuracy find generally similar patterns of results, and these patterns are consistent with the findings in other areas of investigation, including studies of neurophysiological processes and animal learning. Indeed, the degree of coherence is remarkable, and it underlies the expectation that a major synthesis in the understanding of emotional expression and inhibition is under way.

The same statements, alas, cannot be made for studies of nonverbal receiving ability. In contrast with the sending accuracy studies, different measures of receiving ability relate to each other very little or not at all. It was noted in the last chapter that "deceptiveness" is more homogeneous than is the ability to detect deception; that, for example, the ability to detect leakage is not related to the ability to detect deception. There is reason to believe that nonverbal receiving ability is based upon a host of different variables, which have only begun to be understood.

It might be argued that investigators in this area have been too much involved with the construction of empirical tests of receiving ability, and too little concerned with the theoretical nature of what really must be involved with receiving ability. However, these tests have not entirely failed, and even when they have, their failures have pointed the way to the important theoretical contributions.

This chapter first discusses the relationship of nonverbal receiving ability to the broader area of person perception, briefly reviewing the history of studies of accuracy in person perception and focusing particularly upon the methodological problems that were identified in the early literature in that area. It then reviews some of the recent attempts to measure accuracy in emotion recognition, or emotion receiving ability, which may be considered to be a special case of accuracy in person perception which avoids some of the complexities and methodological problems of the latter. However, emotional receiving ability has complexities and methodological problems of its own. Some of the reasons for the complexities in emotional receiving ability are suggested, and current approaches to these complexities are examined. A model of nonverbal receiving ability is then proposed, which recalls the discussion of the evolution of receiving ability presented in Chapter 2, involving both direct "person perception" and mediated "person cognition." Finally, the chapter examines the possible relationship between emotional receiving ability, cerebral lateralization, and the evolution of symbolic communication.

STUDIES OF ACCURACY IN PERSON PERCEPTION

EARLY STUDIES

The Difference-Score Paradigm

The issue of accuracy in person perception, or "empathy," has been one of the classic issues in social and personality psychology for many years. It has long been recognized that an essential aspect of the ability to interact with others in a mutually rewarding way involves the ability to accurately predict how the other will respond. It has been assumed that the more accurate this prediction, the better the skill in interaction. The early studies assumed that this ability to predict must involve the ability to discern the enduring personality, attitudes, and values of the other. If one knew these enduring characteristics, it was reasoned that one could accurately predict the behavior of the other in a wide variety of situations.

This model of person perception was combined with the contemporary interest in psychometric measurement to produce what might be called the difference-score paradigm. In this, the characteristics of the person (P) are first measured to provide a *criterion* measure of personality, attitudes, and/or values. P is then presented in some way to the subjects, or judges (Js)—that is, P may be introduced in person, a film of P may be shown, or P's behavior may be described in some way. Using this information about P, the Js attempt to guess P's position on the criterion measure. Thus if the criterion involves religious attitudes, the Js might try to guess how religious P is from this sample of P's behavior. The accuracy of each J is measured quite simply by taking the difference between J's rating on the scale of religiosity and P's actual position on this scale.

A great many studies were done through the 1930s and into the early 1950s using this paradigm (cf. Bruner & Tagiuri, 1954; Cline, 1964). However, the literature never really led to a greater understanding of the accuracy in person perception. Only a few findings seemed to be stable from study to study: For example, females usually tended to be slightly more accurate judges than males, and Js who were similar to the P in their own characteristics were more accurate than Js who were dissimilar to the P. However, very little light was shed on the childhood determinants of accuracy in person perception, or personality correlates, or techniques to increase accuracy, so that the potential practical benefits of measuring accuracy in person perception—choosing better potential clinicians, teaching persons with difficulty in relating to others to be more accurate, and so forth—were never realized. It gradually became apparent that this was due to methodological problems with the difference-score paradigm itself. Several methodological problems were recognized from the first, one being the validity of the measurement of the criterion, another being the issue of how best to present the P to the panel of Js. However, the apparently simple difference scores concealed much more serious methodological problems.

Assumed Similarity

One of the most important of these problems was pointed out by Hastorf and Bender (1952). This was that the greater apparent accuracy of Js similar to the P was not because they could better discern the characteristic of the P, but rather, they appeared to be more accurate because the Js, lacking real information on which to base the judgments they were called upon to make, simply assumed that the P was similar to themselves. Thus a religious J appeared to be more accurate than a nonreligious J when confronted with a religious P, not because the former was better at "reading" the religious P, but because both Js, lacking real information about P's religiosity, simply assumed that P was similar to themselves. Since the religious J happened to be more similar to the P, the difference score made it appear that he or she was more "accurate in person perception" than the nonreligious J.

Other Problems

The problem of assumed similarity was devastating to the difference-score paradigm, rendering a whole area of study virtually meaningless in one stroke. However, there were other problems as well. Cronbach (1955) pointed out that the apparently simple difference-score measure also concealed effects attributable to the ways in which the Js used the rating scales, and also the J's "stereotype accuracy," or the accuracy of a J's notions about where people in general fall on the criterion measure. Thus, a J who has an accurate idea of about how religious people are in general would tend to appear more accurate in person perception on this measure than Js who incorrectly assume that everyone is more or less religious than they actually are. The incorrect stereotype would introduce a bias into the difference scores which would have nothing to do with the J's ability to perceive the characteristics of *that particular* P, which Cronbach calls "differential accuracy" and which is the concept on which the notion of accuracy in person perception is based (Cline, 1964).

ALTERNATIVE PARADIGMS

The problems with the difference-score approach to person perception have been addressed by multivariate techniques which seek to analyze the difference scores into meaningful components, including stereotype and differential accuracy (Cline, 1964). However, other investigators have been impressed by the other problems inherent in the method, such as the criterion problem, and the general questioning of the extent to which personality and other characteristics really do remain stable across situations (Mischel, 1968, 1969). This questioning, plus the resurgence of research on nonverbal communication and emotion during the late 1960s, contributed to the attractiveness of a new approach to the measurement of "empathy": accuracy in emotion recognition.

APPROACHES TO EMOTION RECEIVING ABILITY

MEASURING TECHNIQUES

A number of techniques designed to measure emotion receiving ability, often derived directly from studies of nonverbal communication accuracy, have been advanced in recent years. These include the Affective Sensitivity (AS) Test of Kagan and his colleagues (Campbell, Kagan, & Krathwohl, 1971; Kagan, 1978); the Brief Affect Recognition Test (BART) described by Ekman and Friesen (1974b); the Communication of Affect Receiving Ability Test (CARAT) described by Buck (1976b); the Rosenthal *et al.* (1979) Profile of Nonverbal Sensitivity (PONS); and the Social Interpretation Task (SIT) of Archer and Akert (1977). All of these instruments are based upon the same general notion: that nonverbal receiving ability involves the ability to decode the states of others via nonverbal cues, and that a reasonable way to approach the measurement of nonverbal receiving ability is to present judges with samples of nonverbal behavior, ask them questions about it, and assess the accuracy of their replies.

The Affective Sensitivity Test

The original version of the AS Test showed videotapes of brief excerpts of actual client–counselor interactions. For each excerpt, the subject was required to indicate what the client was feeling given three alternatives, one of which was considered correct. The criteria for accuracy involved the client's recall of his or her actual feelings during the interaction, and the judgments of expert observers.

A more recent version of the test shows excerpts of interactions between professionals and clients, teachers and pupils, therapists and clients, and physicians and patients. Following each of the 30 excerpts, the subject answers several questions about the thoughts and feelings of the interactants by choosing between five alternatives. In each case, one alternative is considered most correct, receiving two points; one is considered incorrect, receiving no points; and three are considered partially correct, receiving one point. The points are summed for a total score and for 13 subscores involving logically similar types of items (i.e., those involving males vs. females).

The early version of the AS Test has been demonstrated to distinguish between effective and ineffective counselors (Campbell *et al.*,

1971), and the instrument as a whole has face validity. However, some of the complexities (and frustrations) involved in constructing measures of nonverbal sensitivity are illustrated by the fact that scores on the later version of the test do not correlate significantly with scores on the original version ($r = .06$; Kagan, 1978). Apparently the two versions are measuring different things, the nature of which is not clear.

The Brief Affect Recognition Test

The BART instrument includes 70 black-and-white slides showing seven types of facial expressions, six of which were selected to represent the primary affects of happiness, sadness, fear, anger, surprise, and disgust, plus a neutral expression. These slides are presented briefly (for 1/30 second) via a tachistoscope, with the justification that the short exposure given the photograph is similar to the brevity of spontaneously emitted facial cues. The task of the subject is to judge the expression, with the criteria of accuracy being based upon Ekman and Friesen's extensive studies of judgments of posed expressions. Seven scores are derived from BART: one for overall accuracy and one for each of the six primary affects.

One of the major advantages of the BART is that it involves measures of the sensitivity to different emotions, the importance of which have been well documented. One of the major disadvantages is that it has not proved amenable to group administration, since a tachistoscopic presentation has been found to be necessary. Also, tachistoscopic proficiency has been found to be a major factor in the accuracy scores. This has necessitated the use of another test, the Facial Interpretation Test (FIT) consisting of slides of faces with the mouth and eyes in stages of being open or closed, to partial out the effects of tachistoscopic proficiency from the BART scores (O'Sullivan & Hagar, 1980).

The Communication of Affect Receiving Ability Test

The CARAT instrument uses as items selected videotaped sequences taken via the slide-viewing technique, showing senders as they view affective color slides. The task of the receiver is to guess (without audio cues) which kind of slide the sender viewed on each trial, with the criterion of accuracy being the actual slide viewed. The final instrument has 32 items involving four kinds of slides—sexual, scenic, unpleasant, and unusual—and 25 different stimulus persons.

The CARAT is unique among tests of nonverbal receiving ability in that it was assembled using standard item analysis techniques. That is relevant to the present discussion because the process of item analysis theoretically leads to the construction of an internally homogeneous test, and this did not prove to be the case. Six hundred items were originally available. These were reduced to 108 items in an initial selection, which was further refined into two 40-item test forms. These were shown to large groups of subjects (108 and 182 subjects, respectively) and an item analysis was performed in which those items which showed the highest correlations with the total score were retained. The internal consistency of a 20-item operational test derived from this procedure, as indexed by coefficient alpha, was .57. The 47 "best" items from these two 40-item forms were then given to a new sample of 164 subjects, and a 32-item final form was derived which, with minor modifications, remains the final form of the CARAT. Unfortunately, the internal consistency of the instrument was not improved, with the coefficient alpha of the final version estimated to be .56. The test–retest reliability of the CARAT, on the other hand, has been found to be satisfactory ($r = .79$ and $.80$ in two samples). CARAT scores were higher in samples of male business and fine arts majors than in science majors, they were slightly higher in undergraduate females than males, and recent research has found CARAT scores to be positively correlated with Rotter's (1966) interpersonal trust scale (Buck, 1976b; Sabatelli, Buck, & Dreyer, 1983a).

The CARAT is the only test of nonverbal receiving ability which employs videotapes of the spontaneous response to emotional stimuli. It employs a number of stimulus persons and a variety of emotions, the criterion of accuracy is straightforward, and the task is easily understood by the subjects (cf. Buck, 1976b). However, the failure to improve coefficient alpha with item analysis raises questions about whether it is in fact possible to construct an internally homogeneous test of nonverbal receiving ability in an instrument such as the CARAT. Perhaps receiving ability is not a single unidimensional ability, but rather involves a number of abilities; for example, one's ability to receive from males might differ from one's ability to receive from females, or one's abilities to receive negative and positive emotional cues might differ. We shall discuss some of the possible components of nonverbal receiving abilities below.

Derivatives of the CARAT are possible, presenting only the events of the slide period, for example, or adding the content-filtered audio track of the subject's description during the talk period. Such derivatives may begin to approach the problem of addressing different kinds of receiving abilities. However, work on such derivatives has only begun recently, in contrast to the several derivatives of PONS that have done much to add to the usefulness of that technique. Also, the version of the CARAT available for use to other investigators is of marginal technical quality, again in contrast to the wide availability of the PONS.

The Profile of Nonverbal Sensitivity

The PONS instrument developed by Rosenthal et al. (1979) involves 20 emotional responses, posed by a single individual, which were designed to vary along dominance–submission and positive–negative dimensions. Such dimensions were used in analyses of interaction made by Carson (1969), Leary (1955, 1957), and others. These responses are each presented 11 times in three different video forms (face only, body only, face plus body) and two audio forms (content-filtered voice and randomized spliced voice), resulting in 220 stimulus scenes, each of which lasts 2 seconds. The task of the subject is to choose which of two emotional situations is being posed on each trial. The instrument yields a total score, and also a "profile" of scores reflecting a person's relative sensitivity to, for example, facial versus bodily cues, or to dominance cues expressed in the face.

A number of versions of the PONS have been developed for particular purposes. For example, a short form exists which includes only facial and bodily cues; the brief-exposure PONS tests sensitivity to brief presentations of visual cues (median exposure 250 milliseconds; Rosenthal et al., 1979); the Nonverbal Discrepancy Test (NDT) shows facial and bodily enactments paired with altered-voice enactments that are entirely consistent, moderately discrepant, or completely discrepant with one another (DePaulo et al., 1978); the Measure of Verbal and Nonverbal Sensitivity (MOVANS) shows visual and altered-voice enactments paired with verbal transcripts, the whole of which are discrepant or nondiscrepant to different extents (Blanck & Rosenthal, 1981, 1982). The task of the subject in the latter two procedures is to rate the stimulus in positiveness and dominance as well as degree of discrepancy, with the goal of determining skill at recognizing discrepancy and which channels are used to judge positiveness and dominance when discrepancy exists. These versions of the PONS have been used in much research, and have led to many insights into the process of nonverbal receiving ability.

The Social Interpretation Task

The SIT technique involves 20 brief videotaped segments showing naturally occurring situations (i.e., two people talking) which, although the participants were aware of the camera, were otherwise unposed. Audio as well as visual cues are present. For each segment, the subject is asked a question which has a definitely correct answer, for example: Is the person on the telephone talking to a man or a woman? Which of the two women is the mother of the nearby child? (Archer & Akert, 1977).

RELATIONSHIPS BETWEEN MEASURES

Several of the measures of nonverbal receiving ability have problems with internal consistency—the new version of the AS Test does not correlate significantly with the old; coefficient alpha of the CARAT was not improved by item analysis; abilities on different channels of the PONS are often inconsistent; and so forth. Studies of the relationships between these measures have similarly been disappointing. Buck and Carroll (1974) found a .02 correlation between the CARAT and the long form of the PONS; Klaiman (1979) found a significant correlation between the CARAT and the face score of the PONS short form for females (r (109) $= .24$, $p < .01$) but not for males (r (97) $= .09$). Fields and O'Sullivan (1976) found a disappointing pattern of correlations between the PONS, BART, and SIT. Apparently these instruments are sensitive to different aspects of nonverbal receiving ability, or, to put it another way, nonverbal receiving ability is not a unidimensional construct, but involves many different "abilities," as suggested above. This is consistent with the evidence presented in the last chapter that the abilities to detect leakage and deception are not significantly related to one another. The next section shall discuss the nature of these abilities.

COMPLEXITIES OF NONVERBAL RECEIVING ABILITY

In discussing the methods of studying spontaneous sending accuracy in Chapter 5, it was suggested that each procedure has its strengths and weaknesses, and that they should be considered alternatives rather than competing techniques. The same point could be made with regard to the measures of receiving ability. However, whereas the measures of spontaneous sending accuracy relate to one another in coherent ways, the measures of receiving ability do not. Apparently the empirical approach of presenting people with samples of nonverbal behavior and measuring their ability to decode it is not sufficient to capture the complexities of nonverbal receiving ability. Some of these complexities, and recent approaches to their analysis, are discussed in this section.

RECEIVING SPONTANEOUS VERSUS SYMBOLIC BEHAVIOR

I have argued that the distinction between spontaneous and symbolic behaviors is crucial for the analysis of sending accuracy. There is evidence that it is important for the analysis of receiving ability as well. LaRusso (1978) employed Miller's communication paradigm to prepare videotapes of spontaneous expressions of the anticipation of shock versus no shock. She then asked the same senders to pose anticipating shock versus no shock. These videotapes were shown to 24 paranoid patients and 24 normal subjects, who judged whether the sender was anticipating shock or not. "Correct" answers were scored on the spontaneous trials if the subject correctly guessed if the shock was to be presented or not, and on the posed trials if the subject guessed that the subject was going to receive a shock when the sender posed anticipating shock. The results indicated that the paranoid patients were superior to the normals of the spontaneous stimuli, but inferior to them on the posed stimuli (see Figure 7.1). LaRusso

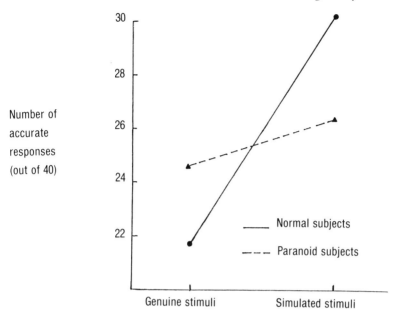

Figure 7.1. Mean accuracy scores showing interaction of Group (paranoid–normal) × Tape Condition (genuine–simulated). From Figure 1 in "Sensitivity of Paranoid Patients to Nonverbal Cues" by L. LaRusso, *Journal of Abnormal Psychology*, 1978, 87, 463–471. Copyright 1978 by the American Psychological Association. Reprinted by permission.

suggests that the paranoid patients have a greater sensitivity to genuine nonverbal cues than normals, but that they are less accepting of stereotyped social presentations. She points out that the apparently lower accuracy of the paranoid patients on the posed trials may actually indicate a high degree of perceptiveness: They may have "seen through" the act and in fact their labeling of many simulated shock trials as involving "no shock" may have been, on one level, quite correct.

This finding suggests that the ability to read spontaneous cues differs in significant ways from the ability to read the stereotyped symbolic cues that are derived from display rules involved in the nonverbal "presentation of self." This is further substantiated by results considered below suggesting that the common finding of superior receiving ability in women may apply only to symbolic displays.

If one is interested in measuring sensitivity to spontaneous displays, one should use instruments which involve spontaneous behavior in their stimuli. Of the tests mentioned above, the BART and PONS clearly involve posed expression, the AS and SIT instruments involve the audiovisual presentation of conversational behaviors with both spontaneous and symbolic elements, and the CARAT as presently constituted involves both spontaneous behaviors (during the slide period) and a silent presentation of conversational behaviors (during the talk period). It may be useful to develop instruments which involve "pure" spontaneous versus highly symbolic behavior.

LEAKAGE AND DECODING RULES

The above observation illustrates the fact that nonverbal receiving ability involves more than the direct perception of emotion in others, and that expectations about expressive presentations must be taken into account as well. We defined "decoding rules" above as cultural rules or expectations about the attention to, and interpretation of, emotional displays. A great deal of work has been done in this area by Rosenthal and his colleagues, using derivatives of the PONS.

Sex Differences in Accommodation

One of the most intriguing findings in this area involves the inter-pretation of sex differences in nonverbal receiving ability. Much research has suggested that women generally score higher than men in tests of receiving ability (Hall, 1978). However, Rosenthal and DePaulo (1979a, 1979b) have suggested that this effect may be restricted to the more obvious, less "leaky" nonverbal cues. We saw in the last chapter that they suggest, following Ekman and Friesen (1969b, 1974a), that different nonverbal channels can be ordered according to their leakiness, with the face being the most controlled and least leaky, the body being more leaky than the face; tone of voice being more leaky than the body; very brief exposures of "micro-momentary" facial/bodily cues being more leaky; and discrepancies between different channels being the more difficult to control and therefore the most leaky of all.

In regard to the sex difference in nonverbal receiving ability, Rosenthal and DePaulo (1979a, 1979b) present evidence that, as nonverbal cues become less controlled and more leaky, women progressively lose their advantage over men in their nonverbal receiving ability scores. They hypothesize that women learn not to "eavesdrop" on the leaky nonverbal cues of others, that they in effect see only what the other wishes them to see. In this sense, Rosenthal and DePaulo suggest that women are more "polite" and accommodating in their interactions with others. In effect, women learn *not* to detect deception. Rosenthal and DePaulo present evidence that women who are not so nonverbally accommodating are judged by others as having less successful interpersonal outcomes, and that sex differences in accommodation are greater in women who are socially and personally more vulnerable, and in cultures where women are less liberated and more oppressed. Recently, Blanck, Rosenthal, Snodgrass, DePaulo, and Zuckerman (in press) have found evidence consistent with a social learning interpretation of the sex difference in accommodation. As young girls grow older, they progressively lose more of their advantage over males on leaky channels, while they gain more of an advantage on less leaky channels. Apparently this reflects their learning about when it is and is not socially appropriate to decode different nonverbal communications.

It is noteworthy that several studies have failed to find a significant female advantage in decoding spontaneous expression (Buck *et al.*, 1972, 1974; Manstead *et al.*, 1982), and Fugita *et al.* (1980) found that females were better than males in decoding posed but not spontaneous expressions. These findings make sense in terms of Rosenthal and DePaulo's analysis, for spontaneous expressions are more likely to contain leaky cues (Manstead *et al.*, 1982).

The Development of Decoding Rules

This brings us to another aspect of the analysis of leakage and decoding rules—the analysis of the development of decoding rules. Blanck and Rosenthal (1982) have reviewed studies analyzing the development of strategies for decoding discrepant multichannel messages. They suggest that nonverbal sensitivity becomes increasingly differentiated with age (DePaulo & Rosenthal, 1979a; Zuckerman, Blanck, DePaulo, & Rosenthal, 1980) and that children learn to rely more heavily on leakier, less controllable channels when discrepancies are perceived in a message, because they apparently learn that these channels express the true underlying meaning of the message (Blanck,

Rosenthal, Snodgrass, DePaulo, & Zuckerman, 1982). Also, Blanck, Zuckerman, DePaulo, and Rosenthal (1980) have found evidence of sibling similarity of nonverbal skill and style on the NDT, suggesting that common family experiences may produce similar decoding styles.

Other investigators have also studied the course of the development of nonverbal receiving ability. For example, Abramovich and Daly (1979) have studied children's use of immediacy cues in determining whether two persons shown on a videotape know one another, and Daly, Abramovich, and Pliner (1980) have found that children whose mothers are good senders tend to be good receivers. Also, Pendleton and Snyder (1982) have studied the development of the ability to articulate a decoding strategy in children attempting to decode the preferences of a videotaped child for a hidden toy.

These studies have broad implications which go beyond the analysis of receiving ability *per se*, in that they are relevant to the analysis of the development of the processes of person perception and attribution, an area which has been neglected until recently. They also may be articulated with more extensive areas of developmental investigation, such as studies of the development of cognitive supports for social behavior. Examples of the latter include Selman's (1971, 1973) analysis of role-taking ability from a Piagetian framework and by extension the whole area of the development of moral judgment (Kohlberg, 1963, 1964; Piaget, 1932). The analysis of different aspects of receiving ability may offer clues to the development of the building blocks of these larger skills, and provide insights about the factors which influence this development.

SPECIFIC NONVERBAL RECEIVING ABILITY

Another potential problem of the measures of nonverbal receiving ability is that they all assess sensitivity to persons that the receiver has no relationship with and has never met. Such sensitivity to the generalized other, or "general nonverbal receiving ability," may be quite different from an individual's sensitivity to the expressions of a person with whom he or she has an ongoing relationship. For example, it may be that clinicians develop a special sensitivity to their own clients, parents to their own children, lovers to their own mates, and that this sensitivity need not necessarily generalize to other persons. Thus, "specific nonverbal receiving ability," defined as the ability to accurately decode the nonverbal behavior of a person with whom one has a specific relationship, may differ in significant ways from the abilities measured by these instruments (cf. Buck, 1979b; Buck & Lerman, 1979).

There is considerable evidence that people often decode the expressions of persons known to them more accurately than they decode unknown persons. Children decode the expressions of their own mothers more accurately than those of unknown mothers (Abramovich, 1977), and the expressions of known peers more accurately than those of unfamiliar children (Abramovich & Daly, 1979). Also, mothers decode the expressions of their children more accurately than do undergraduates (Buck, 1975) and more accurately than they decode the expressions of other children (Zuckerman & Przewuzman, 1979).

There is evidence that specific nonverbal receiving ability also has relationships with relevant variables which are different from, and perhaps more meaningful than, those of general nonverbal receiving ability. For example, Buck and Lerman (1979) found relationships between clinical training and the ability to decode the spontaneous expression of one's own client, while relationships between clinical training and the ability to decode the clients of others, and also ability on the CARAT, were not significant. Also, Sabatelli, Buck, and Dreyer (1980, 1982) studied specific receiving ability (ability to decode the partner) and general receiving ability (CARAT score) in dating and married couples, finding that neither specific nor general receiving ability were related to the length or reported quality of the relationship in dating couples (1980). However, in married couples there were interesting relationships between the ability to decode the spouse and the quality of the relationship. Specifically, it was found that spouses were more accurate at decoding their partner's expressions than was a panel of undergraduate judges, and although sensitivity to the spouse *per se* was not significantly correlated with reports of marital satisfaction, it was found that the wife's ability to decode her husband's expressions *on those trials where the undergraduates could not* was positively and significantly related to both the wife's and husband's reported satisfaction with the relationship. In other words, the wife's ability to decode an overtly and obviously expressed message was not significantly related to marital satisfaction, but her sensitivity to expressions which others could not decode was. This result is consistent with findings by Gottman (1979a) that "private message systems" are more common among happily than unhappily married couples, and it suggests that global measures even of specific nonverbal receiving ability may not be sufficiently sensitive to subtle aspects of nonverbal communication.

This suggests a significant limitation upon attempts to develop general tests of nonverbal receiving ability, particularly when they are based upon the nonverbal behavior of unknown persons. To the extent that nonverbal receiving ability is based upon cues which are idiosyncratic and specific to a given sender, *any* measure of general receiving ability may produce findings that are incomplete and perhaps misleading. Clearly more data on how nonverbal receiving ability varies across relationships would be welcome, and would greatly increase our understanding of the whole process of person perception.

Another study relevant to specific nonverbal receiving ability investigated the receivers' physiological responses to painful facial displays of spouses versus unknown others. There is considerable evidence that observers show evidence of autonomic arousal to grimaces and other pain displays (Berger, 1962; Craig & Lowrey, 1969; Vaughan & Lanzetta, 1980). Block (1981) showed videotapes of the pain versus neutral displays of pain patients and two performers to the spouses of the pain patients, while heart-rate and skin-conductance responses were monitored. Pain displays produced greater skin-conductance responding than did neutral displays. Also, subjects who reported being satisfied with their marriage responded with greater skin-conductance responses to the pain displays of the spouse than did less satisfied subjects.

RECEIVING ABILITY AND SENDING ACCURACY

An observation by Sabatelli *et al.* (1979) introduces another potential complexity to the analysis of nonverbal receiving ability. This study investigated the relationship between nonverbal communication accuracy and cognitive style, with the general expectation that nonverbal receiving ability would be related to field dependence. This expectation was based upon the description of field-dependent persons as being more oriented toward external, social cues, and it was felt that such persons should be more experienced with and able to respond to nonverbal cues in others. Thus, it has been found that field-dependent persons spend more time looking at the faces of the persons with whom they are interacting (Konstadt & Forman, 1965; Nevill, 1974). However, the Sabatelli *et al.* (1979) results indicated no significant relationships between cognitive style and receiving ability. Instead, field-dependent persons were found to be significantly better *senders* on the slide-viewing technique. While we saw in Chapter 5 that more recent work has replicated this finding only for males (Sabatelli *et al.*, 1983b), this finding suggested an interesting possibility: that the most controllable way of being a good receiver is to be a good sender.

In other words, if a person actively sends out information in the form of nonverbal expression, it is likely that others will reciprocate, in a way analogous to the reciprocity of self-disclosure that has been noted by Ehrlich and Graeven (1971). Field-dependent persons have been found to be more verbally self-disclosing (Sousa-Poza, Rohrberg, & Shulman, 1973), and this suggests that they may be more nonverbally self-disclosing as well. Beyond this, this suggests the possibility of an interactional view of nonverbal receiving ability in which one determines the probability of encountering meaningful cues from others by providing meaningful cues to others. Such a possibility can only be evaluated in interactional settings where both sending accuracy and receiving ability are assessed.

ATTENTION TO NONVERBAL CUES

Still another problem with existing measures of nonverbal receiving ability is that they all specifically or implicitly instruct the subject to attend to the nonverbal cues contained in the instrument. There is no assurance that a person who attends to nonverbal cues while taking a test will also do so in "real life," so that the receiving ability score obtained may bear little or no relationship to the person's actual tendency to attend to, and receive information from, others.

The Education of Attention

The education of attention has been discussed at several points: in Chapter 2 in the context of the analysis of perceptual skill from the viewpoint of Gibson's (1966, 1977, 1979) theory of perception, in Chapter 4 in the context of the analysis of responses that differ in accessibility, and in Chapter 6 in the context of the basis of "leakiness" of different response channels and the ability to detect deception. In essence, the education of attention involves the perceptual selection of information from oneself and the environment. Information from more "accessible" response systems is generally more salient than those from less accessible response systems. However, there may be cultural and individual differences in this learning: One can learn to attend to information that others ignore, as persons from India may learn to attend to bodily cues that are ignored by most Westerners, and as patients with biofeedback may learn to attend to normally "inaccessible" cues.

This concept is critical to the analysis of nonverbal receiving ability, for, as we noted above, a person skilled in nonverbal receiving ability may differ from a less skilled receiver not only in the ability to decode an emotion display once it is perceived, but also in the tendency to attend to emotional displays at all. Also, a "poor receiver" who ignores the emotional displays of others may be successful when instructed to attend to such displays in a test situation. It will be recalled that, in the last chapter, we noted the Kraut and Poe (1980) findings concerning the ability of subjects to detect deception in a "customs inspection" situation, and the argument that deception–detection is stimulus driven, with individual differences in detection ability being relatively unimportant. A consideration of the education of attention suggested an important qualification to this conclusion: it would be the case only when receivers are attending to and attempting to detect deception. The ability to appropriately direct one's attention in the face of complex cues in a "real life" situation is an extremely important basis for individual differences in receiving ability, be it for customs inspectors, interrogators, priests, parents, or psychotherapists.

The Segmentation Technique

One way to assess the attentional focus of the individual is to employ the kind of behavior segmentation technique discussed in Chapter 5, in which subjects are instructed to watch a film and indicate by pressing a button when a "meaningful event" occurs (Dickman, 1963; Newtson, 1976). Since the definition of what is meaningful is left to the subject, it allows an analysis of the subject's pattern of attention to the film.

For example, Goodman (1980) used a videotape of a person showing both instrumental actions (sitting down, picking up a magazine, lighting a cigarette, etc.) and emotional expressions (frowning, smiling, shaking the head, shrugging the shoulders, etc.) In one condition (*Action Focus*) subjects were instructed to press the button when the person on the videotape showed meaningful actions, in another (*Emotion Focus*) they were told to press when the person showed emotions, in a third (*No Focus*) they were not specifically instructed to focus on either actions or emotions, and examples of both were given in the instructions, leaving them free to respond to either. Consensual points (CPs) were defined in a way similar to Buck *et al.* (1982), as intervals in which a higher than expected (1 standard deviation above the mean) number of observers pressed the button. In the Goodman (1980) study, the intervals were 3 seconds long.

Results indicated that the pattern of button presses in the Action Focus and Emotion Focus conditions were quite different, with subjects in the Action Focus condition pressing to instrumental actions and those in the Emotion Focus condition pressing to emotional expressions. Interestingly, the pattern of CPs in the No Focus condition was quite similar to that of the Action Focus condition and dissimilar from the Emotion Focus condition, suggesting that under the circumstances of this study, these subjects attended to instrumental actions, and at least consciously ignored the emotional expressions.

Analysis of Events at CPs

Three still photographs were taken over the 3-second CP intervals and analyzed to determine the nature of the changes taking place. Ten "action-oriented CPs" from the Action Focus and No Focus conditions, and ten "emotion-oriented CPs" from the Emotion Focus condition were so analyzed. From inspection of the photographs and videotape, Goodman defined four types of change: (1) *change in object interaction* was scored if the target person began or ended interaction with an object in the environment, (2) *change in position in space* was scored if the photographs showed a full body movement (e.g., sitting down, standing up, walking), (3) *change in body features* was scored if a body part (head, arm) changed position in a "non-expressive" way, and (4) *change in expression* was scored if facial features changed, or if expressive bodily changes (e.g., shrugging, hand gestures) occurred.

Table 7.1 summarizes the results of this analysis. Action CPs contained significantly more changes in interactions with environmental objects and in bodily position in space, and significantly fewer expressive changes, when compared with emotion CPs. Facial expressions occurred at all of the emotion CPs. For two of them, expressive body changes—shrugging the shoulders and a slumping of the upper body—also occurred. Both action and emotion CPs contained changes in body features.

A Segmentation Approach to Receiving Ability

Goodman's study illustrates the point that people may, because of instructions, pay attention to different aspects of a nonverbal display. It is similarly possible that there are individual differences in these patterns of attention that are due to the process of the education of attention, that is, learning to generally attend to emotional cues or not. This could be assessed by correlating the pattern of button presses produced by a given individual with, for example, the pattern produced by experts who are attending to emotional cues. The higher the correlation, the closer that person would be to organizing the display in a way similar to that of the experts. This would be useful as a teaching device, and in evaluating the attentional focus of the subject. It would also serve as a bridge between two traditional approaches to person perception: the accuracy approach and the process approach.

AN ACCURACY-IN-PROCESS APPROACH TO RECEIVING ABILITY

The Accuracy versus Process Controversy

At the time that studies of accuracy in person perception were under their strongest methodological criticism, Tagiuri and Petrullo (1958) suggested the abandonment of the accuracy approach to person perception entirely in favor of a process approach, stating that "attempts at studying correlates of accuracy have with very few exceptions produced negligible correlations and yielded very little insight into

Table 7.1. Occurrence of Different Types of Change in Action-Oriented and Emotion-Oriented CPs

Type of change	Action-oriented CP	Emotion-oriented CP	Significance of difference
Change in object interaction	9	0	$p < .001$
Change in position in space	4	0	$p < .025$
Change in body features	10	9	NS
Change in expression	3	10	$p < .025$

processes. . . . It is the process rather than its achievement that one must investigate if a broad understanding of the phenomenon is to be reached" (Tagiuri & Petrullo, 1958, quoted by Cline, 1964, p. 239). On the other hand, Crow (1960) has pointed out that the process in question involves accuracy, that it is in fact a "process of functional achievement, and that therefore a focus upon accuracy as well as process is necessary" (cf. Cline, 1964, pp. 239–240).

Segmentation and Accuracy

The segmentation technique allows a unique way to study the *process* of person perception which also allows the analysis of accuracy. In Chapter 5 we described the application of the segmentation technique to videotapes taken via the slide-viewing technique (actually the CARAT instrument itself), which revealed what are apparently qualitative differences in the sending behaviors of adult males versus females (cf. Figure 5.3 and Table 5.1). These studies also investigated the relationships between the receivers' segmentation patterns and receiving ability as measured by the accuracy with which the receiver identifies the slide category viewed by the sender (Buck *et al.*, 1980, 1982). Both revealed that receiving ability on CARAT was negatively related to the number of button presses for female receivers (average $r = -.31$, $p < .01$) but not male receivers (average $r = -.01$). Thus, accurate female receivers tended to segment less finely than did less accurate female receivers while viewing adults, while receiving ability was not related to fineness of segmentation in males. On the other hand, receiving ability and fineness of segmentation were positively correlated for both males and females when viewing the expressions of children (average $r = +.23$, $p < .05$).

The Buck *et al.* (1982) study also assessed the quality of segmentation by determining the number of times a given receiver *hit* on CPs and *missed* CPs (pressed the button more than 1 second away from a CP). These proved to be significantly related to receiving ability only among female receivers, with hits being positively correlated (average $r = +.47$, $p < .05$), and misses negatively correlated (average $r = -.59$, $p < .005$), with receiving ability. The comparable figures for male receivers ($r = +.22$ and $-.13$, respectively) were not significant.

This pattern of findings suggests that, as with sending accuracy, receiving ability is more related to segmentation measures in females than males, suggesting the possibility that receiving ability is related to direct perceptual processing in females and a cognitively mediated processing in males (Buck *et al.*, 1982). We shall examine this question in more detail below.

Another example of an application of the segmentation technique to the analysis of the quality of the process of person perception has been conducted by Brackett and Donnelly (1981). Judges indicated points at which they would intrude into a videotaped conversation between two persons. When both audio and video cues were available, significant consensus was demonstrated and CPs established. The videotapes were then shown to a new group of judges under different conditions of degradation: video only, video plus content-filtered voice, and nondegraded audio–video. The new group showed a pattern of CPs similar to the first group in the nondegraded condition, but the other conditions and particularly the video-only condition showed a significant drop in consensus and a lack of agreement with the first sample. The authors suggest that this inability to determine the proper point to enter a conversation with restricted audio cues is the basis of the difficulty with the conversational turn-taking process experienced by hearing-impaired persons.

SUMMARY

There are at least four conceptually distinct factors that might account for an individual's level of nonverbal receiving ability in a given situation: (1) experience and skill in decoding nonverbal behavior in general, (2) experience and skill in decoding the nonverbal behaviors of a specific person known to the receiver, (3) the nonverbal expressiveness of the receiver, and (4) attention to the nonverbal behaviors of others. The instruments designed to measure nonverbal receiving ability considered above are sensitive only to (1)—the ability to decode a stranger when attention has been specifically directed to nonverbal cues (Buck, 1983a). These studies are interesting and have led to important results, but a full understanding of nonverbal receiving ability will require much more, including at least the expanded study of nonverbal receiving ability in the context of specific relationships, the study of nonverbal receiving ability in interactional settings where sending accuracy may be taken into account, and the study of the perceptual organization of nonverbal displays in circumstances where the subject's attention is not specifically directed to the display. In addition, possible differences in the receiving process for spontaneous and symbolic nonverbal displays are of great interest, for they are consistent with the suggestion that there are two qualitatively different sorts of receiving processes: direct "person perception" versus mediated "person cognition."

THE NATURE OF RECEIVING ABILITY

A MODEL OF RECEIVING ABILITY

This final section recalls the model of receiving ability presented in Chapters 1 and 2, and integrates this view with the discussion in the present chapter. It will be recalled that a distinction was made between knowledge by acquaintance, which involves the self-evident and direct process of sensory awareness, and knowledge by description, which involves the interpretation of sense-data (Russell, 1912). I suggested that this distinction is related to the distinction between spontaneous and symbolic communication. On the sending side, spontaneous communication involves the direct expression of motivational/emotional states; on the receiving side, spontaneous communication involves the direct knowledge by acquaintance of the affective state of another via such expressive behavior. It was argued that such receiving processes are "built-in," having evolutionary roots analogous to the better described roots of sending processes.

Just as the spontaneous expression of motivational/emotional states may be influenced by display rules, so this direct receiving process may be influenced by decoding rules: learned expectations about the attention to the interpretation of nonverbal displays. Thus, two kinds of receiving processes were distinguished: emotion perception or person perception, which is a direct process analogous to knowledge by acquaintance which occurs without the mediation of decoding rules; and emotion cognition or person cognition, which involves cognitive processes of memory, judgment, and so forth, and which is thus knowledge by description.

The person perception process was discussed in terms of Gibson's (1966, 1979) theory of perception, and emotion displays were compared to Gibson's concept of social affordance. The relationship between person perception and cognition was described as similar to the relationship between spontaneous and symbolic communication shown in Figure 1.2: Person perception is present in every case of receiving ability, while person cognition may be virtually absent or present to varying degrees. This conception led to the reinterpretation of the social knowing continuum, which is defined at one end by direct knowledge by acquaintance, where the stimulus absolutely determines the response, and at the other end by mediated knowledge by description (Baron, 1980; Baron & Buck, 1979; Baron & Harvey, 1980).

Thus, the account of the evolution of receiving ability is analogous to the model of sending accuracy presented in Chapter 2; and in general a view of communication is advanced in which biologically based, spontaneous, direct, and nonpropositional processes occur simultaneously with socially based, symbolic, mediated, and propositional processes. Thus in both its sending and receiving aspects emotion communication in humans involves two simultaneous "streams" of spontaneous and symbolic communication.

CEREBRAL LATERALIZATION AND RECEIVING ABILITY

Evidence was presented in Chapter 3 that there is evidence that spontaneous communication is particularly associated with right-hemisphere processing, while symbolic communication is associated with left-hemisphere processing. The discussion in Chapter 3 was couched in terms of sending processes, but there is similar evidence in regard to receiving: the right hemisphere is more involved in responding to the holistic "message" contained in facial and bodily expression and tone of voice, while the left hemisphere is involved with decoding the symbolic, propositional message.

Left-Hemisphere Functions

There is plentiful evidence that the left hemisphere is particularly concerned with the processing of sequential verbal stimuli. Lesions in Wernicke's area, in the left temporal lobe near the auditory sensory area, produce what has been termed "receptive aphasia," involving severe deficits of verbal comprehension. There is also much evidence in studies of normal right-handed subjects that sequential and verbal stimuli are processed particularly in the left hemisphere (cf. Tucker, 1981).

Right-Hemisphere Functions

There is also plentiful evidence that the right hemisphere is particularly sensitive to holistic stimuli, employing a kind of pattern recognition in contrast to the sequential processing of the left hemisphere. Also, it appears that the right hemisphere is particularly sensitive to emotional meaning in such holistic displays. This evidence comes both from studies of normal right-handed subjects and brain-damaged patients.

In right-handed subjects, several studies employing dichotic listening tasks have shown that whereas the right ear (i.e., the left hemisphere) is known to be more sensitive to the content of speech—*what* was said—the left ear (i.e., the right hemisphere) better recognizes emotional expression in speech—*how* it was said (Carmon & Nachshon, 1973; Haggard & Parkinson, 1971; Safer & Leventhal, 1977). Also, many studies have demonstrated that there is a left-visual-field (i.e., a right hemisphere) superiority for the recognition and processing of faces, and recent studies have found that this is particularly true of faces expressing emotion (Buchtel, Campari, DeRisio, & Rota, 1978; Campbell, 1978; Heller & Levy, 1981; Landis *et al.*, 1979; Ley & Bryden, 1979; Safer, 1981; Suberi & McKeever, 1977).

In brain-damaged patients, it has been found that right-hemisphere-damaged patients have particular difficulty in the comprehension of affective speech, although they generally have no problems with propositional speech (Heilman *et al.*, 1974; Tucker *et al.*, 1977b). Also, right-hemisphere-damaged patients have particular difficulties with the recognition and discrimination of emotional faces and pictures (Cicone *et al.*, 1980; DeKosky *et al.*, 1980), and they do poorly on the PONS test (Benowitz *et al.*, 1980).

IMPLICATIONS

Sex Differences

This view of nonverbal receiving ability involves the simultaneous functioning of a direct, biologically based, nonpropositional system based particularly on the right hemisphere, and a mediated, learned, propositional system based particularly on the left hemisphere. It might be noted that the sex differences found by Buck *et al.* (1980, 1982) in the relationships between receiving ability measures and segmentation measures suggests that females and males differ in the way these systems are organized. Receiving may be based upon a more direct perception-based syncretic–cognitive processing in females and a more mediated, analytic cognitive processing in males. Whether such a difference may be based upon learned or innate factors is unclear. There are known sex differences in cerebral lateralization, but their origin and the implications of their presence have only begun to be understood (cf. Moore & Haynes, 1980; Trotman & Hammond, 1979). However, this is a very important area for future research.

Message Discrepancies

Other implications of the present view involve what happens when spontaneous and symbolic expressions are discrepant from one another. Some of these are suggested in the example given by Galin (1974) of the "double bind" communication situation in which a parent simultaneously gives to a child a loving verbal message and a contradictory, highly negative message via facial/bodily expression and tone of voice. Because of their different cognitive skills, the two hemispheres extract different information from the experience, and therefore have different response tendencies—the left hemisphere would tend to approach, the right hemisphere to flee.

If the conflict involved is not strong, the child might be able to deal with the discrepancy in some way. In fact, it has been suggested that such discrepancies may be associated with humor (cf. Blanck & Rosenthal, 1982). However, if the conflict is real and strong, maladaptive responses may result. Since the response tendencies of the left hemisphere typically dominate those of the right hemisphere, it is likely that they will be most reflected in overt behavior. However, if the left hemisphere is unable to inhibit the response tendencies of the right hemisphere completely, the conflicting information may somehow become blocked, and would in effect be "repressed" and become "unconscious."

A number of investigators have studied how discrepant messages are "resolved," where resolution is defined in terms of the subject's overt understanding of the message (cf. Bugental, 1974; Mehrabian & Ferris, 1967; Mehrabian & Weiner, 1967). For example, Volkmar, Hoder, and Siegel (1980) gave children visual and auditory messages simultaneously encouraging them to approach and stay away—for example, the experimenter might smile broadly, beckon to the child with the hand, and nod the head while saying "stay away" in a cold tone of voice, or might frown, shake the head, and motion the child away while pleasantly saying "come here." Results indicated that more children conformed to the auditory than the visual messages, and that the messages could be arranged in a unidimensional hierarchy in terms of the child's approach tendencies.

By focusing upon the overt understanding of mixed messages, such studies do not address their possible "unconscious" effects. In effect, they concentrate upon a symbolic communication process, ignoring spontaneous influences.

CONCLUSIONS

This chapter has briefly noted the problems in the history of the study of person perception, and has reviewed several measures of nonverbal receiving ability which have attempted to circumvent these problems. They have had uneven success. Although designed to assess similar phenomena, the instruments have not correlated highly with one another and internal consistency has been a problem in some cases. This chapter has suggested a number of complexities of nonverbal receiving ability which might explain this state of affairs, including the possible differences between the reception of spontaneous and symbolic behavior, the complexities introduced by the decoding rules, the problem that these instruments involve the expressions of strangers, the possible impact of sending accuracy upon receiving ability, and the difficult problem that these measures direct attention to nonverbal cues. The latter problem was addressed by the suggestion that an accuracy-in-process view of nonverbal receiving ability may be possible through the use of the segmentation procedure.

It was concluded that at least four distinct factors might account for an individual's level of receiving ability in a given situation: general skill and experience at decoding; skill and experience at decoding a specific individual; the nonverbal expressiveness of the receiver; and attention to nonverbal cues. Present tests of receiving ability assess only the first kind of factor. The model of receiving ability presented in Chapters 1 and 2 was reconsidered, together with the material on cerebral lateralization and sending accuracy, and introduced evidence that cerebral lateralization is relevant to receiving ability as well. A model of communication consisting of two simultaneous streams—a simultaneous stream based particularly upon right-hemisphere functioning and a symbolic stream based particularly upon left-hemisphere functioning—was presented.

From this point of view, the nature of a receiving ability test which may yet assess a relatively unidimensional process may be suggested: a test specifically designed to measure the ability to receive spontaneous expression. Since spontaneous expression, by definition, is innate and universal to the human species, it could be argued that the use of unknown stimulus persons would be justified. The factor of the sender's tendency to attend to nonverbal cues in others could be assessed by employing the segmentation technique without specifically directing the receiver's attention to nonverbal cues for at least part of the test. The factor of receiver's nonverbal expressiveness would have to be dealt with separately. The most important feature of such an instrument would reside in the nature of the stimuli: they would necessarily be spontaneous, with symbolic behaviors removed as much as is possible. In other words, they should show the spontaneous expressions of a solitary person to affective stimuli, in a situation where the sender does not know that he or she is being filmed. Such an instrument would of course be able to measure only one aspect of the complex phenomenon of nonverbal receiving ability, but there is reason to believe that it is an important aspect.

Another feature of the present analysis is its illustration of the fundamental importance of the education of attention to many aspects of the emotional communication process. It is important in the analysis of sending accuracy, in that the education of attention is involved in determining the accessibility of different aspects of the sender's behavior to the sender, and therefore determines among other things the "leakiness" of various behaviors in the sender. It is also important in the analysis of receiving ability, in determining the saliency of different aspects of the other's behavior to the receiver, and therefore among other things determining the receiver's abilities at the detection of leakage and deception. It allows an "accuracy-in-process" view of receiving ability which may avoid some of the problems posed by views which stress only accuracy or process without considering the importance of the other. Also, we shall see in the next chapter that the concept of the education of attention offers a fresh perspective on, and suggests new approaches to, the analysis of human interaction.

PART FOUR

EMOTION COMMUNICATION AND SOCIAL INTERACTION

8

THE ANALYSIS OF INTERACTION

Thus far we have developed a view of human emotion with the following major features: (1) that emotion involves three kinds of "readout" of motivational/emotional systems organized in the nervous system; (2) that general response accessibility has had a major influence upon how this readout has evolved; (3) that in addition to accessibility, the education of attention helps to determine the actual access to a response, that is, our awareness of the response in ourselves and in others; (4) that one can distinguish an "animal model" of emotion and emotional development, encompassing phenomena which can be seen in both animals and humans, from "emotional education" based upon the unique human capacity for language and its ability to support formal logic and reasoning.

This analysis of emotion is associated with an analysis of communication which distinguishes spontaneous communication—a nonvoluntary emotional readout on the part of the sender and pickup on the part of the receiver—and symbolic communication, which involves a specific voluntary message. It is argued that the term "nonverbal communication" is misleading, because symbolic communication behaviors may be "nonverbal" in the sense that they are not composed of words, yet "verbal" in the sense that they are structured linguistically, or organized to support linguistic structures. Spontaneous communication in the sender has been associated with subcortical and paleocortical systems, where the expression of motivational/emotional states is mediated by excitatory and inhibitory mechanisms, and with right-hemisphere processing. Symbolic communication has been associated with learned and culturally patterned display rules ("deception") and with left-hemisphere processing. In the receiver, spontaneous communication involves "direct perception"; symbolic communication is mediated by learned "decoding rules."

This section examines the implications of this view of emotion and communication for the analysis of social behavior, and specifically for the analysis of human interaction. This area has received much attention in recent years. There has been a great increase in the number and quality of methods for examining the complex flow of human interaction. Some of these are reviewed in the present chapter, and I shall attempt to show the relevance of the present model of emotion and communication to the understanding of the results of these studies.

THE ANALYSIS OF INTERACTION

The study of human social interaction is an exceedingly complex area, one suited more to coverage within a book than within a chapter. It is also an area which is undergoing rapid expansion and change at the present time, and it is therefore difficult to summarize and pick out important trends. As Duncan and Fiske (1977) have suggested, the field is in one sense flourishing, and in another sense floundering, in a rich variety of conceptual perspectives and methodological approaches. However, no discussion of emotion communication would be complete without some consideration of how this functions within interactional settings.

This chapter first considers a model which formally analyzes and describes the components that are concealed within apparently simple interaction data. It then discusses what has been called the "structural approach" to the analysis of communication in interaction, and also some of the approaches that employ experimental manipulations. Next, it discusses some of the major contemporary approaches to the study of social interaction, including naturalistic observation studies and methods of time series analysis. Finally, it considers the implications of the view of emotion and communication developed in this book—particularly the distinction between spontaneous and symbolic communication—to the analysis of social interaction. Specifically, it is argued that two kinds of structure appear simultaneously in social interaction—structure based upon spontaneous processes and structure based upon symbolic processes.

COMMUNICATION IN AN INTERACTIONAL CONTEXT

THE SOCIAL RELATIONS MODEL

Even the most apparently simple interaction data have at least two aspects: Any interaction involves both the characteristics of the individual interactants and dyadic characteristics involving the nature of the specific relationship between any two individuals (Wilmot, 1980). A potential solution to the problem of analyzing individual versus dyadic characteristics has been suggested in the social relations model of interaction by David Kenny and his colleagues (cf. Kenny, 1981; Kenny & Nasby, 1980; Montgomery & Kenny, 1982; Warner, Kenny, & Stoto, 1979). This model is illustrated in Figure 8.1. In brief, Kenny argues that *any* measure of behavior taken during a dyadic interaction can be analyzed into four components: (1) the average level of the behavior across all dyads (Greek μ); (2) the general tendency of one partner (i) to "send" that behavior to all partners

Figure 8.1. The Kenny model of interaction applied to nonverbal communication.

$$X_{ij} = \mu + \alpha_i + \beta_j + \gamma_{ij} \quad \leftarrow \text{Communication of i to j.}$$

$$X_{ji} = \mu + \alpha_j + \beta_i + \gamma_{ji} \quad \leftarrow \text{Communication of j to i.}$$

Observed communication accuracy of i to j and j to i.

General level of communication accuracy within the group (A constant).

General sending accuracy of i and j.

General receiving ability of i and j.

Specific communication within the dyad. i to j and j to i.

(Greek α); (3) the general tendency of the other partner (j) to "receive" that behavior from all partners (Greek β); and (4) the specific level of that behavior within the ij dyad, after these general tendencies have been controlled (Greek γ).

Let us consider the communication process between i and j. Xij represents the total communication accuracy score when i is sending to j; Xji represents the communication accuracy score when j is sending to i. Xij has four components in the model: (1) the general level of communication accuracy for all senders and receivers in the group in question (the grand mean μ); (2) i's general sending accuracy (α); (3) j's general receiving ability (β); and (4) the specific communication accuracy of i to j when these general factors are subtracted out (γ). The latter expression may be regarded as a formal definition of *specific communication accuracy*, that is, communication accuracy which is specific to a given dyad, which was discussed in the last chapter. Conversely, the communication accuracy when j is sending to i (Xji) involves the general sending accuracy of j, the general receiving ability of i, and the specific communication accuracy of j to i.

To investigate specific communication accuracy, it is crucial to obtain separate estimates of these factors. Kenny and his colleagues have shown that simple dyadic designs, in which measures are obtained from only one dyad, are insufficient to obtain these estimates. In its stead, a "round-robin" design, or other special design in which a subject interacts with two or more others, is required. In the full round robin, measures are taken of two members of a dyad as they interact with others as well as with each other (Warner et al., 1979). This is illustrated in Figure 8.2. This design allows the measurement of each person's general tendencies to "send" and "receive" the attribute in question as well as the contribution of the specific dyad.

Kenny and Nasby (1980) have applied this analysis to measures of liking within dyads. They note that the notion of reciprocity of liking is a basic assumption in several theories of social interaction, particularly social exchange (Homans, 1961) and cognitive consistency (Heider, 1958; Newcombe, 1956) theories. Thus, if A likes B, there should be some tendency for B to reciprocate and like A. However, studies of the relationship between the liking of A for B and B for A have not always shown the strong positive correlations that would be expected. For example, Walster, Aronson, Abrahams, and Rottmann (1979) in a study of dating found a zero-order correlation between

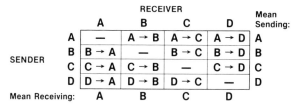

				RECEIVER		Mean
		A	B	C	D	Sending:
	A	—	A → B	A → C	A → D	A
SENDER	B	B → A	—	B → C	B → D	B
	C	C → A	C → B	—	C → D	C
	D	D → A	D → B	D → C	—	D
Mean Receiving:		A	B	C	D	

Figure 8.2. The round-robin design.

how much a woman likes her date and how much he likes her ($r = .03$) and between whether a man wants to date his partner again and whether she wants to date him ($r = .07$). From these numbers it would appear that the liking of one for the other is not necessarily reciprocated.

Kenny and Nasby contend, however, that these small reciprocity correlations are the result of the failure of these studies to take into account the general tendencies of the two partners to like others (i.e., to "send liking") and to be liked by others (to "receive liking"). Using a round-robin design to estimate these general tendencies, and remove them from the measure of liking specific to the dyad, resulted in a positive and significant reciprocity correlation of .62. In other words, if general tendencies to give and receive liking are removed from the data, there is a strong tendency to like those who like you.

AN INTERACTIONAL APPROACH TO COMMUNICATION ACCURACY

The application of the Kenny and Nasby (1980) reasoning to the problem of nonverbal communication is straightforward, and it allows us to analyze the communication process in a new and more complete way, going beyond the simple dyadic design in the analysis of interaction and dramatically demonstrating the complexity that lies behind the apparently simple measures taken from dyads.

We saw in the last chapter that there are at least two ways in which nonverbal receiving ability may be altered by relationship effects. First, the ability accurately to receive information from persons with whom one has a specific relationship history differs from general nonverbal receiving ability; second, receiving ability may be dynamically influenced by the receiver's own sending accuracy in the context of an ongoing interaction. These aspects of receiving ability must be assessed in settings where persons with specified relationships with the receiver play the role of sender. The level of sensitivity to that person may then be compared with sensitivity to strangers to arrive at an estimate of specific nonverbal receiving ability. That was the procedure used in the Buck and Lerman (1979) and Sabatelli *et al.* (1979, 1980, 1982, 1983a, 1983b) studies.

The Kenny model provides an efficient technique for analyzing and organizing the data resulting from such studies, partitioning the effects into variance due to general sending accuracy, general receiving ability, and specific relationship effects. Efforts are now under way to apply this analysis to data collected in the Sabatelli *et al.* studies. However, such data will not directly address the issue of the dynamic relationship between sending accuracy and receiving ability in the context of an actual interaction. This would require the analysis of both sending accuracy and receiving ability in an actual interactional setting in which the receiver could influence the behavior of the other via the receiver's own expressiveness. Receivers in the Buck and Lerman and in the Sabatelli *et al.* studies viewed videotapes of the sender—there was no dynamic interchange. A measurement situation in which the receiver can directly influence the sender, and in which simultaneous measures of sending accuracy and receiving ability can be taken, has not yet been devised. A truly complete approach to communication accuracy, however, would appear to require such an analysis. We shall consider this below, after examining various approaches to the analysis of interaction.

THE STRUCTURAL APPROACH TO COMMUNICATION IN INTERACTION

DESCRIPTION

The *structural* approach to interaction is based upon a view of communication which has developed since the early 1950s. This approach views communication as a multichannel system in which people of a given cultural tradition use a common code consisting not only of language but also of gesture, facial expression, interpersonal spacing, touch, odor, and so on. This code is used for conveying meaning between persons of that tradition, but its true nature is much broader: It is involved in the regulation of all types of transaction, and functions to maintain the social order and social control (Scheflen, 1974).

This multibehavioral coding system is learned and culturally patterned, and does not include spontaneous emotional expression *per se*. In fact, adherents of this approach have criticized other researchers in "nonverbal communication" for focusing exclusively upon emotional expression without considering how nonverbal behaviors interact with language and are patterned by culture (Scheflen, 1972, 1973, 1974). Thus Scheflen (1974) points out that nonverbal behaviors can be considered to be idiosyncratic expressions of personality or emotion only "if they are not usual in some cultural category" (p. 110). In our terms, the structural approach focuses particularly upon symbolic behavior: To the extent that emotional expression is seen as important, it functions within the traditions of a given culture. The unique bases of spontaneous expression are not considered. In effect, the structural approach to interaction is similar to the expanded view of deception discussed in the last chapter, in that it focuses upon the interpersonal "rules" established within a culture which, among other things, govern emotional display and decoding.

The structural approach analyzes this multichannel system by relating various measures of communication behavior to one another, as opposed to relating them to "external variables" such as sex, personality, and situational factors. In this way the structuralists seek to describe the internal structure of communication behavior. They emphasize the immense complexity of this structure: Thus Birdwhistell (1970) has suggested that one would have to record 10,000 bits of information per second to account for the behaviors of two human infants. Duncan (1969) has noted the essential differences of the "structural" and "external variable" approaches. The latter shall be considered in the next section.

HISTORICAL BACKGROUND

The structural approach has its roots in systems theory and information theory concepts developed during and after World War II (see Chapter 1). It was applied to the analysis of the communicative functions of nonverbal behavior by the efforts of a number of investigators from a variety of disciplines, including anthropologists, linguists, and psychiatrists. One of the pioneers in this area is Ray Birdwhistell. An anthropologist by professional affiliation, Birdwhistell became interested in the role of body movement in communication while stationed in England during the war. He became convinced that much meaning is conveyed by such behaviors, and that, as with language, this meaning is specific to the given cultural group. He coined the term *kinesics* to describe the science of communication via body movement, and published the first major work in the field, *Introduction to Kinesics*, in 1952.

The structural approach and its method of *context analysis* (see Chapter 5) were formalized in 1956 at Palo Alto by a group including anthropologists Birdwhistell and Gregory Bateson, linguists Charles Hockett and Norman McQuown, and psychoanalysts Frieda Fromm-Reichmann and Henry Brosin. The result of this collaboration was a book entitled *The Natural History of an Interview* (McQuown, Bateson, Birdwhistell, Brosin, & Hockett, 1971), which includes detailed transcriptions of portions of conversation between anthropologist Gregory Bateson and members of a middle-class American family. Phonetic, paralinguistic, and kinesic transcription systems were used, and the communicative behaviors of the different participants carefully aligned over time. Work on the monograph was essentially completed in 1959, but it did not become publicly available until 1971. Nevertheless, the work has been highly influential and was often cited even while unpublished (Duncan & Fiske, 1977). To a great extent, it has set the agenda for studies of human interaction, suggesting many of the phenomena to be studied.

THE LINGUISTIC-KINESIC ANALOGY

Birdwhistell and other structuralists see a fundamental analogy between kinesics and structural linguistics (Sapir, 1921). This analogy is illustrated in Figure 8.3. Structural linguists see language as composed of discrete units arranged hierarchically, with *phones* (constituting all human elemental vocalizations) being organized successively into *phonemes* (the elements of spoken language), *morphemes* (with arbitrarily assigned meanings), *sentences*, and so on. The ability to decode language depends upon one's knowledge of the meaning of

Kinesic Units	Linguistic Units	Hierarchical Structure

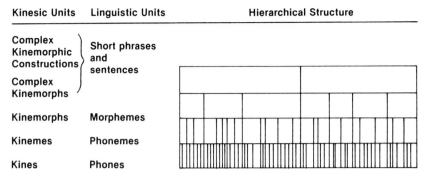

Figure 8.3. Illustration of the hierarchical structure of kinesic and linguistic units.

the morphemes (e.g., the vocabulary) and the rules of *grammar* which determine how the smaller units are organized into larger structures. The "magic" of language is that, through a few phonemes (56 in English; no more than 100 in all human languages), and a few hundred thousand morphemes, a virtually infinite variety of sentences may be constructed via the grammatical rules.

Birdwhistell sees kinesics as analogously involving heirarchically organized units, including *kines* (constituting all detectable human movement), *kinemes* (which are elements analogous to linguistic phonemes), *kinemorphs* (with arbitrary meanings which are determined by the culture), *complex kinemorphs*, and *complex kinemorphic constructions* (which are analogous to short phrases and sentences). He argues that the heirarchy of linguistic units is functionally related to an analogous hierarchy of kinesic units.

Scheflen (1974) has taken this analogy further, suggesting that larger linguistic units (point-units, positions, and performances) are related to analogous kinesic units. He has contributed an instructive example of this using part of an extensively investigated interview between a mother, her schizophrenic daughter, and two psychiatrists (cf. Scheflen, 1973, 1974). The interview began with the mother and daughter sitting on a couch, facing the psychiatrists (see Figure 8.4). The mother sat with her legs crossed at the ankles, oriented toward a point in space intermediate between the two psychiatrists, so that she could easily look from one to the other. In this position, she began to recount the family history. According to Scheflen, this activity of giving the history constituted the linguistic aspect of the "position,"

Therapist   Mother   Patient   Therapist

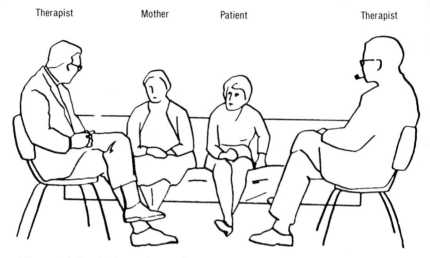

Figure 8.4. Spatial frame from a family psychotherapy session. From Figure 6.4 in *Communication Structure: Analysis of a Psychotherapy Transaction* by A. E. Scheflen, Bloomington, Ind.: Indiana University Press, 1973. Reprinted by permission.

while the mother's particular posture and orientation constituted the kinesic aspect. In the course of this discussion, the following "point-unit" occurred. The mother was describing a psychotic episode in which the daughter asked to be helped upstairs, saying: "Help me upstairs. Imagine, a young girl like that! Help me upstairs." The first and third sentences were stated in a voice which quoted and mockingly imitated that of her daughter, the second was stated scornfully in a way which clearly gave the mother's opinion on the matter. These constituted the linguistic (and paralinguistic) aspects of the "point-unit." The kinesic aspect was this: For the duration of the three sentences, the mother had been looking at the psychiatrist on her right. At the end, she briefly dropped her eyes and shifted her gaze to the other psychiatrist.

Shortly after this, the daughter interrupted her mother with an objection, and one of the psychiatrists turned toward the daughter and began an exchange. This temporarily ended the "giving history" portion of the interview. The mother responded kinesically by uncrossing her ankles and turning toward the girl, so that the new linguistic position was now associated with a new kinesic posture.

In general, Scheflen argues that communication behavior is hierarchically organized, and that this organization is manifested in both linguistic and kinesic behaviors. He has given a number of persuasive examples of this, similar to the one recounted above, and there appears to be little challenge to the validity of the observation. Scheflen argues in addition that this organization is responsible for more than the simple transmission of meaning between individuals, and that in fact it is responsible for the maintenance of the social order.

COMMUNICATION BEHAVIOR AND THE SOCIAL ORDER

One of the most important insights of the structuralists is that the behaviors that reveal the hierarchical structure of communication do not simply aid the transmission of meaning: they also comment about what is being communicated—a function termed *metacommunication* by Bateson (1955)—and they give information about each of the interactants and their relationship with one another and with what is being said.

Taken together, these functions constitute the basis of the social order in the informal interpersonal transaction. Scheflen (1972) notes that a formal social transaction has an established "program" in which the roles of different persons are assigned, the goals of the transaction are stated, and the course of action is organized and defined. Thus, at a formal assembly such as a church service, graduation ceremony, or faculty meeting, different persons play the established roles of moderator, priest, participant, and so forth; a formal program, such as that codified in the rules of Parliamentary Practice, tells one when to stand up, sit down, sing, pray, debate, and so forth. All of these formal elements are relevant to and tend to support the "official" goals of the transaction.

Scheflen suggests that the nonlanguage aspects of communication behavior function in analogous ways to "program" the informal transaction: informing the participants of their roles vis à vis one another; the degrees of dominance, intensity, and intimacy in their relationship; and the goals of the interaction. They also organize the flow of behavior so that each knows, for example, when to begin the interaction, when to speak and when to listen, and when to end the interaction. In essence, these nonlanguage behaviors define the "official" *context* of the informal transaction, and they do so to a great extent by establishing the *frame* for the interaction and providing *markers* to regulate its progress.

Frames

The interaction is framed in space and time by body placements which provide a temporary physical territory within which the interaction occurs. Spatial frames are illustrated in Figure 8.5, which shows a "bird's eye" view of a cocktail party. Suppose the person entering the room at the top left does not know anyone at the party, and must decide how and with whom to enter conversation. It is unlikely that the newcomer will join the group of four at the bottom left, because of the nature of the spatial frame that they have established. They are standing close to one another, and are oriented toward one another as directly as is possible. This, in Scheflen's (1972) terms, is a *closed frame*, and it tends to indicate that the group in question is engaged in an intense interaction and would react poorly to disruption. The group members are probably indicating this in other ways as well. For example, it is likely that they are keeping their glances within the group, so that it would be hard to catch the eye of one of the members. It is also likely that they are speaking in relatively low voices, so that it is hard to catch snatches of the

Figure 8.5. Spatial frames.

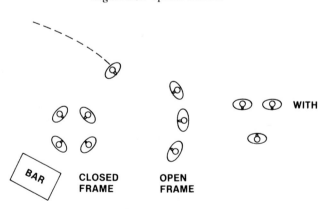

CLOSED FRAME   OPEN FRAME   WITH

BAR

conversation. It also is possible that the group members are moving in synchrony with one another, as we shall consider below.

The group in the middle, in contrast, is showing an *open frame* in their interactional behavior. Their bodies are oriented out into the room, rather than toward one another; they are probably looking around the room rather than at one another, and if they are talking it is probably in short statements in a relatively loud voice, so that it would be relatively easy to catch the drift of their conversation, catch the eye of one of the interactants, and thus join in.

The grouping on the right is illustrating another of Scheflen's (1972) concepts: the *with*. The couple at the top has a "shoulder-to-shoulder" orientation toward the individual at the bottom, and are thus announcing by their frame that they are "with" one another and should thus be treated as a social unit rather than as individuals. This grouping is often seen on campuses, particularly in the spring. Scheflen notes that individuals have other ways to maintain their relationship with one another at parties. If they go off on their own, couples tend to reestablish contact with one another periodically through the party, if only by a brief glance. A marriage partner who does not keep in such contact with his or her spouse during a party may have difficulties during the ride home.

Markers

Whereas frames establish a physical context within which an inter-action occurs, markers aid in its temporal organization. Markers are positive signals by which units in the stream of communication are delimited (Bateson, 1971). These kinesic and paralinguistic behaviors "punctuate" the stream of speaking and listening much as written language is punctuated, allowing the interactants to affect and respond to the temporal ordering of the communication process. Some of the most important markers are relevant to the turn-taking mechanism, allowing the interactants to determine when it is time for a speaking turn and when to remain silent. Duncan (1972) has noted for example that *turn-yielding signals* occur when a speaker is finished with his or her turn. Examples of such signals include the relaxation of a pre-viously tensed gesture, looking up at the listener just as a thought is completed, a drawl or a drop in pitch or loudness at the final syllable, and so forth. At this point, a listener has the choice of remaining silent, taking a speaking turn, or "communicating in the back channel," which in effect gives the turn back to the speaker. Examples of the latter include nodding, saying "yeah" or "uh-huh," restating the speaker's point, and asking for clarification. Client-centered psychotherapists, who attempt to allow the client to disclose and deal with his or her own problems through talking them out, use much back channel communication to encourage the client to continue speaking.

Contextuals and Transcontextuals

Communication behaviors that occur during the interaction are termed *contextuals* if they are appropriate to the "official" definition or program of the transaction. They tend to preserve the lawful organization of the transaction around this program. Acts inappropriate to this program are termed *transcontextuals*. These are often carried over from other contexts. For example, if one is joking with a friend and suddenly remembers the plight of a sick relative, acts appropriate to the latter context may occur and interfere with the "official" joking transaction. The other may use countermeasures, termed *monitors*, to preserve the original definition of the transaction.

INTERACTIONAL SYNCHRONY

One of the major findings of the structuralists, which is consistent with their holistic view of communication behavior, has been their demonstration of synchrony between different communication behaviors. Condon and Ogsten (1966) described synchrony between a speaker's linguistic and kinesic behaviors, noting that when carefully analyzed on slow-motion film, points of change in body motion correspond with points of linguistic importance: "As a person talks . . . [the] body moves in a series of configurations of change which are precisely correlated with that serial transformation of 'phone into syllable into word' of speech" (p. 339). In addition, Condon and Ogsten found that the kinesic and linguistic behaviors of interactants are often synchronized with one another: "The speaker and listener also display body movement organizations of change which are isomorphic with the articulated organization of speech" (p. 339).

As noted in Chapter 4, Condon found such synchrony in the behavior of infants when listening to recorded samples of human speech. Kendon (1970) demonstrated such synchrony in a group of interactants at an English pub, showing that it can occur even between persons who are not looking at one another. This may indicate that persons are interacting with one another even though this is not "officially" acknowledged. Synchrony was particularly evident when an interaction was being initiated or disbanded. Also, as noted in Chapter 5, Birdwhistell found evidence that nodding by a therapist is experienced as conveying understanding by a client only if the nodding is in synchrony with the rhythms of the client's discourse.

All in all, it appears that synchrony may be an important signal in the interaction process, showing that the interactants are quite literally "with" one another at a given point in their exchange. Unfortunately, methods of demonstrating synchrony are laborious, and some have argued that their reliability may be unsatisfactory (McDowall, 1978, 1979; Rosenfeld, 1981). This problem is considered below.

EMOTIONAL BASES OF INTERACTION

Cultural Factors in Interaction

The structural approach has found that communication behaviors reveal the bases of the social order of the informal transaction. As noted above, this has emphasized communication behaviors which in our terms are "symbolic," since they are learned within a culture, even though like language these behaviors are learned so thoroughly that there use becomes virtually automatic and "second nature." Also like language, the rules governing these behaviors exist in every culture but their manifest content differs from culture to culture.

This becomes apparent when persons from different cultures interact. Hall (1966) has given many examples of how differences in these rules can generate cultural misunderstandings. A classic example involves the use of space. All cultures have rules governing the spacing of informal conversations, but the content of these rules differs in different cultures. If a person from a culture with close spacing during conversation (e.g., a southern European or Arab culture) interacts with a person from a culture used to greater distances (e.g., northern European), the former may keep moving forward and the latter backward so that, quite unconsciously, they move across the room. Each might make negative attributions about the other from this experience: The former may think the latter to be cold and distant, while the latter thinks the former to be pushy and intrusive. Clearly an understanding of these unwritten rules is important to cultural understanding, just as is the knowledge of other languages.

The Affective Microscope

Although the structural approach has emphasized symbolic behaviors which operate within a given cultural tradition, it has also revealed the extent to which the social order is grounded in emotional factors. One of the striking findings of the structural approach, which has contributed to much popular interest in nonverbal communication, is the extent to which its careful frame-by-frame analysis of interaction reveals the apparent emotional and motivational tendencies of the participants.

An example of this was pointed out by Peery (1978) in a frame-by-frame analysis of leave-taking by parents at a nursery school. One 3-second sequence of events is illustrated in Figure 8.6. When viewed at normal speed the behavior illustrated seemed unremarkable: A father brought his daughter to the door of the school and waited as she entered. After a few steps, the daughter turned back toward her father, who waved. The daughter then turned back into the schoolroom, while the father left.

The remarkable feature of this seemingly ordinary scene was revealed only when it was viewed in detail using slow motion and frame-by-frame analysis. It then became obvious that the father's "wave" involved a particular "pushing away" form. The beginning was similar to the action of a member of the police stopping traffic. This was associated with the daughter stopping any motion back toward the father (Drawing 4). Then the father brought the hand and arm down in a "pushing" motion, and on precisely the same frame that his action began, the daughter began turning her head away from the father. By Drawing 5, she was no longer looking at the father. Peery states that as one views the .16 second involving Frames 142 through 145, it "almost seems that the father has physically pushed the daughter away," and that despite the fact that there was no physical contact between them, "they look like puppets that are being manipulated by the same strings" (1978, p. 60).

Peery suggests, in company with other structuralists, that the frame-by-frame microanalysis of interaction "magnifies" emotional

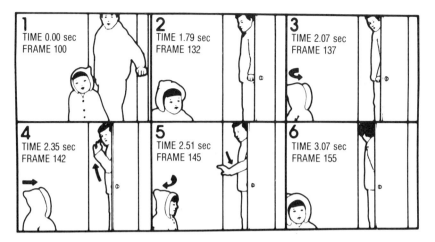

Figure 8.6. Leave-taking sequence between father and preschool daughter, drawn from the film. From Figure 1 in "Magnification of Affect Using Frame-by-Frame Film Analysis" by J. Craig Peery, *Environmental Psychology and Nonverbal Behavior,* 1978, *3,* 58–61. Copyright 1978 by Human Sciences Press, Inc. Reprinted by permission.

behavior just as a lens magnifies its subject, allowing one to draw out emotional components not consciously perceived at normal speed. In essence, frame-by-frame analysis becomes an "affective microscope" allowing the analysis of the rapid flow of affective behavior. It might be suggested, as well, that although these rapid movements may not be consciously perceived, they may be "directly perceived" in the spontaneous receiving process that we have discussed above (see Chapter 2). In any case, this "affective microscope" has revealed the importance in the maintenance of the social order of behaviors that are not perceived at a conscious, symbolic level and that reflect spontaneous emotional expression.

Universal Interaction Behaviors

We have seen that there is evidence that certain facial expressions of emotion are universal to the human species, with analogies to the expressive behaviors of animals, and that this suggests the presence of primary affect systems within the brain. There is also evidence that certain interaction behaviors are universal in humans, and closely related to analogous behaviors in animals. Eibl-Eibesfeldt (1972) has reported evidence of cross-cultural similarities in the actions involved in greeting, begging, flirting, threatening, praying, and so forth. He suggests that these actions have innate origins, although the particular ways that they are used reflect cultural differences as well. Unlike the facial expressions involved with the primary affects, these behaviors are inherently interactive. One can have facial expressions when alone, but it makes no sense to speak of begging, greeting, or flirting alone. The implications of this are important to recognize: Basic features of human interaction, and social organization, may have innate bases just as do basic features of individual emotional expression.

There is evidence from a variety of sources that these basic features of interaction involve courting and dominance, that is, sex and aggression. The structuralists, and particularly Scheflen, have contributed many examples of dominance and courting behaviors in humans which seem analogous to animal behaviors. In one of the most intriguing papers in the area of nonverbal communication, Scheflen (1965) discussed examples of *quasi-courtship* behavior, which he describes as "akin to, or a form of, flirtation behavior" (1973, p. 80). These were first discovered during psychotherapy, but can be seen widely in interactions in which persons know one another and are engaged in a common task. One of Scheflen's examples, taken from the psychotherapy session illustrated in Figure 8.4, involved an event in which an attractive female technician walked across the room. One of the therapists turned to watch her, directing his attention away from the young female patient. The latter immediately engaged in "preening" behaviors, pulling at her blouse. The therapist then turned back to the patient and also preened, straightening his tie and pulling up his sock. He then "disclaimed courtship," however, by an ostentatious yawn and look of boredom. Immediately afterward, the patient told him of her interest in an attractive male aide.

Scheflen states that quasi-courtship behavior contains elements of culturally universal courtship behaviors, but that it includes culturally variable *qualifiers* which make it clear that the behavior is not to be taken literally. (The fact that the latter are culturally variable makes for a powerful potential source of cultural misunderstanding: What may be qualified quasi-courtship in one culture may be overt invitation in another.) Scheflen suggests that quasi-courtship is a systems-maintaining device necessary for group cohesion that derives from sexuality but indicates a balance of sexual interest and sexual inhibition.

Affective Dimensions of Interaction

The observations of ethologists such as Eibl-Eibelsfeldt and structuralists such as Scheflen are consistent with studies to be considered below in suggesting two fundamental affective dimensions of interaction: a positive–negative, friendly–unfriendly dimension which may have its roots in courting and sexuality; and a strong–weak, dominant–submissive dimension which may have roots in dominance and aggression. These dimensions are encountered repeatedly in studies of human interaction. The facts that they may involve universal actions, and that they seem analogous to animal behaviors, suggests that these dimensions may constitute innate bases of human social behavior and organization. The emotional bases of interaction shall be further considered below, after describing other approaches to interaction analysis.

CONCLUSIONS

The structural approach has shown how nonlanguage communication behaviors function in the context of the whole interpersonal transaction, and indeed it can be seen as constituting the basis of the social order of the informal transaction. It has also established useful categories with which interaction may be conceptualized, and it has demonstrated the importance of emotional factors in interaction which may have innate bases. The major problem with the approach, as suggested also in Chapter 5, is the laborious and time-consuming nature of its methods of study. These issues are considered below. The next section reviews a number of different approaches to the analysis of interaction which are not within the structuralist tradition.

EXTERNAL VARIABLE APPROACHES TO INTERACTION

DESCRIPTION

Whereas structural approaches investigate the interrelationship between different measures of the interaction process, external variable approaches investigate the relationships between measures of the interaction process and variables external to that process, such as the rewards the interaction afford to the interactants, their feelings toward one another, and so forth (cf. Duncan, 1969). Until recently, the science of social psychology has expended relatively little effort toward the analysis of the process of interaction *per se*. Instead, theoretical models relevant to interaction have been proposed, and hypotheses derived from those models evaluated by manipulative research. For example, models have been proposed which address such topics as impression formation, ingratiation, interpersonal attraction, attribution processes, and equity, all of which are relevant to interaction (cf. Huston & Levinger, 1978). Unfortunately, this research has only rarely involved actual interaction. Also, the research has often been fragmented, with studies in these different areas rarely being related to one another or to broader questions of interaction process (Altman, Vinsel, & Brown, 1981). Thus a coherent view of interaction has not evolved from this research.

Traditional external variable research approaches the complexity of human interaction by attempting to control various aspects of the interaction process. The resulting studies are often highly artificial. For example, some studies have asked subjects to arrange drawings, dolls, or actual persons to investigate the spacing of persons who have different relationships with one another (cf. Little, 1965). Also, subjects have been asked to interact with a physical object (a coat rack, a chair) as if it were another person (Mehrabian, 1968a). Other studies have employed role-playing techniques, instructing subjects to behave in certain ways in interactional settings, and observing the effects of different instructions upon behavior. Still others have employed confederates who are trained to interact with a subject in a controlled manner (Keiser & Altman, 1976). Another major approach to interaction has involved "game" situations, in which preestablished payoff matrices are manipulated to simulate conflict, cooperation, or other kinds of exchange situations (Kelley & Thibaut, 1978; Thibaut & Kelley, 1959).

A number of studies in this tradition have been employed to evaluate two related models which have relevance to interaction, which we shall consider in the next sections: The first is the exchange theory of interaction; the second is the issue of equilibrium versus reciprocity in the interaction process.

EXCHANGE THEORY AND INTERACTION

The Theory

One of the major theoretical approaches which has implications to the study of interaction is exchange theory, identified particularly with George Homans (1961) and Stacey Adams (1963). Homans has described face-to-face interaction as "elementary social behavior," and suggests that it proceeds according to an exchange of rewards and costs between participants. It is assumed that people strive to maximize their rewards and minimize their costs in the course of interaction, but to do so, they must attend to the fact that the other is also trying to maximize rewards and minimize costs. The result is an *exchange* in which each gives up something in order to maintain rewards in the long run.

Each participant brings relevant qualities to an interaction, termed *inputs* by Adams. These include attributes such as education, skill, seniority, age, sex, and physical attractiveness. Each participant also gains some *outcome* from the interaction, which is an overall summary of the rewards and costs involved in the relationship. Homans and Adams suggest that there are general expectations that persons who bring more valuable relevant inputs to an interaction should receive more in terms of outcomes. If skill or education is relevant in a particular situation, and sex or physical attractiveness is not, people should expect that a more skillful person should receive more output (i.e., pay) than a less skillful person, and that sex or physical attractiveness should not determine outcomes. The general expectations by which outcomes are justly distributed in interaction are termed rules of *distributive justice* or *equity*.

Exchange theory has been applied to the analysis of interaction in a variety of ways. For example, it is the basis of interaction studies of approval seeking and intimacy, and it is also central to one of the major theories relevant to interaction: Altman and Taylor's (1973) *social penetration theory* of relationship maintenance and change.

Approval Seeking

One of the major features of the exchange theory of interaction is its emphasis upon notions of interpersonal approach and avoidance. Rosenfeld (1966a, 1966b, 1972) performed a series of studies on instrumental affiliative acts—behaviors intended to elicit approval and approach from others. To identify such behaviors, he instructed subjects to attempt to either win or avoid approval during an interaction with another person. In one study, female subjects interacted with a female confederate; in another, male and female subjects interacted with another (same-sex) subject.

Results indicated that subjects in the approval-seeking condition were much more active than those in the approval-avoiding condition, emitting more nonverbal behaviors and more frequent and longer verbal utterances. In particular, approval-seeking subjects showed more smiles and verbal reinforcers, but fewer negative head shakes. Two measures showed interactions with sex: Approval-seeking males showed more positive head nods, and approval-seeking females showed more gesticulations, while in both cases the trend for the other sex was in the opposite direction. Approval from the other member of the dyad was positively correlated with positive head nods, verbal reinforcers, and references to the other, and negatively correlated with self-manipulations and self-references. Rosenfeld (1966a) also found that subjects high in the need for social approval smiled more during free dyadic interaction with peers.

Intimacy

The higher the rewards and lower the costs involved in an interaction, the stronger the tendency to approach the other. These approach tendencies are often considered to be the basis of the *intimacy level* of the interaction. These may be reflected in a variety of *immediacy behaviors*: eye contact, close spacing, touch, and so forth.

Albert Mehrabian and his colleagues contributed some of the earliest studies of intimacy in the context of their studies of immediacy behavior. For example, Mehrabian (1968a, 1968b) asked subjects to imagine themselves in situations involving different sorts of persons, that is, liked or disliked, male or female persons. Actually, the "person" was also imaginary: An empty swivel chair on rollers stood in for "the other." Mehrabian found that a number of variables ("eye contact," distance, body orientation) were affected by the subject's "liking" for the imaginary addressee.

Intimacy is not, however, a simple function of liking. Any kind of involvement with another, positive or negative, may produce behaviors indicative of intimacy. For example, it is the case that persons who are angry with one another may approach more closely than nonangry persons under some conditions (Meisels & Dosey, 1971), suggesting that close spacing is not confined only to positive interactions. Negative as well as positive emotional involvement may produce close spacing. By the same token, behaviors indicative of intimacy may intensify either positive or negative feelings, depending upon the context. Thus Ellsworth and Carlsmith (1968) demonstrated that, with positive verbal content, frequent eye contact leads to more positive evaluations, while with negative verbal content frequent eye contact is associated with more negative evaluations. Similarly, close interpersonal spacing has been shown to lead to positive or negative evaluations, depending upon the friendliness of the other (Storms & Thomas, 1977).

Patterson (1976) has suggested an "arousal model" of intimacy, in which the approach of another produces general arousal which may be labeled as positive or negative depending upon the context, eventually producing either approach or avoidance tendencies. This model has been widely cited, and has proved useful in organizing many of the empirical findings in the area. However, it can be argued that the concept of "arousal" greatly underestimates the complexity of the motivational and emotional systems that are operative in social interaction, and for that reason, models employing this concept must be oversimplified. Patterson (1982) has discussed a revised version of the arousal model, which shall be discussed below.

Social Penetration Theory

Altman and Taylor's (1973) influential portrayal of relational development is based upon the notion of perceived rewards and costs. They argue that individuals experience a relationship as a cumulative balance of rewards and costs, with greater preponderance of rewards associated with a more satisfying relationship. Individuals also become increasingly able to forecast the rewards and costs that the relationship will offer in the future. Altman and Taylor feel that the verbal and nonverbal exchange of information about the self is particularly important in this exchange of rewards and also in providing feedback about the nature of the relationship that is relevant to the prediction of future rewards.

Altman and Taylor suggest that the information that is shared by participants in a relationship can be characterized by *breadth*, involving the number of topics that is shared, and *depth*, involving the centrality of the topic to one's self-concept. They suggest that relationships gradually proceed toward the involvement of a broader range of more intimate topics. This is the *social penetration* process. It is assumed to be both *directional* and *cumulative*: directional in that relationship growth is assumed to proceed to greater mutual openness, and cumulative in that exchange at more superficial levels is thought to occur before exchange at more intimate levels.

These latter assumptions have been questioned in recent years. They would imply, for example, that there would be an increased efficiency in verbal and nonverbal communication over time and with increased intimacy. This does not necessarily seem to be the case. For example, in their studies of nonverbal communication in dating and married couples cited in the last chapter, Sabatelli *et al.* (1980, 1982) did not find significant relationships between nonverbal communication accuracy and the length of the relationship. They suggest that there may be a ceiling for nonverbal communication accuracy which reaches a plateau once the relationship is well established.

Other evidence from these studies suggested that nonverbal communication accuracy may increase in importance during times of crisis or transition in the relationship. This would be consistent with a more recent statement of social penetration theory by Altman and his colleagues, which is combined with Altman's work on privacy regulation (Altman *et al.*, 1981). This "dialectic" conception of relationship development hypothesizes that a relationship can exhibit reversible, cyclic, and nonlinear processes as well as unidirectional and cumulative processes, resulting in a cycling of "openness and closedness" over the relationship history: "People not only make themselves accessible to one another; they also shut themselves off to one degree or another, break off contact, engage in more distant styles of interaction, and exhibit an ebb and flow of exchange" (Altman *et al.*, 1981, p. 112). For example, if a relationship is established at a point where the two partners' personal needs for openness happen to be increasing, there might be an unusually rapid increase in intimacy. When these openness cycles change toward increasing needs for closedness, however, a decline in intimacy may result, constituting a "crisis" in the relationship.

This dialectic cycling of openness–closedness is characterized with respect to a second dialectic: that of stability and change. The result is a complex and dynamic model which may prove able to deal with many features of relationships, including relationship growth and decline and crises in relationships. It also opens the intriguing possibility of characterizing relationships in terms of the amplitude, frequency, and synchrony characteristics of openness–closedness cycles across time. As we shall see below, this conception is compatible with recent studies employing time-series analyses of interaction, particularly those employing spectral and cross-spectral analyses.

The Development of Norms

One of the central features in a developing relationship is the formation of shared expectations about what behavior is and is not permissible within the relationship. Thibaut and Kelley (1959) conceptualize *norms* as behavioral rules that are accepted to some degree by both members in a relationship. They argue that norms function as substitutes for the exercise of influence based upon personal power. Norms result in more economic and efficient ways to regulate an exchange, in that they are relatively stable across time and are accepted by both persons, thus reducing the need for surveillance over the other to insure that one's interests in the exchange are protected. That is, both parties feel some obligation to adhere to the norm, whether or not the other is present.

Thibaut and Kelley feel that the kinds of norms that arise within a relationship can be predicted from the nature of the exchange involved in the relationship, and that the latter can be simulated via payoff matrices. These describe the rewards and/or costs accrued by each interactant if different outcomes occur. The outcome of each depends not only upon the preferences of the individual, but upon what the partner chooses to do as well. The resulting matrices can be quite complex, and Thibaut and Kelley have described detailed procedures for analyzing different kinds of payoff matrices which quantify the degree of probable conflict or cooperation. Much research was conducted using such matrices during the 1960s and early 1970s under the general rubric of *game theory*, but the approach has in general proved unsatisfactory as a model for human interaction. In particular, it has proved difficult to establish that the apparent value of the various outcomes established by the experimenter is equivalent to their psychological value to the interactants.

EQUILIBRIUM AND RECIPROCITY

The Argyle and Dean Model

A second major model in which an external variable approach has been applied to the analysis of interaction involves the question of equilibrium versus reciprocity in the sequencing of interaction behaviors. As noted above, there are a number of immediacy behaviors which are signals indicative of intimacy, including touch, gaze, positive facial expressions, proximity, and a direct body orientation. Argyle and Dean (1965) suggested that different immediacy behaviors can substitute for one another. Thus if two people were placed farther apart, the resulting loss of intimacy could be compensated for by more gaze or smiling, for example. This model has been termed the *equilibrium* or *compensatory model,* since it assumes that, with increases in one immediacy behavior being compensated for by decreases in another, intimacy will tend to remain at an equilibrium.

This model was initially supported by a number of studies which measured the extent of gaze at different distances of interaction (Argyle, 1975), and it led to a great deal of research (cf. Harper, Wiens, & Matarazzo, 1978; Mehrabian, 1972; Patterson, 1976). It was found that the model works best when there is an established relationship between the participants. Otherwise, it is possible that the level of intimacy will not remain in equilibrium, but rather will change over the course of the interaction. Frequently, this process results in *reciprocity*, where increases in intimacy on the part of A are reciprocated by increases in intimacy on the part of B and vice versa. A reciprocal increase in immediacy behaviors reflects an overall increase in intimacy between A and B, while a reciprocal decrease reflects a decrease in intimacy. Actually, the beginning and ending of any transaction may be seen as involving an increase and decrease in intimacy, respectively, which may be described in terms of reciprocity: A greets B, B responds in kind, they engage in greater gaze, come closer, orient their bodies, and so forth, until an appropriate "equilibrium" level of intimacy is established. The opposite sort of process occurs when the interaction is disbanded.

Message Sequencing

Cappella (1981) has noted that the equilibrium versus reciprocity models are essentially models of *message sequencing*. He defines message sequencing as the process by which messages are exchanged between interaction participants, and more specifically as how inter-speaker influences determine the sequencing of messages during communicative exchanges. Cappella reviews studies relevant to the compensatory and reciprocity models of message sequencing, including five types of behavior that may express affiliation and/or arousal: objective aspects of speech (duration of utterance, latency, pause duration, vocal intensity); immediacy behaviors (proximity, gaze, body orientation, etc.); body movements; verbal intimacy; and infant–caretaker sequences of similar behaviors (Lamb, 1977).

Cappella finds evidence for both compensatory and reciprocity message sequencing effects in his review. As suggested by Argyle and Dean (1965), increasing physical proximity in general appears to have compensating effects, causing the other to gaze less, adopt less direct body postures, move more, speak less, and attempt to re-introduce the normal social distance. In contrast, Cappella reports a reciprocity effect with self-disclosure: Disclosure by one partner tends to beget disclosure by the other, at least within socially defined limits (cf. Rubin, 1975). Cappella also reports reciprocity effects in gaze behavior and in such noncontent aspects of speech as the number of pauses, speaking latency, and vocal intensity. All of these findings are robust, being supported by a variety of studies employing a variety of methodologies. However, Cappella notes that all have limits, and are mitigated and may even be reversed by certain moderator variables, including both individual differences and situational factors. Also, possible individual differences between dyads have not yet been properly assessed.

Cappella notes that, although the two categories of compensatory and reciprocity responses are sufficient to describe most of the studies of mutual influence and message sequencing conducted to date, this dichotomy may soon be obsolete. These studies are based upon methodologies in which expressive behavior is rather grossly manipulated (i.e., high vs. low gaze, far vs. close distances), and mean changes in response are assessed which cannot take individual patterns of response into account. Cappella suggests that emerging methodologies will allow the description of dynamic influence patterns over time during uncontrolled interaction, and will enable investigators to detect more subtle, complex, and individual patterns of response to mutual influence (Cappella, 1980a; Gottman, 1979b). Cappella also notes the limitations of studies which analyze specific expressive or immediacy behaviors in a "one-at-a-time" fashion, arguing that such approaches cannot in themselves lead to an understanding of the simultaneous influence of all expressive/immediacy behaviors. He suggests that more general indices of such behaviors be developed to assess more general involvement in the interaction. Both of these suggestions shall be considered below.

A Sequential Functional Model of Exchange

Patterson's (1976) arousal model of interpersonal intimacy, cited above, was designed to explain compensatory and reciprocal effects in interaction. Patterson (1982) has recently discussed the status of this model, noting that research has not been uniformly supportive (Patterson, Jordan, Hogan, & Frerker, 1981), and has suggested a revised model based upon an expanded functional classification of interaction. Instead of focusing exclusively upon the intimacy function of interaction, Patterson notes that interaction can also serve social-control and service-task functions, and that the behavior of the interactants will differ according to which of the functions is salient.

The intimacy and social-control functions correspond closely to the affective dimensions of interaction identified by the structuralists, that is, liking and dominance. However, Patterson views these as cognitive rather than affective. He suggests that each individual brings to an interaction a preferred level of involvement with the other and cognitions about the functions of the interaction which in turn shape expectations about the other's level of involvement. Discrepancies between the actual and expected involvement will produce instabilities within the interaction. These result in cognitive-arousal processes which lead to changes in nonverbal involvement measures (either compensatory or reciprocal), and possible reassessments of the interaction's function.

Patterson's conviction that these processes are primarily cognitive rather than affective is reflected in his suggestion that thought-listing procedures be employed to provide insight into sequential changes of thoughts and feelings during the interaction (Cacioppo & Petty, 1981). Patterson (1982) reports using such a procedure in conjunction with a video replay of the interaction, in which the subject stops the videotape at the point where a specific thought or feeling is recalled. He states that subjects appear to be candid in these reports. However, one wonders about the extent to which interactants are really aware of the functions of interaction, or their expectations about the other's involvement. The thought-listing procedure could produce thoughts stimulated by the video replay rather than thoughts that were actually present during the interaction.

The findings of the structuralists suggest that subjects are not always informative about the interaction processes that are revealed in their behavior. They suggest that, through a careful analysis of communication behaviors, an observer may have access to affective processes that are not available to the actor. In the thought-listing procedure, subjects may learn more about the interaction by watching it on videotape than they knew when they were actually involved in the interaction.

CONCLUSIONS

The external variable approach, with its methodology of experimental manipulation and control, has done much to advance our understanding of the nature of interaction. However, it can be argued that this methodology has taken us about as far as it can. First, this approach is based solidly upon reinforcement theory: Interaction is seen in terms of rewards and costs. This is consistent with the learning and cognitive traditions that have lately dominated the social sciences, but it cannot deal adequately with the emotional factors identified by the structuralists. The latter reflect spontaneous communication processes which, I have argued, must constitute the foundation of human interaction. The attachment of a newborn infant or the passions of love and hate simply cannot be explained by a rational consideration of rewards and costs.

Second, the external variable approach has attempted to explain interaction without actually observing interaction, or observing it under such controlled circumstances that spontaneous behavior tendencies cannot "contaminate" the results. The most striking example of this is the game research, where outcomes are strictly controlled and possibilities for "nonverbal communication" strictly minimized.

It can be argued that the analysis of the true complexities of human interaction must begin by the observation of such interaction. Such observation has been rendered much easier by the availability of video and computer technology, which can for the first time capture and analyze such a complex process. The next section considers some recent approaches that are beginning to take advantage of the opportunities provided by this technology.

RECENT APPROACHES TO THE ANALYSIS OF INTERACTION

As noted above, the analysis of interaction is an emerging and rapidly evolving field where the important trends are still unclear. However, three tendencies do seem apparent: One is a trend away from manipulative approaches in favor of naturalistic observation, another is an increasing acknowledgment of the importance of nonlanguage behaviors in interaction, a third is a trend toward the analysis of the interaction *process*, using techniques of time-series analysis. This section considers some approaches involving the naturalistic observation of multiple communication behaviors, and recent approaches to the interaction process using sequential and spectral time-series analyses.

NATURALISTIC OBSERVATION

We saw in Chapter 5 that naturalistic observation involves the observation of naturally occurring behavior in a situation where the behavior is, to a certain extent, unconstrained by experimental manipulations and other operations. This approach has been used with great success by ethologists in the study on animal behavior, and the methodology has been gaining increasing acceptance among investigators of human social interaction. Methods which have attempted to manipulate interaction by, for example, using a trained confederate as a "programed" interactant, or asking subjects to role-play during the interaction, have been useful in the analysis of certain aspects of interaction. However, these invasive techniques have come under increasing criticism in recent years by proponents of naturalistic observation.

Naturalistic observation cannot be completely unfocused, however. Any approach employing an observational methodology must specify (1) the nature of the behavior being observed, and (2) the setting in which the observation takes place. The former consideration will determine the particular "slice" of interaction that is captured by the observations. The latter will constrain the nature of the behavior being observed, of course, but it is argued that this should involve the natural constraints imposed by the setting rather than artificial constraints imposed by the experimenter.

The range of possible choices in the naturalistic observation of interaction is exceedingly wide, and the nature and usefulness of one's results are dependent to a great extent upon how one makes these choices. We shall review several approaches to the resolution of these problems: those of Bales (1950, 1970), Duncan and Fiske (1977), and Ickes (Ickes & Barnes, 1977, 1978), and techniques derived from dance notation systems, which have been particularly advocated by Martha Davis (1979).

Bales's Interaction Process Analysis and SYMLOG

One of the earliest and most widely used methods for the analysis of interaction is Bales's (1950) *interaction process analysis* (IPA). This procedure involves raters observing an interaction and recording their observations on a moving tape. Each statement or other communicative behavior noted by the observers is categorized according to a rating scheme which involves 12 categories of interaction. These categories are primarily verbal in nature, such as giving or asking for suggestions or opinions. However, some categories involve nonlanguage behaviors as well, such as "showing tension" or "tension release," or "showing friendliness" or "antagonism."

Bales's system has been widely used and adapted to a variety of settings. It has gradually evolved into a system in which behavior is evaluated along dimensions identified by factor analysis. Borgatta (1962, 1963) suggested adding factors of sociability (affection or friendliness) and assertiveness (dominance or power) to Bales's categories, since, as noted above, these two factors have been repeatedly identified in studies of social interaction (cf. Foa, 1961; Leary, 1957). A revised version of interaction analysis suggested by Bales (1970, 1982) is the *System for the Multiple-Level Observation of Groups* (*SYMLOG*). This technique is based upon the factor analysis of interaction observations, and it yields indices on three dimensions: positive versus negative (similar to friendliness), up versus down (similar to dominance), and forward versus backward. The latter is also termed "instrumentally controlled" versus "emotionally expressive," and is generally similar to a task versus a socioemotional orientation (Stiles, 1978). Bales (1982) has pointed out that similar three-factor spaces appear in Wish, Deutsch, and Kaplan's (1976) classification of social relationships, and Mehrabian's (1972) analysis of emotion.

Duncan and Fiske

Duncan and Fiske (1977) suggest a general model for research on face-to-face interaction which is derived from the structural approach. In the process, they provide a wealth of specific methodological suggestions and comments. They emphasize the importance of an appropriate data base for the study of interaction, criticizing approaches using global categories and dimensions of judgment such as the Bales approach because they are based too strongly upon the observer's judgment of the intent that lies behind the behavior, as opposed to the behavior itself. On the other hand, they argue that it is not useful to include such "elemental" behaviors as moving one's hand while alone or physiological responses. They do not specify exactly what they mean by "elemental" behaviors, although one possible interpretation might be behaviors that in our terms are relatively "inaccessible" to others.

Duncan and Fiske also choose to ignore verbal content, focusing instead on what they term the *act*, which includes those "relatively specific, immediately observable behaviors . . . of which the larger activities are composed" (p. 4). Acts include nods, smiles, leg crossings, eyebrow raises, voice lowerings, throat clearings, completions of syntactic sentences, head scratches, and posture shifts. Duncan and Fiske argue that acts are relatively objective occurrences which require minimal levels of inference and no attribution of meaning or intent as is involved in the judgment of more abstract or global categories. Categories of acts include paralanguage, kinesics, proxemics, olfaction, haptics (touch), artifacts (i.e., involving dress and cosmetics), and language. Duncan and Fiske agree with the basic structuralist assumption that acts are units of behavior arranged hierarchically.

In their research, Duncan and Fiske paired subjects with a stranger in a room where cameras and lights were visible, and a checkerboard pattern was applied to the floor. While some might argue that such a situation is hardly natural, the subjects were paired with other subjects rather than with a confederate, and there were no restrictions on the topic of conversation. It is thus a very controlled setting, but the actual actions of the participants were not controlled or manipulated.

In one study, each of 88 subjects was observed in two conversations, one with a male, one with a female. The interactions were 7½ minutes long, of which the last 5 minutes were coded. A total of 49 acts were observed and scored for frequency, extent, and duration. The covariation of the actions of each interactant were compared with his or her other actions and the actions of the other, and also were related to scores from a variety of self-report instruments.

The results indicated first of all that there was a varying degree of stability in different acts between the first and second interactions, with correlations ranging from +.80 to .00, with a median of +.40. Variables with higher stabilities included the number of filled pauses ("uhs" and "ahs," $r = .80$); the time, extent, and number of smiles ($r = .72$, .71, and .54, respectively); the extent, number, and time spent gazing ($r = .57$, .52, and .53, respectively); and the number of laughs ($r = .52$). Given the brevity of these interactions, and the fact that they involved different partners of different sex, these findings are interesting, suggesting relatively large and stable individual differences in these behaviors.

Significant sex differences were also observed: Males held the floor longer, and the length of the speaking turns when males spoke with males was significantly longer than those for any other combination. Females smiled, laughed, and gazed at the partner more than did males, while males shifted their seat position and leg position more than females. Differences between the first and the second interaction were interpreted in part as due to the subject being somewhat less at ease in the first conversation; if this was the correct interpretation, males appeared to show their discomfort by bodily movements, females by smiling and laughing. Interestingly, males also showed larger variation in behavior, as seen by larger standard deviations on about three-fourths of the variables.

Because Duncan and Fiske's subjects participated in two interviews, their behavior can be analyzed by Kenny's social relations model discussed above. Preliminary analyses of this kind have been carried out, suggesting the presence of large "sender effects," that is, considerable stability of behavior across different interactions. This may have been enhanced by the fact that both interactions involved strangers. In addition, there is evidence of some "receiver effects": Some persons, for example, are more smiled at than are others (Kenny, 1981). These results may be relevant to the notion of individual differences in interaction strategy. Further results from this interesting type of analysis will be forthcoming.

Ickes's Paradigm

Another paradigm which employs a naturalistic observational approach to the study of interaction, with some similarities with that of Duncan and Fiske, has been employed by Ickes and his colleagues (Ickes & Barnes, 1977, 1978). In Ickes's studies, strangers are brought to a laboratory room supplied with a couch and coffee table. The subjects are invited to sit down, are told that the experimenter forgot some questionnaires, and are asked to "get to know one another" while the experimenter retrieves them. They are then left alone for 5 minutes. Unknown to them, their interaction is recorded on a hidden television camera, and when the experimenter returns, they are told that the most important phase of the study is over.

A number of behaviors are coded from the resulting videotapes, many of them similar to Duncan and Fiske's acts (e.g., number of smiles, gaze direction). Ickes's research has investigated the effects of a number of "external variables" on the interaction process, including sex, race, birth order, and personality variables such as sex-role orientation and self-monitoring. This focus on external variables is in contrast with Duncan and Fiske's more structural approach.

There is evidence that the lack of structure in the Ickes studies may be important in determining the patterns of results. For example, Dabbs and his colleagues have studied the role of self-monitoring in interaction in a study in which same-sex pairs were asked to "get to know one another" in a brief 10-minute conversation (Dabbs, 1979). The subjects were aware that the conversation was being filmed, and in fact they interacted through a .6 m × .6 m box which contained a beam-splitter mirror. The mirror allowed the direct filming of their faces, so that gaze behavior could be assessed. Ickes and Barnes (1977) had found that conversation was difficult when a high self-monitor was paired with a low self-monitor, with the most long silences and self-reported self-consciousness occurring under this circumstance. Dabbs and his colleagues did not find this to be the case, and attributed this to their relatively structured situation as opposed to that of Ickes and Barnes.

Dance Notation Techniques

It should be noted that techniques developed from dance notation systems can also be used to quanitify interaction. We discussed in Chapter 5 the Davis and Weitz (1978) study, which investigated sex differences in conversational behavior using techniques derived from dance notation (see also Hall & Braunwald, 1981; LaFrance & Carmen, 1980). Davis (1979) has described several other studies using a dance notation approach to interaction, and has discussed the potential of using this method of quantifying interaction.

SEQUENTIAL ANALYSIS

Most studies employing naturalistic observation have presented their results in terms of the rates or relative frequencies of occurrence of specific categories of behavior, for example, the number of smiles or instances of gaze direction. However, this kind of analysis loses any sense of the sequence of behavior, and it has been argued that the patterns of such sequences may do much to reveal the implicit structural rules underlying a given type of interaction (Gottman & Parkhurst, 1978). To study these patterns, it is necessary to study the sequence in which behaviors occur.

Sequential analysis originated in Shannon and Weaver's (1949) information theory discussed in Chapter 1. Essentially, it involves the determination of *conditional probabilities* between behaviors. Behaviors are observed across time to determine whether the probabilities of one behavior (e.g., those of interactant A) are altered by the presence or absence of other behaviors (e.g., those of interactant B). The information theory definition of communication presented in Chapter 1 is based upon such an analysis. It will be recalled that a sender's behavior is considered communicative to the extent that it reduces uncertainty in predicting the behavior of a receiver. "The conditional probability that act X2 will be performed by individual B given that A performed X1 is not equal to the probability that B will perform X2 in the absence of X1" (Wilson, 1975, p. 194). Sequential analysis is thus basic to the definition and analysis of communication.

There are many specific ways in which such conditional probabilities may be assembled, depending upon the particular interests and requirements of the investigator. These may range from the simple and descriptive to complex, abstract, and highly mathematical analyses (cf. Cappella, 1980b; Warner, 1979). Bakeman and Dabbs (1976) and Bakeman (1978) have discussed analyses of recurring patterns in several types of data, and Sackett (1977) has described a lag sequence analysis which can accommodate *lags*, which are defined as events or time units occurring between sequential events. The theory of Markov chains can also be used to identify conditional probabilities, although in practice this may be time consuming and produce quantities of data which are difficult to summarize and comprehend (Gottman & Notarius, 1978; Sackett, 1977).

It is impossible to summarize the qualities, advantages, and disadvantages of these many techniques here. Instead, as in the last section, several recent concrete examples of studies using these techniques will be examined. These include studies of the sequencing of conversation by Cappella (1979, 1980a; Cappella & Planalp, 1981) and studies of marital interaction by Gottman and his colleagues (Gottman, Markman, & Notarius, 1977; Gottman & Parkhurst, 1978).

Talk–Silence Sequences

One of the earliest traditions in the analysis of interaction process is the analysis of periods of talk and silence, which is found in the work of Chapple (1940). Chapple's interaction chronograph (1939) measured 12 types of "action" and "inaction" during the course of dyadic interaction. Also, an early application of sequential analysis to the study of interaction was the study by Jaffe and Feldstein (1970), in which the talk and silence sequences in a dyadic interaction were computer coded and subjected to sequential analysis via Markov models.

Cappella (1979, 1980a) has continued this tradition of focusing exclusively upon the sequence of periods of talk and silence, without regard to content. In a useful review of this literature, he reports that there are strong individual differences in overall talk and silence responses, and that a given individual tends to show a relatively consistent pattern of talk and silence both within conversations and between conversations with a given partner. Thus, some persons appear to be generally more "talkative" than others, and this level of talkativeness shows a certain degree of stability. However, talkativeness can be altered by such situational factors as cognitive load, stress, and the attractiveness of the partner. In addition, there is evidence of mutual influences between interactants, so that changes in one person's level of talkativeness can influence the talkativeness of the other (Cappella, 1979).

Given these findings, Cappella suggests four models of talk–silence sequencing which can be evaluated by sequential analyses. The first is a first-order Markov chain model designed to account for within-conversation talk and silence sequences. The other three models are proposed to account for such sequences between conversations, that is, as a person switches partners. These latter models address the fundamental question of deriving dyadic behavior from the qualities of the individuals making up the dyad. It might be noted that the Kenny social relations model (SRM) described above may give a more direct and comprehensive account of these questions than does Cappella's approach. It will be recalled that the SRM analyzes behavior into that attributable to sender effects, receiver effects, and unique dyad effects, as opposed to Cappella's approach of finding evidence for various models which themselves are only indirectly related to actual behavior. However, it is useful to follow Cappella's reasoning in this case, to gain another perspective on the complexity of interaction which can be compared with that of Kenny.

The first of Cappella's between-conversations models is the *independent decision* model, which assumes (1) that an individual's tendency to talk or remain silent is consistent across conversations, and (2) that this tendency is independent of the other's tendency to talk or remain silent. In the SRM, this would be equivalent to all behavior being due to sender effects. The second, *incremental* model relaxes the "consistency across conversations" assumption, allowing change for new occasions or partners. Specifically, it stipulates that a person's probability of talking will shift up or down in response to a new conversational situation. In the terms of the SRM, such changes could be due to either receiver or unique dyad effects. The third, *regulation* model relaxes the "independence of action" assumption, allowing change in response to the overt behaviors of the partner. Specifically, it states that a person's probability of talking will show general consistency across situations and partners, but that it will change within the conversation in response to the partner's probability of talking. Cappella notes that this kind of mutual influence has been little studied, and that there are many potential complications to this sort of analysis. One involves the question of whether the influence of the partner's behavior is immediate or delayed. If delayed, a lag sequence analysis would be appropriate, but the duration of the lag is not known.

To test these models, Cappella studied talk–silence sequences in 30-minute conversations between college student volunteers. Each engaged in three such conversations: the first with a same-sex partner, the second with an opposite-sex partner, the third with a different same-sex partner. Results indicated that the Markov model was a valid representation of the talk–silence sequencing within the conversation on a dyad-by-dyad basis. This suggests that dyads' probabilities of changing talk–silence states are consistent over the conversation, and that individuals are consistent with the conversation. Cappella concludes that this strong consistency is an "important structural baseline for the conversations" and that it is apparently based upon biological, cognitive, or personality factors (Cappella, 1980a, p. 142).

Regarding the modeling of the between-conversation sequences, Cappella (1980a) finds that certain behaviors are consistent across partners: specifically the tendency to break or continue speech and the tendency to talk while the other has the floor. These thus appear to follow the "independent decision" model most clearly (i.e., strong sender effects). Other behaviors follow the "incremental model" assumptions, changing with changing partners. These include the behaviors underlying the breaking or continuing of mutual silences, and the duration of vocalizations. Cappella (1980a) notes that other research has shown that these aspects of conversation are particularly susceptible to such factors as perceived partner's warmth, anxiety, and cognitive load.

Regarding the "regulation model" of mutual influence, Cappella and Planalp (1981) found that the extent of direct interspeaker influence is small but detectable. The nature of the influence differs from dyad to dyad, and includes both positive (matching or reciprocating) and negative (compensating) influences. For example, they report matching on switching pause duration, suggesting that when one partner responds quickly after the other finishes a turn, the other reciprocates and also responds more quickly. In essence, the tempo of the conversation seems to be picked up by the partners from each other. Also, duration was found to show matching effects in some dyads, but compensating effects in others. Cappella and Planalp suggest that matching may result from attempts by partners to equalize participation in the discussion, while compensation may result from one partner being verbose, while the other in effect opts out of the conversation.

Cappella and Planalp (1981) conclude that any general explanation of interspeaker influence must be able to account for both matching and compensation effects—and the conditions that give rise to each—and for between-dyad differences. They also note that such an explanation must involve little cognitive processing and a relatively "automatic" mechanism, given the short time intervals and low order of awareness that interactants have of the process. They tentatively suggest an "arousal-based" explanation: When the other's behavior is within expected limits, arousal would be moderate and pleasurable and matching would occur, while if the other's activity exceeded expected limits, arousal would be excessive and aversive and compensation would occur. Unfortunately, this explanation was only briefly discussed. It did not specify what was meant by "arousal," and it did not make clear why pleasurable situations would necessarily be associated with matching and aversive situations with compensation.

Sequential Analysis of Marital Interaction

Gottman (1979a) has provided an extensive analysis of interactions of married couples, including the sequential analysis of verbal and nonverbal behaviors. In this work, he and his colleagues have investigated the interacting influences of person typologies (husband vs. wife), relationship typologies ("stressed" clinic couples vs. nonclinic couples), and situation typologies (high- vs. low-conflict tasks). Such an interactional approach has many potential advantages (Montgomery, 1981). It has suggested, for example, that differences between stressed and nonstressed couples may be revealed more clearly by high-conflict than low-conflict tasks (Gottman, Notarius, Markman, Bank, Yoppi, & Rubin, 1976).

Differences in sequential behaviors between clinic and nonclinic couples have proved particularly interesting. Gottman *et al.* (1977) have demonstrated that nonclinic couples often begin a discussion with a "validation sequence," in which a neutral description of a problem is followed by an expression of agreement. This tends to continue in a cyclic manner, with the couple avoiding negative exchanges. The discussion is often ended with a "contract sequence," in which expressions of agreement are interspersed with proposals for solving the problem.

"Stressed" couples from a clinic sample, in contrast, often begin a discussion with a "cross-complaining loop," in which a description of one problem is followed by the description of another. Subsequently, a "negative exchange loop" is likely. This loop involves "mindreading," in which one spouse attributes thoughts, feelings, motives, attitudes, or actions to the other. In the negative exchange loop, mindreading with negative affect is followed by the statement of a problem, often with negative affect. The clinic couples are not likely to enter a contract sequence at the end of the discussion. Gottman et al. conclude that the sequential analysis suggests that the two groups of couples "do not simply differ in response frequencies, but they traverse essentially different terrains in their interaction" (p. 476).

It is interesting to compare these findings with models of negotiation and decision making that have been proposed in the small-group literature (i.e., Bales & Strodtbeck, 1951; Fisher, 1974). For example, the cycling through validation sequences and ending with a contract sequence seems quite compatible with the four-phase model of decision making (orientation–conflict–emergence–reinforcement) suggested by Fisher (1974). It is possible that the sequential analysis of natural conversation may be used to develop and evaluate such models.

The results and impact of the complex sequential analyses of Gottman and his colleagues can only be suggested here. Also, there is insufficient space to detail the interesting and important sequential analyses of child–child interaction (Gottman & Parkhurst, 1978), or of mother–infant interaction, which were pioneered in an early study by Rosenfeld (1973; cf. Rosenfeld & Remmers, 1981), and have been reviewed by Cappella (1981). Suffice it to say that these studies demonstrate that the sequential approach can discern phenomena that cannot be handled by other approaches. The next section examines a set of techniques which have been suggested as a new and general approach to sequential analysis: techniques of spectral and cross-spectral analysis.

SPECTRAL AND CROSS-SPECTRAL ANALYSIS

A *time series* refers to a sequential pattern of responses for a specific subject over a period of time. Gottman (1979b, 1981) has discussed the statistical techniques required to analyze cyclic patterns in both continuous and categorical time series data.

Single Time Series

The procedure used to describe the role of periodic variations or rhythms in making up the patterns of responses in a time series is termed *spectral analysis*. Essentially, spectral analysis decomposes the variation observed in the time-series data into component frequencies or periodicities associated with specific rhythms (cf. Gottman, 1979b; Porges, Bohrer, Cheung, Drasgow, McCabe, & Keren, 1980). This involves the partitioning of the data into a set of sine waves which vary in *frequency*, or length of cycle; *phase*, or starting point; and *amplitude*, which is an index of the relative importance of the wave in the time series (cf. Warner, 1982). Any time series can be thus partitioned into a set of sine waves, as is illustrated in Figure 8.7.

The result of spectral analysis is a set of *power density scores* which estimate the variance attributed to each specific component frequency. These are combined in a *spectral density function* which yields power density scores over a range of different frequencies. The dominant or most characteristic frequency, which contributes the most to the variance of the time-series data is termed the *peak power*

Figure 8.7. General characteristics of sine waves.

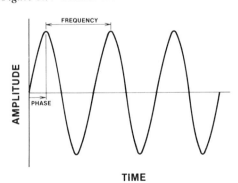

TIME

density. Significance tests are available which assess whether a specific frequency is accounting for more variance than one would expect from chance (cf. Bohrer & Porges, 1982). The percent of total variance in a time series associated with a specific band of frequencies is a measure of the *stability* of the time series.

Two Time Series

The comparison of the cyclic patterns associated with two different time series is known as *cross-spectral analysis*. Essentially, this allows the description of the extent to which the two time series are similar to one another. The cross-spectral analysis generates two kinds of statistics: *coherence* and *phase spectrum*. The coherence statistic involves the ability to predict one time series from another across a range of frequencies. Porges *et al.* (1980) have described a *weighted coherence* statistic which estimates the amount of variance in one series that can be accounted for by variation in the other within a given frequency range. In other words, it summarizes the "proportion of shared variances between two systems over an entire band of frequencies" (p. 14).

The phase spectrum indicates whether the frequency components of one time series "lead" or "lag" the same frequency components in the other time series. This may be useful in making inferences about which series may be "driving" the other: If one series consistently leads a second coherent series, it is possible that the second is being "driven" by the first. Gottman and Ringland (1981) have used this technique to study dominance patterns. A consideration of coherence and phase spectrum thus allow a description of relationships between two time series.

An Example

A useful example of cross-spectral analysis has been provided by Porges *et al.* (1980), using the phenomenon of respiratory sinus arrhythmia, in which heart-rate is known to be related to changes in respiration. Thus, as one breathes in, heart-rate tends to increase, while as one breathes out, it tends to decrease. The physiological mechanism by which this occurs is not completely understood, but there is evidence that this coupling of heart-rate and respiration is based in the brain stem.

The results of a spectral analysis of heart rate and respiration, respectively, are shown in Figure 8.8A. Figure 8.8A shows the "raw" records illustrating the cyclical variation of heart rate and respiration over time. Figure 8.8B presents the spectral density functions showing the power density over a range of frequencies. It will be noted that both heart rate and respiration have a peak power density at the same frequency—about .3 Hz or 18 breaths per minute—which is the dominant frequency for both systems. However, the stability of the heart-rate data is lower in that a number of frequencies are prominently involved in addition to the dominant frequency. This is consistent with the fact that heart rate is affected by a number of influences besides respiration, such as temperature and blood pressure.

The results of a cross-spectral analysis are presented in Figure 8.8C. This describes the correlation of the two time series, or the proportion of variance accounted for by the influence of one series on the other, at each specific frequency. The weighted coherence statistic that Porges *et al.* (1980) describe summarizes this proportion of shared variance in a single statistic which may be taken to reflect the "general coupling" of the two processes in question. In this case of respiratory sinus arrhythmia, coherence may reflect the degree of integration within the brain stem. Porges and his colleagues have found evidence that the coherence between respiration and heart rate is lower in hyperactive than normal children, and that the drug methylphenidate, which has positive effects upon cognitive processes and social behaviors in hyperactive children at certain doses, also increases coherence (Porges, Bohrer, Keren, Cheung, Franks, & Drasgow, 1981).

Categorical Data

Most investigators of social interaction collect categorical rather than continuous data, where each category is classified as present or absent for a specific subject during each period of time. Thus one might classify a smile as present or absent for each second of interaction. In effect, this produces a time series of 1's and 0's for each category of behavior that is observed (cf. Gottman & Bakeman, 1978).

Categorical data are typically handled by the sorts of sequential analyses described above. However, Gottman (1979b) has generalized the spectral analytic methods to the analysis of categorical observation data, including the use of the coherence and phase-spectrum

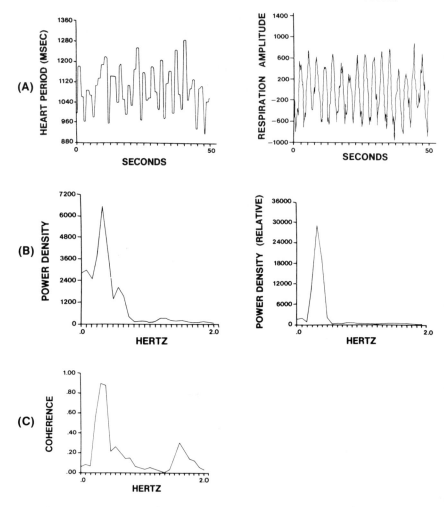

Figure 8.8. Example of time series analysis. (A) Left: Second-by-second heart period values (time intervals between sequential heartbeats). Right: Second-by-second measures of respiration amplitude (changes in chest circumference). (B) Left: Spectral density function of the heart period data. Right: Spectral density function of the respiration data. (C) The coherence spectrum between the heart period data and respiration data. From Figures 4, 5, 6, 7, and 8 in "New Time Series Statistic for Detecting Rhythmic Co-Occurrence in the Frequency Domain: The Weighted Coherence and Its Application to Psychophysiological Research" by S. W. Porges, R. E. Bohrer, M. N. Cheung, F. Drasgow, P. M. McCabe, and G. Keren, *Psychological Bulletin*, 1980, 88, 580–587. Copyright 1980 by the American Psychological Association. Reprinted by permission.

statistics. As an illustration, he used data from the Gottman *et al.* (1977) study cited above. In another illustration of the potential usefulness of this approach, Dabbs (1979) has shown that conversations about social matters have shorter cycles of speaking than do conversations about cognitive matters. In other words, statements tend to be shorter when discussing social, as opposed to task-oriented, topics.

Nonstationarity

Rebecca Warner (1982) has pointed out a significant limitation of spectral analysis: that it is not sensitive to changes in cycling over time. Instead, it simply summarizes the extent to which different cycles appear in the data. For example, if a phenomenon cycles at .5 Hz for the first half of an observation period, and at .25 Hz for the second half, the spectral analysis would simply show peak power densities at .5 and .25 Hz. Such changes in cycle frequency, amplitude, or phase relationship over time are termed *nonstationarity* (cf. Gottman, 1981). Warner suggests the technique of band-pass filtering as an exploratory technique in such cases, in which a given filter passes only data that match the characteristics of the filter. A preliminary spectral analysis is made to choose the filters. For example, .5- and .25-Hz filters would be employed in the above example after the preliminary spectral analysis. The former filter would pass the data from the first half of the observation period; the second would pass data from the second half.

CONCLUSIONS

We have discussed a number of approaches to the analysis of interaction. This section suggests several conclusions from this discussion which may hopefully point toward areas of future interest and research. Specifically, it suggests that the segmentation methodology discussed in Chapter 5 may be profitably applied to the analysis of interaction, and may avoid certain problems involved with current methods. Also, it discusses the substantive issue of the role of emotion communication in interaction, which has been underplayed particularly by approaches based upon exchange theory.

A SEGMENTATION APPROACH TO INTERACTION

Let us summarize and recall some of the points raised in earlier sections of this chapter. We noted that a truly dynamic approach to communication must involve an interactional setting in which the sender and receiver can influence one another directly. The resulting data will be a complex mix of individual sending and receiving tendencies and unique dyadic effects, which must be analyzed by techniques resembling those of the Kenny social relations model. We also noted the importance of the concept of synchrony, and the difficulties in measuring it, as well as the general problem of the laboriousness of the structural approach. Later, we noted Cappella's and Gottman's criticisms of studies which assess specific behaviors in a "one-at-a-time" fashion, arguing instead for more global measures. Such a practice might, on the other hand, lead to the same problems of observer reliability and validity which led Duncan and Fiske among others to opt to study concrete acts.

A number of these difficulties might be avoided by an approach to interaction based upon the segmentation technique discussed in Chapter 5. It will be recalled that this technique involves asking raters to press a button when, in their opinion, "something meaningful" occurs in the stream of behavior, and that raters tend to agree about the location of these "meaningful" points. This approach has been used with success to analyze the complex flow of spontaneous facial expression (Buck et al., 1980, 1982), and there seems to be no reason why it could not be applied to the analysis of interaction as well. Reuben Baron, Kathleen Reardon, and I, with several students, are currently analyzing a videotape of a short (3-minute) interaction between a woman and man. Students segmented the videotape in several conditions; that is, they were told to attend to either the man or the woman, or both interactants, and the former could see the other interactant in one condition but not in another. Figure 8.9 illustrates the segmentation pattern that has resulted. It is interesting that the ability to see the other interactant had very little effect upon the segmentation pattern. That is, the segmentation pattern for those segmenting the woman's behavior was similar whether or not the man was hidden from view.

This technique has several useful features that are relevant to the points summarized above. First, it produces a representation of the behavior stream that is readily analyzable by time-series tech-

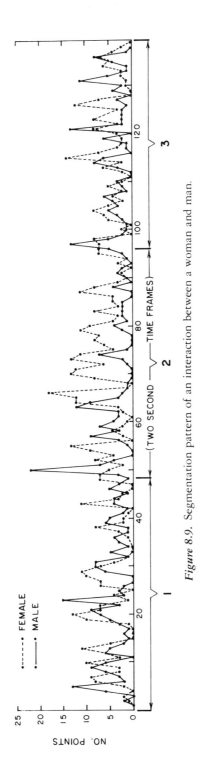

Figure 8.9. Segmentation pattern of an interaction between a woman and man.

niques such as spectral and cross-spectral analysis. It thus appears to be potentially able to detect subtle, complex, and individual patterns of response, the importance of which has been pointed out by Cappella (1980b), Gottman (1979b), and others. Second, the consensually meaningful points identified by this technique are not tied to specific acts: One might be based upon a facial expression, another upon a hand movement, another upon a shift in posture, and so forth. At the same time, these points by definition involve events that are consensually recognized as meaningful by receivers, and the extent of this consensus can be mathematically specified. It thus involves a relatively simple judgment task with a minimum of inference, as advocated by Duncan and Fiske (1977), while on the other hand it is not tied to the analysis of possibly trivial act and can be sensitive to rare events. Third, the segmentation technique may lead to useful and specific ways to define synchrony, in terms of the co-occurrence of consensually meaningful points for two interactants. Perhaps the most useful aspect of this approach, however, is that it does not require the investigator to make *ad hoc* decisions on what is important in the stream of interaction, but instead allows the naïve perceiver to point to the events of importance. It can thus be employed to study both the interaction itself, and the perceiver of the interaction.

THE EMOTIONAL BASES OF INTERACTION

The segmentation technique is also relevant to a substantive issue raised by our review: the relative neglect of the emotional bases of interaction (i.e., spontaneous communication) in favor of the analysis of learned cognitive factors (i.e., symbolic communication). One of the fundamental arguments in this book is that spontaneous behavior is basic to all communication. Its importance has been demonstrated in the detailed frame-by-frame analyses of the structuralists. Human interaction, then, should reflect the simultaneous influence of spontaneous and symbolic processes.

Spontaneous and Symbolic Communication in Interaction

A representation of how spontaneous and symbolic communication occur in interaction, which incorporates the readout model of emotion, is presented in Figure 8.10. It includes the two sources of behavioral

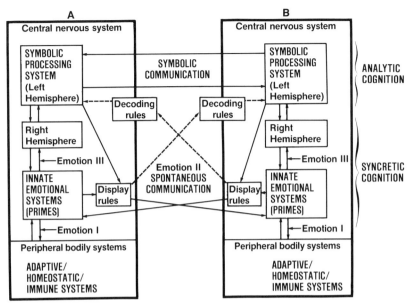

Figure 8.10. A representation of spontaneous and symbolic communication in interaction, incorporating the readout model of emotion.

organization and regulation which have appeared repeatedly in this book: analytic cognition associated with the left hemisphere which, in humans, is dominated by language; and syncretic cognition associated with the right hemisphere and innate emotional systems. The former is the basis for symbolic communication. The latter is read out in the three forms introduced in Figure 2.3: to the body in the form of adaptive and homeostatic responses, to others in the form of spontaneous communication, and to consciousness in the form of subjective experience.

In interaction, these systems result in two streams of communication: symbolic communication, involving the exchange of ideas, and spontaneous communication, involving the exchange of feelings. Individuals A and B simultaneously influence one another via the encoding and decoding of learned symbols and via innate sending and receiving mechanisms. The streams may interact, in that the individual may become consciously aware of the other's spontaneous display (dashed lines). The symbolic stream, however, cannot directly influence emotion in the other—it must first be decoded by the receiver.

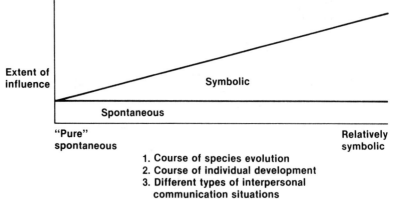

Figure 8.11. Relationship of spontaneous and symbolic communication across three topics.

The Relative Influence of Spontaneous and Symbolic Communication

A number of studies have attempted to assess the relative importance of "verbal" and "nonverbal" behaviors in communication. For example, Mehrabian and his colleagues have estimated that the "facial channel" is weighed more heavily than the "verbal channel" or "vocal channel" in forming judgments about attitudes (Mehrabian & Ferris, 1967; Mehrabian & Weiner, 1967). These studies have been criticized by those who argue that these results are based too narrowly upon the particular tasks involved in the study, and that the facial channel may not be as important when judging nonemotional beliefs or other more "cognitive" judgments.

This may well be the case: One might suggest that different interaction situations should be expected to differ in the degree to which spontaneous versus symbolic communication is involved. If fact, the nature of the relationship between spontaneous and symbolic behavior across different kinds of interaction situations may be described with a figure similar to ones we have encountered before (see Figure 8.11). In essence, this suggests that the relative influences of spontaneous and symbolic communication in different interaction situations should be expected to differ according to the nature of the interaction: that in some situations symbolic communication will be more important than spontaneous and vice versa. However, as before it must be recognized that there can be no pure symbolic communication. All interaction situations involve spontaneous communication, if only to a minor extent.

The Segmentation Technique

This returns us to the segmentation technique. We noted in Chapter 5 that the Goodman (1980) study demonstrated that perceivers instructed to segment according to action events and those instructed to segment according to emotion events created very different patterns of segmentation. It may be that these instructions encourage the perceiver to attend to relatively symbolic and relatively spontaneous cues, respectively, so that the different segmentation patterns reflect the different symbolic and spontaneous organizations in the behavior. This technique could easily be applied to interaction, and it may provide a direct way to assess the relative importance of spontaneous and symbolic behavior in an interaction situation, as well as perhaps the ebb and flow of their relative importance over time. The result could be a fundamentally new approach to the analysis of the interaction process, which is able to efficiently analyze the complex emotional factors upon which human interaction is based and their interplay with the symbolic communication process.

SUMMARY

This chapter has examined the complexity of interaction data, and the social relations model, which analyzes that complexity into components associated with individual sending tendencies, individual receiving tendencies, and unique dyadic effects. It then reviewed two of the major approaches to the analysis of interaction: structural approaches and external variable approaches. In general, the structural approaches have been able to deal holistically with the complexity of their subject, but at the cost of using tedious, detailed, and expensive methods of analysis. The external variable approaches have avoided these problems by using experimental controls to "simplify" the interaction situation, but at the cost of losing the complexity of their subject.

This chapter then examined recent approaches to the analysis of interaction, with the caution that this is a recently emerging area of research in which the major trends and techniques are not yet readily apparent. However, it appears that significant trends include the naturalistic observation of interaction, with an emphasis upon non-language behaviors and upon the analysis of the communication *process*, using techniques of time-series analysis. I suggested that the segmentation approach can be usefully applied in such analyses, and that it has the distinct advantage of being able to focus upon behaviors that are consensually deemed meaningful, as opposed to behaviors that are preselected as meaningful by the investigator. I also suggested that this combination of techniques can efficiently analyze the interplay between spontaneous and symbolic communication behaviors in interaction, and that such an analysis would be uniquely valuable in studying the emotional bases of human behavior and human interaction.

REFERENCES

Abramovich, R. Children's recognition of situational aspects of facial expressions. *Child Development*, 1977, *48*, 459–463.

Abramovich, R., & Daly, E. M. Inferring the attributes of a situation from the facial expressions of peers. *Child Development*, 1979, *50*, 586–589.

Abrams, R. D. Denial and depression in the terminal cancer patients: A clue for management. *Psychoanalytic Quarterly*, 1971, *45*, 394–404.

Adams, S. Toward an understanding of inequity. *Journal of Abnormal and Social Psychology*, 1963, *67*, 422–436.

Alper, S., Buck, R., & Dreyer, A. Nonverbal sending accuracy and receiving ability in preschool children. *Research Relating to Children*, 1978, *41*, 89. (Abstract)

Altman, I., & Taylor, D. A. *Social penetration*. New York: Holt, Rinehart & Winston, 1973.

Altman, I., Vinsel, A., & Brown, B. Dialectic conceptions in social psychology: An application to social penetration and privacy regulation. In L. Berkowitz (Ed.), *Advances in experimental social psychology* (Vol. 14). New York: Academic, 1981.

Anderson, C. D. Expression of affect and physiological response in psychosomatic patients. *Journal of Psychosomatic Research*, 1981, *25*, 143–149.

Andrew, R. J. The origin and evolution of the calls and facial expressions of the primates. *Behaviour*, 1963, *20*, 1–109.

Andrew, R. J. The origins of facial expressions. *Scientific American*, 1965, *213*, 88–94.

Archer, D., & Akert, R. M. Words and everything else: Verbal and nonverbal cues in social interpretation. *Journal of Personality and Social Psychology*, 1977, *35*, 443–449.

Argyle, M. *Bodily communication*. New York: International Universities Press, 1975.

Argyle, M., & Dean, J. Eye contact, distance, and affiliation. *Sociometry*, 1965, *28*, 289–304.

Arnold, M. *Emotion and personality*. New York: Columbia University Press, 1960.

Averill, J. R. An analysis of psychophysiological symbolism and its influence on theories of emotion. *Journal for the Theory of Social Behaviors*, 1974, *4*, 147–190.

Averill, J. R. On the paucity of positive emotions. In K. R. Blankenstein, P. Pliner, & J. Polivy (Eds.), *Assessment and modification of emotional behavior.* New York: Plenum, 1980.

Averill, J. R., Opton, E. M., Jr., & Lazarus, R. S. Cross cultural studies of psychophysiological responses during stress and emotion. *International Journal of Psychiatry*, 1969, *4*, 33–102.

Bakeman, R. Untangling streams of behavior: Sequential analysis of observational data. In G. P. Sackett (Ed.), *Observing behavior* (Vol. 2). Baltimore: University Park Press, 1978.

Bakeman, R., & Dabbs, J. M. Social interaction observed: Some approaches to the analysis of behavior streams. *Personality and Social Psychology Bulletin*, 1976, *2*, 335–345.

Baker, A. H., Mishara, B., Kostin, I., & Parker, L. Kinesthetic aftereffect and personality: A case study of issues involved in construct validation. *Journal of Personality and Social Psychology*, 1976, *34*, 1–13.

Baker, A. H., Mishara, B., Kostin, I. W., & Parker, L. Menstrual cycle affects kinesthetic aftereffect, an index of personality and perceptual style. *Journal of Personality and Social Psychology*, 1979, *37*, 234–241.

Baker, A. H., Mishara, B., Parker, L., & Kostin, I. When "reliability" fails, must a measure be discarded? The case of kinesthetic aftereffect. *Journal of Research in Personality*, 1978, *12*, 262–273.

Baldwin, A. L. *Theories of child development.* New York: Wiley, 1967.

Bales, R. F. *Interaction process analysis.* Reading, Mass.: Addison-Wesley, 1950.

Bales, R. F. *Personality and interpersonal behavior.* New York: Holt, Rinehart & Winston, 1970.

Bales, R. F. *IPA and SYMLOG.* Paper delivered at the meeting of the Eastern Communication Association, Hartford, Conn., May 1982.

Bales, R. F., & Strodtbeck, F. L. Phases in group problem solving. *Journal of Abnormal and Social Psychology*, 1951, *46*, 485–495.

Bandura, A. *Social learning theory.* Englewood Cliffs, N.J.: Prentice-Hall, 1977.

Bandura, A., & Walters, R. H. *Social learning and personality development.* New York: Holt, Rinehart & Winston, 1963.

Barden, R. C., Zelko, F. A., Duncan, S. W., & Masters, J. C. Children's consensual knowledge about the experiential determinants of emotions. *Journal of Personality and Social Psychology*, 1980, *39*, 968–976.

Baron, R. M. Social knowing from an ecological event perspective: A consideration of the relative domains of power for cognitive and perceptual modes of knowing. In J. Harvey (Ed.), *Cognition, social behavior, and the environment.* Hillsdale, N.J.: Erlbaum, 1980.

Baron, R. M., & Buck, R. *A Gibsonian-event perception approach to the meaning of the nonverbal communication of emotion.* Paper presented at the symposium, "The Meaning of Nonverbal Communication," American Psychological Association Convention, New York, 1979.

Baron, R., & Harvey, J. H. Contrasting perspectives on social knowing: An overview. *Personality and Social Psychology Bulletin*, 1980, *6*, 502–506.

Bateson, G. The message: "This is play." In B. Schaffner (Ed.), *Group processes* (Vol. 2). New York: Macy, 1955.

Bateson, G. Chapter 1. In N. A. McQuown, G. Bateson, R. L. Birdwhistell, H. W. Brosin, & C. F. Hockett, (Eds.), *The natural history of an interview* (Collection of Manuscripts on Cultural Anthropology, 15). Chicago: University of Chicago Department of Photoduplication, 1971. (Microfilm)

Bear, D. M. *Anatomy and pathology of emotion.* Presentation at the Boston Veterans Administration Hospital, November 1980.

Bear, D. M., & Fedio, P. Quantitative analysis of interictal behavior in temporal lobe epilepsy. *Archives of Neurology,* 1977, *34,* 454–467.

Beecher, M. D., Peterson, M. R., Zoloth, S. R., Moody, D. B., & Stebbins, W. C. Perception of conspecific vocalizations by Japanese macaques. *Brain, Behavior and Evolution,* 1979, *16,* 443–460.

Benowitz, L. I., Bear, D. M., Rosenthal, R., & Mesulam, M. *Sensitivity to nonverbal communication after unilateral brain damage.* Unpublished manuscript, Harvard University, 1980.

Benson, H. *The relaxation response.* New York: Morrow, 1975.

Berger, S. Conditioning through vicarious instigation. *Psychological Review,* 1962, *69,* 450–466.

Berkowitz, L. Aggressive cues in aggressive behavior and hostility catharsis. *Psychological Review,* 1964, *71,* 104–122.

Best, C., & Taylor, N. *The physiological basis of medical practice* (8th ed). Baltimore: Williams & Wilkins, 1966.

Birdwhistell, R. *Introduction to kinesics.* Louisville, Ky.: University of Louisville Press, 1952.

Birdwhistell, R. L. *Kinesics and context.* Philadelphia: University of Pennsylvania Press, 1970.

Blake, M. J. F. Relationship between circadian rhythm of body temperature and introversion–extraversion. *Nature,* 1967, *215,* 896–897.

Blanck, P., & Rosenthal, R. *Measuring sensitivity to verbal and nonverbal discrepant and consistent multichannel messages: The MOVANS test.* Paper presented at the meeting of the Eastern Psychological Association, New York, 1981.

Blanck, P. D., & Rosenthal, R. Developing strategies for decoding "leaky" messages: On learning how and when to decode discrepant and consistent social communications. In R. Feldman (Ed.), *The development of nonverbal behavior in children.* New York: Springer Verlag, 1982.

Blanck, P. D., Rosenthal, R., Snodgrass, S. E., DePaulo, B. M., & Zuckerman, M. Longitudinal and cross-sectional age effects in nonverbal decoding skill and style. *Developmental Psychology,* 1982, *18,* 491–498.

Blanck, P. D., Rosenthal, R., Snodgrass, S. E., DePaulo, B. M., & Zuckerman, M. Sex differences in eavesdropping on nonverbal cues: Developmental changes. *Journal of Personality and Social Psychology,* in press.

Blanck, P., Zuckerman, M., DePaulo, B., & Rosenthal, R. Sibling resemblances in nonverbal skill and style. *Journal of Nonverbal Behavior,* 1980, *4,* 219–226.

Blest, A. D. The concept of ritualization. In W. H. Thorp & O. L. Zangwill (Eds.), *Current problems in animal behaviors.* Cambridge: Cambridge University Press, 1961.

Block, A. R. An investigation of the response of the spouse to chronic pain behavior. *Psychosomatic Medicine,* 1981, *43,* 415–422.

Block, J. A study of affective responsiveness in a lie detection situation. *Journal of Abnormal and Social Psychology*, 1957, *55*, 11–15.

Blumberg, S. H., Solomon, G. E., & Perloe, S. I. *Display rules and the facial communication of emotion*. Unpublished manuscript, Haverford College, 1981.

Bohrer, R. E., & Porges, S. W. The application of time-series statistics to psychological research: An introduction. In G. Keren (Ed.), *Statistical and methodological issues in psychology and social sciences research*. Hillsdale, N.J.: 1982.

Borgatta, E. A systematic study of interaction process scores, peer and self-assessments, personality and other variables. *Genetic Psychology Monographs*, 1962, *65*, 219–291.

Borgatta, E. A new systematic interaction observation system: Behavior scores system (BSS system). *Journal of Psychological Studies*, 1963, *14*, 24–44.

Borod, J., & Caron, H. Facedness and emotion related to lateral dominance, sex and expression type. *Neuropsychologia*, 1980, *18*, 237–241.

Borod, J., Caron, H., & Koff, E. Facial asymmetry related to quantitative measures of handedness, footedness, and eyedness. *Neuropsychologia*, in press.

Borod, J., & Koff, E. *Facial asymmetry and lateral dominance in normal and brain-damaged adults*. Paper presented at the meeting of the International Neuropsychological Society, Pittsburgh, February 1982.

Boyanowski, E. O., Newtson, D., & Walster, E. Effects of murder on movie preference. *Proceedings of the 80th Annual Convention of the American Psychological Association*, 1972, *7*, 235–236.

Brackett, D., & Donnelly, J. *Interruptions: The role of non-verbal, paralinguistic, and linguistic cues*. Paper presented at the American Speech–Language–Hearing Association Convention, Los Angeles, November 1981.

Brazelton, T. B. *Neonatal behavioral assessment scale*. London: Spastics International Medical Publications, 1973.

Bremer, F. Cerveau "isolé" et physiologie du sommeil. *Comptes Rendus des Séances de la Société de Biologie*, 1935, *118*, 1235–1241.

Brener, J. Sensory and perceptual determinants of voluntary visceral control. In G. E. Schwartz & J. Beatty (Eds.), *Biofeedback: Theory and research*. New York: Academic, 1977.

Brener, J., & Jones, J. M. Interoceptive discrimination in intact humans: Detection of cardiac activity. *Physiology and Behavior*, 1974, *13*, 763–767.

Brener, J., & Ross, A. Cardiac discrimination and heart rate control. *Psychophysiology*, 1980, *17*, 323. (Abstract)

Bridges, K. M. B. Emotional development in early infancy. *Child Development*, 1932, *3*, 324–341.

Brobeck, J. R., Tepperman, J., & Long, C. N. H. Experimental hypothalamic hyperphagia in the albino rat. *Yale Journal of Biology and Medicine*, 1943, *15*, 831–853.

Brugger, M. Fresstreib als hypothalamisches symptom. *Helvetica Physiologica et Pharmacologica Acta*, 1943, *1*, 183–198.

Bruner, J. *The pragmatics of language acquisitions*. Paper presented at the meeting of the Society for Experimental Social Psychology, East Lansing, Mich., November 16, 1979.

Bruner, J., & Taguiri, R. The perception of people. In G. Lindzey (Ed.), *Handbook of social psychology* (Vol. 2). Reading, Mass.: Addison-Wesley, 1954.

Bryden, M. P., Ley, R. G., & Sugarman, J. H. A left-ear advantage for identifying the emotional quality of tonal sequences. *Neuropsychologia*, 1982, *20*, 83–87.

Buchsbaum, M. Self regulation of stimulus intensity. In G. E. Schwartz & D. Shapiro (Eds.), *Consciousness and self-regulation* (Vol. 1). New York: Plenum, 1976.

Buchsbaum, M., & Silverman, J. Stimulus intensity control and the cortical evoked response. *Psychosomatic Medicine*, 1968, *30*, 12–22.

Buchtel, H., Campari, F., DeRisio, C., & Rota, R. Hemispheric differences in the discrimination reaction time to facial expressions. *Italian Journal of Psychology*, 1978, *5*, 159–169.

Buck, R. W. Nonverbal communication of affect in children. *Journal of Personality and Social Psychology*, 1975, *31*, 644–653.

Buck, R. *Human motivation and emotion*. New York: Wiley, 1976. (a)

Buck, R. A test of nonverbal receiving ability: Preliminary studies. *Human Communication Research*, 1976, *2*, 162–171. (b)

Buck, R. Nonverbal communication accuracy in preschool children: Relationships with personality and skin conductance. *Journal of Personality and Social Psychology*, 1977, *33*, 225–236.

Buck, R. The slide-viewing technique for measuring nonverbal sending accuracy: A guide for replication. *Catalog of Selected Documents in Psychology*, 1978, *8*, 63. (Abstract)

Buck, R. Individual differences in nonverbal sending accuracy and electrodermal responding: The externalizing–internalizing dimension. In R. Rosenthal (Ed.), *Skill in nonverbal communication: Individual differences*. Cambridge, Mass.: Oelgeschlager, Gunn & Hain, 1979. (a)

Buck, R. Measuring individual differences in the nonverbal communication of affect: The slide-viewing paradigm. *Human Communication Research*, 1979, *6*, 47–57. (b)

Buck, R. Nonverbal behavior and the theory of emotion: The facial feedback hypothesis. *Journal of Personality and Social Psychology*, 1980, *38*, 811–824.

Buck, R. The evolution and development of emotion expression and communication. In S. Brehm, S. Kassin, & F. Gibbons (Eds.), *Developmental social psychology*. New York: Oxford, 1981. (a)

Buck, R. Sex differences in psychophysiological responding and subjective experience: A comment. *Psychophysiology*, 1981, *18*, 349–350. (b)

Buck, R. *A theory of spontaneous and symbolic expression: Implications for facial lateralization*. Paper presented at the symposium, "Asymmetries in Facial Expression: Method and Meaning," International Neuropsychology Society convention, Pittsburgh, February 4, 1982. (a)

Buck, R. Spontaneous and symbolic nonverbal behavior and the ontogeny of communication. In R. S. Feldman (Ed.), *The development of nonverbal behavior in children*. New York: Springer Verlag, 1982. (b)

Buck, R. Recent approaches to the study of nonverbal receiving ability. In J. Weimann & R. Harrison (Eds.), *Nonverbal communication: The social interaction sphere*. New York: Sage, 1983. (a)

Buck, R. Emotional development and emotional education. In R. Plutchik & H. Kellerman (Eds.), *Emotion in early development*. New York: Academic, 1983. (b)

Buck, R., Baron, R., & Barrette, D. The temporal organization of spontaneous nonverbal expression: A segmentation analysis. *Journal of Personality and Social Psychology*, 1982, *42*, 506–517.

Buck, R., Baron, R., Goodman, N., & Shapiro, N. The unitization of spontaneous nonverbal behavior in the study of emotion communication. *Journal of Personality and Social Psychology*, 1980, *39*, 522–529.

Buck, R., & Carroll, J. *CARAT and PONS: Correlates of two tests of nonverbal sensitivity.* Unpublished paper, Carnegie–Mellon University, 1974.

Buck, R., & Duffy, R. Nonverbal communication of affect in brain-damaged patients. *Cortex*, 1980, *16*, 351–362.

Buck, R., & Lerman, J. General vs. specific nonverbal sensitivity and clinical training. *Human Communication*, Summer 1979, 269–274.

Buck, R., Miller, R. E., & Caul, W. F. Sex, personality and physiological variables in the communication of emotion via facial expression. *Journal of Personality and Social Psychology*, 1974, *30*, 587–596.

Buck, R., & Parke, R. The behavioral and physiological response to the presence of a friendly or neutral person in two stressful situations. *Journal of Personality and Social Psychology*, 1972, *24*, 143–153.

Buck, R., & Reardon, K. *Emotional education and the coping process.* Unpublished manuscript, University of Connecticut, 1983.

Buck, R., Savin, V. J., Miller, R. E., & Caul, W. F. Nonverbal communication of affect in humans. *Proceedings of the 77th Annual Convention of the American Psychological Association*, 1969, *4*, 367–368.

Buck, R., Savin, V., Miller, R. E., & Caul, W. F. Nonverbal communication of affect in humans. *Journal of Personality and Social Psychology*, 1972, *23*, 362–371.

Bugental, D. E. Interpretations of naturally occurring discrepancies between words and intonation: Modes of inconsistency resolution. *Journal of Personality and Social Psychology*, 1974, *30*, 125–133.

Cacioppo, J. T., & Petty, R. E. Social psychological procedures for cognitive response assessment: The thought-listing technique. In T. V. Merluzzi, C. R. Glass, & M. Genest (Eds.), *Cognitive assessment.* New York: Guilford, 1981.

Campbell, R. Asymmetries in interpreting and expressing a posed facial expression. *Cortex*, 1978, *14*, 327–342.

Campbell, R. J., Kagan, N., & Krathwohl, D. R. The development and validation of a scale to measure affective sensitivity (empathy). *Journal of Counseling Psychology*, 1971, *18*, 407–412.

Cannon, W. B. *Bodily changes in pain, hunger, fear, and rage.* New York: Appleton, 1915.

Cannon, W. B. The James–Lange theory of emotion: A critical examination and an alternative theory. *American Journal of Psychology*, 1927, *39*, 106–124. (Reprinted in M. Arnold (Ed.), *The nature of emotion.* Baltimore: Penguin, 1968.)

Cannon, W. B. *The wisdom of the body.* New York: Norton, 1932.

Cannon, W. B., & Britton, S. W. Studies on the conditions of activity in endocrine glands: XV. Pseudoaffective medulliadrenal secretion. *American Journal of Physiology*, 1925, *72*, 283–394.

Cappella, J. N. Talk–silence sequences in informal conversations: I. *Human Communication Research*, 1979, *6*, 3–17.

Cappella, J. N. Talk and silence sequences in informal conversations: II. *Human Communication Research*, 1980, 6, 130–145. (a)

Cappella, J. N. Structural equation modeling: An introduction. In P. R. Monge & J. N. Cappella (Eds.), *Multivariate techniques in communication research*. Academic, 1980. (b)

Cappella, J. N. Mutual influence in expressive behavior: Adult–adult and infant–adult dyadic interaction. *Psychological Bulletin*, 1981, 89, 101–132.

Cappella, J. N., & Planalp, S. Talk and silence sequences in informal conversations: III. Interspeaker influence. *Human Communication Research*, 1981, 7, 117–132.

Carmon, A., & Nachshon, I. Ear asymmetry in perception of emotional and nonverbal stimuli. *Acta Physiologica*, 1973, 37, 351–357.

Carrigan, P. M. Extraversion–introversion as a dimension of personality. *Psychological Bulletin*, 1960, 57, 329–360.

Carson, R. C. *Interaction concepts of personality*. Chicago: Aldine, 1969.

Chapple, E. D. Quantitative analysis of the interaction of individuals. *Proceedings of the National Academy of Sciences*, 1939, 25, 58–67.

Chapple, E. D. Personality differences as described by invariant properties of individuals in interaction. *Proceedings of the National Academy of Sciences*, 1940, 26, 10–14.

Cicone, M., Wapner, W., Foldi, N. Zurif, E., & Gardner, H. The relation between gesture and language in aphasic communication. *Brain and Language*, 1979, 8, 324–349.

Cicone, M., Wapner, W., & Gardner, H. Sensitivity to emotional expressions and situations in organic patients. *Cortex*, 1980, 16, 145–147.

Cline, V. B. Interpersonal perception. In B. A. Maher (Ed.), *Progress in experimental personality research* (Vol. 1). New York: Academic, 1964.

Cofer, C. N., & Appley, M. H. *Motivation: Theory and research*. New York: Wiley, 1964.

Cohen, J. *Statistical power analysis for the behavioral sciences* (Rev. ed.). New York: Academic, 1977.

Condon, W. S. *Communication and order: The micro-rhythm hierarchy of speaker behavior*. Paper presented at the Convention of School Psychologists, New York, 1973.

Condon, W. S. An analysis of behavior organization. In S. Weitz (Ed.), *Nonverbal communication* (2nd ed.). New York: Oxford, 1979.

Condon, W. S. The relation of interactional synchrony to cognitive and emotional processes. In M. R. Key (Ed.), *The relationship of verbal and nonverbal communication*. New York: Mouton, 1980.

Condon, W. S., & Ogston, W. D. Sound film analysis of normal and pathological behavior patterns. *Journal of Nervous and Mental Disease*, 1966, 143, 338–347.

Condon, W. S., & Sander, L. W. Synchrony demonstrated between movement of the neonate and adult speech. *Child Development*, 1974, 45, 456–462.

Coursey, R. D., Buchsbaum, M. S., & Murphy, D. L. Platelet MAO activity and evoked potentials in the identification of subjects biologically at risk for psychiatric disorders. *British Journal of Psychiatry*, 1979, 134, 372–381.

Courville, J. Rubrobulbar fibers to the facial nucleus and the lateral reticular facial nucleus and the lateral reticular nucleus. *Brain Research*, 1966, 1, 317–337.

Cox, D. N. Psychophysiological correlates of sensation seeking and socialization during reduced stimulation (Doctoral dissertation, University of British Columbia, Canada, 1977). *Dissertation Abstracts International*, 1978, *39*, 372B.

Craig, K., & Lowrey, H. J. Heart rate components of conditioned vicarious autonomic responses. *Journal of Personality and Social Psychology*, 1969, *11*, 381–387.

Crider, A. Review of *The nervous body: An introduction to the autonomic nervous system and behavior* by C. Van Toller. *Psychophysiology*, 1980, *17*, 327–328.

Cronbach, L. J. Processes affecting scores on "understanding of others" and "assumed similarity." *Psychological Bulletin*, 1955, *52*, 177–193.

Crow, W. J. *Process vs. achievement and generality over objects and judging tasks.* Paper presented at the American Psychological Association Symposium on New Frontiers in Person Perception Research, 1960.

Cunningham, M. R. Personality and the structure of the nonverbal communication of emotion. *Journal of Personality*, 1977, *45*, 564–584.

Dabbs, J. M. Temporal patterning of speech and gaze in social and intellectual conversations. In S. Feldstein (Chair), *Temporal aspects of speech.* Symposium presented at the International Conference on Social Psychology and Language, Bristol, England, 1979.

Daitzman, R. J., & Zuckerman, M. Disinhibitory sensation seeking, personality, and gonadal hormones. *Personality and Individual Differences*, 1980, *1*, 103–110.

Daitzman, R. J., Zuckerman, M., Sammelwitz, P. H., & Ganjam, V. Sensation seeking and gonadal hormones. *Journal of Biosocial Science*, 1978, *10*, 401–408.

Daly, E. M., Abramovich, R., & Pliner, P. The relationship between mothers' encoding and their children's decoding of facial expressions of emotion. *Merrill–Palmer Quarterly*, 1980, *29*, 25–34.

Dana, C. L. The autonomic seat of emotions: A discussion of the James–Lange theory. *Archives of Neurology and Psychiatry*, 1921, *6*, 634–639.

Darwin, C. *Origin of species.* New York: Modern Library, 1936. (Originally published, 1859.)

Darwin, C. *Expression of the emotions in man and animals.* New York: Philosophical Library, 1955. (Originally published, 1872.)

Davis, C., Cowles, M., & Kohn, P. *Strength of the nervous system and augmenting-reducing: Paradox lost.* Unpublished manuscript, York University, 1982.

Davis, M. Laban analysis of nonverbal communication. In S. Weitz (Ed.), *Nonverbal communication* (2nd ed.). New York: Oxford, 1979.

Davis, M., & Weitz, S. *Systematic observation of role distinctions in conversational behavior.* Paper presented at the convention of the Eastern Psychological Association, New York, 1977.

Davis, M., & Weitz, S. *Sex differences in nonverbal communication: A Laban analysis.* Paper presented at the meeting of the American Psychological Association, Toronto, Ontario, Canada, September 1978.

Deets, A., & Harlow, H. F. *Early experience and the maturation of agonistic behavior.* Paper presented at the convention of the American Association for the Advancement of Science, New York, December 28, 1971.

DeKosky, S. T., Heilman, K. M., Bowers, D., & Valenstein, E. Recognition and discrimination of emotional faces and pictures. *Brain and Language*, 1980, *9*, 206–214.

Delgado, J. M. R. *Physical control of the mind.* New York: Harper & Row, 1969.

Denenberg, V. H. Critical periods, stimulus input, and emotional reactivity: A theory of infantile stimulation. *Psychological Review,* 1964, *71,* 335–351.

Denenberg, V. H. The effects of early experience. In E. S. E. Hafex (Ed.), *The behaviour of domestic animals.* London: Bailliere, Tindall & Cassell, 1969.

Denenberg, V. H. Hemispheric laterality in animals and the effects of early experience. *Behavioral and Brain Sciences,* 1981, *4,* 1–49.

Denenberg, V. H., Garbanati, J., Sherman, G., Yutzey, D. A., & Kaplan, R. Infantile stimulation induces brain lateralization in rats. *Science,* 1978, *201,* 1150–1152.

DePaulo, B. M., & Rosenthal, R. Age changes in nonverbal decoding skills: Evidence for increasing differentiation. *Merrill–Palmer Quarterly,* 1979, *25,* 145–150. (a)

DePaulo, B. M., & Rosenthal, R. Ambivalence, discrepancy, and deception in nonverbal communication. In R. Rosenthal (Ed.), *Skill in nonverbal communication.* Cambridge, Mass.: Oelgeschlager, Gunn & Hain, 1979. (b)

DePaulo, B. M., & Rosenthal, R. Measuring the development of nonverbal sensitivity. In P. B. Read & C. Izard (Eds.), *Measuring emotions in infants and children.* New York: Cambridge University Press, 1980.

DePaulo, B., Rosenthal, R., Eisenstat, R., Rogers, P., & Finkelstein, S. Decoding discrepant nonverbal cues. *Journal of Personality and Social Psychology,* 1978, *36,* 313–323.

DePaulo, B., Zuckerman, M., & Rosenthal, R. *Modality effects in the detection of deception.* Unpublished manuscript, University of Virginia, 1981.

DeRenzi, E., & Spinnler, H. Facial recognition in brain-damaged patients. *Neurology,* 1966, *16,* 145–152.

Dickman, H. R. The perception of behavior units. In R. G. Barker (Eds.), *The stream of behavior.* New York: Appleton-Century-Crofts, 1963.

Dimberg, U. Emotional conditioning to facial stimuli: A psychobiological analysis. *Abstracts of Uppsala Dissertations from the Faculty of Social Sciences,* 1983, *29.*

Dimberg, U., & Ohman, A. The effects of directional facial cues on electrodermal conditioning to facial stimuli. *Psychophysiology,* 1983, *20,* in press.

Dittman, A. T. The body movement–speech rhythm relationship as a cue to speech encoding. In A. W. Siegman & B. Pope (Eds.), *Studies in dyadic communication.* New York: Pergamon, 1972.

Duffy, R. J., & Buck, R. A study of the relationship between propositional (pantomime) and subpropositional (facial expression) extraverbal behaviors in aphasics. *Folia Phonicatrica,* 1979, *31,* 129–136.

Duffy, R. J., & Duffy, J. R. Three studies of deficits in pantomimic expression and pantomimic recognition in aphasia. *Journal of Speech and Hearing Research,* 1981, *24,* 70–84.

Duffy, R. J., Duffy, J. R., & Pearson, K. Pantomime recognition in aphasics. *Journal of Speech and Hearing Research,* 1975, *18,* 115–132.

Duffy, R. J., & Liles, B. Z. A translation of Finklnburg's (1970) lecture on aphasia as "asymbolia" with commentary. *Journal of Speech and Hearing Disorders,* 1979, *44,* 156–168.

Duffy, J. R., Watt, J., & Duffy, R. J. Path analysis: A strategy for investigating multiple causal relationships in communication disorders. *Journal of Speech and Hearing Research,* 1981, *24,* 474–490.

Duncan, S. Nonverbal communication. *Psychological Bulletin*, 1969, *72*, 118–137.

Duncan, S. Some signals and rules for taking speaking turns in conversations. *Journal of Personality and Social Psychology*, 1972, *23*, 283–292.

Duncan, S., & Fiske, D. W. *Face-to-face interaction*. Hillsdale, N.J.: Erlbaum, 1977.

Ehrlich, H. J., & Graeven, D. B. Reciprocal self-disclosure in a dyad. *Journal of Experimental Social Psychology*, 1971, *7*, 389–400.

Eibl-Eibesfeldt, I. *Ethology: The biology of behavior*. New York: Holt, Rinehart & Winston, 1970.

Eibl-Eibesfeldt, I. Similarities and differences between cultures in expressive movements. In R. A. Hinde (Ed.), *Nonverbal communication*. Cambridge: Cambridge University Press, 1972.

Ekman, P. (Ed.). *Darwin and facial expression: A century of research in review*. New York: Academic, 1973.

Ekman, P. About brows: Emotional and conversational signals. In M. von Cranach, K. Foppa, W. Lepenies, & D. Ploog (Eds.), *Human ethology*. London: Cambridge University Press, 1979.

Ekman, P. Asymmetry in facial expression. *Science*, 1980, *209*, 833–834.

Ekman, P., & Friesen, W. V. The repertoire of nonverbal behavior: Categories, origins, usage and coding. *Semiotica*, 1969, *1*, 49–98. (a)

Ekman, P., & Friesen, W. V. Nonverbal leakage and clues to deception. *Psychiatry*, 1969, *32*, 88–105. (b)

Ekman, P., & Friesen, W. V. Constants across cultures in the face and emotion. *Journal of Personality and Social Psychology*, 1971, *17*, 124–129.

Ekman, P., & Friesen, W. V. Detecting deception from the body or face. *Journal of Personality and Social Psychology*, 1974, *29*, 288–298. (a)

Ekman, P., & Friesen, W. V. Nonverbal behavior and psychopathology. In R. J. Friedman & H. M. Katz (Eds.), *The psychology of depression: Contemporary theory and research*. New York: Wiley, 1974.

Ekman, P., & Friesen, W. V. *Unmasking the face*. Englewood Cliffs, N.J.: Prentice-Hall, 1975.

Ekman, P., & Friesen, W. V. Measuring facial movement. *Environmental Psychology and Nonverbal Behavior*, 1976, *1*, 56–75.

Ekman, P., & Friesen, W. V. *Facial Action Coding System (FACS): A technique for the measurement of facial action*. Palo Alto: Consulting Psychologists Press, 1978.

Ekman, P., Friesen, W. V., & Ancoli, S. Facial signs of emotional experience. *Journal of Personality and Social Psychology*, 1980, *39*, 1125–1134. (a)

Ekman, P., Friesen, W. V., & Ellsworth, P. *Emotion in the human face*. New York: Pergamon, 1972. (a)

Ekman, P., Friesen, W. V., O'Sullivan, M., & Scherer, K. Relative importance of face, body, and speech in judgments of personality and affect. *Journal of Personality and Social Psychology*, 1980, *38*, 270–277. (b)

Ekman, P., Friesen, W. V., & Scherer, K. Body movement and voice pitch in deceptive interaction. *Semiotica*, 1976, *16*, 23–27.

Ekman, P., Friesen, W. V., & Tomkins, S. S. Facial affect scoring technique: A first validity study. *Semiotica*, 1971, *3*, 37–58.

Ekman, P., Hagar, J., & Friesen, W. The symmetry of emotional and deliberate facial action. *Psychophysiology*, 1981, *18*, 101–106.

Ekman, P., Liebert, R. M., Friesen, W. V., Harrison, R., Zlatchin, C., Malmstrom, E. J., & Baron, R. A. Facial expressions of emotion while watching televised violence as predictors of subsequent aggression. In G. A. Comstock, E. A. Rubenstein, & J. P. Murray (Eds.), *Television and social behavior* (Vol. V). Rockville, Md.: National Institute of Mental Health, 1972. (b)

Ekman, P., Sorenson, E. R., & Friesen, W. V. Pan-cultural elements in the facial displays of emotion. *Science*, 1969, *164*, 86–88.

Elkind, D. Cognitive growth cycles in mental development. In J. K. Cole (Ed.), *Nebraska Symposium on Motivation*. Lincoln: University of Nebraska Press, 1971.

Elliott, R. Tonic heart rate: Experiments on the effects of collative variables lead to a hypothesis about its motivational significance. *Journal of Personality and Social Psychology*, 1969, *12*(3), 211–228.

Elliott, R. The significance of heart rate for behavior: A critique of Lacey's hypothesis. *Journal of Personality and Social Psychology*, 1972, *22*, 398–409.

Ellsworth, P. C., & Carlsmith, J. M. Effects of eye contact and verbal content on affective response to a dyadic interaction. *Journal of Personality and Social Psychology*, 1968, *10*, 15–20.

Ellsworth, P. C., & Tourangeau, R. On our failure to disconfirm what nobody ever said. *Journal of Personality and Social Psychology*, 1981, *40*, 363–369.

Eshkol, N., & Wachmann, A. *Movement notation*. London: Weidenfeld & Nicholson, 1958.

Eysenck, H. J. *The biological basis of personality*. Springfield, Ill.: Thomas, 1967.

Feij, J. A., Orlebeke, J. F., Gazendam, A., & van Zuilen, R. *Sensation seeking: Measurement and psychophysiological correlates*. Paper presented at the Conference on the Biological Basis of Temperament: Need for Stimulation, Warsaw, Poland, September 1979.

Feldman, R. S. Nonverbal disclosure of teacher deception and interpersonal affect. *Journal of Educational Psychology*, 1976, *68*, 807–816.

Feldman, R. S., Jenkins, L., & Popoola, O. Detection of deception in adults and children via facial expressions. *Child Development*, 1979, *50*, 350–355.

Feldman, R. S., & White, J. Detecting deception in children. *Journal of Communication*, 1980, *30*, 121–128.

Field, T. Individual differences in the expressivity of neonates and young infants. In R. W. Feldman (Ed.), *Development of nonverbal behavior in children*. New York: Springer Verlag, 1982.

Field, T. M., & Walden, T. A. Perception and production of facial expressions in infancy and early childhood. In H. Reese & L. Lipsett (Eds.), *Advances in child development and behavior* (Vol. 16). New York: Academic, 1982.

Field, T., Woodson, R., Greenberg, R., & Cohen, D. Discrimination and imitation of facial expressions in neonates. *Science*, 1982, *218*, 179–181.

Fields, B., & O'Sullivan, M. *Convergent validation of five person perception measures*. Paper presented at a meeting of the Western Psychological Association, 1976.

Finklnburg, F. Niederrheinische Gesellschaft, Sitzung vom 21. Marx 1870 in Bonn. *Berliner Klinische Wochenschrift*, 1870, *7*, 449–450, 460–462.

Fisher, B. A. *Small group decision making.* New York: McGraw-Hill, 1974.

Flannery, J. G. Alexithymia: I. The communication of physical symptoms. *Psychotherapy and Psychosomatics*, 1977, *28*, 133.

Flor-Henry, P. Psychosis, neurosis and epilepsy. *British Journal of Psychiatry*, 1974, *124*, 144–150.

Flor-Henry, P. On certain aspects of the localization of the cerebral systems regulating and determining emotion. *Biological Psychiatry*, 1979, *14*, 677–698.

Foa, U. G. Convergences in the analysis of the structure of interpersonal behavior. *Psychological Review*, 1961, *68*, 341–353.

Fowles, D. C. The three arousal model: Implications of Gray's two-factor learning theory for heart rate, electrodermal activity, and psychopathy. *Psychophysiology*, 1980, *17*, 87–104.

Fraiberg, S. Blind infants and their mothers: An examination of the sign system. In M. Lewis & L. A. Rosenblum (Ed.), *The effect of the infant on its caregiver.* New York: Wiley, 1974.

Frank, J. D. *Persuasion and healing.* Baltimore: Johns Hopkins Press, 1961.

Frankenhaeuser, M. Psychoneuroendocrine sex differences in adaptation to the psychosocial environment. In L. Zechella (Ed.), *Clinical psychoneuroendocrinology in reproduction* (Serono Symposium, 1977). New York: Academic, 1978.

Frankenhaeuser, M., von Wright, M., Collins, A., von Wright, J., Sedvall, G., & Swahn, C. Sex differences in psychoneuroendocrine reactions to examination stress. *Psychosomatic Medicine*, 1978, *40*, 334–343.

Freud, A. *The ego and the mechanisms of defense.* New York: International Universities Press, 1966.

Freud, S. *Psychopathology of everyday life.* New York: New American Library, 1959. (Originally published, 1904.)

Freud, S. Fragment of an analysis of a case of hysteria. In *Collected papers* (Vol. 3). New York: Basic Books, 1959. (Originally published, 1905.)

Freud, S. *The problem of anxiety.* New York: Psychoanalytic Quarterly Press, 1936. (Originally published, 1926.)

Friedman, R. Proto-rhythms from nonverbal to language and musical acquisition. In M. R. Key (Ed.), *The relationship of verbal and nonverbal communication.* New York: Monton, 1980.

Friedman, H. S., DiMatteo, M. R., & Taranta, A. A study of the relationship between individual differences in nonverbal expressiveness and factors of personality and social interaction. *Journal of Research in Personality*, 1980, *14*, 351–364. (a)

Friedman, H. S., Prince, L. M., Riggio, R. E., & DiMatteo, M. R. Understanding and assessing nonverbal expressiveness: The Affective Communication Test. *Journal of Personality and Social Psychology*, 1980, *39*, 333–351. (b)

Friedman, H. S., Riggio, R. E., & Segall, D. O. Personality and the enactment of emotion. *Journal of Nonverbal Behavior*, 1980, *5*, 35–48. (c)

Frodi, A. M. Contribution of infant characteristics to child abuse. *American Journal of Mental Deficiency*, 1981, *85*, 341–349.

Frodi, A. M., & Lamb, M. E. Fathers' and mothers' responses to the faces and cries of normal and premature infants. *Developmental Psychology*, 1978, *14*, 490–498.

Fugita, B. N., Harper, R. G., & Wiens, A. N. Encoding–decoding of nonverbal emotional messages: Sex differences in spontaneous and enacted expressions. *Journal of Nonverbal Behavior*, 1980, *4*, 131–145.

Gainotti, G. Emotional behavior and hemispheric side of the lesion. *Cortex*, 1972, *8*, 41–55.

Gainotti, G., & Lemmo, M. Comprehension of symbolic gestures in aphasia. *Brain and Language*, 1976, *3*, 451–460.

Galaburda, A. M. *Architectonic structure of language areas in humans*. Paper presented at the Aphasia Research Center, Boston Veterans Administration Hospital, 1980.

Galaburda, A. M., & Geschwind, N. Anatomical asymmetries in the adult and developing brain and their implications for function. *Advances in Pediatrics*, 1981, *28*, 271–292.

Galin, D. Implications for psychiatry of left and right cerebral specialization: A neurophysiological context for unconscious processes. *Archives of General Psychiatry*, 1974, *31*, 572.

Gallagher, D., & Shuntich, R. J. Encoding and decoding of nonverbal behavior through facial expressions. *Journal of Research in Personality*, 1981, *15*, 241–252.

Garbanati, J. A., Sherman, G. F., Rosen, G. D., Hofmann, M., Yutzey, D. A., & Denenberg, V. H. *Handling in infancy, brain laterality, and muricide in rats*. Unpublished manuscript, University of Connecticut, 1980.

Gardner, R., & Gardner, B. Teaching sign language to a chimpanzee. *Science*, 1969, *165*, 664–672.

Gazzaniga, M. S. The split brain in man. In T. Teyler (Ed.), *Altered states of awareness*. San Francisco: Freeman, 1972.

Gellhorn, E. Motion and emotion: The role of proprioception in the physiology and pathology of emotions. *Psychological Review*, 1964, *71*, 457–472.

Gellhorn, E. *Principles of autonomic–somatic integrations*. Minneapolis: University of Minnesota Press, 1967.

Gerson, A. C., & Perlman, D. Loneliness and expressive communication. *Journal of Abnormal Psychology*, 1979, *88*, 258–261.

Geschwind, N. The borderland of neurology and psychiatry: Some common misconceptions. In D. F. Benson & D. Blumer (Eds.), *Psychiatric aspects of neurologic disease*. New York: Grune & Stratton, 1975. (a)

Geschwind, N. The apraxias: Neural mechanisms of disorders of learned movement. *American Scientist*, 1975, *63*, 188–195. (b)

Geschwind, N. Specializations of the human brain. *Scientific American*, 1979, *241*, 180–199. (a)

Geschwind, N. *Neurological denial syndromes*. Paper presented at the University of Connecticut, October 31, 1979. (b)

Geschwind, N. *The neurological vampire and the philosophical cross*. Paper presented at the Massachusetts Institute of Technology, October 1980.

Gibson, E. J. *Principles of perceptual learning and development*. New York: Appleton-Century-Crofts, 1969.

Gibson, J. J. *The senses considered as perceptual systems*. Boston: Houghton-Mifflin, 1966.

Gibson, J. J. The theory of affordances. In R. E. Shaw & J. Bransford (Eds.), *Perceiving, acting and knowing: Toward an ecological psychology.* Hillsdale, N.J.: Erlbaum, 1977.

Gibson, J. J. *The ecological approach to visual perception.* Boston: Houghton-Mifflin. 1979.

Glickman, S. E., & Schiff, B. B. A biological theory of reinforcement. *Psychological Review*, 1967, *74*, 81–109.

Goffman, E. *The presentation of self in everyday life.* Garden City, N.Y.: Doubleday Anchor, 1959.

Goldman, D., Kohn, P., & Hunt, R. Sensation seeking, augmenting–reducing, and absolute auditory threshold: A strength-of-the-nervous-system perspective. *Journal of Personality and Social Psychology*, 1983, *45*, 405–411.

Goodall, J. *In the shadow of man.* New York: Dell, 1971.

Goodall, J. Life and death at Gombe. *National Geographic*, 1979, *155*, 592–621.

Goodglass, H., & Kaplan, E. Disturbances of gesture and pantomime in aphasia. *Brain*, 1963, *86*, 703–720.

Goodman, N. R. *Determinants of the perceptual organization of ongoing action and emotion behavior.* Unpublished doctoral dissertation, University of Connecticut, 1980.

Gorenstein, E. E., & Newman, J. P. Disinhibitory psychopathology: A new perspective and a model for research. *Psychological Review*, 1980, *87*, 301–315.

Gottman, J. *Marital interaction: Experimental investigations.* New York: Academic, 1979. (a)

Gottman, J. Detecting cyclicity in social interaction. *Psychological Bulletin*, 1979, *86*, 338–348. (b)

Gottman, J. *Time-series analysis: A comprehensive introduction for social scientists.* New York: Cambridge University Press, 1981.

Gottman, J., & Bakeman, R. The sequential analysis of observational data. In M. Lamb, S. Suomi, & G. Stephenson (Eds.), *Methodological problems in the study of social interaction.* Madison: University of Wisconsin Press, 1978.

Gottman, J., Markman, H., & Notarius, C. The topography of marital conflict: A sequential analysis of verbal and nonverbal behavior. *Journal of Marriage and the Family*, 1977, *39*, 461–477.

Gottman, J., & Notarius, C. The sequential analysis of observational data using Markov chains. In T. Kratochwill (Ed.), *Strategies to evaluate change in single subject research.* New York: Academic, 1978.

Gottman, J., Notarius, C., Markman, H., Bank, S., Yoppi, B., & Rubin, M. Behavior exchange theory and marital decision making. *Journal of Personality and Social Psychology*, 1976, *34*, 14–23.

Gottman, J., & Parkhurst, J. T. *A developmental theory of friendship and acquaintanceship processes.* Paper presented at the Minnesota Symposium on Child Psychology, Minneapolis, October 1978.

Gottman, J., & Ringland, J. The analysis of dominance and bidirectionality in social development. *Child Development*, 1981, *52*, 393–412.

Graves, C. A., & Natale, M. The relationship of hemispheric preference, as measured by conjugate lateral eye movements, to accuracy of emotional facial expression. *Motivation and Emotion*, 1979, *3*, 219–234.

Gray, J. A. *The psychology of fear and stress.* New York: McGraw-Hill, 1971.

Gray, J. A. The psychophysiological nature of introversion-extraversion: A modification of Eysenck's theory. In V. D. Nebylitsyn & J. A. Gray (Eds.), *Biological bases of individual behavior.* New York: Academic, 1972.

Gray, J. A. Drug effects on fear and frustration: Possible limbic site of action of minor tranquilizers. In L. L. Iversen, S. D. Iversen, & S. H. Snyder (Eds.), *Handbook of psychopharmacology* (Vol. 8: *Drugs, neurotransmitters, and behavior).* New York: Plenum, 1977.

Green, H. D., & Walker, A. E. The effects of the ablation of the cortical motor face area in monkeys. *Journal of Neurophysiology,* 1938, *1,* 262-280.

Greer, S., Morris, R., & Pettingale, K. W. Psychological response to breast cancer: Effect on outcome. *Lancet,* 1979, *1,* 785-787.

Grossman, S. P. *A textbook of physiological psychology.* New York: Wiley, 1967.

Grossman, S. P. The biology of motivation. *Annual Review of Psychology,* 1979, *30,* 209-242.

Gubar, G. Recognition of human facial expressions judged live in a laboratory setting. *Journal of Personality and Social Psychology,* 1966, *4,* 108-111.

Gur, R. C., & Sackeim, H. A. Self deception: A concept in search of a phenomenon. *Journal of Personality and Social Psychology,* 1979, *37,* 147-153.

Gur, R. E., & Gur, R. C. Defense mechanisms, psychosomatic symptomatology, and conjugate lateral eye movements. *Journal of Consulting and Clinical Psychology,* 1975, *43,* 416-420.

Hackett, T. P., & Weisman, A. D. Denial as a factor in patients with heart disease and cancer. *Annals of the New York Academy of Sciences,* 1969, *164,* 802-817.

Hager, J. C., & Ekman, P. Methodological problems in Tourangeau and Ellsworth's study of facial expression and experience of emotion. *Journal of Personality and Social Psychology,* 1981, *40,* 358-362.

Haggard, E. A., & Isaacs, F. S. Micromomentary facial expressions as indicators of ego mechanisms in psychotherapy. In L. A. Gottschalk & A. H. Averbach (Eds.), *Methods of research in psychotherapy.* New York: Appleton Century Crofts, 1966.

Haggard, M. P., & Parkinson, A. M. Stimulus and task factors as determinants of ear advantages. *Quarterly Journal of Experimental Psychology,* 1971, *23,* 168-177.

Hall, E. T. *The hidden dimension.* New York: Doubleday, 1966.

Hall, J. A. Gender effects in decoding nonverbal cues. *Psychological Bulletin,* 1978, *85,* 845-857.

Hall, J. A., & Braunwald, K. G. Gender cues in conversations. *Journal of Personality and Social Psychology,* 1981, *40,* 99-110.

Hall, J. A., & Halberstadt, A. G. Masculinity and femininity in children: Development of the Children's Personal Attributes Questionnaire. *Developmental Psychology,* 1980, *16,* 270-280.

Hare, R. D. Acquisition and generalization of a conditioned fear response in psychopathic and nonpsychopathic criminals. *Journal of Psychology,* 1965, *59,* 367-370. (a)

Hare, R. D. Psychopathy, fear arousal and anticipated pain. *Psychological Reports,* 1965, *16,* 499-502. (b)

Hare, R. D. Temporal gradient of fear arousal in psychopaths. *Journal of Abnormal Psychology,* 1965, *70,* 442-445. (c)

Hare, R. D. *Psychopathy: Theory and research.* New York: Wiley, 1970.

Hare, R. D. Electrodermal and cardiovascular correlates of psychopathy. In R. D. Hare & D. Schalling (Eds.), *Psychopathic behavior: Approaches to research.* New York: Wiley, 1978.

Hare, R. D., & Craigen, D. Psychopathy and physiological activity in a mixed-motive game situation. *Psychophysiology,* 1974, *11,* 197–206.

Hare, R. D., & Quinn, M. J. Psychopathy and autonomic conditioning. *Journal of Abnormal Psychology,* 1971, *77,* 223–235.

Harlow, H. F. Love in infant monkeys. *Scientific American,* 1959, *200,* 68–74.

Harlow, H. F. *Learning to love.* San Francisco: Albion, 1971.

Harlow, H., McGaugh, J., & Thompson, R. F. *Psychology.* San Francisco: Albion, 1971.

Harlow, H. F., & Zimmerman, R. R. The development of affectional responses in infant monkeys. *Proceedings of the American Philosophical Society,* 1958, *102,* 501–509.

Harper, R. G., Wiens, A. N., & Fugita, B. *Individual differences in encoding–decoding of affect and emotional dissimulation.* Paper presented at the convention of the American Psychological Association, San Francisco, 1977.

Harper, R. G., Wiens, A. N., & Matarazzo, J. D. *Nonverbal communication.* New York: Wiley, 1978.

Harper, R. G., Wiens, A. N., & Matarazzo, J. D. The relationship between encoding–decoding of visual nonverbal emotional cues. *Semiotica,* 1979, *28,* 171–192.

Harrison, A. A., Hwalek, M., Raney, D. G., & Fritz, J. G. Cues to deception in an interview situation. *Social Psychology,* 1978, *41,* 156–161.

Hass, H. *The human animal.* New York: Dell, 1970.

Hastorf, A. H., & Bender, I. E. A caution respecting the measurement of empathic ability. *Journal of Abnormal and Social Psychology,* 1952, *47,* 574–576.

Heath, R. G. Pleasure responses of human subjects to direct stimulation of the brain: Physiologic and psychodynamic considerations. In R. G. Heath (Ed.), *The role of pleasure in behavior.* New York: Hoeber Medical Division, Harper & Row, 1964. (a)

Heath, R. G. (Ed.). *The role of pleasure in behavior.* New York: Hoeber Medical Division, Harper & Row, 1964. (b)

Heath, R. G., & Mickle, W. A. Evaluation of seven years' experience with depth electrode studies in human patients. In E. R. Ramey & D. S. O'Doherty (Eds.), *Electrical studies on the unanesthetized brain.* New York: Hoeber, 1960.

Hebb, D. O. Drives and the C.N.S. (conceptual nervous system). *Psychological Review,* 1955, *62,* 243–254.

Heider, F. *The psychology of interpersonal relations.* New York: Wiley, 1958.

Heil, J. What Gibson's missing. *Journal of the Theory of Social Behavior,* 1979, *9,* 265–269.

Heilman, K. M., Coyle, J. M., Gonyea, E. F., & Geschwind, N. Apraxia and agraphia in a left-hander. *Brain,* 1973, *99,* 21–28.

Heilman, K. M., Scholes, R., & Watson, R. T. Auditory affective agnosia. *Journal of Neurology, Neurosurgery and Psychiatry,* 1974, *38,* 69–72.

Heimburger, R. F., Whitlock, C. C., & Kalsheck, J. E. Stereotoxic amygdalectomy for epilepsy with aggressive behavior. *Journal of the American Medical Association,* 1966, *198,* 741–745.

Heller, W., & Levy, J. Perception and expression of emotion in right-handers and left-handers. *Neuropsychologia*, 1981, *19*, 263–272.

Hess, W. R. Stammgarglien-reizversuche. *Berichte ueber die Gesamte Physiologie*, 1928, *42*, 554.

Hetherington, A. N., & Ranson, S. W. The spontaneous activity and food intake of rats with hypothalamic lesions. *American Journal of Physiology*, 1942, *136*, 609–617.

Hiatt, S., Campos, J., & Emde, R. Facial patterning and infant emotional expression: Happiness, surprise, and fear. *Child Development*, 1979, *50*, 1020–1035.

Hochberg, J. Perception: Toward the recovery of a definition. *Psychological Review*, 1956, *63*, 400–405.

Hohmann, G. Some effects of spinal cord lesions on experimental emotional feelings. *Psychophysiology*, 1966, *3*, 143–156.

Homans, G. C. *Social behavior: Its elementary forms.* New York: Harcourt, Brace, & World, 1961.

House, E. L., & Pansky, B. *A functional approach to neuroanatomy* (2nd ed.). New York: McGraw-Hill, 1967.

Huston, T. L., & Levinger, G. Interpersonal attraction and relationships. *Annual Review of Psychology*, 1978, *29*, 115–156.

Ickes, W., & Barnes, R. D. The role of sex and self-monitoring in unstructured dyadic interactions. *Journal of Personality and Social Psychology*, 1977, *35*, 315–330.

Ickes, W., & Barnes, R. D. Boys and girls together—and alienated: On enacting stereotyped sex roles in mixed-sex dyads. *Journal of Personality and Social Psychology*, 1978, *36*, 669–680.

Ippolitov, F. V. Interanalyzer differences in the sensitivity–strength parameter for vision, hearing, and cutaneous modalities. In V. D. Nebylitsyn & J. A. Gray (Eds.), *Biological bases of individual behavior.* New York: Academic, 1972.

Izard, C. *The face of emotion.* New York: Appleton-Century-Crofts, 1971.

Izard, C. E. *Human emotions.* New York: Plenum, 1977. (a)

Izard, C. E. Personal communication, 1977. (b)

Izard, C. E. *Emotion as motivation: An evolutionary–developmental perspective.* Colloquium presented at the University of Connecticut, April 11, 1979. (a)

Izard, C. E. *The Maximally Discriminative Facial Movement Coding System (Max).* Newark, Del.: Instructional Resources Center, University of Delaware, 1979. (b)

Izard, C. E. Differential emotions theory and the Facial Feedback Hypothesis of emotion activation. *Journal of Personality and Social Psychology*, 1981, *40*, 350–354.

Izard, C. E., Huebner, R. R., Risser, D., McGinnes, G. C., & Dougherty, L. M. The young infant's ability to produce discrete emotion expressions. *Developmental Psychology*, 1980, *16*, 132–140.

Jackson, D. N. *Personality Research Form manual.* New York: Research Psychologists Press, 1974.

Jacobson, E. *Progressive relaxation.* Chicago: University of Chicago Press, 1938.

Jacobson, E. Muscular tension and the stimulation of effort. *American Journal Psychology*, 1951, *64*, 112–117.

Jaffe, J., & Feldstein, S. *Rhythms of dialogue.* New York: Academic, 1970.

James, W. What is an emotion? *Mind*, 1884, *9*, 188–205. (Reprinted in M. Arnold (Ed.), *The nature of emotion*. Baltimore: Penguin, 1968.)

James, W. *The principles of psychology* (Vol. 1). New York: Holt, 1890.

Johanson, M., Risberg, J., Silfverskiold, P., Hagstadius, S., & Smith, G. *Regional cerebral blood flow in anxiety*. Paper presented at the meeting of the International Neuropsychological Society, Pittsburgh, February 3–6, 1982.

Johnson, R. N. *Aggression in man and animals*. Philadelphia: Saunders, 1972.

Jones, H. E. The galvanic skin reflex in infancy. *Child Development*, 1930, *1*, 106–110.

Jones, H. E. The galvanic skin response as related to overt emotional expression. *American Journal of Psychology*, 1935, *47*, 241–251.

Jones, H. E. The study of patterns of emotional expression. In M. Reymert (Ed.), *Feelings and emotions*. New York: McGraw-Hill, 1950.

Jones, H. E. The longitudinal method in the study of personality. In I. Iscoe & H. W. Stevenson (Eds.), *Personality development in children*. Chicago: University of Chicago Press, 1960.

Jurgens, U. Neural control of vocalization in nonhuman primates. In H. D. Steklis & M. J. Raleigh (Eds.), *Neurobiology of social communication in primates*. New York: Academic, 1979.

Jurgens, U., & von Cramon, D. On the role of the anterior cingulate cortex in phonation: A case report. *Brain and Language*, 1982, *15*, 234–248.

Kagan, N. I. *Affective sensitivity test: Validity and reliability*. Paper presented at the meeting of the American Psychological Association, San Francisco, 1978.

Katkin, E. S., Blascovich, J., & Goldbrand, S. Empirical assessment of visceral self-perception: Individual and sex differences in the acquisition of heartbeat discrimination. *Journal of Personality and Social Psychology*, 1981, *40*, 1095–1101.

Katkin, E. S., Morell, M. A., Goldband, S., & Bernstein, G. L. Individual differences in visceral and external signal discrimination. *Psychophysiology*, 1980, *17*, 322–323. (Abstract)

Katz, R. C. Perception of facial affect in aphasia. In R. H. Brookshire (Ed.), *Clinical aphasiology: Conference proceedings 1980*. Minneapolis: BRK Publishers, 1980.

Keiser, G. J., & Altman, I. Relationship of nonverbal behavior to the social penetration process. *Human Communication Research*, 1976, *2*, 147–161.

Kelley, H. H., & Thibaut, J. W. *Interpersonal relations: A theory of interdependence*. New York: Wiley, 1978.

Kelly, G. A. *The psychology of personal constructs*. New York: Norton, 1955.

Kendon, A. Movement coordination in social interaction: Some examples described. *Acta Psychologica*, 1970, *32*, 100–125.

Kendon, A. Gesticulation and speech: Two aspects of the process of utterance. In M. R. Key (Ed.), *The relationship of verbal and nonverbal communication*. New York: Monton, 1980.

Kenny, D. A. Personal communication, 1981.

Kenny, D. A. Interpersonal perception: A multivariate round robin analysis. In M. Brewer & B. Collins (Eds.), *Scientific inquiry and the social sciences*. San Francisco: Jossey-Bass, 1981.

Kenny, D. A., & Nasby, W. Splitting the reciprocity correlation. *Journal of Personality and Social Psychology*, 1980, *38*, 249–256.

Key, M. R. (Ed.). *The relationship of verbal and nonverbal communication*. New York: Monton, 1980.

Kilbride, J. E., & Yarczower, M. Recognition and imitation of facial expressions: A cross-cultural comparison between Zambia and the United States. *Journal of Cross-Cultural Psychology*, 1980, *11*, 281–296.

Kimura, D. Acquisition of a motor skill after left-hemisphere damage. *Brain*, 1977, *100*, 527–542.

Kimura, D. Neuromotor mechanisms in the evolution of human communication. In H. D. Steklis & M. J. Raleigh (Eds.), *Neurobiology of social communication in primates*. New York: Academic, 1979.

Kimura, D., & Archibald, Y. Motor functions of the left hemisphere. *Brain*, 1974, *97*, 337–350.

King, H. E. Psychological effects of excitation in the limbic system. In D. E. Sheer (Ed.), *Electrical stimulation of the brain*. Austin: University of Texas Press, 1961.

Klaiman, S. *Selected perceptual, cognitive, personality, and socialization variables as predictors of nonverbal sensitivity*. Doctoral dissertation, University of Ottawa, 1979.

Kleck, R. E., Vaughan, R. C., Cartwright-Smith, J., Vaughan, K. B., Colby, C., & Lanzetta, J. Effects of being observed on expressive, subjective, and physiological reactions to painful stimuli. *Journal of Personality and Social Psychology*, 1976, *34*, 1211–1218.

Kluver, H., & Bucy, P. C. "Psychic blindness" and other symptoms following bilateral temporal lobectomy in rhesus monkeys. *American Journal of Physiology*, 1937, *119*, 352–353.

Kluver, H., & Bucy, P. C. An analysis of certain effects of bilateral temporal lobectomy in the rhesus monkey with special reference to "psychic blindness." *Journal of Psychology*, 1938, *5*, 33–54.

Kluver, H., & Bucy, P. C. Preliminary analysis of functions of the temporal lobe in monkeys. *Archives of Neurology and Psychiatry (Chicago)*, 1939, *42*, 979–1000.

Koenig, O. Das aktionssystem der Bartmeise (*Panurus biarmicus* L). *Oesterreichische Zoologische Zeitschrift*, 1951, *3*, 247–325.

Koff, E., Borod, J., & White, B. Asymmetries for hemiface size and mobility. *Neuropsychologia*, 1981, *19*, 825–830.

Kohlberg, L. Moral development and identification. In H. W. Stevenson (Ed.), *Child psychology*. Chicago: University of Chicago Press, 1963.

Kohlberg, L. Development of moral character and moral ideology. In M. L. Hoffman & L. W. Hoffman (Eds.), *Review of child development research*. New York: Russell Sage Foundation, 1964.

Kolb, B., & Milner, B. Observations on spontaneous facial expression after focal cerebral excisions and after intracarotid injection of sodium amytal. *Neuropsychologia*, 1981, *19*, 505–514. (a)

Kolb, B., & Milner, B. Performance of complex arm and facial movements after focal brain lesions. *Neuropsychologia*, 1981, *19*, 491–503. (b)

Konstadt, N., & Forman, E. Field dependence and external directedness. *Journal of Personality and Social Psychology*, 1965, *1*, 490–493.

Kotsch, W. E., Izard, C. E., & Walker, S. *Experimenter-manipulated facial patterns and emotion experience*. Unpublished manuscript, University of Delaware, 1978.

Kraut, R. E. Verbal and nonverbal cues in the perception of lying. *Journal of Personality and Social Psychology*, 1978, *36*, 380–391.

Kraut, R. E. Humans as lie detectors: Some second thoughts. *Journal of Communication*, 1980, *30*, 209–216.

Kraut, R. E. Social presence, facial feedback, and emotion. *Journal of Personality and Social Psychology*, 1982, *42*, 853–863.

Kraut, R. E., & Johnston, R. Social and emotional messages of smiling: An ethological approach. *Journal of Personality and Social Psychology*, 1979, *37*, 1539–1553.

Kraut, R. E., & Poe, D. Behavioral roots of person perception: Deception judgments of customs inspectors and laymen. *Journal of Personality and Social Psychology*, 1980, *39*, 784–798.

Kunst-Wilson, W. R., & Zajonc, R. B. Affective discrimination of stimuli that cannot be recognized. *Science*, 1980, *207*, 557–558.

Lachman, S. J. *Psychosomatic disorders*. New York: Wiley, 1972.

LaFrance, M., & Carmen, B. The nonverbal display of psychological androgyny. *Journal of Personality and Social Psychology*, 1980, *38*, 36–49.

Lagerspetz, K. M. J., & Engblom, P. Immediate reactions to TV violence by Finnish pre-school children of different personality types. *Scandinavian Journal of Psychology*, 1979, *20*, 43–53.

Lagerspetz, K. M. J., Wahlroos, C., & Wendelin, C. Facial expressions of pre-school children while watching televised violence. *Scandinavian Journal of Psychology*, 1978, *19*, 213–222.

Laird, J. D. Self-attribution of emotion: The effects of expressive behavior on the quality of emotional experience. *Journal of Personality and Social Psychology*, 1974, *29*, 475–486.

Lamb, M. E. A re-examination of the infant social world. *Human Development*, 1977, *20*, 65–85.

Landis, T., Assal, G., & Perret, E. Opposite cerebral hemisphere superiorities for visual associative processing of emotional facial expressions and objects. *Nature*, 1979, *278*, 739–740.

Lange, C. G. *Uber Gemutsbewegunguen*. Leipzig, 1887.

Lanzetta, J. T., Cartwright-Smith, J., & Kleck, R. E. Effects of nonverbal dissimulation on emotional experience and autonomic arousal. *Journal of Personality and Social Psychology*, 1976, *33*, 354–470.

Lanzetta, J. T., & Kleck, R. E. Encoding and decoding of nonverbal affect in humans. *Journal of Personality and Social Psychology*, 1970, *16*, 12–19.

Lanzetta, J. T., & Orr, S. P. Influence of facial expressions on the classical conditioning of fear. *Journal of Personality and Social Psychology*, 1980, *39*, 1081–1087.

LaRusso, L. Sensitivity of paranoid patients to nonverbal cues. *Journal of Abnormal Psychology*, 1978, *8*, 463–471.

Lazarus, R. S. *Psychological stress and the coping process*. New York: McGraw-Hill, 1966.

Lazarus, R. S., & Alfert, E. Short-circuiting of threat by experimentally altering cognitive appraisal. *Journal of Abnormal and Social Psychology*, 1964, *69*, 195–205.

Leary, T. The theory and measurement methodology of interpersonal communication. *Psychiatry*, 1955, *18*, 147–161.

Leary, T. *Interpersonal diagnosis of personality*. New York: Ronald, 1957.

Lesser, I. M. A review of the alexithymia concept. *Psychosomatic Medicine*, 1981, *43*, 531–543.

Lester, D. *A physiological basis for personality traits.* Springfield, Ill.: Thomas, 1974.

Levine, S. An endocrine theory of infantile stimulation. In A. Ambrose (Ed.), *Stimulation in early infancy.* London: Academic, 1969.

Lewis, M., & Rosenblum, L. A. (Eds.). *The effect of the infant on its caregiver.* New York: Wiley, 1974.

Ley, R. G., & Bryden, M. P. Hemispheric differences in processing emotions and faces. *Brain and Language,* 1979, *7,* 127–138.

Lindsley, D. B. Emotion. In S. S. Stevens (Ed.), *Handbook of experimental psychology.* New York: Wiley, 1951.

Lindsley, D. B. Psychophysiology and motivation. In M. R. Jones (Ed.), *Nebraska Symposium on Motivation.* Lincoln: University of Nebraska Press, 1957.

Linehan, E. J. The trouble with dolphins. *National Geographic,* 1979, *155,* 506–541.

Lippold, O. C. J. Electromyography. In P. H. Venables & I. Martin (Eds.), *Manual of psychophysiological methods.* New York: Wiley, 1967.

Little, K. B. Personal space. *Journal of Experimental Social Psychology,* 1965, *1,* 237–247.

London, H., & Nisbett, R. E. *Thought and feeling: Cognitive alteration of feeling states.* Chicago: Aldine, 1974.

Losow, J. *Nonverbal communication accuracy. Individuals vs. dyads.* Unpublished MA thesis, University of Connecticut, 1981.

Lykken, D. T. A study of anxiety in the sociopathic personality. *Journal of Abnormal and Social Psychology,* 1957, *55,* 6–10.

Lykken, D. T. Psychology and the lie detector industry. *American Psychologist,* 1974, *29,* 725–739.

Lykken, D. T. The detection of deception. *Psychological Bulletin,* 1979, *80,* 47–53.

MacLean, P. D. Contrasting functions of limbic and neocortical systems of the brain and their relevance to psychophysiological aspects of medicine. In E. Gellhorn (Ed.), *Biological foundations of emotion.* Glenview, Ill.: Scott, Foresman, 1968.

MacLean, P. D. The hypothalamus and emotional behavior. In W. Haymaker, E. Anderson, & W. J. H. Nauta (Eds.), *The hypothalamus.* Springfield, Ill.: Thomas, 1969.

MacLean, P. D. The limbic brain in relation to the psychoses. In P. H. Black (Ed.), *Physiological correlates of emotion.* New York: Academic, 1970.

MacLean, P. D. Effects of lesions of globus pallidus on species-typical display behavior of squirrel monkeys. *Brain Research,* 1978, *149,* 175–196.

Malmo, R. B., Kohlmeyer, W., & Smith, A. A. Motor manifestations of conflict in interview. *Journal of Abnormal and Social Psychology,* 1956, *52,* 268–271.

Mandler, G. *Mind and emotion.* New York: Wiley, 1975.

Mandler, G., Mandler, J. M., & Uviller, E. T. Autonomic feedback: The perception of autonomic activity. *Journal of Abnormal and Social Psychology,* 1958, *56,* 367–373.

Mann, R. D. *The relationship between personality characteristics and individual performance in small groups.* PhD thesis, University of Michigan, 1958.

Manstead, A. S. R., MacDonald, C. J., & Wagner, H. L. *Nonverbal communication of emotion via spontaneous facial expressions.* Unpublished manuscript, University of Manchester, 1982.

Manstead, A. S. R., & Wagner, H. L. Arousal, cognition, and emotion: An appraisal of two-factor theory. *Current Psychological Reviews,* 1981, *1,* 35–54.

Maranon, G. Contribution à l'étude de l'action émotive de l'adrénaline. *Revue Française d'Endocrinologie*, 1924, *2*, 300–325.

Mark, V. H., & Ervin, F. R. *Violence and the brain.* New York: Harper & Row, 1970.

Markov, P. O. A study of interoception in human subjects. *Uchenye Zapiski Leningradskogo Gosudarstvennogo Universiteta, Seriya Biologicheskikh Nauk*, 1950, *22*, 345–368.

Marsh, R. C. (Ed.). *Bertrand Russell: Logic and knowledge.* London: George Allen & Unwin, 1956.

Marshall, G. D., & Zimbardo, P. G. Affective consequences of inadequately explained physiological arousal. *Journal of Personality and Social Psychology*, 1979, *37*, 953–969.

Maslach, C. Negative emotional biasing of unexplained arousal. *Journal of Personality and Social Psychology*, 1979, *37*, 970–988.

Mason, W. A. The effects of social restriction on the behavior of rhesus monkeys: III. Tests of gregariousness. *Journal of Comparative and Physiological Psychology*, 1961, *54*, 287–290.

Mateer, C., & Kimura, D. Impairment of nonverbal oral movements in aphasia. *Brain and Language*, 1977, *4*, 262–276.

McCaul, K. D., Holmes, D. S., & Solomon, S. Facial expression and emotion. *Journal of Personality and Social Psychology*, 1982, *42*, 145–152.

McClelland, D. C. *The achieving society.* Princeton: Van Nostrand, 1961.

McClelland, D. C. *Motives as sources of long-term trends in life and health.* Paper presented at the symposium, "The Shape of Future Research on the Person in Society," Wesleyan University, April 2, 1982.

McClelland, D. C., & Winter, D. G. *Motivating economic achievement.* New York: Free Press, 1969.

McDowall, J. J. Interactional synchrony: A reappraisal. *Journal of Personality and Social Psychology*, 1978, *36*, 963–975.

McDowall, J. J. Microanalysis of filmed movement: The reliability of boundary detection by observers. *Environmental Psychology and Nonverbal Behavior*, 1979, *3*, 77–88.

McGeer, P. L., & McGeer, E. G. Chemistry of mood and emotion. *Annual Review of Psychology*, 1980, *31*, 273–307.

McGuiness, D., & Pribram, K. The neuropsychology of attention: Emotional and motivational controls. In M. C. Wittrock (Ed.), *The brain and psychology.* New York: Academic, 1980.

McQuown, N. A., Bateson, G., Birdwhistell, R. L., Brosin, H. W., & Hockett, C. F. (Eds.). *The natural history of an interview* (Collection of Manuscripts on Cultural Anthropology, 15). Chicago: University of Chicago Department of Photoduplication, 1971. (Microfilm)

Mead, G. H. *Mind, self, and society.* Chicago: University of Chicago Press, 1934.

Mehrabian, A. Inference of attitudes from the posture, orientation, and distance of a communicator. *Journal of Consulting and Clinical Psychology*, 1968, *32*, 296–308. (a)

Mehrabian, A. Relationship of attitude to seated posture, orientation, and distance. *Journal of Personality and Social Psychology*, 1968, *10*, 26–30. (b)

Mehrabian, A. *Nonverbal communication.* Chicago: Aldine-Atherton, 1972.

Mehrabian, A., & Ferris, S. R. Inference of attitudes from nonverbal communication. *Journal of Consulting Psychology*, 1967, *31*, 248–252.

Mehrabian, A., & Weiner, M. Decoding of inconsistent communications. *Journal of Personality and Social Psychology*, 1967, *6*, 109–114.

Meisels, M., & Dosey, M. Personal space, anger arousal, and psychological defense. *Journal of Personality*, 1971, *39*, 333–334.

Milgram, S. Behavioral study of obedience. *Journal of Abnormal and Social Psychology*, 1963, *67*, 371–378.

Milgram, S. *Obedience to authority: An experimental view.* New York: Harper & Row, 1974.

Miller, N. E. The learning of visceral and glandular responses. *Science*, 1969, *163*, 434–445.

Miller, N. E. Biofeedback and visceral learning. *Annual Review of Psychology*, 1978, *29*, 373–404.

Miller, R. E. Experimental studies of communication in the monkey. In L. Rosenblum (Ed.), *Primate behavior: Developments in field and laboratory research* (Vol. 2). New York: Academic, 1971.

Miller, R. E. Social and pharmacological influences on nonverbal communication in monkeys and man. In L. Krames, T. Alloway, & P. Pliner (Eds.), *Nonverbal communication.* New York: Plenum, 1974.

Miller, R. E., Banks, J., & Kuwahara, H. The communication of affects in monkeys: Cooperative reward conditioning. *Journal of Genetic Psychology*, 1966, *108*, 121–134.

Miller, R. E., Banks, J., & Ogawa, N. Communication of affect in "cooperative conditioning" of rhesus monkeys. *Journal of Abnormal and Social Psychology*, 1962, *64*, 343–348.

Miller, R. E., Banks, J., & Ogawa, N. Role of facial expression in "cooperative-avoidance conditioning" in monkeys. *Journal of Abnormal and Social Psychology*, 1963, *67*, 24–30.

Miller, R. E., Caul, W. F., & Mirsky, I. A. Communication of affects between feral and socially isolated monkeys. *Journal of Personality and Social Psychology*, 1967, *7*, 231–239.

Miller, R. E., Murphy, J. V., & Mirsky, I. A. Nonverbal communication of affect. *Journal of Clinical Psychology*, 1959, *15*, 155–158.

Mischel, W. *Personality and assessment.* New York: Wiley, 1968.

Mischel, W. Continuity and changes in personality. *American Psychologist*, 1969, *24*, 1012–1018.

Mishara, B., & Baker, A. H. Kinesthetic aftereffect scores are reliable. *Applied Psychological Measurement*, 1978, *2*, 239–247.

Mogenson, G. J., & Phillips, A. G. Motivation: A psychological construct in search of a physiological substrate. In J. M. Sprague & A. N. Epstein (Eds.), *Progress in psychobiology and physiological psychology.* New York: Academic, 1976.

Monrad-Krohn, G. H. On the dissociation of voluntary and emotional innervation in facial paresis of central origin. *Brain*, 1924, *47*, 22–35.

Monrad-Krohn, G. H. On facial dissociation. *Acta Psychiatrica et Neurologica Scandinavica*, 1939, *14*, 557–566.

Montgomery, B. *Toward a person by context interactionist perspective of marital communication.* Paper presented at the meeting of the Eastern Communication Association, Pittsburgh, 1981.

Montgomery, B., & Kenny, D. A. *An interactionist approach to small group research: Analyzing peer assessments.* Paper presented at the Pennsylvania State University Conference on Small Group Research, April 1982.

Moore, W. H., & Haynes, W. O. A study of alpha hemispheric asymmetries for verbal and nonverbal stimuli in males and females. *Brain and Language,* 1980, *9,* 338–349.

Moruzzi, G., & Magoun, H. W. Brain stem reticular formation and activation of the EEG. *Electroencephalography and Clinical Neurophysiology,* 1949, *1,* 455–473.

Moscovitch, M., & Olds, J. Asymmetries in spontaneous facial expressions and their possible relation to hemispheric specialization. *Neuropsychologia,* 1982, *20,* 71–81.

Moyer, K. E. *The physiology of hostility.* Chicago: Markham, 1971.

Mullen, B., & Suls, J. The effectiveness of attention and rejection as coping styles: A meta-analysis of temporal differences. *Journal of Psychosomatic Research,* 1982, *26,* 43–49.

Murphy, D. L. Technical strategies for the study of catecholamines in man. In E. Usdin & S. Snyder (Eds.), *Frontiers in catecholamine research.* Oxford: Pergamon, 1973.

Murphy, D. L., *et al.* Biogenic amine related enzymes and personality variations in normals. *Psychological Medicine,* 1977, *7,* 149–157.

Myers, R. E. Comparative neurology of vocalization and speech: Proof of a dichotomy. *Annals of the New York Academy of Sciences,* 1976, *280,* 745–757.

Narabayashi, H., & Uno, M. Long range results of stereotoxic amygdalectomy for behavior disorders. *Confina Neurologica,* 1966, *27,* 168–171.

Nebylitsyn, V. D. *Fundamental properties of the human nervous system.* New York: Plenum, 1972.

Nebylitsyn, V. D., & Gray, J. A. (Eds.). *Biological bases of individual behavior.* New York: Academic, 1972.

Neisser, U. *Cognition and reality.* San Francisco: Freeman, 1976.

Nemiah, J. C., & Sifneos, P. E. Psychosomatic illness: A problem in communication. *Psychotherapy and Psychosomatics,* 1970, *18,* 154–160.

Netter, F. H. *Nervous system.* New York: Ciba, 1962.

Nevill, D. Experimental manipulation of dependency motivation and its effects on eye contact and measures of field dependency. *Journal of Personality and Social Psychology,* 1974, *29,* 72–79.

Newcombe, T. M. The prediction of interpersonal attraction. *American Psychologist,* 1956, *11,* 575–586.

Newlin, D. B. Hemisphericity, expressivity, and autonomic arousal. *Biological Psychology,* 1981, *12,* 13–23.

Newtson, D. Foundations of attribution: The perception of ongoing behavior. In J. H. Harvey, W. J. Ickes, & R. F. Kidd (Eds.), *New directions in attribution research* (Vol. 1). New York: Wiley, 1976.

Newtson, D., Engquist, G., & Bois, J. The objective basis of behavior units. *Journal of Personality and Social Psychology,* 1977, *35,* 847–862.

Notarius, C. I., & Levenson, R. W. Expressive tendencies and physiological response to stress. *Journal of Personality and Social Psychology*, 1979, *37*, 1204–1210.

Notarius, C., Wemple, C., Ingraham, L., Burns, T., & Kollar, E. Multichannel responses to an interpersonal stressor: Interrelationships among facial display, heart rate, self-report of emotion, and threat appraisal. *Journal of Personality and Social Psychology*, 1982, *43*, 400–409.

Nottebohm, F. Ontogeny of bird sound. *Science*, 1970, *167*, 950–956.

Nottebohm, F. Asymmetries in neural control of vocalization in the canary. In S. Harnard, R. W. Doty, L. Goldstein, J. Jaynes, & G. Krauthamer (Eds.), *Lateralization in the nervous system*. New York: Academic, 1977.

Nottebohm, F. Origins and mechanisms in the establishment of cerebral dominance. In M. S. Gazzaniga (Ed.), *Handbook of behavioral neurobiology* (Vol. 2). New York: Plenum, 1979.

Obrist, P. A. The cardiovascular–behavioral interaction—As it appears today. *Psychophysiology*, 1976, *13*, 95–107.

Obrist, P. A., Webb, R. A., Sutterer, J. R., & Howard, J. L. The cardiac–somatic relationship: Some reformulations. *Psychophysiology*, 1970, *6*, 569–587. (a)

Obrist, P. A., Webb, R. A., Sutterer, J. R., & Howard, J. L. Cardiac deceleration and reaction time: An evaluation of two hypotheses. *Psychophysiology*, 1970, *6*, 695–706. (b)

Odom, R. D., & Lemond, C. M. Developmental differences in the perception and production of facial expressions. *Child Development*, 1972, *43*, 359–369.

O'Hair, H. D., Cody, M. J., & McLaughlin, M. L. Prepared lies, spontaneous lies, Machiavellianism, and nonverbal communication. *Human Communication Research*, 1981, *47*, 325–329.

Ohman, A., & Dimberg, U. Facial expressions as conditioned stimuli for electrodermal responses: A case of "preparedness?" *Journal of Personality and Social Psychology*, 1978, *36*, 1251–1258.

Olds, J. Differential effects of drives and drugs on self-stimulation in different brain sites. In D. Sheer (Ed.), *Electrical stimulation of the brain*. Austin: University of Texas Press, 1961.

Olds, J., & Milner, P. Positive reinforcement produced by electrical stimulation of septal area and other regions of rat brain. *Journal of Comparative and Physiological Psychology*, 1954, *47*, 419–427.

Olds, J., & Olds, M. E. The mechanisms of voluntary behavior. In R. Heath (Ed.), *The role of pleasure in behavior*. New York: Harper & Row, 1964.

Olds, J., & Olds, M. E. Drives, rewards, and the brain. In T. M. Newcombe (Ed.), *New directions in psychology* (Vol. 2). New York: Holt, 1965.

Olds, M. E., & Fobes, J. L. The central basis of motivation: Intracranial self-stimulation studies. *Annual Review of Psychology*, 1981, *32*, 523–576.

Olds, M. E., & Olds, J. Approach–avoidance analysis of the rat diencephalon. *Journal of Comparative Neurology*, 1963, *120*, 259–295.

Orne, M. T. The efficacy of biofeedback therapy. *Annual Review of Medicine*, 1979, *30*, 489–503.

O'Sullivan, M., & Hagar, J. *Measuring person perception: New techniques, old problems*. Unpublished manuscript, San Francisco, 1980.

Papez, J. W. A proposed mechanism of emotion. *Archives of Neurology and Psychiatry*, 1937, 38, 725–743.

Parisi, S. *Five-, seven-, and nine-month-old infants' facial responses to 20 stimulus situations*. Unpublished master's thesis, Vanderbilt University, 1977.

Patterson, M. L. An arousal model of interpersonal intimacy. *Psychological Review*, 1976, 83, 235–245.

Patterson, M. L. A sequential functional model of nonverbal exchange. *Psychological Review*, 1982, 89, 231–249.

Patterson, M. L., Jordan, A., Hogan, M. B., & Frerker, D. Effects of nonverbal intimacy on arousal and behavioral adjustment. *Journal of Nonverbal Behavior*, 1981, 5, 184–198.

Pavlov, I. P. [*Conditioned reflexes*] (G. V. Anrep, trans.). Oxford: Clarendon, 1927.

Peery, J. C. Magnification of affect using frame-by-frame film analysis. *Environmental Psychology and Nonverbal Behavior*, 1978, 3, 58–61.

Pendleton, K. L., & Snyder, S. S. Young children's perceptions of others. *Journal of Nonverbal Behavior*, 1982, 4, 220–237.

Penfield, W., & Roberts, L. *Speech and brain mechanisms*. Princeton, N.J.: Princeton University Press, 1959.

Pennebaker, J. W. *The psychology of physical symptoms*. New York: Springer Verlag, 1982.

Petrie, A. *Individuality in pain and suffering*. Chicago: University of Chicago Press, 1967.

Piaget, J. *The child's conception of physical causality*. London: Routledge & Kegan Paul, 1930.

Piaget, J. *The moral judgment of the child*. Glencoe, Ill.: Free Press, 1948. (Originally published, 1932.)

Piaget, J. Piaget's theory. In P. Mussen (Ed.), *Handbook of child development* (Vol. 1). New York: Wiley, 1971.

Piaget, J., & Inhelder, B. *The psychology of the child*. New York: Basic Books, 1969.

Pickett, L. W. An assessment of gestural and pantomimic deficit in aphasic patients. *Acta Symbolica*, 1974, 5, 69–86.

Pierloot, R., & Vinck, J. A pragmatic approach to the concept of alexithymia. *Psychotherapy and Psychosomatics*, 1977, 28, 156.

Ploog, D. W. Biological basis for instinct and behavior: Studies on the development of social behavior in squirrel monkeys. In J. Wortis (Ed.), *Recent advances in biological psychiatry* (Vol. 8). New York: Plenum, 1966.

Ploog, D. Neurobiology of primate audio-vocal behavior. *Brain Research Reviews*, 1981, 3, 35–61.

Plutchik, R. *The emotions: Facts, theories and a new model*. New York: Random House, 1962.

Plutchik, R. *Emotion: A psychoevolutionary synthesis*. New York: Harper & Row, 1980.

Podlesny, J. A., & Raskin, P. C. Physiological measures and the detection of deception. *Psychological Bulletin*, 1977, 84, 782–799.

Porges, S. W., Bohrer, R. E., Cheung, M. N., Drasgow, F., McCabe, P., & Keren, G. New time-series statistic for detecting rhythmic co-occurrence in the frequency domain: The weighted coherence and its application to psychophysiological research. *Psychological Bulletin*, 1980, *88*, 580–587.

Porges, S. W., Bohrer, R. E., Keren, G., Cheung, M., Franks, G. J., & Dragow, F. The influence of methylphenidate on spontaneous autonomic activity and behavior in children diagnosed as hyperactive. *Psychophysiology*, 1981, *18*, 42–48.

Pribram, K., & McGuinness, D. Arousal, attention, and effort in the control of attention. *Psychological Review*, 1975, *82*, 116–149.

Prideaux, E. The psychogalvanic reflex: A review. *Brain*, 1920, *43*, 50–73.

Prkachin, K. M., Craig, K. D., Papageorgis, D., & Reith, G. Nonverbal communication deficits and response to performance feedback in depression. *Journal of Abnormal Psychology*, 1977, *86*, 224–234.

Prokasy, W., & Raskin, D. *Electrodermal activity in psychological research.* New York: Academic, 1973.

Raskin, P. C., & Podlesny, J. A. Truth and deception: A reply to Lykken. *Psychological Bulletin*, 1979, *86*, 54–59.

Razran, G. The observable unconscious and the inferable conscious in current Soviet psychophysiology. *Psychological Review*, 1961, *68*, 81–147.

Reardon, K. K. *Persuasion: Theory and context.* Beverly Hills, Calif.: Sage, 1981.

Reardon, K. K., & Buck, R. *Emotion, reason, and communication in coping with cancer.* Unpublished manuscript, University of Connecticut, 1983.

Redmond, D. E., Jr., & Murphy, D. L. Behavioral correlates of platelet monoamine oxidase (MAO) activity in rhesus monkeys. *Psychosomatic Medicine*, 1975, *37*, 80.

Redmond, D. E., Jr., Murphy, D. L., & Baulu, J. Platelet monoamine oxidase activity correlates with social affiliative and agonistic behaviors in normal rhesus monkeys. *Psychosomatic Medicine*, 1979, *41*, 87–100.

Reuter-Lorenz, P., & Davidson, R. J. Differential contributions of the two cerebral hemispheres to the perception of happy and sad faces. *Neuropsychologia*, 1981, *19*, 609–613.

Riggs, G., Winter, P., Ploog, D., & Mayer, W. Effects of deafening on the vocal behavior of the squirrel monkey. *Folia Primatologica*, 1972, *17*, 404–420.

Riskind, J. H., & Gotay, C. C. Physical posture: Could it have regulatory or feedback effects on motivation and emotion? *Motivation and Emotion*, 1982, *6*, 273–298.

Rosenfeld, H. M. Instrumental affiliative functions of facial and gestural expressions. *Journal of Personality and Social Psychology*, 1966, *4*, 65–72. (a)

Rosenfeld, H. M. Approval-seeking and approval-inducing functions of verbal and nonverbal responses in the dyad. *Journal of Personality and Social Psychology*, 1966, *4*, 597–605. (b)

Rosenfeld, H. M. The experimental analysis of interpersonal influence processes. *Journal of Communication*, 1972, *22*, 424–442.

Rosenfeld, H. M. *Time series analysis of mother–infant interaction.* Presented at a symposium on the Analysis of Mother–Infant Interaction Sequences, Annual Meeting of the Society for Research in Child Development, Philadelphia, 1973.

Rosenfeld, H. M. Whither interactional synchrony? In K. Bloom (Ed.), *Prospective issues in infancy research.* Hillsdale, N.J.: Erlbaum, 1981.

Rosenfeld, H. M., & Remmers, W. W. Searching for temporal relationships in mother–infant interactions. In B. L. Hoffer & R. N. St. Clair (Eds.), *Developmental kinesics; The emerging paradigm.* Baltimore: University Park Press, 1981.

Rosenthal, R., & DePaulo, B. M. Sex differences in eavesdropping on nonverbal cues. *Journal of Personality and Social Psychology,* 1979, *37,* 273–285. (a)

Rosenthal, R., & DePaulo, B. M. Sex differences in accommodation in nonverbal communication. In R. Rosenthal (Ed.), *Skill in nonverbal communication.* Cambridge, Mass.: Oelgeschlager, Gunn & Hain, 1979. (b)

Rosenthal, R., Hall, J. A., DiMatteo, M. R., Rogers, P. L., & Archer, D. *Sensitivity to nonverbal communication: The PONS test.* Baltimore: Johns Hopkins University Press, 1979.

Rosenzweig, M. R., Bennett, E. L., & Diamond, M. C. Brain changes in response to experience. *Scientific American,* 1972, *226,* 22–29.

Rosvold, H. E., Mirsky, A. F., & Pribram, K. H. Influence of amygdalectomy on social behavior in monkeys. *Journal of Comparative and Physiological Psychology,* 1954, *47,* 173–178.

Rotter, J. B. Generalized expectancies for internal versus external control of reinforcement. *Psychological Monographs,* 1966, *80* (1, Whole No. 609).

Routtenberg, A. The reward system of the brain. *Scientific American,* 1978, *239*(5), 154–164.

Rubin, Z. Disclosing oneself to a stranger: Reciprocity and its limits. *Journal of Experimental Social Psychology,* 1975, *11,* 233–260.

Russell, B. *The principles of mathematics.* London: Allen & Unwin, 1903.

Russell, B. *Problems of philosophy.* New York: Oxford, 1912.

Russell, B. *Human knowledge: Its scope and limits.* New York: Simon & Schuster, 1948.

Russell, B. *An outline of philosophy.* Cleveland: World Publishing, 1961.

Russell, J. A. Affective space is bipolar. *Journal of Personality and Social Psychology,* 1979, *37,* 345–356.

Russell, J. A., & Mehrabian, A. Evidence for a three-factor theory of emotions. *Journal of Research in Personality,* 1977, *11,* 273–294.

Ryle, G. *The concept of mind.* New York: Barnes & Noble, 1949.

Saarni, C. Children's understanding of display rules for expressive behavior. *Developmental Psychology,* 1979, *15,* 424–429.

Saarni, C. Social and affective functions of nonverbal behavior: Developmental concerns. In R. W. Feldman (Ed.), *Development of nonverbal behavior in children.* New York: Springer Verlag, 1982.

Sabatelli, R., Buck, R., & Dreyer, A. Communication via facial cues in intimate dyads. *Personality and Social Psychology Bulletin,* 1980, *6,* 242–247.

Sabatelli, R., Buck, R., & Dreyer, A. Locus of control, interpersonal trust, and nonverbal communication accuracy. *Journal of Personality and Social Psychology,* 1983, *44,* 399–409. (a)

Sabatelli, R., Buck, R., & Dreyer, A. Nonverbal communication accuracy in married couples: Relationships with marital complaints. *Journal of Personality and Social Psychology,* 1982, *43,* 1088–1097.

Sabatelli, R., Dreyer, A., & Buck, R. Cognitive style and the sending and receiving of facial cues. *Perceptual and Motor Skills,* 1979, *49,* 203–212.

Sabetelli, R., Dreyer, A., & Buck, R. Cognitive style and marital complaints. *Journal of Personality*, 1983, *51*, 192–201. (b)

Sackeim, H. A. Self-deception, self-esteem, and depression: The adaptive value of lying to oneself. In J. Masling (Ed.), *Empirical studies of psychoanalytic theory.* Hillsdale, N.J.: Erlbaum, 1982.

Sackeim, H., & Gur, R. Self-deception, self-confrontation, and consciousness. In G. Schwartz & D. Shapiro (Eds.), *Consciousness and self-regulation: Advances in research* (Vol. 2). New York: Plenum, 1978.

Sackeim, H. A., Gur, R. C., & Saucy, M. C. Emotions are expressed more intensely on the left side of the face. *Science*, 1978, *202*, 434–435.

Sackeim, H. A., Greenberg, M. C., Weiman, A. L., Gur, R. C., Hungerbuhler, J. P., & Geschwind, N. Hemispheric asymmetry in the expression of positive and negative emotions: Neurological evidence. *Archives of Neurology*, 1982, *39*, 210–218.

Sackett, G. P. Monkeys reared in isolation with pictures as visual input: Evidence for an innate releasing mechanism. *Science*, 1966, *154*, 1468–1473.

Sackett, G. P. The lag sequential analysis of contingency and cyclicity in behavioral interaction research. In J. Osofsky (Ed.), *Handbook of infant development.* New York: Wiley, 1977.

Safer, M. A. Sex and hemisphere differences in access to codes for processing emotional expressions and faces. *Journal of Experimental Psychology: General*, 1981, *110*, 86–100.

Safer, M. A., & Leventhal, H. Ear differences in evaluating emotional tones of voice and verbal content. *Journal of Experimental Psychology: Human Perception and Performance*, 1977, *3*, 75–82.

Sagan, C. *Cosmos.* New York: Random House, 1980.

Sales, S. Need for stimulation as a factor in social behavior. *Journal of Personality and Social Psychology*, 1971, *19*, 124–134.

Sales, S. Need for stimulation as a factor in preference for different stimuli. *Journal of Personality Assessment*, 1972, *36*, 55–61.

Sales, S., & Throop, W. F. Relationship between kinesthetic aftereffect and "strength of the nervous system." *Psychophysiology*, 1972, *9*, 492–497.

Sapir, E. *Language.* New York: Harcourt, 1921.

Schachter, S. *The psychology of affiliation.* Stanford: Stanford University Press, 1959.

Schachter, S. The interaction of cognitive and physiological determinants of emotion state. In L. Berkowitz (Ed.), *Advances in experimental social psychology* (Vol. 1). New York: Academic, 1964.

Schachter, S. Some extraordinary facts about obese humans and rats. *American Psychologist*, 1970, *26*, 129–144.

Schachter, S., & Singer, J. E. Cognitive, social, and physiological determinants of emotional state. *Psychological Review*, 1962, *69*, 379–399.

Schachter, S., & Singer, J. E. Comments on the Maslach and Marshall–Zimbardo experiments. *Journal of Personality and Social Psychology*, 1979, *37*, 989–995.

Schallert, T., Whishaw, I., Ramirez, V., & Teitelbaum, P. Compulsive, abnormal walking caused by anticholinergics in akinetic, 6-hydroxydopamine-treated rats. *Science*, 1978, *199*, 1461–1463.

Scheflen, A. E. Quasi-courtship behavior in psychotherapy. *Psychiatry*, 1965, *28*, 245-257.

Scheflen, A. E. *Body language and social order*. Englewood Cliffs, N.J.: Prentice-Hall, 1972.

Scheflen, A. E. *Communicational structure: Analysis of a psychotherapy interaction*. Bloomington: Indiana University Press, 1973.

Scheflen, A. E. *How behavior means*. Garden City, N.Y.: Anchor, 1974.

Schildkraut, J. J., & Kety, S. S. Biogenic amines and emotion. *Science*, 1967, *156*, 21-30.

Schlosberg, H. The description of facial expressions in terms of two dimensions. *Journal of Experimental Psychology*, 1952, *44*, 229-237.

Schneider, W., & Shiffrin, R. Controlled and automatic information processing: I. Detection, search, and attention. *Psychological Review*, 1977, *84*, 1-66.

Schooler, C., Zahn, T. P., Murphy, D. L., & Buchsbaum, M. S. Psychological correlates of monoamine oxidase in normals. *Journal of Nervous and Mental Disease*, 1978, *166*, 177-186.

Schwartz, G. E., Brown, S. L., & Ahern, G. Facial muscle patterning and subjective experience during affective imagery: Sex differences. *Psychophysiology*, 1980, *17*, 75-82.

Schwartz, G. E., Davidson, R. J., & Maer, F. Right hemisphere lateralization for emotion in the human brain: Interactions with cognition. *Science*, 1975, *190*, 286-288.

Schwartz, G. E., Fair, P. L., Greenberg, P. S., Freedman, M., & Klerman, J. L. Facial electromyography in the assessment of emotion. *Psychophysiology*, 1974, *11*, 237.

Schwartz, G. E., Fair, P. L., Salt, P., Mandel, M. R., & Klerman, G. L. Facial expression and imagery in depression: An electromyographic study. *Psychosomatic Medicine*, 1976, *38*, 337-347.

Seligman, M. E. P. *Helplessness: On depression, development and death*. San Francisco: Freeman, 1975.

Selman, R. The relation of role-taking to the development of moral judgment in children. *Child Development*, 1971, *42*, 79-92.

Selman, R. *A structural analysis of the ability to take another's social perspective— Stages in the development of role taking ability*. Paper presented at the Society for Research in Child Development, Philadelphia, 1973.

Selman, R., & Byrne, D. *Manual for scoring stages of role-taking in moral and non-moral social dilemmas*. Unpublished manuscript, Harvard University, 1972.

Selye, H. *The physiology and pathology of exposure to stress*. Montreal: Acta, 1950.

Selye, H. *The stress of life*. New York: McGraw-Hill, 1978.

Sem-Jacobson, C. W. Depth-electroencephalographic stimulation of the human brain and behavior. Springfield, Ill.: Thomas, 1968.

Shannon, C. E., & Weaver, W. *The mathematical theory of communication*. Urbana: University of Illinois Press, 1949.

Shearer, S. L., & Tucker, D. M. Differential cognitive contributions of the cerebral hemispheres in the modulation of emotional arousal. *Cognitive Theory and Research*, 1981, *5*, 85-93.

Shennum, W. A. Field-dependence and facial expression. *Perceptual and Motor Skills*, 1976, *43*, 179-184.

Siegman, A. W., & Pope, B. *Studies in dyadic communication.* New York: Pergamon, 1972.

Sifneos, P. E. The prevalence of "alexithymic" characteristics in psychosomatic patients. *Psychotherapy and Psychosomatics,* 1973, *22,* 255–262.

Skinner, B. F. *Science and human behavior.* New York: Macmillan, 1953.

Smokler, I. A., & Shevrin, I. Cerebral lateralization and personality style. *Archives of General Psychology,* 1979, *36,* 949–954.

Snyder, M. Self-monitoring of expressive behavior. *Journal of Personality and Social Psychology,* 1974, *30,* 526–537.

Snyder, M. Self-monitoring processes. In L. Berkowitz (Ed.), *Advances in experimental social psychology* (Vol. 12). New York: Academic, 1979.

Sommers, S. Emotionality reconsidered: The role of cognition in emotional responsiveness. *Journal of Personality and Social Psychology,* 1981, *41,* 553–561.

Sousa-Poza, J. F., Rohrberg, R., & Shulman, E. Field dependence and self-disclosure. *Perceptual and Motor Skills,* 1973, *36,* 735–738.

Spiesman, J. C., Lazarus, R. S., Mordkoff, A. M., & Davison, L. A. Experimental reduction of stress based on ego-defense theory. *Journal of Abnormal and Social Psychology,* 1964, *68,* 367–380.

Sroufe, L. A. Socioemotional development. In J. D. Osofsky (Ed.), *Handbook of infant development.* New York: Wiley, 1979.

Stein, L. *Reciprocal action of reward and punishment mechanisms.* Washington: U.S. Government Printing Office, 1968.

Steklis, H. D., & Raleigh, M. J. Behavioral and neurobiological aspects of primate vocalization and facial expression. In H. D. Steklis & M. J. Raleigh (Eds.), *Neurobiology of social communication in primates.* New York: Academic, 1979.

Stellar, E. The physiology of motivation. *Psychological Review,* 1954, *61,* 5–22.

Sternbach, R. A. *Principles of psychophysiology.* New York: Academic, 1966.

Stiles, W. B. Verbal response modes and dimensions of interpersonal roles: A method of discourse analysis. *Journal of Personality and Social Psychology,* 1978, *36,* 693–704.

Storms, M. D. Videotape and the attribution process: Reversing actors' and observers' points of view. *Journal of Personality and Social Psychology,* 1973, *27,* 165–175.

Storms, M. D., & Thomas, G. C. Reactions to physical closeness. *Journal of Personality and Social Psychology,* 1977, *35,* 412–418.

Streeter, L. A., Krauss, R. M., Geller, V., Olson, C., & Apple, W. Pitch changes during attempted deception. *Journal of Personality and Social Psychology,* 1977, *35,* 345–350.

Strelau, J. Nervous system type and extraversion–introversion: A comparison of Eysenck's theory with Pavlov's typology. *Polish Psychological Bulletin,* 1970, *1,* 17–24.

Suberi, M., & McKeever, W. F. Differential right hemispheric memory of emotional and non-emotional faces. *Neuropsychologia,* 1977, *15,* 757–768.

Suomi, S. J., & Harlow, H. F. Social rehabilitation of isolate-reared monkeys. *Developmental Psychology,* 1972, *6,* 487–496.

Sweet, W. H., Ervin, F. R., & Mark, V. H. The relationship of violent behavior to focal cerebral disease. In S. Garattini & E. B. Sigg (Eds.), *Aggressive behavior.* Amsterdam: Excerpta Medica, 1969.

Szpiler, J. A., & Epstein, S. Availability of an avoidance response as related to autonomic arousal. *Journal of Abnormal Psychology,* 1976, *87,* 73–82.

Tagiuri, R., & Petrullo, L. (Eds.). *Person perception and interpersonal behavior.* Stanford, Calif.: Stanford University Press, 1958.

Teitelbaum, P. Disturbances of feeding and drinking behavior after hypothalamic lesions. In M. R. Jones (Ed.), *Nebraska Symposium on Motivation.* Lincoln: University of Nebraska Press, 1961.

Teplov, B. M. The problem of types of human higher nervous activity and methods of determining them. In V. D. Nebylitsyn & J. A. Gray (Eds.), *Biological bases of individual behavior.* New York: Academic, 1972.

Terzian, H. Behavioural and EEG effects of intracarotid sodium amytal injections. *Acta Neurochirurgica (Wien),* 1964, *12,* 230–239.

Terzian, H., & Ceccotto, C. Su un nuova metodo per la determinazione e lo studio della dominanza emisferica. *Giornale di Psichiatria et di Neuropatologia,* 1959, *87,* 889–924.

Thibaut, J. W., & Kelley, H. H. *The social psychology of groups.* New York: Wiley, 1959.

Thoman, E. How a rejecting baby affects mother–infant synchrony. In *Parent–infant interaction* (Ciba Foundation Symposium 33). New York: Associated Scientific Publishers, 1975.

Thoman, E. B. Affective communication as the prelude and context for language learning. In R. L. Schiefelbusch & D. Bricker (Eds.), *Early language: Acquisition and intervention.* Baltimore: University Park Press, 1981.

Thomas, A., Chess, S., & Burch, H. G. The origin of personality. *Scientific American,* 1970, *223,* 102–109.

Tinbergen, N. Comparative studies of the behaviour of gulls (Laridae): A progress report. *Behaviour,* 1959, *15,* 1–70.

Tomkins, S. *Affect, imagery, and consciousness: The positive affects* (Vol. 1). New York: Springer, 1962.

Tomkins, S. *Affect, imagery, and consciousness: The negative affects* (Vol. 2). New York: Springer, 1963.

Tomkins, S. S. Script theory: Differential magnification of affects. In H. E. Howe, Jr., & R. A. Dienstbier (Eds.), *Nebraska Symposium on Motivation* (Vol. 26). Lincoln: University of Nebraska Press, 1979.

Tomkins, S. S. The role of facial response in the experience of emotion: A reply to Tourangeau and Ellsworth. *Journal of Personality and Social Psychology,* 1981, *40,* 355–357.

Tourangeau, R., & Ellsworth, P. C. The role of facial response in the experience of emotion. *Journal of Personality and Social Psychology,* 1979, *37,* 1519–1531.

Trotman, S. C. A., & Hammond, G. R. Sex differences in task-dependent EEG asymmetries. *Psychophysiology,* 1979, *16,* 429–431.

Truex, R. C. *Human neuroanatomy.* Baltimore: Williams & Wilkins, 1959.

Tucker, D. M. Lateral brain function, emotion, and conceptualization. *Psychological Bulletin,* 1981, *89,* 19–46.

Tucker, D. M., & Newman, J. P. Lateral brain function and the cognitive inhibition of emotional arousal. *Cognitive Theory and Research*, 1981, *5*, 197–202.

Tucker, D. M., Roth, R. S., Arneson, B. A., & Buckingham, V. Right hemisphere activation during stress. *Neuropsychologia*, 1977, *15*, 697–700. (a)

Tucker, D. M., Stenslie, C. E., Roth, R. S., & Shearer, S. L. Right frontal lobe activation and right hemisphere performance decrement during a depressed mood. *Archives of General Psychiatry*, 1981, *38*(2), 169–174.

Tucker, D. M., Watson, R. T., & Heilman, K. M. Discrimination and evocation of affectively intoned speech in patients with right parietal disease. *Neurology*, 1977, *27*, 947–950. (b)

Tucker, D., & Williamson, P. Asymmetric neural control systems in human self-regulation. *Psychological Review*, 1984, *91*.

Ursin, H., & Kaada, B. R. Functional localization within the amygdala complex within the cat. *Electroencephalography and Clinical Neurophysiology*, 1960, *12*, 120.

Valenstein, E. S. *Brain control*. New York: Wiley, 1973.

Valenstein, E. S., Cox, V. C., & Kakolewski, J. K. Re-examination of the role of the hypothalamus in motivation. *Psychological Review*, 1970, *77*, 16–31.

Varney, N. R. Linguistic correlates of pantomime recognition in aphasic patients. *Journal of Neurology, Neurosurgery and Psychiatry*, 1978, *41*, 564–568.

Vaughan, K. B., & Lanzetta, J. T. Vicarious instigation and conditioning of facial expressive and autonomic responses to a model's expressive display of pain. *Journal of Personality and Social Psychology*, 1980, *38*, 909–923.

Volkmar, F. R., Hoder, L., & Siegel, A. E. Discrepant social communications. *Developmental Psychology*, 1980, *16*, 495–505.

von Frisch, K. Honeybees: Do they use direction and distance information provided by their dancers? *Science*, 1968, *158*, 1072–1076.

von Holst, E., & von Saint Paul, U. Electrically controlled behavior. *Scientific American*, 1962, *205*, 50–59.

Wada, J., & Rasmussen, T. Intracarotid injection of sodium amytal for the lateralization of cerebral speech dominance. *Journal of Neurosurgery*, 1960, *17*, 266–282.

Waid, W. M. Skin conductance response to both signaled and unsignaled noxious stimulation predicts level of socialization. *Journal of Personality and Social Psychology*, 1976, *34*, 923–929.

Waid, W. M., Orne, E. C., Cook, M. R., & Orne, M. T. Meprobamate reduces accuracy of physiological detection of deception. *Science*, 1981, *212*, 71–73.

Waid, W. M., Orne, M. T., & Wilson, S. K. Effects of level of socialization on electrodermal detection of deception. *Psychophysiology*, 1979, *16*, 15–22. (a)

Waid, W. M., Orne, M. T., & Wilson, S. K. Socialization, awareness, and the electrodermal response to deception and self-disclosure. *Journal of Abnormal Psychology*, 1979, *88*, 663–666. (b)

Walster, E., Aronson, V., Abrahams, D., & Rottmann, L. Importance of physical attractiveness in dating behavior. *Journal of Personality and Social Psychology*, 1979, *10*, 1742–1757.

Warner, R. M. Periodic rhythms in conversational speech. *Language and Speech*, 1979, *22*, 381–396.

Warner, R. M. *Statistical methods for analysis of nonverbal behavior.* Unpublished manuscript, University of New Hampshire, May 28, 1982.

Warner, R. M., Kenny, D. A., & Stoto, M. A new round robin analysis of variance for social interaction data. *Journal of Personality and Social Psychology,* 1979, *10,* 1742–1757.

Watson, M. Relationship between the suppression of emotional behaviors and physiological arousal. *Journal of Psychosomatic Research,* 1981, *25,* 451. (Abstract)

Weil, J. L. *A neurophysiological model of emotional and intentional behavior.* Springfield, Ill.: Thomas, 1974.

Weiner, M., Devoe, S., Rubinow, S., & Geller, J. Nonverbal behavior and nonverbal communication. *Psychological Review,* 1972, *79,* 185–214.

Weinstein, E. A., & Bender, M. B. Integrated facial patterns elicited by stimulation of the brainstem. *Archives of Neurology and Psychiatry,* 1943, *50,* 34–42.

Weitz, S. *Nonverbal communication* (2nd ed.). New York: Oxford, 1979.

Wenger, M. A., & Bagchi, B. K. Studies of autonomic functions in practitioners of yoga in India. *Behavioral Science,* 1961, *6,* 312–323.

Wenger, M. A., Bagchi, B. K., & Anand, B. K. Experiments in India on "voluntary" control of the heart and pulse. *Circulation,* 1961, *24,* 1319–1325.

Werner, H. The concept of development from a comparative and organismic point of view. In D. B. Harris (Ed.), *The concept of development.* Minneapolis: University of Minnesota Press, 1957.

Whalen, R. E. *Sexual motivation. Psychological Review,* 1966, *72,* 151–163.

White, J. C. Autonomic discharge from stimulation of the hypothalamus in man. *Research Publications of the Association for Research in Nervous and Mental Disease,* 1940, *20,* 854–863.

White, R. W. Motivation reconsidered: The concept of competence. *Psychological Review,* 1959, *66,* 297–333.

Whitehead, W. E., Drescher, V. M., & Blackwell, B. Lack of relationship between Autonomic Perception Questionnaire scores and actual sensitivity for perceiving one's heart beat. *Psychophysiology,* 1976, *13,* 176. (Abstract)

Whitehead, W. E., Drescher, V. M., Heiman, P., & Blackwell, B. Relation of heart rate control to heart beat perception. *Biofeedback and Self-Regulation,* 1977, *2,* 371–392.

Wilmot, W. W. *Dyadic communication* (2nd ed.). Reading, Mass.: Addison-Wesley, 1980.

Wilson, E. D. *Sociobiology: The new synthesis.* Cambridge, Mass.: Belknap, 1975.

Wilson, W. R. Feeling more than we can know: Exposure effects without learning. *Journal of Personality and Social Psychology,* 1979, *37,* 811–821.

Wilson, W. P., & Nachold, B. S. The neurophysiology of affect. *Diseases of the Nervous System,* 1972, *33,* 13–18.

Winter, P., Handley, P., Ploog, D., & Schott, D. Ontogeny of squirrel monkey calls under normal conditions and under acoustic isolation. *Behaviour,* 1973, *47,* 230–239.

Winton, W. M., Putnam, L. E., & Krauss, R. M. *On the relation between facial expressiveness and physiological reactivity.* Paper presented at the meeting of the American Psychological Association, New York, September 1979.

Wish, M., Deutsch, M., & Kaplan, S. J. Perceived dimensions of interpersonal relations. *Journal of Personality and Social Psychology*, 1976, *33*, 409–420.

Witkin, H. A., Goodenough, D. R., & Oltman, P. K. Psychological differentiation: Current status. *Journal of Personality and Social Psychology*, 1979, *37*, 1127–1145.

Wolff, H. H. The concept of alexithymia and the future of psychosomatic research. *Psychotherapy and Psychosomatics*, 1977, *28*, 376.

Yarczower, M., & Daruns, L. Social inhibition of spontaneous facial expressions in children. *Journal of Personality and Social Psychology*, 1982, *43*, 831–837.

Yarczower, M., Kilbride, J. E., & Hill, L. A. Imitation and inhibition of facial expression. *Developmental Psychology*, 1979, *15*, 453–454.

Zajonc, R. B. Feeling and thinking: Preferences need no inferences. *American Psychologist*, 1980, *35*, 151–175.

Zeskind, P. S., & Lester, B. M. Acoustic features and auditory perceptions of the cries of newborns with prenatal and perinatal complications. *Child Development*, 1978, *49*, 580–589.

Zhorov, P. A., & Yermolayeva-Tomina, L. B. Concerning the relation between extraversion and the strength of the nervous system. In V. D. Nebylitsyn & J. A. Gray (Eds.), *Biological bases of individual behavior*. New York: Academic, 1972.

Zuckerman, Marvin. *Sensation seeking: Beyond the optimal level of arousal*. Hillsdale, N.J.: Erlbaum, 1979. (a)

Zuckerman, Marvin. Sensation seeking and risk taking. In C. E. Izard (Ed.), *Emotions in pesonality and psychopathology*. New York: Plenum, 1979. (b)

Zuckerman, Marvin, Buchsbaum, M. S., & Murphy, D. L. Sensation seeking and its biological correlates. *Psychological Bulletin*, 1980, *88*, 187–214.

Zuckerman, Miron. Personal communication, 1980.

Zuckerman, Miron, Blanck, P. D., DePaulo, B. M., & Rosenthal, R. Developmental changes in decoding discrepant and nondiscrepant nonverbal cues. *Developmental Psychology*, 1980, *16*, 220–228.

Zuckerman, Miron, DeFrank, R. S., Hall, J. A., Larrance, D. T., & Rosenthal, R. Facial and vocal cues of deception and honesty. *Journal of Experimental Social Psychology*, 1979, *15*, 378–396. (a)

Zuckerman, Miron, Hall, J. A., DeFrank, R. S., & Rosenthal, R. Encoding and decoding of spontaneous and posed facial expressions. *Journal of Personality and Social Psychology*, 1976, *34*, 966–977.

Zuckerman, Miron, Larrance, D., Hall, J., DeFrank, R., & Rosenthal, R. Posed and spontaneous communication via facial and vocal cues. *Journal of Personality*, 1979, *47*, 712–733. (b)

Zuckerman, Miron, Lipets, M. S., Koivumaki, J. H., & Rosenthal, R. Encoding and decoding nonverbal cues of emotion. *Journal of Personality and Social Psychology*, 1975, *32*, 1068–1076.

Zuckerman, Miron, & Przewuzman, S. Decoding and encoding facial expressions in preschool-age children. *Environmental Psychology and Nonverbal Behavior*, 1979, *3*, 147–163.

AUTHOR INDEX

Abrahams, D., 290, 371n.
Abramovich, R., 268, 269, 339n., 346n.
Abrams, R. D., 247, 339n.
Adams, S., 307, 339n.
Ahern, G., 76, 368n.
Akert, R. M., 259, 263, 339n.
Alfert, E., 157, 358n.
Alper, S., 188, 195, 205, 339n.
Altman, I., 306, 307, 309, 310, 339n., 356n.
Anand, B. K., 145, 372n.
Ancoli, S., 173, 348n.
Anderson, C. D., 229, 339n.
Andrew, R. J., 35–37, 339n.
Apple, W., 235, 369n.
Appley, M. H., 147, 345n.
Aquinas, T., 147
Archer, D., 106, 259, 263, 339n., 366n.
Archibald, Y., 102, 357n.
Argyle, M., 312, 313, 339n.
Aristotle, 147
Arneson, B. A., 107, 371n.
Arnold, M., 71, 339n.
Aronson, V., 290, 371n.
Assal, G., 106, 358n.
Averill, J. R., 158, 340n.

Bagchi, B. K., 145, 372n.
Bakeman, R., 322, 329, 340n., 352n.
Baker, A. H., 218
Baldwin, A. L., 151, 340n.
Bales, R. F., 317, 318, 326, 340n.
Bandura, A., 140, 340n.
Bank, S., 325, 352n.
Banks, J., 135, 361n.
Barden, R. C., 154, 157, 340n.
Barnes, R. D., 317, 321, 355n.

Baron, R. A., 173, 349n.
Baron, R. M., 21, 42, 45, 111, 183, 193, 278, 332, 340n., 344n.
Barrette, D., 183, 192, 193, 344n.
Bateson, G., 178, 294. 297, 299, 340n., 341n., 360n.
Baulu, J., 226, 365n.
Bear, D. M., 95, 106, 109, 341n.
Beecher, M. D., 163, 164, 341n.
Bender, I. E., 257, 354n.
Bender, M. B., 94, 372n.
Bennett, E. L., 161, 366n.
Benowitz, L. I., 106, 280, 341n.
Berger, S., 270, 341n.
Berkowitz, L., 137, 341n.
Bernstein, G. L., 50, 356n.
Best, C., 74, 341n.
Birdwhistell, R. L., 8, 178–180, 293–295, 301, 341n., 360n.
Blackwell, B., 49, 50, 372n.
Blake, M. J. F., 220, 341n.
Blanck, P., 263, 267, 268, 281, 341n.
Blascovich, J., 50, 356n.
Blest, A. D., 36, 341n.
Block, A. R., 270, 341n.
Block, J., 199, 206, 210, 342n.
Blumberg, S. H., 189, 342n.
Bohrer, R. E., 327–330, 342n., 364n., 365n.
Bois, J., 183, 362n.
Borgatta, E., 317, 342n.
Borod, J., 105, 106, 342n., 357n.
Bowers, D., 106, 346n.
Boyanowski, E. O., 153, 342n.
Brackett, D., 276, 342n.
Braunwald, K. G., 321, 353n.
Brazelton, T. B., 208, 342n.

375

SUBJECT INDEX